Michael Ferrebee Sadler

The Revelation of Saint John the Divine

With Notes Critical and Practical

Michael Ferrebee Sadler

The Revelation of Saint John the Divine
With Notes Critical and Practical

ISBN/EAN: 9783337779863

Printed in Europe, USA, Canada, Australia, Japan

Cover: Foto ©Lupo / pixelio.de

More available books at **www.hansebooks.com**

THE REVELATION OF ST. JOHN THE DIVINE.

WITH NOTES CRITICAL AND PRACTICAL.

BY THE REV. M. F. SADLER,
RECTOR OF HONITON AND PREBENDARY OF WELLS.

SECOND EDITION, REVISED.

LONDON:
GEORGE BELL AND SONS.
1894.

INTRODUCTION.

WE must examine the authenticity of the Apocalypse in the same way as we have that of other books of the rest of the New Testament. The authenticity of any book which entitles it to form part of the Sacred Canon depends upon its reception by the Church from the first. With respect to the book of the Revelation we have Justin Martyr (about A.D. 140) writing as follows: "And further, there was a certain man with us whose name was John, one of the Apostles of Christ, who prophesied, by a Revelation that was made to him, that those who believed in our Christ should dwell a thousand years in Jerusalem, and that thereafter the general, and, in short, the eternal resurrection and judgment of all men should likewise take place" ("Dialogue with Trypho," sect. 81). Now it is very remarkable that this is the only place in which Justin mentions an Apostle by name. Throughout his works which are extant he constantly refers to the Apostles, and the companions of the Apostles, but does not name any one of them; and this is the solitary place in which he refers to an Apostle by name.

The ecclesiastical memory of Justin Martyr must have reached to the times of St. John himself. If he was martyred—say in or about 150—he must have conversed with many middle-aged or old men who were contemporary with the Apostle in his later years; so that it was impossible for him to have been mistaken as to the authorship of a work attributed to the Apostle.

Then we have Irenæus, about A.D. 170 or 180, that is, he lived within less than a century after the time to which early writers assign the date of the Apocalypse. I have now before me an index of his quotations from, or references to, Scripture, and from this I gather that he refers to the Apocalypse thirty-one times. I have examined each of these, and some of the results are as follows. In by far the greater part of these places he not only refers to the book, but quotes it as the work of the Apostle John. "John also, the Lord's disciple, when beholding the sacerdotal and glorious advent of His kingdom, says in the Apocalypse, 'I turned to see the voice that spake with me. And being turned, I saw seven golden candlesticks,'" &c. (Irenæus, "Against Heresies," iv. 11). "On this account also does John declare in the Apocalypse, 'And his voice as the sound of many waters'" ("Against Heresies," iv. 14). Again also, "But when John could not endure the sight (for he says, 'I fell at his feet as dead,')," &c. (iv. 11). Also i. 26, "The character of these men is very plainly pointed out in the Apocalypse of John as teaching that it is a matter of indifference to practise adultery and to eat things sacrificed to idols. Wherefore the Word has also spoken of them thus: 'This thou hast, that thou hatest the deeds of the Nicolaitanes, which I also hate.'" (Also v. 10, 2; iv. 20, 3; iii. 11, 8; iv. 20, 11; iv. 17, 5; v. 30, 2; iv. 18, 6; ii. 31, 3, &c.)

But Irenæus himself may be reckoned a contemporary of St. John, being acquainted with his (John's) disciple Polycarp: writing thus: "But Polycarp also was not only instructed by Apostles, and conversed with many who had seen Christ, but was also by Apostles in Asia appointed Bishop of the Church in Smyrna, *whom I also* saw in my early youth" (Irenæus, "Against Heresies," iii. 3, 4).

Melito, Bishop of Sardis about A.D. 171, is mentioned by Eusebius as having amongst many other works written one on the Revelation of St. John. Also Theophilus, Bishop of Antioch, as having written "against the heresy of Hermogenes," in which he makes use of testimony from the Revelation of St. John, besides certain other catechetical works. And speaking of Apollonius, in the end of Cent. ii., Eusebius says, "He quotes also the Revelation of John as testimony."

Tertullian.—The references to the Apocalypse in the writings of Tertullian are exceedingly numerous. It will suffice to give three or four. Thus, "If thou doubtest this consider what the Spirit saith unto the churches. To the Ephesians he imputeth that they have *left their first* love: those of Thyatira he reproacheth with fornication, and the eating of things sacrificed to idols. The Sardians, he accuseth of works not perfect," &c. ("On Penitence," chap. viii.) Again ("Prescription against Heretics," xxxiii.), "But John in the Revelation is commanded to chastise them which eat things sacrificed to idols," &c. Also in "On the Crowns," xv., "To him that overcometh, saith he, I will give a crown of life. . . . The angel also receiveth a crown of victory, going forth on a white horse to conquer. And another is adorned with a rainbow encircling him like a meadow in the heavens. The elders also sit wearing crowns," &c.

Clement of Alexandria, "And although here upon earth he be not honoured with the first seat, he will sit down on the four-and-twenty thrones, judging the people, as St. John says in the Apocalypse" ("Miscellanies," vi. 13). Again, "The Apocalypse says also that the Lord Himself appeared wearing such a robe. It says also, 'I saw the souls of those that had witnessed beneath the altar, and there was given to each a white robe" ("Instructor," ii. 11). Again, "Thus the Lord Himself is called Alpha and Omega, the beginning and the end" ("Miscellanies," vi. chap. 16).

Origen, "Once more John, in teaching us the difference between what ought to be committed to writing and what not, declares that he heard seven thunders instructing him on certain matters, and forbidding him to commit these words to writing" ("Against Celsus," vi. chap. 6). Again, "He will more worthily transfer all the saints from a temporal to an everlasting Gospel, according to the designation employed by John in the Apocalypse, of 'an everlasting Gospel," ("De Principiis," iv. ch. 1).

Cyprian, "Also in the Apocalypse, 'And I saw in the right hand of God a book written within, and on the back, sealed with seven seals.'" In an index to the Scripture passages quoted in Cyprian's works I find sixty-four references to the Revelation.

It seems useless to load pages with more instances of the Old Fathers quoting the Apocalypse as Scripture. The reader will find in Alford, and the "Speaker's Commentary," quotations from many others, as Hippolytus, Victorinus, Ephrem Syrus, Epiphanius, Basil, Hilary of Poitiers, Athanasius, Gregory of Nyssa, Didymus, Ambrose, and Augustine. Altogether there is no book of the Bible which has more decisive testimony in its favour than this one.

We have now to come to testimonies on the opposite side, those which impugn its authenticity—that it was not the work of the Apostle St. John.

The first of these was an obscure sect called the Alogi, whose principal characteristic was that they opposed the Montanists. They are not mentioned by Eusebius, and what we learn about them is from Epiphanius. In their zeal against Montanism they denied the existence of spiritual gifts in the Church, and rejected the Revelation as being not the work of St. John, but of Cerinthus. But by far the most important testimony against the Revelation is from Dionysius of Alexandria, about 240 A.D., described as the most influential as well as the ablest bishop of that age. Eusebius, who himself desired to show that the Apocalypse should not be considered the writing of John, the son of Zebedee, though he acknowledged its inspiration, gives a lengthened extract from Dionysius as follows: " Some, indeed, before us, have set aside and have attempted to refute the whole book, criticizing every chapter, and pronouncing it without sense and without reason. They say that it has a false title, for it is not a work of John. Nay, that it is not even a revelation, as it is covered with such a dense and thick veil of ignorance that not one of the Apostles and not one of the holy men, or those of the Church, could be its author. But that Cerinthus, the founder of the sect of the Cerinthians, so called from him, wishing to have reputable authority for his own fiction, prefixed the title. For this is the doctrine of Cerinthus, that there will be an earthly reign of Christ; and as he (Cerinthus) was a lover of the body, and altogether sensual in those things which he so eagerly craved, he dreamed that he would revel in the gratification of the sensual appetite, in eating and drinking and marrying. . . . For my part I would not venture to set this book (of the Revelation) aside, as there are many brethren that value it much; but having formed a conception of its subject as exceeding my capacity, I considered it also as containing a certain concealed and wonderful intimation in each particular. For though I do not understand, yet I suspect that some deeper sense is enveloped in the words, and these I do not measure and judge by my private reason; but allowing more to faith, I have regarded them as too lofty to be comprehended by me, and those things that I do not understand I do not reject, but I wonder the more that I cannot comprehend."

After this he examines (these are the words of Eusebius) the whole book of the Revelation, and after proving that it is impossible that it should be understood according to the obvious and literal sense, he proceeds, "The prophet, as I said, having completed the whole prophecy, he pronounces those blessed that should observe it as also himself. 'For blessed,' says he, 'is he that keepeth the words of the prophecy of this book, and I John, who have seen and heard these things.' I do not therefore deny that he was called John, and that this was the writing of one John, and I agree that it was the work, also, of some holy and inspired man. But I would not easily agree that this was the Apostle, the son of Zebedee, the brother of James, who is the author of the Gospel and the Catholic Epistle that bears his name. But I conjecture, both from the general tenor of both and the form and complexion of the composition, and the execution of the whole book that it is not from him. For the Evangelist never prefixed his name, never proclaims himself, either in the Gospel or in his Epistle."

A little further he adds, "But John never speaks as of himself (in the first person) nor as of another (in the third), but he that wrote the Apocalypse declares himself immediately in the beginning: 'The Revelation of Jesus Christ which he (God) gave unto him, to show to his servants quickly. And he sent and signified it by his angel to his servant John, who bare record of the word of God and of his testimony (of Jesus Christ) and of all things that he saw.'

"Besides this he wrote an Epistle, 'John to the seven churches of Asia: Grace and peace to you.' But the Evangelist does not prefix his name even to his general Epistle, but without any introduction or circumlocution begins from the very mystery of the Divine Revelation: 'that which was from the beginning, which we have heard, which we have seen with our eyes;' . . . . but neither in the second nor third Epistle ascribed to John (the Apostle), though they are very brief, is the name of John presented. But anonymously it is written *the presbyter*. But the other did not consider it sufficient to name himself but once, and then to proceed in his narrative, but afterwards again resumes: 'I John, your brother and partner in tribulation, and in the kingdom and patience of Jesus, was on the island called Patmos, on account of the word of God, and the testimony of Jesus.' And likewise at the end (of the book) he says, 'Blessed is he that keepeth the words of the prophecy of this book, and I am John, that saw and heard these things.'

"That it is a John that wrote these things we must believe him as he says it; but what John it is is uncertain. For he has not said that he was (as he often does in the Gospel) the beloved disciple of the Lord, neither the one leaning on his bosom, nor the brother of James, nor he that himself saw and heard what the Lord did and said. For he certainly would have said one of these particulars, if he wished to make himself clearly known. But of all this there is nothing, he only calls himself our brother and companion, and the witness of Jesus, and blessed on account of seeing and hearing these revelations.

"I am of opinion there were many of the same name with John the Apostle, who for their love and admiration and emulation of him, and their desire at the same time, like him, to be beloved of the Lord, adopted the same epithet, just as we find the name of Paul and of Peter to be adopted by many among the faithful.

"There is also another John, surnamed Mark, mentioned in the book of the Acts. . . . . But whether this is the one that wrote the Apocalypse I could not say. . . . . I think, therefore, that it was another, one of those in Asia. For they say that there are two monuments at Ephesus, and that each one bears the name of John, and from the sentiments and the expressions, as also their composition, it might be very reasonably conjectured that this one is different from that. For the Gospel and Epistle mutually agree. They commence in the same way; for the one says, 'In the beginning was the Word;' the other, 'That which was from the beginning.' The one says, 'And the Word was made flesh and dwelt (tabernacled) among us, and we saw his glory, the glory as of the only-begotten of the Father;' the other says the same things a little altered, 'That which we have heard, which we have seen with our eyes, which we have looked upon, and our hands have handled of the Word of life, and the life was manifested.' These things, therefore, are premised, alluding, as he has shown in the subsequent parts, to those who say that the Lord did not come into the flesh. Wherefore also he has designedly subjoined, 'What we have seen we testify, and declare to you that eternal life,' &c.

"But the attentive reader will find the expressions, *the life, the light,* frequently occurring in both; in both he will find the expressions, *fleeing from darkness, the truth, grace, joy, the flesh and blood of the Lord, the judgment, forgiveness of sins, the love of God to us, the commandment given to us to love one another, that we ought to keep all the commandments, the conviction of the world, the devil, of Antichrist, the promise of the Holy Spirit, the adoption of God (i.e., the adoption made by God) the faith to be exhibited by us in all matters, the Father and the Son,* everywhere occurring in both, and altogether throughout, to attentive observers, it will be obvious that there is one and the same complexion and character in the Gospel and Epistle. Very different and remote from all this is the Apocalypse; not even touching or even bordering upon them in the least, I might say, not even containing a syllable in common with them. But the Epistle, to say nothing of the Gospel, has not made any mention or given any intimation of the Apocalypse, or does the Apocalypse mention the Epistle, whereas Paul indicates something of his revelations in his Epistle, which, however, he never recorded in writing.

"We may also note how the phraseology of the Gospel and the Epistle differs from the Apocalypse. For the former are written not only irreprehensibly, as it regards the Greek language, but are most elegant in diction, in the arguments, and the whole structure of the style. It would require much to discover any barbarism or solecisms or any odd peculiarity of expression at all in them. For, as is to be presumed, he was endued with all the requisites for his discourse, the Lord having given him both that of knowledge and that of expression and style. That the latter, however, saw a revelation, and received knowledge and prophecy, I do not deny. But I perceive that his dialect and language is not very accurate Greek, but that he uses barbarous idioms, and in some places solecisms, which it is now unnecessary to select: for neither would I have anyone suppose that I am saying these things by way of derision, but only with the view to point out the great difference between the writings of these men" (Eusebius, "Eccles. History," vii. ch. 25, Cruse's Translation).

I have given this place in full, because it is the first and only passage worth speaking of in the Ante-Nicene Fathers which questions the Apostolic origin of this book. Now it is to be remarked that Dionysius entirely confines himself to certain internal considerations, ignoring the testimony of those who preceded him, to the external and ecclesiastical testimony for the Apostolic authorship. To begin with, what value can we attach to the surmise that if St. John wrote the book he could not put his name to it because he did not put his name to his Gospel or his Epistle. What right has anyone to push aside the authenticity of a well-accredited book for such a reason. Is an author bound never to vary in his mode of asserting the fact of his authorship. Now when I say an author I must in a way correct myself, and ask, who is the real author of this book? Evidently not John, but Jesus. "The Revelation of Jesus Christ, which God gave unto him. . . . . I John, who also am your brother, and companion in tribulation. . . . . And I turned to see the voice that spake with me. . . . · And in the midst of the seven candlesticks one like unto the Son of man. . . . . Write the things which thou hast seen. . . . . Unto the angel of the church of Ephesus write; These things saith he that holdeth the seven stars. . . . . Unto the angel of the church in Smyrna write; These things saith the first and the last," and so on with each Epistle the real author is the Lord and St. John is only the amanuensis.

After the third chapter the writer begins the relations of vision. " I looked, and, behold, a door. . . . . I was in the spirit. . . . . I saw in the right hand of him that sat on the throne. . . . . I saw four angels. . . . . I saw the seven angels. . . . . I saw another mighty angel." Then he speaks of what he himself had to see, but it is equally mysterious, in the spirit, equally transcendental, equally inexplicable. Then the great wonder in heaven; then the beast rising from the sea; then seven angels having the seven last plagues; then the harlot; then the fall of the harlot; then the new heaven and the new earth. Then the conclusion, which so unhinged the blessed Apostle that he was on the point of committing an act of idolatrous worship. Then at last the Lord resumes, "Behold, I come quickly. . . . I am Alpha and Omega. . . . . I Jesus have sent mine angel to testify unto you these things."

Such were the things which the Apostle was made the instrument of communicating. We know that they for the moment so unhinged his mind that he was twice on the very eve of forgetting his first duty to God. How can we—how can Dionysius of Alexandria—possibly lay down rules as to what he was (if he was the true John) to begin it all with? Why must he exclude his own name? Why must he say to himself before he began, " I must not begin with my own name," and yet—though he does use his own name—yet all that he says is in another's Name? Will anyone dare say he has added a single word from himself out of his own moral consciousness to anything which he has been commissioned to reveal?

Now this seems to me to put altogether out of court all arguments, drawn from diversity of vocabulary, of idiom, and such things, respecting the authorship of the Revelation and the Gospel as compared with one another. The one—the Gospel—is the most matter-of-fact book; the other—the Revelation—is the most visionary book in the whole Bible. I say the most visionary perfectly reverently, because it is a book entirely occupied (except chaps. ii. and iii.) with visions of the most transcendental character to which no two expositors have given the same meaning. How can we assert that a communication of such things must be in such or such a form? If the visions are such as they are described as being it is certain that the narrator would be intensely affected by them, and if so he would express them more in the style of his native Hebrew or Aramaic than in the Greek, which he had acquired later in life by pains and labour.

But there are a considerable number of remarkable similarities of expression which are to be found in the language of the Gospel and Apocalypse which are not to be found elsewhere in the New Testament. The first of these is that in both books (and to this we may add the Epistle of St. John) the term *Logos* is applied to our Lord. In the Gospel, "In the beginning was the Word, and the Word was made flesh;" in the Apocalypse xix. 13, "And his name is called The Word of God."

It is very remarkable that a word denoting His humiliation and sacrifice—the term Lamb—is only applied to our Lord by St. John in his Gospel and in the Revelation. One would have thought that it would have been applied to Him multitudes of times, but it is not. It is not applied to him in the Hebrews where we should have most expected it; only in the Gospel, "Behold the Lamb ($αμνος$) of God," and in the Revelation under the diminutive ($αρνιον$). It is true that the word $αμνος$ is applied to Him by the Baptist, not by the Evangelist, and is only recorded by the Evangelist. But it is not recorded by any other of the Evangelists (Matthew, Mark, Luke), and the fact that St. John records it betokens his love for it, for the idea underlying it. St. Paul comes near to it when he says, "Christ our Passover is sacrificed for us;'

but he seems to have been restrained from using the name of "Lamb."

The word "to tabernacle" (σκηνόω) is only used in the Gospel of John (i. 14) and in the Apocalypse (xxi. 3), and if the use of mere words can be cited as implying identity of authorship this should be, for in its associations it is a remarkable word. Then the word αληθινος, "that which is true," has been noticed as being Johannine, being used in the Gospel and Epistle thirteen times, in the Apocalypse ten times, and only once in all the rest of the New Testament. Then "to overcome," νικᾷν, is also almost exclusively Johannine. It occurs once in St. Luke xi. 22, three times in Romans, one of which is a quotation from the Old Testament, six times in the first Epistle of St. John, and sixteen times in the Revelation.

And what is to me most significant of identity of authorship, the piercing of the Messiah, prophesied of in Zechariah, is quoted or alluded to both in John xix. 37, and in Rev. i. 7, and in each case with the same verb, ἐξεκέντησεν, which is not the same as that used by the prophet in the Septuagint, κατωρχησαντο. This seems to me far more decisive in favour of identity of authorship than having in common any number of mere verbal agreements.

There is another remarkable coincidence between the Gospel and the Apocalypse which I have not seen noticed in any expositor. In the Gospel and in the Apocalypse, alone of the books of the New Testament, does the Lord promise to give to the believer His Spirit under the figure of living water; in the Apocalypse as the water of life, but evidently alluding to the same Spirit. Thus in St. John, speaking to the woman of Samaria (iv. 14): "If thou knewest the gift of God, and who it is that saith to thee, Give me to drink, thou wouldest have asked of him, and he would have given thee living water;" and again, verse 14, "Whosoever shall drink of the water that I shall give him shall never thirst;" and again, "If any man thirst, let him come to me and drink;" "But this spake he of the Spirit," &c. Now it is very remarkable that this figure of the Spirit under this refreshing aspect, as given by Christ, is never used elsewhere in the New Testament except in the Revelation; one would have supposed that so very obvious a figure of the refreshing Spirit would have pervaded the New Testament, but it is confined to the Gospel of St. John and the Revelation. Thus, "The Lamb that is in the midst of the throne shall feed them, and lead them unto living fountains of waters;" again

(xxii. 17), "And let him that is athirst come. And whosoever will let him take of the water of life freely." And again, "He shewed me a pure river of water of life ... proceeding out of the throne of God and of the Lamb" (xxii. 1).

There is another remarkable doctrinal and also verbal correspondence between the Gospel and the Apocalypse. In the Gospel the existence in the past eternity of the eternal Word is described by the imperfect ἠν. Thus, "In the beginning *was* (ἦν), the Word and the Word was (ἦν) with God, and the Word was (ἦν) God, the same was (ἦν) in the beginning with God," ἦν τὸ φῶς τὸ ἀληθινόν. ἐν τῷ κόσμῳ ἦν, &c.

Now in the Apocalypse a most anomalous form is used to express the past eternal existence of God, " I am Alpha and Omega, the Beginning and the End, saith the Lord, which is and which was (ὁ ὢν καὶ ὁ ἦν), and which is to come." Such a use of ἦν is strictly Johannine. Nothing approaching to it is to be found in any other inspired writer.

The time and place of writing is next to be considered. There is very satisfactory evidence for this also, and that by Irenæus, who writes (v. 30), "As to the name of Antichrist, if it were necessary that his name should be distinctly revealed in this present time, it would have been announced by him who beheld the Apocalyptic vision; for that was seen no very long time since, but almost in our day, towards the end of Domitian's reign."

Clement of Alexandria writes: "After the death of the tyrant, John went from the isle of Patmos to Ephesus," and he also adds that "John remained with the Presbyters of Asia till the time of Trajan." Clement also says, "After that the tyrant was dead, coming from the isle of Patmos to Ephesus, he went also, when called, to the neighbouring regions of the Gentiles," &c. (Eusebius, "Eccles. Hist.," iii. 23).

To these we may add Origen, who writes, "And the King of the Romans, as tradition informs us, condemned John, when bearing witness as a martyr in the isle of Patmos on account of the word of truth;" and John himself informs us concerning his own martyrdom, not telling us who it was that condemned him, but using these words in his Apocalypse, "'I John your brother and companion in the tribulation, and kingdom, and patience of Jesus, became a sojourner in the isle that is called Patmos, on account of the Word of God.'"

Victorinus (A.D. 380), also wrote a comment on the Apocalypse, in which he says, "When John saw this he was in the isle of Patmos, condemned to the mines by Domitian Cæsar." In two other places he mentions the same time and place, so that we have no greater certainty respecting the writing of any book of Scripture as to author, time, or place, than we have for this.

We have to consider, in the next place, For what purpose was the Apocalypse given? This is told us expressly in the first verse, "to shew unto His servants things which must shortly come to pass." Now this has been most mischievously understood, as if the "shortly" meant during the lifetime of the Apostle, or in the reigns of Nero, Galba, Otho, and Vitellius, whereas it must be understood in that very mysterious, but most certainly revealed sense, that the Lord when He comes the second time will come quickly, suddenly, as in a moment, taking both the world and the Church by surprise. Thus He says (ii. 5), "I will come unto thee quickly, and will remove thy candlestick out of its place." And again, to the Church of Pergamos, "Repent, or else I will come to thee quickly" (ii. 16). And again (iii. 11), "Behold, I come quickly; hold that fast which thou hast." Again, in the last chapter, verse 7, "Behold I come quickly: blessed is he that watcheth," and again (12), "Behold, I come quickly, and my reward is with me." And in verse 20, "He which testifieth these things saith, Surely I come quickly." How then can He be said to come quickly, seeing that there are twenty chapters of visions which must be accomplished before He comes? No, it is not so, for these visions are not a continuous history of the Church. On the contrary, they are constantly broken by intimations of the actual coming of the end, and we have apparently to begin again, and then the end comes a second time, and we begin again, and the end comes a third time, and again we begin with another vision, and again the end comes.

Now we will enumerate some of these "comings of the end."

(1.) At the end of the sixth chapter we read: "And I beheld when he had opened the sixth seal, and lo there was a great earthquake, and the sun became black as sackcloth of hair, and the stars of heaven fell unto the earth .... and the heavens departed as a scroll, and the kings of the earth .... and every bondman, and every freeman hid themselves in the dens, &c. .... hide us from the face of him that sitteth upon the throne, and from the wrath of the Lamb, for the great day of his wrath is come" (vi. 12-17).

There is not throughout Scripture a sublimer description of "the end;" but it is only under one aspect—in its aspect of terror to the wicked. Any attempt to explain it as the defeat of the heathen in the time of Constantine seems to me absurd, as well as blasphemous.

(2.) At the conclusion of the next chapter there is as evident an account of "the end," but only as it bears upon the reward of the righteous. They are "before the throne of God, and serve him day and night in his temple: and he that sitteth on the throne shall dwell among them. They shall hunger no more. . . . For the Lamb which is in the midst of the throne shall feed them, and shall lead them unto living fountains of waters: and God shall wipe away all tears from their eyes" (vii. 15-17). If the reader turns to the twenty-first chapter, he will find that these are all the descriptions of the final blessedness of the true people of God. Let him look to verses 3 and 4 of that chapter and he will find that they are anticipated here.

(3.) "At the sounding of the trumpet of the seventh angel" (xi. 15-18). This is undoubtedly a description of the consummation, "And the seventh angel sounded; and there were great voices in heaven, saying, The kingdoms of this world are become the kingdoms of our Lord, and of his Christ; . . . Thou hast taken to thee thy great power, and hast reigned. And the nations were angry, and thy wrath is come, and the time of the dead, that they should be judged, and that thou shouldest give reward unto thy servants the prophets, and to the saints."

(4.) In the fourteenth chapter there is undoubtedly a vision of the end: "And I looked, and behold a white cloud, and upon the cloud one sat like unto the Son of man, having on his head a golden crown, and in his hand a sharp sickle. . . . Thrust in thy sickle and reap: for the time is come for thee to reap; for the harvest of the earth is ripe" (xiv. 14).

(5.) In the sixteenth chapter there is another vision of the end: "A great voice out of the temple of heaven, from the throne, saying, It is done. . . . There was a great earthquake. . . . And the great city was divided into three parts, and the cities of the nations fell. . . . And every island fled away, and the mountains were not found" (xvi. 17).

(6.) In the nineteenth chapter there is a vision of an appearance of the Son of God: "And I saw heaven opened, and behold a white horse; and he that sat upon him was called Faithful and True, and in righteousness he doth judge and make war. His eyes were as a flame of fire." This may not be a vision of the final catastrophe, for though in a sense He comes to judge, yet it may not be the final judgment, but it is an appearance of Jesus Christ in glory.

(7.) The end is described in the next chapter, the twentieth, verse 11: "I saw a great white throne.... I saw the dead, small and great, stand before God, and the books were opened .... and the dead were judged out of those things which were written in the books, according to their works."

So that this book of the Revelation is not a continuous historical vision, leading to the final consummation, but the consummation bursts upon the world six or seven times—the final judgment, and Second Coming, or what seems equivalent to it, comes seven times. How are we to account for such a thing? Now it is clear that this is in strict accordance with what the Lord teaches us respecting the suddenness of His Second Coming, and that we are to be on the watch for Him, and to welcome Him whenever He appears. He leaves the time of His coming uncertain, that we may be always on the watch. This is described in His discourse in St. Mark xiii. 32: "But of that day and that hour knoweth no man, no, not the angels which are in heaven, neither the Son, but the Father. Take ye heed, watch and pray: for ye know not when the time is: For the Son of man is as is a man taking a far journey, who left his house, and gave authority to his servants, and to every man his work, and commanded the porter to watch. Watch ye therefore: for ye know not when the master of the house cometh, at even, or at midnight, or at the cockcrowing, or in the morning: lest coming suddenly, he find you sleeping."

The first of the things of immeasurable importance "which must shortly come to pass" is the Second Coming. That is the thing to be looked for, whatever be the significance of each successive vision.

Now the imminence of the Second Advent is impressed upon us by some words interjected, as it were, in the account of the pouring out of the sixth vial. After describing the unclean spirits like frogs coming out of the mouth of the dragon, and the beast, and the false prophet, the Lord is represented as saying suddenly, "Behold I come as a thief, Blessed is he that watcheth and keepeth his garments" (xvi. 15-17). This is said apparently without connection with what goes before, and with what follows.

So that to impress upon believers the imminence of the Second Advent is one of the chief purposes of the Apocalypse.

But, besides this, we are taught that all things which affect the nations of the world are not due to mere natural causes, though God may employ natural causes according to His will, but to the personal will of God. He sees that nations require correction; that for the sake of others they require to be made severe examples of His wrath, and He acts accordingly. He uses natural means to effect this, just as iron, and the substances which compose gunpowder, are used by men to exercise their wrath upon one another, but it is all His doing. The famines which accompany the rider on the black horse, and the pestilences which follow the rider on the livid horse, may be due to natural or secondary causes; but the primary cause, no matter how remote, is the will of God alone, who foresees wickedness, and pre-ordains and prepares punishment.

It is the impression produced by this view of the judgments of God, as attributable solely to His will, and brought about solely by His power, which constitutes the value of this book to believers. A man may not understand the historical significance of any one of the visions, and yet may be deeply impressed with the significance of one and all of them, that all are from God.

A godly man of great intelligence, by no means a fanatic, said to me in the middle of the Franco-Prussian war, just after the invasion of France: "The great hail, sir! the great hail!" Now this man's judgment might be wrong, but his heart was right. His judgment might be wrong respecting the interpretation of Rev. xvi. 21; but his heart was right in leading him to acknowledge the hand of God in it all.

Another lesson which we get from the Revelation—a lesson which is palpably on its surface—is, that God has a world of active, powerful, and holy intelligences which He employs in His government of the universe. It teaches us as no other book of the Bible, except the book of Daniel, does, that He has constituted the services of angels, as well as those of men, in a wonderful order. Do the angels only act mechanically in sounding the trumpets, or pouring out the vials? No; we may be sure that under God they help to inflict the judgments which come upon the earth at each sounding of a trumpet, or each emptying of a vial. At one time I was tempted to think that the book itself was given to us simply to teach us, that whilst God does all things by His own power and by

His own will, He does all things by the interposition of angelic beings, so that the universe, in every department of it, is not ruled mechanically, but by willing and obedient agents.[1]

Another lesson which the Apocalypse teaches us abundantly is, that the Church, like her divine Master, cannot attain to her glorified state, her eternal rest, except by passing through tribulation. Every one of the visions, as far as I can remember, implies tribulation. It is true that in certain visions the instruments of evil are not allowed to touch or to harm those who have the seal of God on their foreheads; but the general impression produced by the whole book is that the righteous, the forgiven, the accepted, the sanctified, are those who have come out of "the tribulation, the great one," who by their own co-operating, have washed their robes, and made them white in the Blood of the Lamb.

The judgments of God are upon the earth, and seem to be upon the righteous and the wicked alike. This is certainly to be gathered from the words of Christ. "In those days shall be affliction, such as was not from the beginning of the creation which God created unto this time, neither shall be. And except that the Lord had shortened those days, no flesh should be saved: but for the elect's sake, whom he hath chosen, he hath shortened the days" (Mark xiii. 19, 20).

So that any unlearned but devout Christian who does not understand the historical sequences of any one of the visions, will yet gather from the book itself these four truths.

1. That the Coming of Christ is ever imminent.

2. That God orders all things by His ever-watchful providence, which alike controls the revolutions of empires and the fall of sparrows.

3. That God acts in all things by His angels, so that there is no mere mechanical direction of events in the universe.

4. And that the normal state of Christians—that by which they are disciplined for a happy eternity—is by suffering and distress. All these blessed lessons, I repeat, are totally independent of the historical significance of the visions. They are, as it were, on the surface, and seem to impress the devout reader, whether he be

---

[1] Sir Isaac Newton declares that he cannot conceive any power or force residing in one ball of matter to attract to itself another ball of matter at a distance from it, having no connection with it, and he implies that such attraction is due to a spiritual force, that is, the force exercised by spirit, not by matter.

learned or unlearned, with some of the highest truths respecting God's government of the world.

It will be now necessary for me to make a few remarks respecting:
1. The numerals used in the Apocalypse.
2. The times noted during which certain events are to take place; and
3. The references in the Apocalypse to the Old Testament prophecies.

1. The numbers. There can be no doubt that the numbers in the Apocalypse, especially 3, 4, 7, and 12, are to be taken symbolically. But what do we mean by this? Do we mean that the fact that they are symbolical makes them uncertain, so that 3 may mean some other number than 3, or 4 than 4? By no means. Each numeral signifies the number which it represents, and no other. The symbolical reference or meaning is the reason on account of which it is chosen. Thus in the Trisagion, the thrice holy of ch. iv. 8, the three refers to the ever-blessed Three. They chant Holy three times, because of the three Persons of the Trinity.

Archdeacon Lee (in "Speaker's Commentary") writes well: "It is but natural, indeed, that the essential character of the Triune God, as He has revealed Himself, should be impressed upon His works. And so in the record of Revelation three is the numerical 'signature' of the Divine Being, and of all that stands in any real relation to God; *e.g.*, three angels appear to Abraham (Gen. xviii. 2). The priestly benediction in Numbers vi. 24 is threefold. Each year God's people must appear before Him three times (Exod. xxiii. 14, 17). Above all, there is the Ter Sanctus, the Holy, Holy, Holy, of Isaiah vi. 3."

Again, with respect to Four, "Four is the signature of nature, of the created—of the world . . . . as Kosmos, as the Revelation of God, so far as nature can reveal Him. In Scripture the four rivers of Paradise, the four winds, the four corners of the earth, the four cherubim." Though I cannot agree with those who make the four living ones, the *Zoa* of Rev. iv., to be only symbolical; their number may be symbolical in a sense, but they themselves are real existences.

7. The number seven, $3 + 4$, is the most mysterious and sym-

bolical of all numbers. Lee speaks of it as the note of union between God and the world. There are the seven days of creation, the seven days of the week, the seven years of plenty and famine, the sevenfold compassing of the doomed city; and still more in the New Testament, where we have the seven words from the Cross, the seven petitions of the Lord's Prayer, the seven disciples of John xxi. 2, the seventy disciples of Luke x. 1, the seven deacons, &c.; but the mystical use of "seven" is far more conspicuous in the Revelation than in any other book, witness the seven Spirits before the throne, the seven Churches and their candlesticks, the seven angels, the seven seals, the seven trumpets, the seven vials, and so throughout.

The half of seven. Three and a half is used in the Old Testament to signify a time of tribulation; and, though the number is not specifically mentioned, in the Book of Kings (xvii. 1) as indicating a time of famine, yet it is mentioned by our Lord as such in Luke iv. 25. "The witnesses lay dead three days and a half." This is the same as the time, times and dividing of time of Daniel vii. 25, and the period of the nourishment of the woman in the wilderness is the same, Rev. xii. 14.

The number twelve, being the number of the Patriarchs and the number of the Apostles, is most sacred. Lee speaks of it as the number of the Covenant people in whose midst God dwells, and with whom He has entered into Covenant relations. The introduction of twelve as a factor of other numbers is also to be noted. There are twenty-four courses of the priests, twenty-four elders, forty-eight (12×4) cities of the Levites.

The length and breadth of the city ($12 \times 10 \times 10 \times 10$) 12,000 furlongs.

The height of the wall of the city was 144 cubits (12×12).

The number of the sealed was the square of 12 multiplied by the cube of 10, *i.e.*, 144,000.

I have next to consider, as closely following upon this, the times prophesied during which certain events are to take place.

The first of these is the five months in which the locusts like scorpions were to hurt men (chap. ix. 5-10).

The second is the hour, day, month and year in which the angels loosed from the river Euphrates were to slay the third part of men (ix. 15).

INTRODUCTION. xxiii

The third is the forty and two months in which the holy city should be trodden down of the Gentiles (xi. 2).

The fourth is the one thousand two hundred and threescore days in which the two witnesses are to prophesy clothed in sackcloth (xi. 3).

The fifth is the three days and a half in which the dead bodies of the witnesses shall be unburied, at the end of which the Spirit of life from God shall revive them (xi. 9 and 11).

The sixth is the time in which the woman was fed in the place which God had prepared, one thousand two hundred and threescore days (xii. 6).

The seventh is, perhaps, the same as the last, where the woman is nourished in her place a time and times and half a time, $360 + 720 + 180 = 1260$ (xii. 14).

The eighth is the power to continue, given to the first beast, forty and two months (xiii. 5).

The ninth is the one hour in which the ten kings have received power with the beast (xvii. 12).

The tenth is the thousand years of the reign of Christ with his saints (xx. 6).

In glancing over these the reader will see that the third, the fourth, the sixth, the seventh, and the eighth are the same, for forty and two months are 1,260 days.

A great question which has arisen amongst expositors is this: Are we to understand by these, actual days or years? are we to take a day as in prophetic language standing for one year? I think the two proofs alleged from Scripture, viz., the years of the wanderings of the children of Israel as corresponding to the time of the spying out of the land (Numb. xiv. 34), and the days in which Ezekiel was commanded to lie on his side (Ezekiel, iv. 4-6), are no proof at all that in the language of prophecy a day is to stand for a year. For neither of these places are prophetical. The one occurs in a strictly historical book, and the other in some historical verses of a prophetical book. The reader, of course, must be aware that the use to which these numbers are put is in order that we may know the times and the seasons which the Lord Himself tells us that the Father has placed in His own power (of course in His own power alone), but if so we must know the date at which these years begin; but there is not a date in the Apocalypse which we can even so much as approach to identify with any date in history. Are we to suppose that the third

(Rev. xi. 2), the treading down of the Holy City, the fourth, the testifying of the two witnesses, the sixth, the time of the feeding of the woman, the eighth, the continuance of the beast, are all the same, starting from the same point of time. No expositor has taken any such view. If the date, apparently given in xi. 2, the commencement of the Holy City—the actual Jerusalem—being trodden under foot be A.D. 70, then we ask, did anything approaching to the conclusion of this occur about seventy years after A.D. 1260, *i.e.*, 1330? Did anything which we can identify with the termination of the persecution of the woman, or the discontinuance of the therion occur at this time. For as far as I can see this is the only date in history which synchronizes with any date in the Apocalypse, and it leads to nothing, fixes nothing, settles nothing, for no historical change took place in 1330.

I cannot help reproducing the following words of Dean Alford on this subject in his Introduction or Prolegomena to the Revelation: "I have not pretended to offer any solution of those periods of time so remarkably pervaded by the half of the mystic seven.[1] I am quite unable to say who the two witnesses are; quite unable, in common with all Apocalyptic interpreters, to point out definitely any period in the history of the Church corresponding to the 1,260 days (chap. xii. 6), or any in the history of this world's civil power which shall satisfy the forty-two months of chap. xiii. 5. As far as I have seen every such attempt hitherto made has been characterized by signal failure. One after another the years fixed on for the consummation by different authors have passed away, beginning with the 1836 of Bengel; one after another the expositors who have lived to be thus refuted have shifted their grounds into the safer future. It is not my intention to enter the lists on either side of the vexed 'year-day' question. I have never seen it proved, or even made probable, that we are to take a day for a year in Apocalyptic prophecy; on the other hand, I have never seen it proved or made probable that such mystic periods are to be taken literally, a day for a day. It is a weighty argument against the year-day system that a period of a thousand years (xx. 6, 7) does occur in the prophecy (to which the year-day system is never applied by its advocates, as it would make the length of the millennium three hundred

---

[1] $\frac{7}{2} = 3\frac{1}{2}$, which, according to the year-day system, is $360 + 720 + 180 = 1260 = 4$ months of 30 days each.

and sixty thousand years). It is hardly a less strong one against literal acceptation of days, that the principles of interpretation given us by the seer himself (xvii. 17) seem to require for the reign of the beast a far longer period than this calculation would allow. So that in the apparent failure of both systems I am driven to believe that these periods are to be assigned by some clue of which the Spirit has not yet put the Church in possession."

It will be necessary now to say something respecting the references in the Apocalypse to the Old Testament prophecies.

These are very numerous: I can only notice three. The first shall be Rev. xi. 3, 4, "And I will give power unto my two witnesses, and they shall prophesy a thousand two hundred and threescore days, clothed in sackcloth. These are the two olive trees, and the two candlesticks standing before the God of the earth." Now the prophet Zechariah saw in a vision a candlestick with a bowl on the top of it, and his seven lamps thereon, and seven pipes to the seven lamps, and he saw also two olive trees by it, which apparently supplied the candlestick. There can be no doubt but that the Apocalyptic seer alludes to this vision of Zechariah, but he introduces many features not in Zechariah, particularly that the two witnesses shall prophesy a thousand two hundred and threescore days, clothed in sackcloth; that if any man will hurt them, fire proceedeth out of their mouth, and devoureth their enemies; and they have power to shut heaven, and to turn waters into blood. Now it is to be noticed that the explanation given by Zechariah is only for the encouragement of Zerubbabel, but the power given to St. John's two witnesses and olive trees is for much more; it is for vengeance upon their enemies—or rather upon God's enemies—to smite them with the plagues of Egypt, and at the end of their testimony the beast, *i.e.*, according to the most approved expositors, the "world-power," shall destroy them. So there is a reference to the prophecy of Zechariah and very much more.

This prophecy of Zechariah then seems to have had a very limited fulfilment, and that it waits for a far completer fulfilment in the latter days.

The next must be xx. 8, where the nations that are deceived by Satan are Gog and Magog. This appears to refer (and no doubt does) to Ezekiel xxxviii. 2, 3, "Son of man, set thy face against

Gog, the land of Magog, the chief prince of Meshech and Tubal, and prophesy against him, and say, Thus saith the Lord God; Behold, I am against thee, O Gog . . . . and I will turn thee back, and put hooks into thy jaws. . . . Thou shalt ascend and come like a storm, thou shalt be like a cloud to cover the land, thou, and all thy bands, and many people with thee." Then, after describing that Gog and his hosts would desire to come up to the land of unwalled villages to spoil them, he says, "Art thou he of whom I have spoken in old time by my servants the prophets of Israel, which prophesied in those days many years that I would bring thee against them?"

Now it is quite clear that no such invasion of the land of Israel has taken place in historic times. As I have shown in the commentary, on pages 257 and 258, there was an invasion of northern nations (Scythians) on their way to Egypt which seems not to have affected the interior of Palestine. This prophecy then remains to be fulfilled in its completeness, and it will be fulfilled at the time of the end. It seems to postulate that the Jews or Israelites will have been restored to their land, and that *all* the nations will be gathered against them—rather against the Lord and against His Christ—and that they will be destroyed by supernatural means. It seems as if they would be under the direction of Antichrist—*the* Antichrist—and shall be consumed by the Spirit proceeding from the Lord's mouth, and destroyed with the brightness of His coming (2 Thess. ii. 8).

The last of the three shall be xxii. 1, &c., "And he shewed me a pure river of water of life, clear as crystal, proceeding out of the throne of God and of the Lamb. In the midst of the street of it, and on either side of the river, was there the tree of life, which bare twelve manner of fruits, and yielded her fruit every month: and the leaves of the tree were for the healing of the nations." In this place the seer has unquestionably in his eye the vision in Ezekiel xlvii.,—where the prophet is said to be shown that the waters that issued from the threshold of the Lord's house which sprang from the south side of the altar—then the prophet saw the waters forming a river up to the ancles; then he measured another thousand cubits, and the waters were to the knees; then another, and the waters were to the loins; and then further, and the river could not be passed over ("waters to swim in"). Then he is brought back and he sees on the bank very many trees on the one side and on the other; then in the 12th verse, "Then by the river upon the bank thereof, on this side and on that side, shall grow all trees for meat, whose leaf shall not fade, neither shall the fruit thereof be consumed: it shall bring forth new fruit according to his months, because their waters they issued out of the sanctuary: and the fruit thereof shall be for meat, and the leaf thereof for medicine" ("and the leaves of the trees were for the healing of the nations"). Now what is the relation between these two passages? The prophecy in Ezekiel is much fuller and more circumstantial, but the Apocalyptic vision, without losing altogether its earthly character, is much more spiritual—much more in accordance with the exceeding blessedness of the New Jerusalem as the eternal habitation of the people of God. I believe then that the Apocalyptic vision is the fulfilment, and more than the fulfilment, of the older vision. There never has been any fulfilment as yet of the Ezekiel vision in the Old Jerusalem, but there will be in the New. There has been a spiritual fulfilment, when the Holy Ghost descended and a flood of light and truth spread over all nations, but God Who has created us body and soul and will renew both, promises a time when the outward glory will correspond to the inward sanctity. The tree of life disappeared after Adam's fall: it will reappear when the effects of that fall are undone, when, as the next verse (in the Apocalyptic vision) tells us, "there shall be no more curse."

It will be necessary now to say a few words on the systems of interpretation of the Revelation. They seem naturally to divide themselves into three.

1. The preterist interpretation.
2. The continuous historical interpretation.
3. The futurist.

1. The preterist. According to this scheme the Apocalypse was written to forewarn the contemporaries of the Apostle of what was to take place in his own lifetime. Of course such a scheme of interpretation would apply principally to the destruction of Jerusalem and the distress and afflictions which would befall the Jewish nation, and also Rome during the reigns of the Emperors Nero, Galba, Otho, Vitellius, Vespasian, Titus, and perhaps Domitian. Under this mode of interpretation the Revelation is scarcely a prophetic book. The horizon of a prophet's vision does not

extend, it is assumed, beyond his own lifetime, so that all the things revealed in it are the account of well-known events occurring in Italy or Palestine, which for some reason or other were veiled under the most mysterious enigmatical forms. Of all the suggested interpretations of this book this one appears to me the one most unlikely to be true. According to this view, after the Apocalypse was published its interest for Christians wellnigh ceased. Its only interest to us is that of a book of enigmas, in interpreting which we have to hazard all manner of guesses to explain away awful preternatural figures which after all signify the plainest things; thus, the sounding of his trumpet by the second angel, followed by the burning mountain cast into the sea, and the waters becoming blood, and the third part of the sea becomes blood, and the third part of the fish die. This is explained as the inundation which devastated the coasts of Lydia, and the destruction of fleets, and the waves reddened with the blood of men as at Joppa and on the coasts of the Dead Sea and on the lake of Galilee. But why should such dreadful but plain historical events be wrapped up in the language of extreme mystery, as a burning mountain cast into the sea and turning the third part of the sea into blood? There may be, I allow, certain things which needed to be shrouded in mystery, such as the name of Neron Cæsar, which in this nineteenth century is discovered to be the name of Nero Cæsar, taking the value of the letters of his name as written in Hebrew, but of the greater part of the events hidden under the Apocalyptic figures there was no need whatsoever of shrouding them under visions.

For this and many other reasons I reject altogether the preterist scheme, and I cannot conceive how any persons of ordinary common-sense should have accepted it as it is usually stated *except for for some strong reason in the background.*[1]

The next scheme to be noticed is the historical, or rather continuous historical scheme. This scheme is principally occupied with the Papacy, and with the events which preceded it, and the events which have followed it and greatly modified its power; such as the French Revolution and the French Empire under Napoleon. By far the most elaborate, and, we may say, exhaustive exposition

---

[1] Alcasar, a Jesuit, seems to be the first of such expositors. After him Grotius, Hammond, Bossuet, Wetstein, Moses Stuart, F. D. Maurice.

of this view is Elliot's "Horæ Apocalypticæ" in four thick volumes. I have constantly referred to this work, giving specimens of its (I really must say) outrageous expositions to show the reader how little reliable a system can be which has to resort to such expedients to maintain its continuity.

But the thing which appears to me to discredit utterly this continuous historical view is the way in which it is forced, in order to maintain itself, to get rid of the intimations of the Second Coming of Christ. It seems scarcely credible that such a vision as that of the opening of the sixth seal should be explained by Christian expositors as foretelling the conquests of the Christian Constantine over his heathen antagonists, but so it is. Read the prophecy: "The heavens departed as a scroll when it is rolled together; and every mountain and island were moved out of their places. And the kings of the earth, and the great men, and the rich men, and the chief captains, and the mighty men, and every bondman, and every free man, hid themselves in the dens and in the rocks of the mountains; and said to the mountains and rocks, Fall on us, and hide us from the face of him that sitteth on the throne, and from the wrath of the Lamb; for the great day of his wrath is come; and who shall be able to stand?" (vi. 14-17).

Now it is inconceivable to me that this can be applied by any Christian man to any event but one, but the exigencies of the continuous historical scheme demand that its fulfilment should be at the beginning of the fourth century, and something must be discovered then to suit it no matter how absurdly inappropriate.[1]

3. The futurist scheme lays down that as yet the reality of none of the Apocalyptic visions is accomplished, but they all wait for their consummation to the times immediately preceding the Second Advent. This scheme of exposition seems to me mainly to rely on the obscurity of the visions—on the fact that scarcely any two interpreters have given the same meaning to any one of them. Still, if the book is given to us to bid us look for and expect "things which shall be hereafter," then there are many things

---

[1] The principal expositors of this scheme are Berengard, the Abbot Joachim, the Reformers, as Wickliffe, Luther, Bullinger, Bale, Fox, Brightman, and many others. In more modern times by Mede, who, however, makes many of its visions synchronous, Jurieu, Cressener, Vitringa, Sir Isaac Newton, Whiston, Bengel, and Bishop Newton, and in our times Faber, Elliot in "Horæ Apocalypticæ," and Bishop Wordsworth. Isaac Williams and Dean Vaughan take a spiritualistic view of the whole book.

which have occurred since the rise of Christianity which seem worthy of a place in such a book of prophecy, as, for instance, the submission of the Roman Empire to receive Christianity; the rise and progress of the pretensions of the Bishops of Rome; the extraordinary rapid success of the religion of Mahomet; the Reformation, as it is called, and its—one might almost say—collapse; the French Revolution, culminating in the Empire of Bonaparte, *its* collapse—all these as affecting the Church and a partially-Christianized world seem worthy of a place in prophecy, and if our eyes were opened we should find that they have, or had, a place; but as far as I can see God has as yet not given to us a principle of sequence in which these things find their place.[1]

It will be necessary for me now to point out what sort of scheme of interpretation seems to point towards the true one.

First I must take it for granted that any scheme of interpretation must take into the fullest account the intimations throughout the book of the Lord's Second Coming. Now, as He has not come yet and the opening of the first six seals covers the ground between His First Coming to proclaim His Salvation, and His Second glorious and terrible Advent, the present time in which we live must be under the opening of the seals. I do not say under the opening of one of the seals, for, as I have shown in the exposition, all the horse riders run together—the white horse Rider, the Gospel, is now progressing: there has been a time of continuous war—of scarcity sometimes bordering on famine, and of pestilence, not universal, but in divers places—as if a fourth part of the earth was affected. The opening of the fifth seal evidently betokens what takes place in the unseen world, so we can say nothing about it as regards its effect on this lower world; but still we are evidently living in the seal-opening period.

The sealing period of chap. vii. is not visible in this world, so that we can say nothing about it.

The trumpet soundings of chap. viii. and ix. may be going on now for we are not told, nor have we the least hint given to us, whether the effect of the first trumpet sounding ceases altogether before the

---

[1] The founder of the futurist school seems to have been the Jesuit Ribera. To it, according to Alford, belong the respected names of Dr. Todd, Maitland, Burgh, Isaac Williams (?), and others. The reader will find in the fourth volume of Elliot's "Horæ Apocalypticæ" a most exhaustive history of Apocalyptic interpretation from Victorinus to Bishop Waldegrave in our day.

second trumpet is blown, so that what is meant by the mountain cast into the sea may be synchronous with the hailstorm mingled with fire of verse 7, and the wormwood star of verses 10 and 11, and partial darkening of the sun, moon, and stars of verse 12.

If the effects of the fifth angel-trumpet be the rise and progress of Islamism, and the sixth the rise and progress of the Turkish power, then this may be taking place now and a large portion of mankind may be affected by it.

The vision of chap. x., that of the mighty angel, seems to take place in the unseen world, and its effects on this outer world have not, as far as I can see, been revealed to us.

There is nothing in the history of the world, or of the Church, in the least degree corresponding to the witnessing of the two witnesses. I humbly think that it takes place (or took place) in the unseen world. If the reader desires to see the futility of explaining it of what took place in this lower world, *i.e.*, of the persecutions of the pre-Reformation Protestants, or of the witnessing of the Old and New Testaments, he has only to look to the extract I have given from Mr. Elliot and Bishop Wordsworth in pp. 140-148 in this exposition.

If the vision of chap. xii., of the woman bringing forth the man child, and persecuted by the dragon, refers to the world-long conflict between the serpent and the seed of the woman, intensified by the Incarnation, then of course we are living in it.

If the two theria of chap. xiii. be the fierce and ferocious world-power, and the milder and more cultured world-power of Bishop Boyd-Carpenter and others, then of course the warfare is going on now, and we are living in it.

The events of the first part of chap. xiv. seem to take place in the unseen world.

The two visions of the Son of man on the white cloud, and the angel reaping the vintage of the earth, of course refer to the end and the end only.

Respecting the pouring out of the vials I can say nothing. If they are synchronous they immediately precede the Second Coming. Two or three seem to correspond with the effects of the seven trumpets.

Respecting the vision of Babylon, the great harlot of chaps. xvii. and xviii., if it betokens either a particular fallen Church, or the fall of universal Christendom, or the collapse of modern commerce, as some have thought, it is probable that we are now living in the times indicated. It seems to me certain that no voice answering to that of xviii. 4 ("Come out of her, my people,") has been heard by those most nearly concerned, that is, by godly Romanists.

The vision of chap. xix. seems to take place in the unseen heavenly world.

With respect to the vision of what is called the millennium, in chap. xx., Christ has certainly reigned ever since "all things were put under his feet" at His Ascension. He has reigned in order to discipline His elect, that they may be ready for Him when He comes at the last; and His saints may have reigned under Him, not visibly, but effectually—effectually for the purposes for which He has ordained their reign. One thing, however, seems to me to be certain, that Satan at no time or period since the Coming of Christ has been restrained from deceiving the world, unless in ways which God has not revealed to us.

The MSS. of the Apocalypse are as follows:

ℵ. Codex Sinaiticus.

A. Codex Alexandrinus.

B. Codex Vaticanus 2066, not the celebrated Codex B., but another uncial altogether. It is an uncial copy of the end of the eighth century; the Codex Vaticanus B. of the Gospels and Epistles not containing the Apocalypse. A full account of it for general readers will be found in Scrivener's "Introduction to the Criticism of the New Testament."

C. Codex Ephraemi.

P. Codex Porphyrianus. A palimpsest, containing the Acts, all the Epistles, the Apocalypse, and a few fragments of Maccabees iv. of the ninth century. It was found by Tischendorf in 1863 at St. Petersburg, in the possession of the Archimandrite (now Bishop) Porphyry, who allowed him to take it to Leipsic to decipher (see p. 162 of Scrivener's "Introduction," 3rd edition).

There are 111 Cursive MSS. of the Apocalypse described or noticed in Scrivener's "Introduction," pp. 273-278.

A COMMENTARY.

THE REVELATION OF ST. JOHN THE DIVINE.

CHAP. I.

THE Revelation of Jesus Christ, ^a which God gave unto him, to shew unto his servants

^a John iii. 32. & viii. 26. & xii. 49.

---

1. "The Revelation of Jesus Christ." That is, the Revelation given by Jesus Christ to St. John.

It does not seem to mean the Revelation of the Person and Work of Christ, but of that reality of future things which Christ received of the Father to make known to His people.

"The Revelation." Apocalypse means the uncovering of what is before concealed. It is a word of very frequent use to express much more than such glimpses of the future as are contained in Daniel and this book. Thus, in Rom. ii. 5, we have: "After thy hardness and impenitent heart treasurest to thyself wrath against the day of wrath and apocalypse of the righteous judgment of God." By many modern authors it is confined to books of visions, such as Daniel, Zechariah, and parts of Ezekiel.

"Which God gave unto him." In the words of Christ preserved to us in the Gospel of St. John, the Lord carefully sets before us the Father as the fountain of all knowledge. "I have called you friends; because all things that I have heard of my Father I have made known unto you" (John xv. 15); and again: "The Father which sent me, he gave me a commandment, what I should say and what I should speak" (John xii. 49). This the Lord said lest in declaring His Divine Nature and Attributes

things which ᵇmust shortly come to pass; and ᶜhe sent and signified *it* by his angel unto his servant John: 2 ᵈWho bare record of the word of God, and of the testimony of Jesus Christ, and of all things ᵉthat he saw. 3 ᶠBlessed *is* he that readeth, and they that

ᵇ ch. iv. 1. ver. 3.
ᶜ ch. xxii. 16.
ᵈ 1 Cor. i. 6. ch. vi. 9. & xii. 17. ver. 9.
ᵉ 1 John i. 1.
ᶠ Luke xi. 28. ch. xxii. 7.

---

2. "And" (τε) omitted by ℵ, A., B., C., P., fifty Cursives, Vulg., Copt., Syr., Arm.; retained by few Cursives.

He should in the slightest degree seem to speak or act independently of the Father.

"To shew unto his servants things which must shortly come to pass." "Shortly" (ἐν τάχει), does this mean that the things to be revealed will shortly come to pass in the usual sense of "shortly," or that we are to understand this in the light of 2 Pet. iii. 8: "One day is with the Lord as a thousand years, and a thousand years as one day"? The former rendering is relied upon by the preterists, the latter by those who look upon the series of visions as embodying a continuous history from the Ascension to the Second Advent.

"And he sent and signified it by his angel unto his servant John." This seems to mean that the whole revelation was given through angelic mediation, though only here and there does the angel actually appear as in ch. xvii. 1. This seems analogous to the giving of the law. God speaks on Mount Sinai, and yet the law was "given by angels in the hand of a mediator" (Gal. iii. 19).

"Servant John." The Apostle selected in the wisdom of God to be the instrument of revealing the deepest mysteries of the kingdom.

2. "Who bare record of the word of God, and of the testimony of Jesus Christ." This has been supposed to allude to the Gospel record which was of "the Word of God and of the testimony of Jesus Christ," as God manifest in the flesh.

Most, however, consider the words to allude to the revelation of God's purposes in the book now opening.

"Of all things that he saw," *i.e.*, in vision.

3. "Blessed is he that readeth, and they that hear the words," &c. It is supposed that by "he that readeth" we are to under-

hear the words of this prophecy, and keep those things which are written therein: for ᵍthe time *is* at hand.

4 John to the seven churches which are in Asia: Grace *be* unto you, and peace, from him ʰ which

g Rom. xiii. 11. James v. 8. 1 Pet. iv. 7. ch. xxii. 10.
h Exod. iii. 14. ver. 8.

---

stand the public reader in the Christian assembly, inasmuch as he is alluded to in the singular number, and his hearers in the plural.

"And keep those things which are written therein: for the time," &c. They who keep the things which are written in this book habitually remember that it especially predicts aggregations of evil men, or embodiments of evil principles, acting in concert against God and Christ with the ferocity of evil wild beasts, and so their duty to God is to keep themselves from all union in sin, and to lay to heart the judgments of God against sinners.

4. "John to the seven churches which are in Asia." How is it that the number seven is used here? There were far more than seven churches in proconsular Asia. There was Colosse, to which an Epistle was sent by St. Paul; there was Hierapolis, and Miletus, and Troas, where St. Paul raised Eutychus from the dead. There can be, I think, no doubt but that seven was chosen as a mystic number, signifying the whole and perfect Church of Christ. Seven is chosen in order that it may indicate at once the definite and indefinite. The Church is an infinite body, but in contemplating it we must not lose ourselves in infinitude, but consider it as embracing a *definite* number of smaller bodies, each one known to God and regarded by Him as if there were none else but Himself and it to share His regard.

"Grace be unto you, and peace, from him which is, and which was, and which is to come." St. John has been said to have been guilty of a fault in grammar—a grammatical solecism—because he has treated the most sacred name as an indeclinable noun, ἀπὸ (του) ὁ ὢν και ὁ ἦν και ὁ ἐρχόμενος, which, following the strict rules of grammar ought to have been (after απο) in the genitive; but it is no more a solecism than Moses was guilty of when he sent this message from God to the children of Israel: "I AM hath sent me unto you." The immutability in the words by which the Name of God is expressed has been well set forth by Archbishop Trench as setting forth the immutability of Him Who is the same yesterday

THE SEVEN SPIRITS. [REVELATION.

ⁱ John i. 1.
^k Zech. iii. 9. & iv. 10. ch. iii. 1. & iv. 5. & v. 6.
^l John viii. 14. 1 Tim. vi. 13. ch. iii. 14.
^m 1 Cor. xv. 20. Col. i. 18.

is, and ⁱ which was, and which is to come; ^k and from the seven Spirits which are before his throne;

5 And from Jesus Christ, ^l*who is* the faithful witness, *and* the ^m first begotten of the dead, and

---

and to-day and for ever, so that it is expressed in this absolute resistance to change, or even modification, of the very name; and Wordsworth expresses it as bespeaking the indeclinability of the Divine Essence "with whom is no variableness or shadow of turning" (James i. 17).

"And which is to come." This is not to be taken as signifying the same as "shall be," but as signifying that though He is with His people now He is ever "coming" to them in some new manifestation of grace and goodness.

"And from the seven Spirits which are before his throne." This no doubt refers to the Holy Ghost; the One Spirit in His Essence, and yet the Manifold in His operations. The place is parallel to ch. v. 6. The lamb "having seven horns and seven eyes, which are the seven Spirits of God sent forth into all the earth." An infinite Spirit, the Spirit of God, confronts each personality with His most searching and loving presence, as if there were none in the universe except Himself and the man whom He observes. In the most ancient form of Liturgy, the Clementine, God is said to be One, and yet exceeding all number, $αναριθμητος$, as being absolutely One, and yet One to each intelligence whom He has created. Here the Spirit is seven because there are seven churches, in each of which He dwells wholly and separately.

It is impossible to suppose that these are seven created spirits as angels, because grace and peace cannot come from them, but must come from the Adorable Three in One.

5. "And from Jesus Christ, who is the faithful witness, and the first begotten." He is the faithful Witness because He witnesses—as none other can do—to the absolute truth of God. In the Gospel the Lord constantly refers to His office of Witness. This is a Johannine expression. We may safely say that no scripture writer would have applied this term to our Lord except the beloved disciple.

"And the first begotten of the dead." He is, as St. Paul says,

CHAP. I.] UNTO HIM THAT LOVED US. 5

ⁿ the prince of the kings of the earth. Unto him
ᵒ that loved us, ᵖ and washed us from our sins in
his own blood,

6 And hath ᑫ made us kings and priests unto

ⁿ Eph. i. 20.
ch. xvii. 14. &
xix. 16.
ᵒ John xiii. 34.
& xv. 9. Gal.
ii. 20.
ᵖ Heb. ix. 14.
1 John i. 7.
ᑫ 1 Pet. ii. 5,
9. ch. v. 10.
& xx. 6.

---

5. "Loved." ℵ, A., B., C., forty-five Cursives read, "loves"; P., and a few Cursives read as in Authorized Translation.

"Washed." So B., P., most Cursives, Vulg., Copt., &c.; but ℵ, A., C. read, "loosed us," the difference only one letter.

"become the firstfruits of them that slept" (1 Cor. xv. 20); and again, in Coloss. i. 18: "The first born of the dead."

"And the prince of the kings of the earth." "All power is given unto me in heaven and in earth." "King of Kings and Lord of Lords." In these three sentences the glory of the Lord Jesus is declared. He is the faithful Witness to God and His truth. He is the Author of Everlasting Life, being the first born of the dead. He is the Wielder of all power. Fear not your persecutors, even though they may be emperors, for Christ rules them all, and makes each one accomplish His purposes, not their own.

"Unto him that loved us, and washed us from our sins," &c. Better, perhaps, "him that loves us," in the singular. His love in past time continues in the present, and will last for ever.

"And washed us from our sins in his own blood." Perhaps the true reading is $\lambda \acute{v} \sigma a \nu \tau \iota$, not $\lambda o \acute{v} \sigma a \nu \tau \iota$, "Who has redeemed us by His Blood."

6. "And hath made us kings and priests." Rather, perhaps, "has made us a kingdom—even priests to God." This, with the alterations, is the exact counterpart of Exod. xix. 6: "Ye shall be unto me a kingdom of priests and a holy nation."

In what does the universal priesthood of all Christians consist? Mainly in intercession. There are in all churches, and always have been, certain ministers set apart to minister certain functions, such as Baptism, the Consecration of the Eucharist, Ordination, &c.; but the priesthood of the laity must, of necessity, consist principally in Intercession, and it would be well if they were more frequently reminded of this their sacerdotal duty. They are constantly bid to assert their priesthood as against the ministerial

God and his Father; ʳ to him *be* glory and dominion for ever and ever. Amen.

7 ˢBehold, he cometh with clouds; and every eye shall see him, and ᵗ they *also* which pierced

<small>ʳ 1 Tim. vi. 16.
Heb. xiii. 21.
1 Pet. iv. 11.
& v. 11.
ˢ Dan. vii. 13.
Matt. xxiv.
30. & xxvi. 64.
Acts i. 11.
ᵗ Zech. xii. 10.
John xix. 37.</small>

---

7. "With clouds." "With the clouds."

brethren; but their principal function they are scarcely ever reminded of. A layman who never intercedes for his brethren is worse than an ordained minister who neglects his sacred function of presiding in the congregation.

"To him be glory and dominion." This doxology, addressed to God the Son, is one of the innumerable places where the Godhead of the Son is most surely asserted by implication. It is addressed to One Who shed His Blood, and so is a creature, and yet it would be the height of blasphemy to apply it to a mere creature.

7. "Behold he cometh with clouds." Thus in Daniel: "One like the Son of man came in the clouds of heaven." Thus in St. Matthew xxiv. 30: "They shall see the Son of man coming in the clouds of heaven," and "Hereafter shall ye see the Son of man sitting on the right hand of power, and coming in the clouds of heaven" (xxvi. 64). How is it that such marked stress is laid on His coming in the "clouds"? Evidently to show that His coming will not be a spiritual, but an open, visible appearance, as that of a judge coming to his assize. But may it not be, as Professor Milligan asks, that these are not the mere clouds of the sky, but those clouds of Sinai, of the Shechinah, of the Transfiguration, of the Ascension, which are the recognized signs of Deity?

"And every eye shall see him." Not merely the eyes of the living, but those who have been dead for ages, because the Evangelist goes on to say, "and they also which pierced him." This will be true of those who actually pierced the Lord on Calvary; then it will be true of all the inhabitants of Jerusalem—as Zechariah says; then of those who have pierced the Lord with their sins, as all have, for if He died for all, then all have a part in His Death, both in the guilt which brought it about, and the atonement consequent upon it.

him: and all kindreds of the earth shall wail because of him. Even so, Amen.

8 ᵘ I am Alpha and Omega, the beginning and the ending, saith the Lord, ˣ which is, and which was, and which is to come, the Almighty.

ᵘ Isa. xli. 4. & xliv. 6. & xlviii. 12. ver. 11, 17. ch. ii. 8. & xxi. 6. & xxii. 13.

ˣ ver. 4. ch. iv. 8. & xi. 17. & xvi. 5.

---

8. "The beginning and the ending" omitted by אᶜ, A., B., C., P., forty-five Cursives, Syr., Arm., Æth.; but retained by א*, a few Cursives, Vulg., Copt.

"Saith the Lord." κύριος ὁ Θεός. So א, A., B., C., P., fifty Cursives.

The words "they also which pierced him" are taken from Zechariah xii. 10, and it is much to be remarked that both here and in John xix. 37 the New Testament writer does not adopt, as usual, the Septuagint reading, which runs, "because they have mocked me" (ἀνθ'ὧν κατωρχήσαντο), but "whom they have pierced." This, as Alford, and Lee in the "Speaker's Commentary" remark, is almost a demonstration of the common authorship of the Apocalypse and the Fourth Gospel. This and John xix. 37 are the only places in the New Testament where this prophecy is alluded to.

"And all kindreds of the earth shall wail because of him. Even so, Amen." The tribes or kindreds of the earth are those who are of the earth earthly, who are not reconciled to God through His Merits, and have not taken Him as their Master and Lord.

8. "I am Alpha and Omega, the beginning and the ending, saith the Lord." The title "Lord" is almost always given to the Lord Jesus; and all the words from the beginning of verse 5 relate solely and entirely to Him, so that if we believe in His Essential Godhead we must suppose that these words are spoken by Him of Himself, as undoubtedly they are in xxii. 13.

"Which is, and which was, and which is to come, the Almighty." "Such as the Father is, such is the Son, and such is the Holy Ghost. The Father Almighty, the Son Almighty, and the Holy Ghost Almighty." Archbishop Trench gives a remarkable passage from Clement of Alexandria: "For He is the circle of all power, rolled and united into one unity, wherefore the Word is called the Alpha and Omega, of whom alone the end becomes beginning, and ends again at the original beginning without any break" ("Miscell." iv. 25); and another from Tertullian: "So, too,

THE ISLE CALLED PATMOS. [REVELATION.

y Phil. i. 7. &
iv. 14. 2 Tim.
i. 8.
z Rom. viii.
17. 2 Tim. ii.
12.
a ver. 2. ch.
vi. 9.

9 I John, who also am your brother, and ʸ companion in tribulation, and ᶻ in the kingdom and patience of Jesus Christ, was in the isle that is called Patmos, ᵃ for the word of God, and for the testimony of Jesus Christ.

---

the two letters of Greece, the first and the last, the Lord assumes to Himself as figures of the beginning and end, which concur in Himself, so that just as Alpha rolls on till it reaches Omega, and again Omega rolls back till it reaches Alpha, in the same way He might show that in Himself is both the downward course of the beginning on to the end, and the backward course of the end up to the beginning; so that every economy, ending in Him through Whom it began, through the Word of God that is, Who was made flesh may have an end corresponding to its beginning" ("On Monogamy," ch. v.).

"The Almighty." "Whatsoever things the Father doeth, these also doeth the Son likewise" (John v. 19).

9. "I John, who also am your brother, and companion in tribulation," &c. "Who also am your brother," *i.e.*, in Christ. The three following words are to be taken together, "and partaker with you in the tribulation, and kingdom, and patience which are in Jesus." "Let us not fail," says Trench, "to observe the connection and the sequence, tribulation first and the kingdom afterwards;" on which Richard of St. Victor well remarks, "he rightly puts first, 'in tribulation,' and adds afterwards, 'in the kingdom,' because 'if we suffer with him we shall also reign with him'" (2 Tim. ii. 12).

As yet, however, the tribulation is present, the kingdom is only in hope, therefore he adds to these, as that which is the link between them, "and patience of Jesus Christ." Still it is possible that the kingdom may be the present kingdom of grace. "The kingdom of God is among you." When our Lord, during the great forty days, spoke of the things pertaining to the kingdom of God, He most probably meant the means of grace and the ministry of the Church.

"Was in the isle that is called Patmos." A rocky island, consisting of three peninsulas joined together by very narrow isthmuses, said to be just visible from Miletus; "was" is rather "came to be."

10 ᵇI was in the Spirit on ᶜthe Lord's day, and heard behind me ᵈa great voice, as of a trumpet.

11 Saying, ᵉI am Alpha and Omega, ᶠthe first and the last: and, What thou seest, write in a

ᵇ Acts x. 10.
2 Cor. xii. 2
ch. iv. 2. &
xvii. 3. & xxi. 10.
ᶜ John xx. 26.
Acts xx. 7.
1 Cor. xvi. 2.
ᵈ ch. iv. 1. & x. 8.
ᵉ ver. 8.
ᶠ ver. 17.

---

11. "I am Alpha and Omega, the first and the last, and," omitted by ℵ, A., B., C., fifty Cursives, Vulg., Copt., Syr., Arm., Æth.; retained by only a few Cursives.

"For the word of God, and for the testimony of Jesus Christ." Some moderns, against all ancient authority, say that he went there to preach, but almost all ancient writers who refer to this sojourn say that it was a banishment to an island to which with others on the coast of Asia criminals were transported by way of punishment.

10. "I was in the Spirit." "I was wrapt in mind in a state of spiritual vision or an ecstasy," so that he was in a fit state to receive impressions from the invisible world. St. Paul describes such a state in 2 Cor. xii. 2, as being one in which he did not know whether he was "in the body or out of the body," and was "caught up into paradise and heard unspeakable words which it was not lawful or possible for one to utter."

"On the Lord's day," *i.e.*, on the day of the Resurrection. The weekly Christian festival and day for the Eucharistic celebration.

"And heard behind me a great voice, as of a trumpet." "Not merely," says Professor Milligan, "one with a clear and strong sound, but with a sound inspiring awe and terror, and corresponding in this respect to the distinguishing characteristics of the Lord in the further details of this vision."

11. "Saying, I am Alpha and Omega, the first and the last: and, What thou seest." There can be no doubt that the words, "I am Alpha and Omega, the first and the last," do not form a part of the original text, but have been inserted, together with the following clause, at a very early period, perhaps to take off from the abruptness of commencing the word of the Lord with "What thou seest," &c.

"What thou seest, write in a book, and send it unto the seven churches," &c. He is bid to write it that it may be in a permanent book, and send *it* unto the seven churches which are in Asia; unto Ephesus, and unto Smyrna, and unto Pergamos, and unto Thyatira, and unto Sardis, and unto Philadelphia, and unto Laodicea.

12 And I turned to see the voice that spake with me. And being turned, ^g I saw seven golden candlesticks;

<small>g ver. 20.
Exod. xxv. 37.
Zech. iv. 2.</small>

---

form. It is to be remarked that this command to write is given twelve times (i. 11, 19; ii. 1, 8, 12, 18; iii. 1, 7, 14; xiv. 13; xix. 9; xxi. 5).

He is told to write not what he hears, but what he sees. This must refer, not to the verbal messages sent to the churches, but to the visions which he saw rising before him in succession.

"And send it to the seven churches [which are in Asia]; unto Ephesus." There can be no doubt but that the number seven is to be taken mystically—the writing or Epistle is sent to the perfect Church, the universal, the Catholic Church.

"To Ephesus." Ephesus, being the most important, is placed first, also as being the seat of St. John's own ministry.

"And unto Smyrna." Eight miles to the north of Ephesus. Polycarp, the disciple of St. John, was afterwards its Bishop.

"And unto Pergamos," or rather, "Pergamum," was a city of Mysia, and the most northerly city of the group.

"Thyatira" was in Lydia on the river Lycus. It is mentioned as the city of Lydia in Acts xvi. 14.

"Sardis." The city of Crœsus and the ancient capital of the Lydian kings, situated to the south of Thyatira.

"Philadelphia," a city of Lydia, to the south-east of Sardis.

"Laodicea," to the east of Ephesus. It is the most southern of the seven, so that these cities all lay as it were within a stone's throw of one another. They were all within what may be called the archdiocese or province of the Apostle. They could not have been all the cities over which he had apostolic oversight, so their reduction to the number of seven must have been, as I have said, for some mystical reason.

12. "And I turned to see the voice that spake with me. And being turned," &c. How is it that he did not see the Lord

13 ʰ And in the midst of the seven candlesticks ⁱ *one* like unto the Son of man, ᵏ clothed with a

ʰ ch. ii. 1.
ⁱ Ezek. i. 26. Dan. vii. 13. & x. 16. ch. xiv. 14.
ᵏ Dan. x. 5.

---

first, as His countenance was "as the sun shining in his strength." No doubt he saw the candlesticks first, and then the form of the Lord appeared among them.

The candlesticks should rather be rendered lamp-stands. The figure was taken from the seven-branched candlestick or candelabrum in the temple, but with this difference, that in the temple it was one lamp-stand with seven branches, here there were seven candelabra, or it could not have been said that the Lord was in the midst of them. Some commentators suppose that each lamp-stand had seven branches, but this seems hardly likely.

The candlesticks or lamp-stands signify light-bearers. They hold the oil of the Spirit which alone illuminates.

13. "And in the midst of the seven candlesticks one like unto the Son of man." Why is the Lord said to be in the midst of the candlesticks? As the great priest whose duty it is—like that of His type—to see to the candlesticks, that they are supplied with the oil of Divine grace, that they are trimmed, and that nothing be wanting to them which would hinder them from giving their light.

"The Son of man." This is the only place except Acts vii. 56, where the Lord is called the Son of man by another than Himself. Not only in His Divine Nature as the Son of God, but as the Son of man He is present in or among the churches. He mediates between His Father and them, through His human Nature, "for there is one mediator between God and man, the man Christ Jesus" (1 Tim. ii. 5).

"Clothed with a garment down to the foot." The word in the original is ποδήρη which afterwards became, in ecclesiastical Latin, *poderis*. It seems a mistake to suppose that it is exclusively an ecclesiastical garment; it is rather a garment of supreme dignity, which is signified by its length, which indicates a garment for those who are above the sphere of labour: those who had to labour were obliged to have garments which could be tucked up or girded ("your loins girt about"). Thus, in Isaiah vi. 1, it is said

garment down to the foot, and ¹girt about the paps with a golden girdle.

14 His head and ᵐ*his* hairs *were* white like wool, as white as snow; and ⁿhis eyes *were* as a flame of fire;

¹ ch. xv. 6.
ᵐ Dan. vii. 9.
ⁿ Dan. x. 6. ch. ii. 18. & xix. 12.

---

respecting God that " His train," *i.e.*, the skirts of His robe, "filled the temple."

"And girt about the paps with a golden girdle." His girdle, that is, implied higher dignity than the girdle about His loins, by which the lower garments of those engaged in manual work were girded up.

14. " His head and his hairs were white like wool, as white as snow." This is the description of the Ancient of days, that is, of God the Father, in Daniel vii. 9. "The hair of his head like the pure wool." " It has been said that this whiteness signifies age—the ages of eternity; but this is impossible, for white hairs are the sign of declining bodily strength—the blood does not circulate through the extremities, and therefore not through the hairs, or they would retain their colour. It is rather a part of the transfiguration in light of the glorified Person of the Redeemer, a transfiguration so complete that it reaches to the extremities, to the very hairs of the head " (Trench).

"And his eyes were as a flame of fire." This is taken by Trench and others not as indicating the piercing power of His glance searching men through and through, but as the sign of Divine vengeance. His very glance consumes the sinner. "In the symbolism of Scripture fire is throughout the expression of the Divine anger, and —seeing that nothing moves that anger but sin—it is the expression of Divine anger against sin." I question, however, whether all this is not carried too far; St. John, the beloved one, saw His eyes as a flame of fire, and throughout the Apocalypse, particularly in the latter chapters, He looks upon men with compassion as well as with wrath. Fire is the source of light and warmth, without which nature could not be. When the Holy Spirit descended at Pentecost in the likeness of tongues of fire this was not the symbol of vengeance in any way.

15. "And his feet like unto fine brass, as if they burned in a fur-

15 °And his feet like unto fine brass, as if they burned in a furnace; and ᴾhis voice as the sound of many waters.

16 ᵠAnd he had in his right hand seven stars: and ʳout of his mouth went a sharp two-edged

° Ezek. i. 7.
Dan. x. 6.
ch. ii. 18.
ᴾ Ezek. xliii. 2. Dan. x. 6. ch. xiv. 2. & xix. 6.
ᵠ ver. 20. ch. ii. 1. & iii. 1.
ʳ Isa. xlix. 2. Eph. vi. 17. Heb. iv. 12. ch. ii. 12, 16. & xix. 15, 21.

---

15. "Like unto fine brass." Various meanings given below. The precise meaning of the word is quite unknown (Alford).

"As if they burned in a furnace." πεπυρωμένοι read in B., P., and most Cursives; but πεπυρωμένῳ with ℵ, a few Cursives, Vulg., Copt., Sah., Syr., Æth.

nace." "Like unto chalco-libanus." A word apparently exceedingly difficult to explain. Some have rendered it as mountain brass, some as brass of Mount Lebanon; some, taking the latter part, libanus, in its meaning of frankincense, as brass of the colour of frankincense—than which nothing can be more unlikely. Trench, after noticing all three and other explanations, renders it "the glowing brass." This conclusion is much strengthened by the apexegesis "as if they burned in a furnace," words of explanation immediately added by St. John as probably knowing the difficulty which his readers would find in the unusual term.

"And his voice as the sound of many waters." This is taken from Ezekiel xliii. 2: "Behold, the glory of the God of Israel came from the way of the east: and his voice was like the noise of many waters." "This comparison," says Trench, "is not to be understood of the far and wide publication of the Gospel ('this sound is gone out into all lands') but to the terribleness of the voice with which He will rebuke His foes both within the Church and without."

16. "And he had in his right hand seven stars." The seven churches are here said to be in the hand of Christ, because He has all power over them and He protects them, "no one can pluck them out of my hand." Trench supposes that He holds them as one would hold a wreath.

"And out of his mouth went a sharp two-edged sword." This indicates the word, but not, we are told, the saving word so much as the avenging word. "The whole feeling, the whole sense of the passage with which we have here to do, requires that we should

sword: *and his countenance was as the sun shineth in his strength.

17 And †when I saw him, I fell at his feet as dead. And ᵘhe laid his right hand upon me, saying unto me, Fear not; ˣI am the first and the last:

* Acts xxvi. 13. ch. x. 1.
† Ezek. i. 28.
ᵘ Dan. viii. 18. & x. 10.
ˣ Isa. xli. 4. & xliv. 6. & xlviii. 12. ch. ii. 8. & xxii. 13. ver. 11.

17, and part of 18. "I am the first and the last, and the living one, and I was dead."

take this sword from the mouth as expressing rather the punishing than the convincing power of God's word" (Trench).

"His countenance is as the sun shineth in his strength." Thus He appeared to St. Paul on his way to Damascus. "I saw a light from heaven, above the brightness of the sun" (Acts xxvi., 13).

It is doubtful to me whether this signifies the unendurable brightness of one appearing in vengeance, or the (I was going to say) natural brightness of the Revelation of the Deity.

17. "And when I saw him, I fell at his feet as dead." It was no other than St. John, the beloved disciple who had lain in the bosom of Jesus, who was then utterly prostrated by the extremity of his fear. Whenever the supernatural is revealed the natural quails before it; much more must this be true of the Lord of spiritual existences. When but a created angel appeared in glory to Daniel there remained no strength in him, for his comeliness was turned in him to corruption, and he retained no strength (Dan. x. 8).

"And he laid his right hand upon me, saying unto me, Fear not; I am," &c. The right hand which held the stars. The right hand, whether of God or man, is contemplated in Scripture as that by which the power of God and man is put forth.

"Fear not, I am the first and the last." "This," as Trench says, "is the expression of Absolute Godhead." It is three times applied to Jehovah, in Isaiah xli. 4: "I the Lord, the first, and with the last; I am he;" xliv. 6: "I am the first, and I am the last; and beside me there is no God;" and in xlviii. 12: "I am the first, I also am the last." That the Lord should thus assume it is the most convincing proof that in substance, power, and eternity He is One with the Father. Trench quotes a remarkable passage from Richard of St. Victor: "Ego sum primus et novissimus

18 ʸ*I am* he that liveth, and was dead; and, behold, ᶻI am alive for evermore, Amen; and ᵃhave the keys of hell and of death.

19 Write ᵇthe things which thou hast seen, ᶜand the things which are, ᵈand the things which shall be hereafter;

ʸ Rom. vi. 9.
ᶻ ch. iv. 9. & v. 14.
ᵃ Ps. lxviii. 20. ch. xx. 1.
ᵇ ver. 12, &c.
ᶜ ch. ii. 1, &c.
ᵈ ch. iv. 1, &c.

---

18. "Amen" omitted by ℵ*, A., C.; retained by ℵᶜ, B.
19. "Write therefore the things which thou sawest, and what things they are, and the things which shall be after these."

Primus per creationem, novissimus per retributionem. Primus qui ante me non est formatus Deus; novissimus quia post me alius non erit. Primus quia a me sunt omnia, novissimus quia ad me sunt omnia; a me principio ad me finem. Primus quia Ego sum causa originis; novissimus quia Ego Judex et Finis."

18. "I am he that liveth and was dead; and behold, I am alive for evermore." There should be no break between this and the last clause of the preceding verse. It should run: "I am the first, and the last, and the living one, and I became dead, and behold I am alive for evermore."

"I am the living One—the One who is essentially Life. As the Father hath life in Himself, so hath He given to the Son to have life in Himself."

"And I became dead." "For a very brief space I allowed death to have dominion over me: but it was to redeem man from death by my death."

"And now I am alive for evermore, having the keys of hell and of death." "The possession of the keys exhibits the permanency of my victory."

"I open, and no man shuts, I shut and no man opens." By far the more important MSS. invert the order of our Authorized, and read Death and Hell (Hades). This is the natural order, for it is death which peoples Hades.

19. "Write the things which thou hast seen, and the things which are, and," &c. I cannot but think that "the things which thou hast seen" includes more than the Vision of the Redeemer set forth between the 12th and the 18th verses. It seems to cover all the visions in this book of visions.

"The things which are." This must allude to the things now at

20 The mystery ^e of the seven stars which thou sawest in my right hand, ^f and the seven golden candlesticks. The seven stars are ^g the angels of

^e ver. 16.
^f ver. 12.
^g Mal. ii. 7. ch. ii. 1, &c.

---

this present time occurring. But is it possible to limit these "things which are" to the delivery of the messages to the seven churches? I cannot think so. We cannot say what the time is which is indicated by the "are" in the phrase "things which are." It may be a day or it may be a thousand years.

"And the things which shall be hereafter." "The things which shall come to pass after these things." The time here indicated depends upon the meaning of "these things."

20. "The mystery of the seven stars which thou sawest in my right hand, and the seven golden candlesticks." Upon what do these words depend? It is supposed that they depend upon the word "write." He is to write, or explain, or enunciate the mystery of the stars and candelabra. This he does either now in the latter part of this verse, or in the succeeding two chapters. If the former, then he writes simply the fact that the stars in the Lord's right hand are the angels of the seven churches, and the candlesticks are the seven churches, thus distinguishing between the angels of the churches and the churches themselves. If the latter, then the mystery of the seven stars and churches is the account of their character and of their dangers, and of God's dealings with them.

But what are these angels? They can scarcely be angelic beings or guardian angels, because letters or epistles would not be sent to them by God, neither can they be, as some have supposed, impersonations of the churches, because the church would not require personating, as each church was itself in turn arraigned at the bar of Christ. They must be the chief ministers, or presidents, of each church. When it is said that this Apocalypse was written at a date in which the episcopacy of latter times was not in operation, we answer, that St. John himself had lived in a city, Jerusalem, which was as much under episcopal regimen as any city now existing, and St. Paul had put the first of these churches, Ephesus, under a man who in his absence exercised very stringent episcopal rule over it.

the seven churches: and ᵇ the seven candlesticks which thou sawest are the seven churches.   ᵇ Zech. iv. 2.
Matt. v. 15.
Phil. ii. 15.

The most serious thing as regards bishops is that the stars or angels are held responsible for the religious character of each church, as if the bishop was capable by the example of his holiness of moulding the church, and by his prayers and exertions of keeping it from declension and heresy.

CHAP. II.

UNTO the angel of the church of Ephesus write; These things saith ᵃ he that holdeth the seven stars in his right hand, ᵇ who walketh in the midst of the seven golden candlesticks.   ᵃ ch. i. 16, 20.
ᵇ ch. i. 13.

---

1. "Unto the angel of the church of Ephesus write; These things saith he that holdeth the seven stars." Ephesus is placed the first because of its importance. The Apostle St. Paul had exercised in it a ministry lasting over three years. He had during his absence committed the oversight of it to his first disciple, and St. John, according to the united testimony of Christian antiquity, presided over it for many years. It was very natural then that it should occupy the first place in his thoughts.

The Lord begins His message to each church with one of the titles He assumed in this address, or with one of the Divine or supernatural marks by which He had made Himself known to the Apostle. In the words to the Church of Ephesus it is, "These things saith he that holdeth the seven stars in his right hand, and walketh in the midst of the seven golden candlesticks." As Trench notices, there is a significant alteration. It is not "He that hath," but "He that holdeth the seven stars," and it is not "He that is in the midst," but "He that walketh in the midst." He holdeth the stars so that no one can pluck them out of His hand. He walked in the

2 ^c I know thy works, and thy labour, and thy patience, and how thou canst not bear them

<small>c Ps. i. 6. ver. ix. 13, 19. ch. iii. 1, 8, 15.</small>

midst of the candlesticks; He sits not inertly, He walks up and down amongst them, expressing His unwearied activity, beholding the good and the evil, evermore trimming and feeding with the oil of grace the golden lamps of the sanctuary.

"I know thy works." The Lord begins each of His messages with the same "I know thy works." Whatever these works are—whether good or evil—whether open and manifest, or carried on only in the most secret recesses of the soul, works of repentance, hope, love, adoration, or of envy, covetousness, or evil thought, He knows all.

"And thy labour." I cannot forbear giving some very practical words of Archbishop Trench on this word. "Indeed this word κόπος, signifying as it does not merely labour, but labour unto weariness, may suggest some solemn reflections to everyone who at all affects to be working for his Lord, and as under his Great Taskmaster's eye. This is what Christ looks for, this is what Christ praises in His servants. But how often does labour, which esteems itself labour for Him, stop short of this; take care that it shall never arrive at this point: and, perhaps, in our days none are more tempted continually to measure out to themselves tasks too light and inadequate than those to whom an office and ministry in the Church has been committed. Indeed there is here to them an ever-recurring temptation, and this from the fact that they do for the most part measure out their own day's task to themselves. Others in almost every other calling have it measured out to them; if not the zeal, earnestness, sincerity which they are to put into the performance of it, yet at any rate the outward limits, the amount of time which they shall devote to it, and often the definite quantity of it which they shall accomplish. It is not so with us. We give it exactly the number of hours which we please; we are for the most part responsible to no man; and when labourers thus apportion their own burdens, and do this from day to day, how near the danger that they should unduly spare themselves, and make their burdens far lighter than they should have been."

"And thy patience." This patience may be the endurance of persecution. It may be perseverance in the Divine life, or it may

which are evil: and ᵈ thou hast tried them ᵉ which say they are apostles, and are not, and hast found them liars:

ᵈ 1 John iv. 1.
ᵉ 2 Cor. xi. 13.
2 Pet. ii. 1.

3 And hast borne, and hast patience, and for my name's sake hast laboured, and hast ᶠ not fainted.

ᶠ Gal. vi. 9.
Heb. xii. 3, 5.

4 Nevertheless I have *somewhat* against thee, because thou hast left thy first love.

---

3. "And hadst patience, and didst bear for my name's sake, and hast not been weary" (Revised and Alford).

be, as Bishop Wordsworth suggests, that while the angel is praised because he exercises godly discipline in censure and correction of errors, he yet preaches Christian patience and forbearance towards the "erring."

"And how thou canst not bear them which are evil." This does not mean that they are to persecute them, or render to them the same evil which they have done, but that they should do their utmost to counteract their evil, and bring them by prayer and remonstrance to a right mind, and, if need be, put them out of the Church lest they contaminate others.

"And thou hast tried them which say they are apostles, and are not, and hast found them liars." St. Paul speaks of heretical teachers who claimed to be Apostles. "Such are," he writes, 2 Cor. xi. 13, " false apostles, deceitful workers, transforming themselves into the apostles of Christ." Tertullian relates a story of a presbyter who forged an Epistle of St. Paul, was found out, and was removed from his office ("On Baptism," ch. xvii.). This must have occurred, one would think, whilst St. John was absent from them enduring imprisonment.

3. "[And hast borne], and hast patience, and for my name's sake hast laboured, and hast not fainted." The first clause should be omitted, and the whole is in the Revised, "And thou hast patience, and didst bear for my name's sake, and hast not grown weary." Apparently greater praise could not have been bestowed upon them. And yet the Lord proceeds to say:—

4. "Nevertheless I have somewhat against thee, because thou hast left thy first love." There is nothing in the original answer-

5 Remember therefore from whence thou art fallen, and repent, and do the first works; ᵍor else I will come unto thee quickly, and will remove thy candlestick out of his place, except thou repent.

ᵏ Matt. xxi. 41, 43.

---

5. "Quickly." So B., most Cursives, Syr., Arm.; but omitted by ℵ, A., C., P., Vulg., Copt., &c.

ing to the "somewhat" of our Authorized. It should be read "I have against thee that thou didst leave thy first love." How terrible a charge when taken in connection with the immediately preceding words of praise, "thou hast patience, and didst bear for my name's sake, and hast not grown weary." Terrible I say to us in these days when love has grown cold. Who is sufficient for these things, who is sufficient for keeping up the love of Christ in the soul of man? It is not enough that there should be good works. It is not enough that there should be labour. The works must be works of faith: the labour must be labour of love. There must be a constant endeavour on our part to keep up the warmth of the love of Christ in the soul. Let us think of His Wounds. Let us recount His words on the Cross. Let us be diligent in receiving the Sacrament of His love, and let us be diligent in preparing for it aright.

5. "Remember therefore from whence thou art fallen." Commentators with one consent remind us of God's remonstrance with fallen Israel in Jeremiah ii. 2: "Thus saith the Lord; I remember thee, the kindness of thy youth, the love of thine espousals, when thou wentest after me in the wilderness."

"Repent." A decline from the first fervour of love to Christ needs to be repented of. Constantly need we to pray, "Graft in our hearts the love of thy name."

"And do the first works." The later works of verses 2 and 3 seem to have been works against adversaries of the truth, which it is most needful to contend for, and so, perhaps, these *first* works are works of charity and brotherly love, and private devotion and religion, which, in their zeal for the truth, they had grown somewhat slack in performing. "But," as Trench says, "not the quantity, but the quality of the works was now other and worse than once it had been."

"Or else I will come unto thee quickly, and will remove thy

6 But this thou hast, that thou hatest the deeds of ^h the Nicolaitanes, which I also hate.   ^h ver. 15.

7 ^i He that hath an ear, let him hear what the Spirit saith unto the churches; To him that

^i Matt. xi. 15. & xiii. 9, 43. ver. 11, 17, 29. ch. iii. 6, 13, 22. & xiii. 9.

---

candlestick." This threat means, "I will remove thy light. Thou shalt no longer shed forth the light of my truth, but I will give thy privileges to others who will make a better use of them." It is terrible to think of a church like that of Ephesus, planted by St. Paul, and a generation afterwards watered by St. John, becoming extinct. "How awful for Ephesus the fulfilment of the threat has been every modern traveller who has visited the ruins of that once famous city has borne witness. One who lately did so found only three Christians there, and these sunken in such ignorance and apathy as scarcely to have heard the names of St. John and St. Paul" (Trench).

6. "But this thou hast, that thou hatest the deeds of the Nicolaitanes, which I also hate." It is not merely the opinions, or the heresies, but the deeds of the Nicolaitanes which are hateful to Christ. As there is much difference of opinion respecting these heretics I shall give an account of them in a note at the end of this chapter.

7. "He that hath an ear, let him hear what the Spirit saith unto the churches." He that hath an ear—an opened ear—a circumcised ear, and this springs from a circumcised heart. The heart alive to the things of Christ will make the ear attentive and ready to receive the accents of the Divine Word. Notice also how that such an ear will hear what "the Spirit saith." Christ speaks but by the Spirit. The working of the Son and of the Spirit is never separated. It is the Spirit of the Son proceeding from His human nature. "He shall not speak of himself," the Saviour foretold, "but whatsoever he shall hear, that shall he speak." What a mystery is the Unity of the Trinity, the ever-blessed Three having each His part in every divine act.

"To him that overcometh." This is repeated at the close of each of the seven epistles. In each case its signification is somewhat different, because each church has a different form of temptation. It is the reproduction of the Lord's promise, "He that endureth to the end, the same shall be saved," and of that which He gave

overcometh will I give ᵏ to eat of ¹ the tree of life, which is in the midst of the paradise of God.

ᵏ ch. xxii. 2, 14.
¹ Gen. ii. 9.

---

through His servant, St. Paul, "Fight the good fight of faith; lay hold of eternal life."

"Will I give to eat of the tree of life." Mark, it is the Son of God, the Saviour and Judge, who assigns to each one the reward, as if He be—which He is—the Supreme Arbitrator. The gift of God is eternal life, but here it is the gift of Christ. So that as it is the Spirit Who sends the messages, so the reward is that of the Son; and yet no word is sent, no gift or grace given without or apart from the Father.

"Will I give to eat of the tree of life." In the "tree of life" there is a manifest allusion to Gen. ii. 9. "The tree which disappeared with the disappearance of the earthly paradise reappears with the reappearance of the heavenly, Christ's kingdom being in the highest sense the restitution of all things" (Acts iii. 21). Whatever had been lost through Adam's sin is won back, and that, too, in a higher shape through Christ's obedience. The term, "tree of life," seems often put to indicate the highest blessing. Thus wisdom is said to be a "tree of life to them that lay hold upon her" (Prov. iii. 18), and "the fruit of the righteous is a tree of life" (Prov. xi. 30; also Prov. xiii. 12; xv. 4).

"In the midst of the paradise of God." The word paradise is employed in the Septuagint to denote the Garden of Eden; then in the New Testament it is used by our Lord to signify the good side of Hades, where the souls of the blessed dead shall await the Resurrection; and in one place in the epistles it signifies the third heaven into which St. Paul was caught up and heard the unspeakable words (2 Cor. xii. 3, 4). "We see eminently in it, what we see in so many other words, how revealed religion assumes them into her service, and makes them vehicles of far higher truth than any which they knew at first, transforming and transfiguring them, as in this case, from glory to glory" (Trench).

What is this tree of life? Is it an actual tree, or is it some spiritual power or grace. One holy man says that it is the Cross; another that it is Christ Himself. But in order to overcome, each soul must have previously partaken of the Cross—must have partaken of Christ.

8 And unto the angel of the church in Smyrna write; These things saith ᵐ the first and the last, which was dead, and is alive;

9 ⁿ I know thy works, and tribulation, and poverty, (but thou art ᵒ rich) and *I know* the blasphemy of ᵖ them which say they are Jews, and are not, ᵠ but *are* the synagogue of Satan.

ᵐ ch. i. 8, 17, 18.
ⁿ ver. 2.
ᵒ Luke xii. 21. 1 Tim. vi. 18. James ii. 5.
ᵖ Rom. ii. 17, 28, 29. & ix. 6.
ᵠ ch. iii. 9.

---

9. "Thy works, and." So ℵ, B., most Cursives, Syr., Arm.; but omitted by A., C., P., Vulg., Copt., Æth.

8. "And unto the angel of the church in Smyrna write." Smyrna, it is said, is the only one of the churches which remains. The Church now ministers to half of the population of 160,000.

"These things saith the first and the last, which was dead, and is alive." The title thus assumed by the Lord from i. 17, 18, seems to be assumed by Him in speaking to those who were on the eve of suffering a severe persecution. "I am the first and the last, so that I shall outlive all thy persecutors, to reward thee, and render to them according to their deeds of cruelty and injustice. As I was dead and am now alive, so shall I raise thee from the dead."

9. "[I know thy works], and tribulation, and poverty, (but thou art rich)." "Thy tribulation," *i.e.*, from the persecutions of the heathen, in whose midst they dwelt, instigated most frequently by the Jews.

"And poverty." Poverty, both because the Church was principally recruited from the lower grades of society, and what goods these poor Christians had they were despoiled of by their persecutors.

"But thou art rich." Rich in faith, rich in good works, rich in treasures laid up for them in heaven.

"And I know the blasphemy of them which say they are Jews, and are not." St. John's brother Apostle had said, "He is not a Jew which is one outwardly . . . . but he is a Jew which is one inwardly." Till Christ came and gave His own name to the New Church, no appellation could be more honourable than that of "Jew." He was the elect of God, the heir of His promises, the

10 ʳ Fear none of those things which thou shalt suffer: behold, the devil shall cast *some* of you into prison,

ʳ Matt. x. 22.

---

10. "None of." So ℵ, P., most Cursives, Vulg., Syr.; but A., B., C., read "not" ("fear not").

guardian of His law, but when he rejected Him to Whose Name he was specially chosen to be a witness, nothing could exceed the depth of his fall. He became naturally, as it were, a blasphemer, for for a Jew there was no medium between accepting Christ and blaspheming Him. He must either acknowledge Him to be the Christ, or brand Him as a blasphemer. And so the unbelieving Jew belied his name, his traditions, his prospects, his worship. He repudiated everything to which God had chosen him, and so literally and truly his synagogue was no longer the sacred assembly of the people of God, but the school and camp of God's enemy.

10. "Fear none of those things which thou shalt suffer: behold, the devil shall cast some of you into prison." Here the persecution of Christians is ascribed to the agency of Satan. We sometimes assume that Christians were persecuted because the truths for which they bore witness offended the pride, the prejudices, and the passions of men; and this is most true, but we have not so reached the ground of the matter. There is nothing more remarkable in the records which have come down to us of the early persecutions, and in this point they singularly illustrate the Scripture before us, than the sense which the confessors and martyrs had that these great fights and afflictions through which they were called to pass were the immediate work of the devil, and no mere result of the offended passions, prejudices, or interests of men. The enemies of flesh and blood, as mere tools or instruments, are nearly lost sight of by them in a constant reference to Satan as the invisible but real author of all. And assuredly they were right. Who that reads that story of the persecutions of the Saints at Lyons and Vienne, A.D. 177, happily preserved to us by Eusebius (H. E. v. 1) in the very words of the survivors, that wondrous tale of persistent, inventive cruelty on the part of the heathen, overmatched by a superhuman patience on the part of the faithful, but must feel that there is infinitely more here than a conflict of bad men with good. There is rather on the one side an outbreak from

that ye may be tried; and ye shall have tribulation ten days: ⁸be thou faithful unto death, and I will give thee ᵗa crown of life.

11 ᵘ"He that hath an ear, let him hear what the Spirit saith unto the churches; He that overcometh shall not be hurt of ˣthe second death.

ˢ Matt. xxiv. 13.
ᵗ James i. 12. ch. iii. 11.
ᵘ ver. 7. ch. xiii. 9.
ˣ ch. xx. 14. & xxi. 8.

---

the bottomless pit—the might and malice of the devil making war against God in the person of His saints; on the other a victory, not over evil men only, but over Satan, so transcendent, that it could only have been surpassed when Christ Himself beheld him with the Spirit's eye, fall as lightning from heaven (Luke x. 18).

"Ye shall have tribulation ten days." It is impossible to say what is meant by these ten days. Whether they were only ten days or ten years, or whether they betoken a longer time or a shorter one. Some have imagined that there is a covert allusion to the ten persecutions of the first three centuries.

"Be thou faithful unto death, and I will give thee a crown of life." There has been some difference of opinion whether this "crown" is a kingly or a victor's crown. Commentators mostly incline to the former, though the word used is not *diadema* but *stephanos;* but it appears that kingly crowns took rather the form of the latter. The Lord was evidently intended to be crowned in mockery with a regal crown. The other references in the New Testament are to the crowns of victors, thus 1 Cor. ix. 25, but it is to be remarked that there are no other illustrations taken from heathen customs in this book.

"He that overcometh shall not be hurt of the second death." The reason for this promise seems to be of this sort: though their bodies may be slain by violence and torture, yet they will not be hurt by that death which is really death (Matt. x. 28). By death they will enter into life.

An interesting question arises as to who the angel of the Church of Smyrna was when this letter was addressed to it. It is not at all improbable that it was the famous Polycarp. If Polycarp suffered martyrdom in the year A.D. 168, and he had been, as he asserts before the governor, eighty-six years a Christian at that time, he was probably baptized into Christ about A.D. 82, and

12 And to the angel of the church in Pergamos write;
These things saith ʸ he which hath the sharp sword with two edges;

13 ᵃ I know thy works, and where thou dwellest, *even* ᵃ where Satan's seat *is:* and thou holdest fast my name, and hast not denied my faith, even

ʸ ch. i. 16.

ᵃ ver. 2.

ᵃ ver. 9.

---

13. "Thy works, and." So B. and most Cursives, Arm., and Syriac; but omitted by ℵ, A., C., P., Vulg., Copt.

"Even" (καὶ) omitted by ℵ, B., P., many Cursives; but retained by A., C.

could have been the Bishop of Smyrna in A.D. 96, when this letter was written. Tertullian distinctly tells us that he was consecrated Bishop of Smyrna by St. John. As early as A.D. 108, Ignatius, on his way to his martyrdom at Rome, found Polycarp the Bishop or Angel of the Church at Smyrna. Still more is this within the bounds of probability if we adopt Bishop Pearson's calculation that he suffered about A.D. 147.

12. "And to the angel of the church in Pergamos write; These things saith he which hath the sharp sword with two edges." Pergamos, rather Pergamum, a city noted for its idolatry. In particular it had a magnificent temple, dedicated to Æsculapius, the ruins of which yet remain. The Lord describing Himself as the One Who had the sharp sword with two edges, is supposed to be consonant with the severity of His rebuke of this Church.

13. "I know thy works, and where thou dwellest, even where Satan's seat is." Various conjectures have been hazarded as to what is alluded to in the Lord saying that Satan had his seat in Pergamum. One is that Æsculapius was worshipped there under the figure of a serpent, another that Pergamum was more given to idolatry than any of the other cities, but this can hardly be true of it as compared with Ephesus. Trench confesses his inability to explain the matter, and writes: "All that we can conclude from this language is, that from one cause or another Pergamum enjoyed the bad pre-eminence of being the headquarters in these parts of the opposition to Christ and His Gospel."

"And thou holdest fast my name, and hast not denied my faith, even in those days wherein Antipas was my faithful martyr." It is a singular fact that nothing is known respecting Antipas and

CHAP. II.] ANTIPAS MY FAITHFUL MARTYR. 27

in those days wherein Antipas *was* my faithful martyr, who was slain among you, where Satan dwelleth.

14 But I have a few things against thee, because thou hast there them that hold the doctrine of ᵇBalaam, who taught Balac to cast a stumbling-block before the children of Israel, ᶜto eat things sacrificed unto idols, ᵈand to commit fornication.

15 So hast thou also them that hold the doctrine ᵉof the Nicolaitanes, which thing I hate.

ᵇ Num. xxiv. 14. & xxv. 1. & xxxi. 16. 2 Pet. ii. 15. Jude 11.
ᶜ ver. 20. Acts xv. 29. 1 Cor. viii. 9, 10. & x. 19, 20.
ᵈ 1 Cor. vi. 13, &c.
ᵉ ver. 6.

---

15. "Which I also hate" omitted by most MSS. ℵ, A., B., C., read, ὁμοίως, "in like manner."

his martyrdom through early tradition, though he is thus honourably mentioned by Christ Himself. Later traditions make him to have been Bishop of Pergamum, and by command of Domitian to have been enclosed in a brazen bull, which was made red hot. Tertullian, in his "Scorpiace," simply cites this place, but gives us no further information respecting him.

14. "But I have a few things against thee ... to eat things sacrificed unto idols." The early converts were bound to abstain from things offered to idols, because if they were seen to do so they were held to have partaken in the idolatrous worship ; and so the Nicolaitanes, who are here alluded to, enticed them to take part in the idolatrous feasts, and so to all intents and purposes in the idolatry itself. It was at Balaam's instigation that the Israelites were invited to the sacrificial feasts of Numbers xxv.; and so these seducers are said to hold the doctrine, *i.e.*, the iniquitous teaching of Balaam.

"And to commit fornication." Fornication was almost a part of worship. In Corinth an immense number of prostitutes were priestesses of the temple of Aphrodite; and, in fact, the characters of the principal gods were such that it could hardly have been otherwise.

15. "So hast thou also them that hold the doctrine of the Nicolaitanes." In speaking to the angel of this Church the Lord does not say that He hated the doctrines of the Nicolaitanes, for which thing He commended the Church of Ephesus ; rather He

16 Repent; or else I will come unto thee quickly, and ᶠwill fight against them with the sword of my mouth.

<small>ᶠ Isa. xi. 4.
2 Thess. ii. 8.
ch. i. 16. & ix. 15, 21.
ᵍ ver. 7, 11.</small>

17 ᵍHe that hath an ear, let him hear what the Spirit saith unto the churches; To him that overcometh will I give to eat of the hidden manna, and will give him a white stone, and in the stone ʰ a new name written, which no man knoweth saving he that receiveth *it*.

<small>ʰ ch. iii. 12. & xix. 12.</small>

---

blames the angel for tolerating those who hold the doctrines in question.

16. "Repent; or else I will come unto thee quickly, and will fight against them." He will come to the angel quickly, unless he repents, and will fight against them, that is, those that hold the doctrine of the Nicolaitanes. Milligan writes: "The Lord will come to war against the Nicolaitanes, not against the Church. Against His Church, even in her declension, He cannot war. Her threatened punishment (and is it not enough!) is that the Lord will make war upon His enemies without her, and that not taking part in His struggle she shall lose her part in the victory." Most commentators take no notice of the difficulty.

"The sword of my mouth." This sword seems to signify His punishing and destroying power. He has but to say the word, and they are overwhelmed.

17. "He that hath an ear . . . to him that overcometh will I give to eat of the hidden," &c. The hidden manna seems undoubtedly to refer to that which was hidden in the ark. But what is the reality of this hidden manna; it must be some aspect of eternal life; it must be the interior knowledge of Him Whom to know is eternal life.

"And will give him a white stone, and in the stone a new name written." White is the colour of victory and of purity. The rider on the white horse goes forth conquering and to conquer; the elect are clothed in white robes. With respect to the stone there is more difficulty. The word really seems to some to signify the white pebble cast into the urn as the token or vote of

THE CHURCH IN THYATIRA.

18 And unto the angel of the church in Thyatira write; These things saith the Son of God, ¹ who hath his eyes like unto a flame of fire, and his feet *are* like fine brass;

19 ᵏ I know thy works, and charity, and service, and faith, and thy patience, and thy works; and the last *to be* more than the first.

¹ ch. i. 14, 15.

ᵏ ver. 2.

---

19. "And thy last works to be more than the first." So ℵ, A., C.

acquittal after a trial. This is, with some reason, objected to, as this book is altogether Jewish in its symbols, and seems to exclude all illustrations drawn from the practices of the Gentiles. Trench, who devotes three pages to it, supposes it to contain an allusion to a white stone, in all probability a diamond, enclosed in the breastplate of the high priest, and on which was written the most sacred name of God, the τετραγραμματον, and so this was the Divine acknowledgment that he who received this stone was a high priest to God.

What the new name is most expositors do not even attempt to conjecture. Can it be the name by which Christ knows His own sheep? Can it be a name of God? Can it be a well-known name to which Christ attaches a new significance, differing in the case of each believer?

18. "And unto the angel of the church in Thyatira write; These things saith the Son of God, who hath his eyes like unto a flame of fire, and his feet," &c. It is to be noticed that here only does the Lord call Himself the Son of God. No certain connection can be established between the words by which the Lord here describes Himself (the same as those in i. 14, 15), and his reproof of this Church. It would be idle to mention the conjectures.

19. "I know thy works, and charity [love], and service [or ministry], and faith, and thy patience, and thy last works to be more than the first." This is the opposite of what is said of Ephesus. The love of the Ephesian Church had grown cold, but that of Thyatira had advanced, as was evinced by its works being increased.

20 Notwithstanding I have a few things against thee, because thou sufferest that woman ¹Jezebel, which calleth herself a prophetess, to teach and to seduce my servants ᵐto commit fornication, and to eat things sacrificed unto idols.

21 And I gave her space ⁿto repent of her fornication; and she repented not.

¹ 1 Kings xvi. 31. & xxi. 25. 2 Kin. ix. 9.
ᵐ Ex. xxxiv. 15. Acts xv. 20, 29. 1 Cor. x. 19, 20. ver. 14.
ⁿ Rom. ii. 4. ch. ix. 20.

---

20. "I have a few things against thee." Rather, "I have (this) against thee, to teach and seduce my servants. And she teacheth and seduceth."

20. "Notwithstanding I have a few things against thee, because thou sufferest that woman [or thy wife] Jezebel." It is scarcely possible to suppose that this Jezebel was the actual wife of the bishop or president of this Church. If she had been he would scarcely have been allowed to retain his position of chief teacher. We are to remember that though there is every reason to believe that the angel was the president of the Church, yet that he also was treated as its representative, so that the sins of which the Church as a body was guilty were accounted to be his, as he had not sufficiently purged his Church from them by the exercise of godly discipline and reproof.

Jezebel, no doubt, was a name given to her because of her sin, so closely resembling that of Ahab's wife, who was the leading introducer of idolatry of the worst type among the ten tribes.

"To teach and to seduce my servants to commit fornication, and to eat," &c. To partake in the meal offered to idols was, when it was done knowingly, to partake in the idolatry itself. See notes on 1 Cor. viii. 9, 10.

21. "And I gave her space to repent of her fornication; and she repented not." This could only be said of one who had known the truth, and had been outwardly at least in the pale of the Church. It seems to imply also that the Great Head of the Church had brought His grace to bear upon her so as to convince her of her sin, and yet without effect.¹

---

¹ A remarkable account is given of a form of idolatry in Thyatira in Smith's "Dictionary of the Bible," which is supposed by the writer (Dean Blakesley) to throw light on this reference to Jezebel:—"Another superstition of an extremely curious character which existed at Thyatira seems to have been brought thither by some of

22 Behold, I will cast her into a bed, and them that commit adultery with her into great tribulation, except they repent of their deeds.

23 And I will kill her children with death; and all the churches shall know that ᵒI am he

ᵒ 1 Sam. xvi. 7. 1 Chron. xxviii. 9. & xxix. 17. 2 Chron. vi. 30. Ps. vii. 9. Jer. xi. 20. & xvii. 10. & xx. 12. John ii. 24, 25. Acts i. 24. Rom. viii. 27.

---

22. "Their deeds." So A. and two or three Cursives; but ℵ, B., C., P., most Cursives, &c., read, "her deeds."

22. "Behold, I will cast her into a bed, and them that commit adultery with her," &c. "A bed," that is a bed of sickness, perhaps of death.

"And them that commit adultery with her into great tribulation." This adultery is in all probability spiritual adultery, *i.e.*, idolatry; and "with her" means, not that they committed actual adultery, but were followers of her leading, and instruments of seducing others into idolatry.

23. "And I will kill her children with death." Her children here must be distinguished from those who commit adultery with her of verse 22, and must be those seduced by her and her accomplices.

"And all the churches shall know that I am he," &c. This prerogative to search out and try the hearts and reins is the

---

the corrupted Jews of the dispersed tribes. A fane stood outside the walls dedicated to Sambetha, the name of the Sibyl who is sometimes called Chaldæan, sometimes Jewish, sometimes Persian, in the midst of an enclosure designated the Chaldæan Court (τοῦ χαλδαίου περίβολος). This seems to lend an illustration to the obscure passage in Rev. ii. 20, 21, which Grotius interprets of the wife of the Bishop. The drawback against the commendation bestowed upon the angel of the Thyatirean Church is that he tolerates 'that woman—that Jezebel, who, professing herself to be a prophetess, teaches and deludes my servants into committing fornication and eating things offered to idols.' Time, however, is given her to repent: and this seems to imply a form of religion which had become condemnable from the admixture of foreign alloy, rather than one idolatrous *ab initio*. Now there is evidence to show that in Thyatira there was a great amalgamation of races. . . . But amalgamation of races in pagan nations always went together with a syncretism of different religions, every relation of life having its religious sanction. If the Sibyl Sambetha was really a Jewess, lending her aid to this proceeding, and not discountenanced by the authorities of the Judæo-Christian Church at Thyatira, both the reference and its qualification becomes easy of explanation." This is curious and interesting, but the Lord would scarcely speak of such an one as a pretended Sibyl, one outside of the Church, as having space given her for repentance.

which searcheth the reins and hearts: and ᵖ I will give unto every one of you according to your works.

24 But unto you I say, and unto the rest in Thyatira, as many as have not this doctrine, and which have not known the depths of Satan, as

ᵖ Ps. lxii. 12. Matt. xvi. 27. Rom. ii. 6. & xiv. 12. 2 Cor. v. 10. Gal. vi. 5. ch. xx. 12.

---

24. "But unto you I say, and." "And" omitted by ℵ, A., B., C., P., most Cursives, &c. No authority for retaining it.

---

especial one of God, and God only. Thus the Psalmist, "The righteous God trieth the hearts and reins" (Ps. vii. 9). By assuming to do this Christ most unequivocally asserts his proper Godhead.

"I will give unto every one of you according to your works." No truth of God is asserted in such plain terms as this, and I think none so frequently, and yet there is none so much lost sight of. Some, if they do not deny it, keep it in the background, because they have an idea that it is contrary to or superseded by justification by faith, but the great Apostle, who especially insists upon salvation by grace through faith, as persistently insists upon judgment according to our works; thus Rom. ii. 6, "Who will render to every man according to his deeds;" thus 1 Cor. iii. 8, "Every man shall receive his own reward according to his own labour."

24. "But unto you I say, and unto the rest in Thyatira, as many as have." The conjunction "and" must be omitted, otherwise the Lord seems to speak to two sets of persons, whereas He only speaks to one.

"As many as have not this doctrine, and which have not known the depths," &c. The Gnostics pretended to initiate their disciples into the deepest mysteries of the Divine Nature or workings, interposing successions of æons between God and the universe which He has created. These the Lord characterizes here not as the deep things of God, but as the depths of Satan. Trench, however, supposes that it was a more subtle and ensnaring delusion. "They taught that it was a small thing for a man to despise pleasure, and to show himself superior to it, whilst at the same time he fled from it. The true, the glorious victory was to remain superior to it whilst tasting it to the full; to give the body to all the lusts of the flesh,

they speak; ᵠI will put upon you none other burden.

25 But ʳthat which ye have *already* hold fast till I come.

26 And he that overcometh, and keepeth ˢmy works unto the end, ᵗto him will I give power over the nations :

ᵠ Acts xv. 28.

ʳ ch. iii. 11.
ˢ John vi. 29.
1 John iii. 23.
ᵗ Matt. xix. 28. Luke xxii. 29, 30. 1 Cor. vi. 3. ch. iii. 21. & xx. 4.

---

and yet withal this to maintain the Spirit in a region of its own, uninjured by them, and thus, as it were, to fight against pleasure with the weapons of pleasure itself; to mock and defy Satan even in his own kingdom and domain."

"I will put upon you none other burden." This burden which they were bearing manfully could only be the burden of keeping themselves from the sins to which they were tempted by this Jezebel and her associates; not to join in the smallest approach to idolatry and its ever-attendant abominations of lewdness and impurity. In a nominally Christian state of society like ours we have no idea of the difficulty of keeping from these enticements. Let us imagine the case of one Christian in a family of heathen, and his brothers or sisters continually reminding him that every piece of meat on the table had been offered to an idol, and so in conscience he was bound to abstain from it (1 Cor. x. 27). We can see from this how full of snares to weak Christians was the commonest domestic intercourse.

25. "But that which ye have already hold fast till I come." "That which ye have already"—your works, charity, ministry, faith, patience—"hold fast till I come." Mark how the reward and final establishment in righteousness is not at death but at the Second Coming. We gather from this that the Lord expected, and yet expects, each church to watch and wait for Him—no matter how long His Coming may be delayed.

26. "And he that overcometh, and keepeth my works unto the end, to him will I give," &c. Whatever Christ has, that He shares with His people, even to sitting with Him on His throne (iii. 21).

"Over the nations." That is, over the Gentiles, over the heathen.

27 ᵘ"And he shall rule them with a rod of iron; as the vessels of a potter shall they be broken to shivers: even as I received of my Father.

28 And I will give him ˣ the morning star.

29 ʸ He that hath an ear, let him hear what the Spirit saith unto the churches.

ᵘ Ps. ii. 8, 9. & xlix. 14. Dan. vii. 22. ch. xii. 5. & xix. 15.
ˣ 2 Pet. i. 19. ch. xxii. 16.
ʸ ver. 7.

27. "And he shall rule them with a rod of iron; as the vessels of a potter," &c. Here the Septuagint rather than the Hebrew is followed; the Hebrew being, "Thou shalt bruise or break;" the Septuagint, "Thou shalt tend them like a shepherd, thou shalt rule them." How and at what time this will take place we know not. Such a passage as xx. 4, if taken in the terms in which it is expressed, seems to give ample time and scope for it.

What is the significance of "as the vessels of a potter shall they be broken to shivers?" It may refer to the breaking up of great empires, as the Roman; it can scarcely refer to the destruction of individual offenders.

28. "And I will give him the morning star." The Lord speaks thus of Himself at the end of this book (xxii. 16), "I am the root and the offspring of David, and the bright and morning star." It seems then that in this He promises in some way to give Himself as the Harbinger of everlasting day. St. Peter speaks of the day star having arisen in our hearts; but this must have been anterior to what is promised here.

CHAP. III.

ᵃ ch. i. 4, 16. & iv. 5. & v. 6.

AND unto the angel of the church in Sardis write; These things saith he ᵃ that hath the

1. "And unto the angel of the church in Sardis write." Sardis, once the capital of Lydia, and the kingdom of Crœsus, now absolutely deserted.

"These things saith he that hath the seven Spirits of God." I refer

seven Spirits of God, and the seven stars; ᵇI know thy works, that thou hast a name that thou livest, ᶜand art dead.

ᵇ ch. ii. 2.
ᶜ Eph. ii. 1, 5.
1 Tim. v. 6.

2 Be watchful, and strengthen the things which

---

the reader to what I have written on chap. i. 4. The Spirit of God is absolutely One, and yet infinitely manifold in His operations. He is One, and yet, in dealing with the infinite number of souls on whom He operates, is as if He were sevenfold: sevenfold in the sense of perfect distribution of Himself to each one. See also v. 6. This place asserts two great theological truths. That the Son is Lord and God, and that having the Holy Ghost in His absolute fulness within Him, that Holy Spirit proceeds from Him as well as from His Father.

"And the seven stars." The seven stars are the angels of the seven churches. We must see in this combination (between the Spirits and the churches) a hint of the relation between Christ as the Giver of the Holy Spirit and as the author of a ministry of living men in His Church; this ministry of men resting wholly on their gifts. As Trench, and also as Dean Plumptre writes, " He is able to bring together the gifts of life and the ministry for which those gifts are needed. If those who minister are without gifts it is because they have not asked for them.

"I know thy works, that thou hast a name that thou livest, and art dead." I know thy works that they spring not from a living faith in me.

"That thou hast a name that thou livest, and art dead." A name—that is, a reputation. The Church of Sardis was to all appearance a spiritual church, but not so in the sight of the Searcher of hearts.

"And art dead." Thus St. Paul speaks of one who lived in pleasure as being dead whilst she lived (1 Tim. v. 6). So also the father of the prodigal says: "My son was dead and is alive again."

2. "Be watchful, and strengthen the things which remain, that are ready to die." Watchfulness is the necessary preliminary before there can be any real Christianity, because without constant watchfulness we do not know our own state, and so shall be ever deceiving ourselves.

"Strengthen the things which remain, that are ready to die."

remain, that are ready to die: for I have not found thy works perfect before God.

3 ᵈRemember therefore how thou hast received and heard, and hold fast, and ᵉrepent. ᶠIf therefore thou shalt not watch, I will come on thee as a thief, and thou shalt not know what hour I will come upon thee.

Marginal references: ᵈ 1 Tim. vi. 20. 2 Tim. i. 13. ver. 11. ᵉ ver. 19. ᶠ Matt. xxiv. 42, 43, & xxv. 13. Mark xiii. 33. Luke xii. 39, 40. 1 Thess. v. 2, 6. 2 Pet. iii. 10. ch. xvi. 15.

---

2. "Before God." ℵ, A., B., C., most Cursives, Vulg., Copt., Syr., Æth. read, "Before my God."

How? by prayer, by applying to Him Who has the Spirit without measure to give him that Spirit.

"And strengthen the things which remain." According to some, the parts or members of the Church which remain; according to others, the graces not yet extinct.

"For I have not found thy works perfect before God." Perfect rather means fulfilled. "I have found no works of thine fulfilled before God, none of them have come to maturity."

3. "Remember therefore how thou hast received and heard, and hold," &c. The charge against Sardis is not a perverse holding of untruth, but a heartless holding of the truth, and therefore the Lord is graciously reminding her of the heartiness, the zeal, the love with which she received the truth at the first.

"And hold fast." Hold it fast in heart and soul, ponder over it, make it again thine own by renewed faith.

"And repent." Repent of thy slackness, of thy declension in faith, and of the coldness which has crept over thee.

"If therefore thou shalt not watch, I will come on thee as a thief." This is what the Lord constantly impressed upon the Apostles, even whilst He was with them before His Crucifixion and Ascension. They were ever to be looking for Him, so as to be ready to open the door to Him the moment that He knocked (Luke xii. 36).

But this is said to all the world. Would He come in any sense separately to Sardis, inasmuch as He addresses her as if His Coming would be to her alone? There is a coming of the Son of God to all the world at once, and there is a coming in judgment to each one whose sins call for it, just as there is a coming in mercy when the soul is truly converted.

4 Thou hast ᵍ a few names even in Sardis which have not ʰ defiled their garments; and they shall walk with me ⁱ in white : for they are worthy.

5 He that overcometh, ᵏ the same shall be clothed in white raiment; and I will not ˡ blot out his name out of the ᵐ book of life, but

ᵍ Acts i. 15.
ʰ Jude 23.
ⁱ ch. iv. 4. & vi. 11. & vii. 9, 13.
ᵏ ch. xix. 8.
ˡ Exod. xxxii. 32. Ps. lxix. 28.
ᵐ Phil. iv. 3. ch. xiii. 8. & xvii. 8. & xx. 12. & xxi. 27.

---

4. "Even" omitted by ℵ, A., B., C., P., most Cursives, &c.
5. "The same" (οὗτος). So ℵᶜ, B., P., most Cursives; but ℵ*, A., C., Vulg., Copt., &c., read, οὕτως ("thus").

4. "*Thou hast a few names (even) in Sardis which have not defiled their garments,*" &c. Who have not defiled their garments? It is always assumed that those who are admitted into the Christian Covenant are "washed, sanctified, justified in the Name of the Lord Jesus and by the Spirit of God," and what God imposes upon them is that they should keep this—that they should abide in the state into which they have been admitted, and keep the cleansing or washing once accorded to them. However difficult this may be to realize in this our day, there is absolutely no other principle of addressing the baptized in the New Testament. In no case is there the slightest recognition of an invisible church within the visible into which the members of the merely visible church are to enter if they would be saved.

"*They shall walk with me in white: for they are worthy.*"

5. "*He that overcometh, the same shall be clothed in white raiment.*" White is, of course, the symbol of purity. That they should "walk in white" and "be clothed in white garments" seems to signify that their internal purity and holiness shall be openly manifested; in this world it has been hidden; they have shrunk from any display of it—but in the eternal world it shall be manifested in the splendour of their white attire, and in their shining forth as the sun in the Kingdom of their Father.

"*And I will not blot out his name out of the book of life.*" No meaning can be given to this assertion of the Lord's unless it is possible for those whose names once have been in the book of life to have their names blotted out of that book. Such a fall and such a doom is terrible to think of, but it seems to me that there is no use in arguing against it; but the one thing laid upon us is to pray that

ⁿ I will confess his name before my Father, and before his angels.

6 ᵒ He that hath an ear, let him hear what the Spirit saith unto the churches.

7 And to the angel of the church in Philadelphia write; These things saith ᵖ he that is holy, ᵠ he that is true, he that hath ʳ the key of David, ˢ he that openeth, and no man shutteth; and ᵗ shutteth, and no man openeth;

ⁿ Matt. x. 32. Luke xii. 8.
ᵒ ch. ii. 7.
ᵖ Acts iii. 14.
ᵠ 1 John v. 20. ver. 14. ch. i. 5. & vi. 10. & xix. 11.
ʳ Isa. xxii. 22. Luke i. 32. ch. i. 18.
ˢ Matt. xvi. 19.
ᵗ Job xii. 14.

---

7. "Shutteth." ℵ, A., B., C., most Cursives read, "shall shut."

"Openeth." ℵ, B., read, "shall open," also most Cursives; but A., C., P., Vulg., Arm., Syriac read, "openeth."

God would "lead us not into temptation, but deliver us from evil"—"from the evil one," as one of the old Liturgies has it, "and from all his devices and snares"—and that He would make us perfect, establish, strengthen, settle us.

"I will confess his name before my Father, and before his angels." "He has confessed me in the midst of ridicule and opposition, and persecution, and I will confess his name before my Father, and before His angels." Let souls under scorn and opposition remember this and they will be nerved to undergo all that is laid upon them. Let them remember that the ridicule and scorn is but for a moment, and the honour of the confession before God and good angels is for ever and ever.

7. "And to the angel of the church in Philadelphia write." Philadelphia, a comparatively modern city, built by Attalus Philadelphus, King of Pergamos, who died B.C. 138. In the reign of Tiberius it was nearly destroyed by an earthquake.

"These things saith he that is holy, he that is true." "He that is holy." Christ is spoken of in Daniel ix. 24 as "the most Holy."

"He that is true." Not merely as meaning that He adheres to His promises and will fulfil them, but that He is truly what He represents Himself or is represented to be. For instance, if He be God He is true God; if He be man He is true man; if He be Mediator He in all respects answers to the truth or reality of Mediatorship between God and man.

"He that hath the key of David, he that openeth, and no man

8 ᵘ I know thy works: behold, I have set be- ᵘ ver. 1.
fore thee ˣ an open door, and no man can shut it: ˣ 1 Cor. xvi. 9.
2 Cor. ii. 12.

---

shutteth." "The key of David" means authority over the house of David. Here is a reference to the removal of one of the king's ministers (Shebna), and the substitution of another (Eliakim) in his place, which we find in Isaiah xxii. 20-24: "It shall come to pass in that day, that I will call my servant Eliakim the son of Hilkiah: and I will clothe him with thy robe, and strengthen him with thy girdle, and I will commit thy government into his hand: and he shall be a father to the inhabitants of Jerusalem, and to the house of Judah. And the key of the house of David will I lay upon his shoulder; and he shall open and none shall shut; and he shall shut and none shall open."

It is quite clear that in this passage there is a far greater than Eliakim in the mind of the Prophet or of the Spirit Who inspired him, even the exaltation of the true Steward of the mysteries of God Who shall be faithful in all His house. But has not Christ Himself committed the keys of the kingdom of heaven to His ministers? Yes, but so that in any turn of those keys His own hand should be paramount. His ministers turn the key, but the turning of the key admits only those whom He desires to admit, and excludes those whom He desires to exclude. Trench has two apposite illustrations. "It was in faith of this that Huss, when the greatest council which Christendom had seen for a thousand years delivered his soul unto Satan, did himself confidently commend it to the Lord Jesus Christ; and many a faithful confessor that at Rome or Madrid has walked to the stake, his yellow *San benito* all painted over with devils, in token of those with whom his portion should be, has never doubted that his lot should be indeed with Him Who retains in His own hands the key of David, Who then should open for him, though all who visibly represented here the Church had shut him out, with extreme malediction, at once from the Church militant here on earth and the Church triumphant in heaven."

8. "I know thy works: behold, I have set before thee an open door," *i.e.*, a door of usefulness and an assurance of success. This figure of an open door for the successful preaching of the Gospel is constantly used by St. Paul; thus 1 Cor. xvi. 9: "A great door and effectual is opened unto me, and there are many adversaries."

for thou hast a little strength, and hast kept my word, and hast not denied my name.

^y ch. ii. 9.

9 Behold, I will make ^y them of the synagogue of Satan, which say they are Jews, and are not,

^z Isa. xlix. 23. & lx. 14.

but do lie; behold, ^z I will make them to come and worship before thy feet, and to know that I have loved thee.

10 Because thou hast kept the word of my

"For thou hast a little strength, and hast kept my word, and hast not denied my name." Many expositors omit the article in the English, "thou hast little strength." But, notwithstanding this, no one can shut the door which I have opened before thee.

"And hast kept my word, and hast not denied my name." The merit of the Church of Philadelphia seems to have been its steadfast adherence to the faith once delivered to the saints. The heresies against which they had to contend involved apparently the denial of the very Name of Jesus as the Christ—the only and veritable Son of God.

9. "Behold I will make them of the synagogue of Satan, which say that they are Jews," &c. The same adversaries must be described here as in chap. ii. 9. It must refer, one would think, to those who said that there was no salvation to those who would not conform to Judaism—those against whose machinations St. Paul's whole life was a contention—whose teaching, as I have shown in my notes on the Galatians, involved a real denial of the Divine Nature and eternal Sonship of Christ.

"Behold, I will make them to come and worship before thy feet." This seems a reminiscence of the prophecy in Isaiah xlix. 23: "They shall bow down to thee with their face toward the earth, and lick up the dust of thy feet," &c.

10. "Because thou hast kept [or didst keep] the word of my patience, I also will keep thee," &c. This seems to refer (as Mr. Blunt conjectures) to some past trial of faith which the Church of Philadelphia had gone through. This appears to have been connected with the doctrine of a suffering Messiah which was denied both by the Jews and the Gnostic sects, as the Docetæ.

patience, ᵃI also will keep thee from the hour of temptation, which shall come upon ᵇall the world, to try them that dwell ᶜupon the earth.

11 Behold, ᵈI come quickly: ᵉhold that fast which thou hast, that no man take ᶠthy crown.

12 Him that overcometh will I make ᵍa pillar in the temple of my God, and he shall go no more out: and ʰI will write upon him the name

ᵃ 2 Pet. ii. 9.
ᵇ Luke ii. 1.
ᶜ Isa. xxiv. 17.
ᵈ Phil. iv. 5. ch. i. 3. & xxii. 7, 12, 20.
ᵉ ver. 3. ch. ii. 25.
ᶠ ch. ii. 10.
ᵍ 1 Kings vii. 21. Gal. ii. 9.
ʰ ch. ii. 17 & xiv. 1. & xxii. 4.

"I also will keep thee from the hour of temptation, which shall come upon all the world." Under what circumstances they were kept we are not told. This promise seems look farther than the deliverance of a particular church. It seems to have to do with the deliverance of those who bore certain characters. They had already made their calling and election sure, and their trial had been sufficient.

11. Behold, I come quickly: hold that fast which thou hast," &c. They are like runners in a race; one may gain a prize which another, through weakness or slackening of his speed, may fail to win though it seemed almost within his grasp. But Archbishop Trench seems to give a different turn: "Let no man," Christ would say, "deprive thee of the glorious reward laid up for thee in heaven, of which many, my adversaries and thine, would fain rob thee; but which only one, even thyself, can ever cause thee to lose."

12. "Him that overcometh will I make a pillar in the temple of my God, and he shall go no more out." This has been supposed to refer to the two pillars set up by Solomon in the Temple of Jerusalem, Jachin and Boaz—the first signifying "he shall establish," and the other, "in it is strength"—described in 1 Kings vii. 15-21; but, as Trench says, these were set up not in the Temple but in the porch. The allusion rather is to the candlestick which may be removed out of its place, whereas the pillar cannot. He who is made a pillar "goes no more out." God says respecting him, "This my son shall be in danger no longer," and he has final perseverance assigned to him, for owing to his steadfastness he has won it.

"And I will write upon him the name of my God." This is in allusion to the name of Jehovah engraven on the plate placed

of my God, and the name of the city of my God, *which is* ⁱnew Jerusalem, which cometh down out of heaven from my God: ᵏand *I will write upon him* my new name.

13 ˡHe that hath an ear, let him hear what the Spirit saith unto the churches.

14 And unto the angel of the church ‖ of the

<small>ⁱ Gal. iv. 26.
Heb. xii. 22.
ch. xxi. 2, 10.
ᵏ ch. xxii. 4.

ˡ ch. ii. 7.

‖ Or, in *Laodicea*.</small>

---

on the forehead of the High Priest. All true Christians being priests of God.

"And the name of the city of my God, which is new Jerusalem." The name of the glorious city described in Ezekiel as taking the place of the old Jerusalem is Jehovah Shammah—the Lord is there. The Name of God being written on any one by the Saviour means that that man belongs to God. The name of the Holy City, new Jerusalem, being written on him, implies that he is free of that city. He can without hindrance enter through the gates into the city.

"Which cometh down out of heaven from my God." In chap. xxi. 2 we have a vision of the descent of the Holy City from heaven—not taken up to heaven, but coming down from God out of heaven. The reader will notice that some of the last Revelations of this book are here anticipated—as the writing of God's Name on men's foreheads, and the descent of the new Jerusalem.

"And I will write upon him my new name." In chap. xix. 12 it is said of the rider on the white horse—that is, of the Lord—that He hath a name written that no man knoweth but Himself; but in the next verse that His Name is called the "Word of God."

The new name is not "the Word," by that He was known from everlasting; neither is it "King of Kings and Lord of Lords," but it is some name of mystery, bearing upon the eternal relation of Christ to His Church, which is not yet made known, but which we shall know when we have it written upon us.

14. "And unto the church of the Laodiceans write." Laodicea was a city of Asia Minor, situated 115 miles east of Ephesus. The Church was planted by St. Paul, and to it he sent an Epistle which is either lost or was the same as that to the Ephesians with the

Laodiceans write; ᵐThese things saith the Amen, ⁿthe faithful and true witness, ᵒthe beginning of the creation of God;

15 ᵖI know thy works, that thou art neither cold nor hot: I would thou wert cold or hot.

m Isa. lxv. 16.
n ch. i. 5. & xix. 11. & xxii. 6. ver. 7.
o Col. i. 15.
p ver. 1.

---

14. "Of the Laodiceans;" or, "in Laodicea."

words "in Ephesus" at the beginning omitted (see footnote in my notes on Epistle to the Colossians, p. 78). Some suppose that Archippus, mentioned in Coloss. iv. 17, was yet its bishop, but that is uncertain, for it would imply an episcopate of thirty-three or thirty-four years. It is now utterly destroyed, and in a small hamlet raised near its ruins only three or four Christians could be found.

"These things saith the Amen." From a root signifying "to make firm," and taking a neuter signification, "to be firm," and so to be believed, to be relied on. Here equivalent to the faithful One.

"The faithful and true witness." He witnesses to the truth of God. "I say unto you," he says, "we speak that we do know, and testify that we have seen" (John iii.). Being a person of the ever-blessed Trinity He witnesses as no one else can do to the absolute truth of God.

"The beginning of the creation of God." This is true in two ways, but in two different acceptations, whether we look to the Lord's Divine or to His human Nature.

If we look to His Divine Nature He is the beginning of the creation, because He is its origin. He began it in the sense of bringing it into existence.

But inasmuch as He took upon Himself our full human being "perfect man, of a reasonable soul and human flesh," He was, as to His lower nature, a creature of God, and so He said to Mary Magdalen, "I ascend unto my God and your God." In this nature, being conceived by the Holy Ghost in the womb of the Blessed Virgin, He is the beginning of the creation of God, being the first creature in the sense of being the greatest, the foremost, the principal of all that can call upon God the Father.

15. "I know thy works, that thou art neither cold nor hot. would thou," &c. Archbishop Trench considers "'cold' to mean

16 So then because thou art lukewarm, and neither cold nor hot, I will spue thee out of my mouth.

^q Hos. xii. 8.
1 Cor. iv. 8.

17 Because thou sayest, ^q I am rich, and increased with goods, and have need of nothing;

---

one hitherto untouched by the powers of grace; 'lukewarm' to mean one who has tasted of the good gift . . . . but one in whom that grace has failed to kindle more than the faintest spark."

Bishop Boyd-Carpenter well remarks: "An intermediate state between these is the lukewarm; such as one neither earnest for God, nor utterly indifferent to religion. They are perhaps best described as those who take an interest in religion, but whose worship of their idol of good taste or good form leads them to regard enthusiasm as ill-bred or disturbing; and who have never put themselves to any inconvenience, braved any reproach, or abandoned any comfort for Christ's sake, but hoped to keep well with the world, while they flattered themselves that they stood well with God."

"I would thou wert cold or hot." So, then, because thou art lukewarm, thou art neither fervent in faith, nor entirely unbelieving. But if thou wert still unbelieving there would remain to thee the hope of conversion, whereas now, in that thou doest not the will of God which thou knowest, thou shalt be cast forth from the bosom of my Church.

17. "Because thou sayest, I am rich, and increased with goods, and have need of nothing." What is meant by "I am rich, and increased in goods, and have need of nothing?" Is the allusion to spiritual satisfaction or abundance of temporal goods? The first appears to be most in accordance with the general contents of these Epistles, which have to do with spiritual rather than with worldly things, but inasmuch as the worldly prosperity of Laodicea was remarkable, for when she and other cities in her neighbourhood were destroyed by an earthquake, her citizens undertook of themselves, without any assistance from the Imperial treasury, to rebuild their city, which they did in far more than its original magnificence; and when, along with this, we take into account that temporal prosperity is always assumed by the New Testament writers to have a deleterious effect on the soul's true spirituality, it is very probable that we must join the two. The

and knowest not that thou art wretched, and miserable, and poor, and blind, and naked:

18 I counsel thee ʳto buy of me gold tried in the fire, that thou mayest be rich; and ˢwhite raiment, that thou mayest be clothed, and *that*

ʳ Isa. lv. 1.
Matt. xiii. 44.
& xxv. 9.
ˢ 2 Cor. v. 3.
ch. vii. 13. &
xvi. 15. &
xix. 8.

---

17. "Wretched," &c. With article, "the wretched and miserable."—temporal wealth begat self-consequence and pride, and this entered into the domain of the Spirit, for pride in one thing prepares the way for pride in another. If a man looks with self-satisfaction at his own outward surroundings, he will look with the same satisfaction at his supposed spiritual endowments, and this will ruin all.

"And knowest not that thou art wretched, and miserable, and poor," &c. There is an article before wretched (ὁ ταλαίπωρος) which may be understood before each of these adjectives as emphasizing them. "The wretched, and miserable, and poor, and blind, and naked one." None are so wretched as those who in spiritual things know not their lost condition. Their whole condition is one of self-deception, and on account of this, their spiritual blindness, they imagine they have no need of the great Divine Redeeming Remedy.

18. "I counsel thee to buy of me gold tried in the fire, that thou mayest be rich." We should have thought that the Lord would have rather said, "ask of me," rather than " buy of me:" but in our zeal for the doctrine of free grace we must not conceal from ourselves the fact that there must be a certain zeal and earnestness in the asking. It is not the careless asking—the asking anyhow—but the asking followed by the importunate seeking, and the still more importunate knocking.

What is this "gold"? Trench explains it as meaning faith, and refers to the prayer of the Apostles: "Lord increase our faith;" others as love, without which faith is of no account. But ought we to limit it? Must it not mean that grace in which the soul is poor or deficient?

"And white raiment, that thou mayest be clothed." White raiment is the symbol of forgiveness and of purity. The robes must be washed and made white in the Blood of the Lamb, and

the shame of thy nakedness do not appear; and anoint thine eyes with eyesalve, that thou mayest see.

19 ᵗAs many as I love, I rebuke and chasten: be zealous therefore, and repent.

ᵗ Job v. 17. Prov. iii. 11, 12. Heb. xii. 5, 6. James i. 12.

---

the soul or spirit must be clean in the sight of Him that searcheth the hearts. And yet these two whitenesses, these two purities, are in the sight of God but one. He that hath righteousness imputed has it also imparted, or the imputation is useless.

"And anoint thine eyes with eyesalve, that thou mayest see." We are here reminded how that the Lord on occasion of restoring sight to the blind man, "made clay of the spittle, and anointed the eyes of the blind man with the clay" (John ix. 6).

But what is this anointing which gives or restores sight to the spiritually blind? It seems that it can be only the Holy Spirit, the Illuminator. "Ye were sometime darkness, but now are ye light in the Lord," and the Word of God, which is His instrument. "When thy word goeth forth it giveth light and understanding to the simple." So that if we are to use the Divine eyesalve we must diligently pray for the Spirit, and we must diligently study the Word.

19. "As many as I love, I rebuke and chasten: be zealous therefore, and repent." This is often repeated in the sacred scriptures. Thus in Job. v. 17: "Behold, happy is the man whom God correcteth; therefore despise not thou the chastening of the Almighty." Thus Ps. xciv. 12: "Blessed is the man whom thou chasteneth, O Lord, and teachest him in thy law." Thus Prov. iii. 11-12: "My son, despise not the chastening of the Lord . . . . Whom the Lord loveth he correcteth;" thus Heb. xii. 6, quoting Prov. iii. 10.

"I rebuke and chasten." "I rebuke," so as to bring them to a sense of their sin and to repentance. "I chasten," I discipline them after their repentance by adversity and grace.

"Be zealous therefore." Shake off thy coldness—kindle thy lukewarmness into earnestness and love.

"And repent." Not only sin, but coldness and lukewarmness in the service of Christ have to be repented of if we would be restored to the favour of God.

20 Behold, [u]I stand at the door, and knock: [x]if any man hear my voice, and open the door, [y]I will come in to him, and will sup with him, and he with me.

21 To him that overcometh [z]will I grant to sit

[u] Cant. v. 2.
[x] Luke xii. 37.
[y] John xiv. 23.
[z] Matt. xix. 28. Luke xxii 30. 1 Cor. vi. 2. 2 Tim. ii. 12. ch. ii. 26, 27.

---

20. "Behold, I stand at the door, and knock: if any man hear my voice." "We have a right, so far as we may venture to distinguish between the two, to see in the voice the more inward appeal, the closer dealing of Christ with the soul, speaking directly by His Spirit to the spirit of the man: in the knocking, those more outward gracious dealings of sorrow and joy, of sickness and health, and the like, which He sends, and sending uses for the bringing of His Elect, in one way or another, by smooth paths or by rough, to Himself" (Trench).

"I will come in to him, and will sup with him, and he with me." So John xiv. 23: "My Father will love him, and we will come to him and make our abode with him." Compare the words of the bridegroom, Canticles v. 2: "It is the voice of my beloved that knocketh, saying, Open to me, my sister, my love." In another aspect it constantly recurs in the Pauline Epistles. Thus Coloss. i. 27: "Christ in you, the hope of glory." "Prove your own selves. Know ye not your own selves, how that Jesus Christ is in you, except ye be reprobates?" (2 Cor. xiii. 5).

21. "To him that overcometh will I grant to sit with me on my throne, even as I also," &c. This is a promise far exceeding that to the twelve: "Ye also shall sit upon twelve thrones, judging the twelve tribes of Israel." It is to be remembered that the throne of eastern kings is not a mere two-armed chair, but a large and wide seat that will hold many persons, intended to seat those whom the great king delights to honour by placing them close beside himself.

This is the highest reward which Christ has promised to any of the churches; and the reader will notice that it is given to the Church lowest in spiritual attainments—to one which the Saviour had threatened to cast out of His mouth. "The highest place," as Trench remarks, "is within reach of the lowest; the faintest spark of grace may be fanned into the mightiest flame of Divine love."

with me in my throne, even as I also overcame, and am set down with my Father in his throne.

ᵃ ch. ii. 7.   22 ᵃHe that hath an ear, let him hear what the Spirit saith unto the churches.

"Even as I also overcame, and am set down with my Father in his throne." What is the difference between Christ's throne and God's throne? for a difference there is, and must be understood and acknowledged. Christ's throne is His Priestly or Mediatorial throne, to which He exalts those who have been made by Him priests to God. If they are priests in any real sense it can only be by, in some inferior sense, sharing His Priesthood; but God's throne is the throne of Almighty Power and Grace, and can only be shared by One who is equal with God in Nature and Attributes.

NOTES TO THE SECOND AND THIRD CHAPTERS.

THE ANGELS OF THE CHURCHES.

1. There can be, I think, little doubt but that the angels of these churches are their chief ministers. They cannot well signify angelic beings, for we never read of such having the care or oversight of churches. Such functions God has assigned to men only. But in looking upon them as chief ministers, or bishops, a great mistake has, I am persuaded, been made by some of our best expositors, in that the words of praise or blame in which the angels are addressed by the Lord are supposed to be said to them as individuals, and not as representing their respective churches. The difference between the two is very apparent in the Epistle to the Church at Thyatira, to whom the Lord says: "Unto you (ὑμῖν) I say, unto the rest in Thyatira, as many as have not this doctrine," &c. This is evidently addressed not to the president but to the whole Church. Again to the Church of Smyrna: "Fear none of those things which thou shalt suffer: behold the devil shall cast some of you into prison," &c. Here also is a distinction made between the angel and the persons composing his flock.

This is a matter of considerable moment. The address to each church is undoubtedly in an important sense personal (for the churches are not addressed merely as aggregates as in St. Paul's Epistles), and yet the church is represented as a whole, having, notwithstanding its numbers, a particular character pervading it. So that besides the individual responsibility of each angel, and the individual responsibility of each individual member, each church has a character of its own. Now this corresponds with the way in which in this our day we speak of congregations, or even of dioceses. We constantly speak of a congregation being in a backward or a forward state; of a congregation being generous or niggardly; or of a diocese or congregation being imbued with certain right or wrong principles; but by His addressing the angel rather than the church, and blaming or praising him, the Lord holds him, in a very marked degree, responsible for the moral or spiritual state of the church. If he had been thoroughly alive to his duty, and courageous in fulfilling it, each church reproved would not have been so much to blame as it is.

So that in these addresses of Christ to the churches we have a very high view indeed of ministerial responsibility. The ministers are—God only knows to what extent—answerable for the sins of the people, as they are answerable for their freedom from heresy or false doctrine, and on the other hand they equally share in their praise here and shall share in their reward hereafter. As St. Paul says of the Thessalonian Church, "What is our hope, or joy, or crown of rejoicing? Are not even ye in the presence of our Lord Jesus Christ at his coming?" (1 Thess. ii. 19).

2. It may be well to devote a few words to what has been called the Historico-Prophetical interpretation of these seven Epistles. According to this scheme they are supposed to be not seven actual churches existing eighteen hundred years ago in Asia Minor, but as seven periods of the world's history in which that character was predominant which the Lord praises or blames in His message to each several Church. Thus Brightman—an English divine of the reign of Elizabeth, born 1557, died 1607, a man of great learning and piety—sees in the Church of Ephesus the Apostolic period between A.D. 30-100; the Church of Smyrna, A.D. 100-382; Pergamum, 382-1300; Thyatira, 1300-1520; in Sardis the Lutheran, in Philadelphia the Reformed, and in Laodicea the Anglican Church.

Sir Isaac Newton considers that the Church of Ephesus prefigures the condition of the Catholic Church from St. John to the persecution of Diocletian, A.D. 302; the Epistle to Smyrna, from A.D. 302 to that of Licinius; the Epistle to Pergamum, the Church under Constantine and his sons, A.D. 324-340; the Epistle to Thyatira, the Church under the divided rule of the sons of Constantine, A.D. 340-350; the Epistle to Sardis, the Church under the sole rule of Constantius, A.D. 350-361; the Epistle to Philadelphia, the faithfulness of the Church under Julian, A.D. 361-363; the Epistle to Laodicea, the lukewarmness of the Church under Valentinian and Valeus, A.D. 363-376.

Stier in his "Words of the Risen Saviour," sees in these Epistles the spirit of prophecy embracing in a parallel scheme the times and the histories of the Old Testament and of the New in their entire development. 1. The primitive world and primitive Christianity (Noah—Constantine). 2. The preparation of God's people and the European peoples (Moses—Charlemagne). 3. Israel in its decline and the Romish Church as the tolerated transition (Nebuchadnezzar—Hildebrand). 4. The Babylonish period and the Papal-worldly period (Zerubbabel—Luther). 5. The Persian-Greek period and the Protestant-political age (Alexander—Napoleon). 6. The Greek-Roman period and the Second Reformation. 7. The Advent of Christ and the Millenial Kingdom. These three I owe to Archdeacon Lee's note in "Speaker's Commentary." In Lange's Commentary there is a scheme by a Romanist—Holzhauser: 1. Ephesus: end of the Apostolic age. 2. Smyrna: time of the Martyrs. 3. Pergamos: confession of faith; time of the great Church Fathers from the fourth to the sixth century. 4. Thyatira: laudable condition; time of the Church's domination from Justinian to Charlemagne, warring against worldliness—Jezebel. 5. Sardis: semblances of Christianity: the prevailing condition of the Church at the present time. 6. Philadelphia: destitute of exterior power, yet witnessing a good confession: perhaps our immediate future. Laodicea, *i.e.*, people's judgment. The end. The same may be said against interpreting the seven churches as seven periods which may be said against the continuous historical interpretation of all the rest of the book. No two learned men can agree upon it. It is open to the same objections which lie against all interpretations which demand long periods, that the Divine Inspirer of the Apocalypse recognizes no lapse of time between the Ascension and the Second Advent. A very good examination of it is to be found at the end of Archbishop Trench's "Commentary on the Epistles to the Seven Churches."

THE NICOLAITANES.

The first account of these heretics is in Irenæus i. 26: "The Nicolaitanes are the followers of that Nicolas who was one of the seven first ordained to the diaconate by the Apostles. They led lives of unrestrained indulgence. The character of these men is very plainly pointed out in the Apocalypse of John as teaching that it is a matter of indifference to practice adultery, and to eat things sacrificed to idols. Wherefore the Word has also spoken of them thus: 'But this thou hast, that thou hatest the deeds of the Nicolaitanes, which I also hate.'" (Rev. ii. 6).

Tertullian in a tract entitled "Against all Heresies," not the "De Præscrip. Hæreticorum," says: "A brother heretic emerged to light in Nicolaus. He was one of the seven deacons who were appointed in the Acts of the Apostles. He affirms that darkness was seized with a concupiscence (and indeed a foul and obscene one) after light; out of this permixture it is a shame to say what fetid and unclean combinations arose," &c. A reference is given to the third book of the Miscellanies of Clement of Alexandria in Eusebius, "Eccles. Hist.," iii. 29, but I have not been successful in verifying it. The passage from Eusebius is as follows: "About this time also, for a very short time, arose the heresy of those called Nicolaites, of which also mention is made in the Revelation of John. These boasted of Nicolaus as their founder, one of those deacons who with Stephen were appointed by the Apostles to minister unto the poor, ... I have ascertained, however, that Nicolaus lived with no other woman than the one to whom he was married, but that his daughters continued in the state of virginity to advanced life: that his son also remained uncorrupt. This is very inconsistent with the tradition that he was the founder of an immoral sect." A curious attempt has been made to identify the heresy of the Nicolaitanes with the doctrine of Balaam, denounced by our Lord in ii. 14, on the ground that Nicolaus is the reproduction in a Greek word of Balaam in the Hebrew, but it appears to me that there is no ground whatsoever for the alleged identity. If Balaam, or rather Bilam, means anything, it means one who devours, Bala being a common word signifying "he ate up," or "devoured," but there is no part of it answering to "people" if it is thus taken. Gesenius makes it signify "one not of the people," that is, a stranger; but Balaam would have his name given years before he was summoned by Balak to curse Israel. Nicolas was a common Greek proper name, and signifies conqueror of the people, that is, of the people against whom he fought, as we must suppose, his enemies.

I do not attempt to deny that the doctrine of the Nicolaitanes was the doctrine of Balaam, but still I hold it upon grounds very different from this absurd derivation of their respective names.

CHAP. IV.

AFTER this I looked, and behold, a door *was* opened in

1. "Opened." It stood open—he did not see it opened.

1. "After this I looked, and behold, a door was opened," &c. It may be well to say a few words in introduction to our remarks on the visions in these fourth and fifth chapters. They are visions, but if sent by a God of truth they must represent realities. What are the things which St. John now saw? Are they spiritual hieroglyphics, having no reality in themselves but only to be understood as representing other things? Take, for instance, the "sea of glass." The great MSS. omit "as it were," and read simply "and before the throne a sea of glass." Did St. John see before him what appeared to him, and what he could not distinguish from "a sea of glass," clear as crystal, or, did he see any of the things which are said to be signified by this sea of glass? Thus Ebrard thinks "that as the stormy sea represents the godless nations, so here the pure and calm sea represents creation in its true relation to its creator." De Burgh sees here, and in chap. xv. 2, a reference to the molten sea or great basin of brass in Solomon's temple (1 Kings vii. 23-26, 38) now introduced in order to typify the puri-

heaven: and ᵃ the first voice which I heard *was*   ᵃ ch. i. 10.

---

fication in baptism of all who are made kings and priests. Now this vision takes its place with those in Isaiah vi. and Ezekiel i. as a vision of God. God, Who fills all things (rather in Whom are all things), is here pleased to localize Himself as it were. The infinite Deity, for His own all-wise purposes, represents Himself as a great king holding a court. If He does this it is only natural that He should not appear alone in absolutely solitary majesty, but that He should be surrounded with those to whom He has assigned places very near to Himself. Now He chooses to represent Himself not as filling all space, if such a thing is imaginable, but as sitting upon a throne; before this throne there is a space, and this space the Evangelist sees filled up with this glassy sea. What the spiritual or typical meaning of it is we are not told, but St. John saw it as there. It afterwards appears as affording a place for the whole army of the conquerors over sin and evil, so that they may celebrate their triumph in the most immediate presence of God (Rev. xv. 2).

This then will illustrate what I think is the nature of these visions. They describe the court of God—His immediate Presence—the heavenly Holy of Holies, as they would appear to one who from his holiness and purity was able to bear the sight. Whether these were phenomena only, behind which there were certain realities, certain noumena, we cannot inquire. We take them as St. John saw them, for it is evidently intended that we should do so. If it be objected that some of the things represented are below the dignity of the immediate court or presence-chamber of God, we say that it is impossible for us to assert anything of the sort. It is quite possible that St. John, in seeing these things, might have his sense of space annihilated, just as in describing other things in this book he had his sense of time taken away. No one, not even Raphael, has been able to put on canvas the forms of the four living ones; but this does not undo the fact that creatures so near to God would be beyond all conception beautiful, majestic, terrible to eyes of flesh and blood.

1. "After this I looked [or I saw], and behold a door was opened in heaven." Not in the act of being opened, but standing open.

as it were of a trumpet talking with me; which said, ᵇCome up hither, ᶜand I will shew thee things which must be hereafter.

2 And immediately ᵈI was in the spirit: and, behold, ᵉa throne was set in heaven, and *one* sat on the throne.

3 And he that sat was to look upon like a

ᵇ ch. xi. 12.
ᶜ ch. i. 19. & xxii. 6.
ᵈ ch. i. 10. & xvii. 3. & xxi. 10.
ᵉ Isa. vi. 1. Jer. xvii. 12. Ezek. i. 26. & x. 1. Dan. vii. 9.

---

3. "And he that sat was." "Was" omitted by ℵ, A., B., P., some Cursives, Vulg., Syriac, &c.

"And the first voice which I heard was, as it were, of a trumpet talking with me." That is, the voice was not like the still small voice which Elijah heard, but loud, clear, sonorous, penetrating.

"Which said." Who said? The One Who caused His voice to be heard as a trumpet—no other than the Lord.

"Which said, Come up hither, and I will shew thee things which," &c. This is the message in the Apocalypse—not the things then occurring, not the destruction of Jerusalem, not the foundation of the Christian Church, but the things which needed one to whom the future was naked and open to reveal.

2. "And immediately I was in the spirit." That is, the Spirit of God. "So exalted and permeated by Spirit, that I saw with the eyes of my spirit what the Spirit of God saw within me."

This constituted his ascent, as it were, in obedience to the call "Come up hither."

"And behold, a throne was set in heaven, and one sat on the throne." Mark, the throne first appears, and then One Whose appearance is not described Who sat upon it.

3. "And he that sat was to look upon like a jasper and a sardine stone." He that sat must be God the Father, for the Lord had said, "I have overcome, and am set down with my Father on his throne." According to the truth of the imagery of this book it cannot be God the Son, for in the next chapter He comes forward to take the roll book out of the hands of Him that sat upon the throne.

It has been made a question whether He that sat upon the throne was the Father, or the Triune God. But the Godhead of

jasper and a sardine stone: 'and *there was* a rainbow round about the throne, in sight like unto an emerald.   f Ezek. i. 28.

4 ᵍ And round about the throne *were* four and   g ch. xi. 16.
twenty seats: and upon the seats I saw four and

God is in the Father, and is by Him communicated to the Son and the Holy Ghost.

3. "And he that sat (was) to look upon like a jasper and a sardine stone." What does this mean? It is impossible to suppose that the Evangelist compared the Personal Appearance of the Almighty to a jewel, no matter how set, no matter how bright. The fact of course is, that, like the children of Israel of old, he saw no similitude; what was before his eyes was that "light which no man can approach unto" in which God dwelt. But this light must appear to his eyes as pure white light, as of the stone here called the jasper, or as having some other colour, as the sardine stone, very probably the brightest red. These colours may have been mixed, or their rays might be separated, but the light which proceeded from the Deity was, in the sight of St. John, in some sense two.

"And there was a rainbow round about the throne, in sight like unto an emerald." The rainbow is the sign of God's covenanted mercies, but it is also the most beautiful thing in nature; so that, quite apart from its typical meaning, if God intended to convey to a mortal yet in the flesh some idea of the outward material glory with which He chose to surround Himself, He would encircle His throne with the rainbow.

"In sight like unto an emerald." This is generally taken as if the brightness of the emerald predominated. Alford says: "The form is that of the covenant bow, the colour even more refreshing and more directly symbolizing grace and mercy."

4. "And round about the throne were four and twenty seats [thrones]: and," &c. Notice that here again the thrones are seen apparently before those who sat upon them. It seems as if the thrones were there and had to be won by the foremost conquerors in the war with sin and evil.

"And upon the seats I saw four and twenty elders sitting." Did they compass the throne in a circle (it is quite possible), or were

twenty elders sitting, ʰ clothed in white raiment; ⁱ and they had on their heads crowns of gold.

ʰ ch. iii. 4, 5. & vi. 11. & vii. 9, 13, 14. & xix. 14.
ⁱ ver. 10.

4. "They had" omitted by ℵ, A., B., P., most Cursives, Vulg., Arm., Syriac.

they placed in front in a half-circle, twelve on each side, and who were the occupants? It seems agreed on all hands that in some way they represent the Catholic Church in its two divisions—that of the Old and that of the New Dispensation. But I trust that it may be lawful to inquire into the likelihood of this.

It is supposed that the twenty-four consist of the twelve Patriarchs and the twelve Apostles; but are the twelve Patriarchs the actual Patriarchs, the sons of Jacob? Is it possible that Reuben, the first of the Patriarchs, was on a throne close to the throne of God; and in this case what place is left for such men as Enoch, Noah, Melchizedec, Abraham, Moses, Joshua?

Again, taking the second twelve to be New Testament saints, is it possible to assign them to the twelve, leaving out St. Stephen, St. John the Baptist, St. Paul, St. Barnabas?

Must we not apply to all such lists of names the words of the Lord, "Many that are first shall be last; and the last first" (Matt. xix. 30), particularly since He said this immediately after His promise of one of twelve thrones to each of the twelve?

All seem to be agreed that these twenty-four are not angelic natures but human beings, but they must have been human beings who occupy these thrones not by creation, much less by mere favour, but because they have won places so near to God by holiness and self-endurance.

"Clothed in white raiment." As if they were priests to God—the white raiment being the vestment of priests.

"And they had on their heads crowns of gold." This may signify that they were kings as well as priests. But it may also signify that they had gotten a victory and were each rewarded with a bright and imperishable crown.

That these were real intelligences and not merely emblematical figures is plain from what is said in the next chapter, where, in verse 5, we are told that one of these elders consoled St. John when he wept because no one was worthy to open the book.

5 And out of the throne proceeded *k* lightnings and thunderings and voices: *l* and *there were* seven lamps of fire burning before the throne, which are *m* the seven Spirits of God.

6 And before the throne *there was* *n* a sea of

k ch. viii. 5. & xvi. 18.
l Ex. xxxvii. 23. 2 Chr. iv. 20. Ezek. i. 13. Zech. iv. 2.
m ch. i. 4. & iii. 1. & v. 6.
n Ex. xxxviii. 8. ch. xv. 2.

---

5. "And out of the throne proceeded lightnings and thunderings and voices." Out of the throne, from God Himself proceeded these voices of God, which were His decrees to His angelic messengers who, when they heard them, proceeded to carry them into execution. These are the voices heard from Mount Sinai; there were "thunders and lightnings, and a thick cloud upon the mount, and the voice of the trumpet exceeding loud" (Exod. xix. 16). These were the voices of Psalm xxix.: "The voice of the Lord is upon the waters: the God of glory thundereth. The voice of the Lord is powerful: the voice of the Lord is full of majesty." The thunderings and lightnings were not the utterance of God in anger, but meant to impress those who heard them with His irresistible power. God here surrounds Himself with the features of the natural world which are grandest and most appalling; unless he has utterly hardened his heart, nothing strikes a man so much with his own helplessness as the lightning and the thunder of God's power. In some way unknown to us the lightnings and thunders appear to be the natural accompaniments of God's presence.

"And there were seven lamps of fire burning before the throne, which are the seven Spirits of God." These seven Spirits are the One Spirit in His sevenfold operations, and seven being the complete, the perfect number, it signifies that the presence and operations of the One Spirit are as if He were present in His absolute fulness and entirety to each one of those with whom He has to do. He is not divided amongst those upon whom He acts, but He acts upon each one indivisibly as if He were a separate person confronting each one (see notes on i. 4).

6. "And before the throne there was a sea of glass like unto crystal." I have noticed this sea of glass in the introductory remarks (p. 52). I believe that the Apostle saw it as he describes it, and if the throne of God and the four-and-twenty thrones were there, so was this "sea of glass like unto crystal." Various explanations have

glass like unto crystal: °and in the midst of the throne, and round about the throne, *were* four beasts full of eyes before ᵖ and behind.

° Ezek. i. 5.
ᵖ ver. 8.

---

been given as to what it typifies—nearly all different; I have given two on p. 52. One commentator thinks that it represents the waters of baptism: "It may be that the standing upon the sea of glass mingled with fire (xv. 2) signifies that the whole spiritual life, even to its final glory, stands upon the foundation given in baptism of water and of the spirit." Another, "That as the waters on which the scarlet woman sits, represent the unguided, unreasoning, and unprincipled thoughts of men, so the calm glass-like sea, which is never in storm but only interfused with flame (xv. 2), represents the counsels of God, those purposes of righteousness and love often fathomless but never obscure; always the same, though sometimes glowing with holy anger."

"And in the midst of the throne, and round about the throne, were four beasts [living ones] full of eyes before and behind." Now here again I must recall the reader to that which, beyond all controversy, the Evangelist describes; he describes the court of God. Now, inasmuch as between God and all created things there is a gulf profound, impassable, illimitable, he might have been led to describe the throne of the Almighty as existing in a boundless void, which would aptly represent His essential separation from all creature existences; but, instead of this, he is led to describe God as bringing certain created intelligences very near to Himself. There are three occasions in which God is pleased to reveal to men the court of His immediate presence, Isaiah vi., Ezekiel i., and this place; and in each of these He represents Himself as bringing certain created intelligences close to His throne. I firmly believe, then, that no matter what these living ones typify, they represent themselves; they are existences who have won a place very close to the throne of God.

"Full of eyes before and behind." If this means anything it signifies that their power of vision is infinite. They were seen by the Evangelist as if they were all eye, all observation, they received knowledge, not as we do, slowly and imperfectly, but from all parts of God's universe at once—nothing could be hidden from them. In this they were as near as possible to Him to

7 ᑫ And the first beast *was* like a lion, and the second beast like a calf, and the third beast had a face as a man, and the fourth beast *was* like a flying eagle.

ᑫ Num. ii. 2, &c. Ezek. i. 10. & x. 14.

Whom the Psalmist said: "The darkness and light to thee are both alike."

7. "And the first living one was like a lion, and the second living one like a calf [it may as well be translated ox], and the third living one had a face as a man," &c. It has generally been assumed that these living ones represent all animated nature uniting in glorifying God, "All thy works praise thee, O Lord," but there is, to me at least, one insurmountable difficulty in this, which is that the third living one has the human countenance. Now, if his praise corresponds to his appearance, his must be the only intelligent praise offered to God by any of the four creatures, the idea of which is not to be entertained for a moment.

The meaning, if it is lawful to express it in words, seems to be something of this sort. The creatures had not each of them a human face, one had; and this fact shows that they were different from the rest of the angelic host who all come to us in the likeness of man.

Now we must carefully remember that St. John in this and in all the rest of this book describes things as they appeared to him. Only one of these countenances appeared to him human. The rest of the faces were more like the creatures mentioned by him. There is an infinite variety in the human face as manifesting the interior character; the human face may exhibit the character of a good angel, or that of an intensely evil spirit. Now there is a certain nobility in the countenances of each of the three non-human creatures here described, which nobility no doubt was, to the seeming of St. John, its characteristic, its feature, and its grandeur and beauty. We acknowledge this when we say that such an one has the face of a lion or the eye of an eagle. If we said this, as we do every day, we should say it in praise, not in disparagement.

I believe then that these living ones whom God Himself has placed so near to His throne are all intelligence, all activity, all grandeur and beauty. They have been called representatives of creation. It may be that they are rather types of it which the

8 And the four beasts had each of them ʳ six wings about him; and *they were* full of eyes ˢ within: and †they rest not day and night, saying, ᵗ Holy,

ʳ Isa. vi. 2.
ˢ ver. 6.
† Gr. *they have no rest.*
ᵗ Isa. vi. 3.

noblest of earthly countenances are formed upon. I have written all this because I believe these creatures to be real, and it requires very great care in making them out to be representations or types lest we destroy their reality.¹

8. "And the four living ones had each of them six wings about him." How these wings were affixed to their bodies we know not. The living creatures in Ezekiel i. had but four, but the seraphim in Isaiah had, like these, six; and it is very remarkable that of their six wings they employed four in adoration, "with twain he covered his face, and with twain he covered his feet, and with twain he flew." Whether these similarly used their wings we are not told, but it seems to me very probable. It is to be remarked that these only of angelic beings are said to have wings. The wings of course represent their power of progression to obey the behests of God, just as the eyes in every part of them represent their powers of observation and intellect.

"And they were full of eyes within." Alford takes κυκλόθεν with ἔσωθεν, and says upon this, "the object of St. John being to show that the six wings in each case did not interfere with that which he had before declared, viz., that they were full of eyes before and behind. Round the outside of each wing, and up the inside of each (half-expanded) wing, and of the part of the body also which was in that inside recess, they are full of eyes." But surely this is too elaborate. One commentator explains the eyes within as doubling the contemplative concentration and unity of the Divine Omniscience; another, the never-resting, wakeful activity of organic life. Most commentators, however, pass it over without notice.

"And they rest not day and night, saying, Holy, holy, holy, Lord God Almighty, which was, and is, and is to come." This is

---

¹ For instance, their reality is utterly destroyed if they are assumed to be figures of the four Gospels. Are they the books of the four Gospels, or are they the writers? If the former, then they are very imperfect, for they give but a very small part of the words and deeds of Christ. When we are amongst the blessed in the unseen world, we shall learn from eye-witnesses a hundred times more than we have learnt from the Evangelists. John xxi. 25.

holy, holy, ᵘLord God Almighty, ˣwhich was, and is, and is to come.

9 And when those beasts give glory and honour and thanks to him that sat on the throne, ʸwho liveth for ever and ever,

ᵘ ch. i. 8.
ˣ ch. i. 4.
ʸ ch. i. 18. & v. 14. & xv. 7.

---

9. "Give"—"shall give."

the Trisagion adopted into its Liturgies by every branch of the Church of Christ, its use reaching far back into a time when there was no central authority to compel, or even to recommend, obedience in the Church, so that its use dates from the origin or first planting of each church, which was generally by an Apostle or Apostolic man, a companion of an Apostle. It is the highest act of praise offered to God by those that are nearest to His throne, and yet it is the simplest.

The threefold repetition of "Holy" has always been held to point to the mystery of the ever-blessed Trinity, and for this reason this chapter has been chosen for the Epistle for Trinity Sunday. There is a difference between the concluding words in Isaiah and in the Apocalypse. In Isaiah it is "the whole earth is full of his glory." Here it is "which was, and is, and is to come." Mr. Blunt remarks that inasmuch as the older form in Isaiah is adopted in the oldest type of Liturgy—in that of St. James, used in Jerusalem—it is probable that the main body of this Liturgy was settled before the Apocalypse was written. So that at every celebration of the Eucharist we are permitted to join in the highest worship of angels.

The root idea of holiness is separation. The consecrated or hallowed person or thing is separated to the service of God. Thus the tabernacle and its vessels, and the robes of the priests, and the altar were all hallowed, as separated, by the very fact of their dedication, from all profane uses. So that the creatures nearest to God proclaim in their ceaseless anthem the infinite separation in essence between themselves and God; so that, so close as He has put them to Himself, He is yet infinitely above them.

9. "And when those living ones give glory and honour and thanks." "Give" is in the future tense, "shall give," and implies

10 ªThe four and twenty elders fall down before him that sat on the throne, ªand worship him that liveth for ever and ever, ᵇand cast their crowns before the throne, saying,

11 ᶜThou art worthy, O Lord, to receive glory and honour and power: ᵈfor thou hast created all things, and for thy pleasure they are and were created.

ᵃ ch. v. 8, 14.
ª ver. 9.
ᵇ ver. 4.

ᶜ ch. v. 12.

ᵈ Gen. i. 1.
Acts xvii. 24.
Eph. iii. 9.
Col. i. 16.
ch. x. 6.

---

10. "Fall down"—"shall fall down." "Sat"—"sitteth." "Worship"—"will worship," ℵ, A., B. "And cast"—"will cast."

the eternal repetition of the act; whenever they give praise then their praise is seconded by the elders, for we read:

10. "The four and twenty elders [shall] fall down before him that sat [sitteth] on the throne." Note the lowliness of the adoration of these exalted ones. They fall down, that is, they prostrate themselves.

"And cast their crowns before the throne." Tacitus ("Ann.," xv. 29) tells how Tiridates cast down his diadem (*insigne regnum*) in homage before the effigy of Nero; so also Dion Cassius (lib. xxxvi.) tells how Tigranes cast down his diadem before Pompeius (Archdeacon Lee in "Speaker's Commentary"), so that this was not an unusual sign of homage to the supreme power.

11. "Thou art worthy, O Lord, to receive glory and honour and power: for thou hast created all things." This is an act of praise to God the Creator. In the next chapter the praise is to the Redeemer. In the succession of time creation comes before redemption, for things must have existed and been brought into being before they could be redeemed.

"And for thy pleasure they are and were created." ℵ, A., &c., read "they were," meaning they existed and were created. This seems to mean, "No sooner didst Thou will their being than they were, and by the contemporaneous act of creation they took forms and were manifested."

Such was the act of praise to God as the Creator. And now the book of God's providence is unrolled.

CHAP. V.

AND I saw in the right hand of him that sat on the throne ᵃa book written within and on the backside, ᵇsealed with seven seals.

2 And I saw a strong angel proclaiming with a loud voice, Who is worthy to open the book, and to loose the seals thereof?

ᵃ Ezek. ii. 9, 10.
ᵇ Isa. xxix. 11. Dan. xii. 4.

---

1. "And I saw in the right hand of him that sat on the throne." The appearance or form of Him that sat on the throne is not described by St. John. Of course, because it was unlawful to make any image or figure of the Father, and so there could be no description given of Him. Still, out of the excess of light in which God was, His right hand was to be seen, and on this (not in it) lay a book or roll written on both sides—both within—that is, in the usual place of writing, and without, on the back side; so that every part of the book was covered with writing.

"Sealed with seven seals." This implies that the roll or scroll was made up of seven pieces of parchment. The outer one the first, the innermost the seventh.

Were, then, all the seven seals visible? It would seem that they were; and so there was a thread—or something of such a kind—which was sealed in each seal, and the end of which reached to the outside of the whole roll, so that one could immediately tell where each part of the roll began.

What were the contents of each part of the roll? We cannot tell. It may have been the events that occurred at each opening of the successive seals, or, which is more probable, the interpretation of their mysteries.

2. "And I saw a strong angel." Supposed to be Gabriel, because his name signifies mighty or strong God; but if it was so well known a messenger of God I think his name would have been recorded as that of Michael is.

"Proclaiming with a loud voice, Who is worthy to open the

3 And no man ᶜin heaven, nor in earth, neither under the earth, was able to open the book, neither to look thereon.

ᶜ ver. 13.

4 And I wept much, because no man was found worthy to open and to read the book, neither to look thereon.

5 And one of the elders saith unto me, Weep not: behold

---

4. "And to read" omitted by ℵ, B., P., forty Cursives, Vulg., Copt., Syriac, Arm., Æth.; retained by only two or three Cursives.

book, and to loose," &c. Who is able to make known the mysteries of God's providence? Who is able to unfold the book of His secret counsels?

3. "And no man in heaven, nor in earth, neither under the earth," &c. "No man," *i.e.* no one; man is not expressed.

"Was able to open the book." This seems to mean "was worthy." No created intelligence, no mere creature was worthy. This is one of those almost innumerable places which set forth the Divine Nature of the Eternal Son, and, so far as that Divine Nature is concerned, the gulf between Him and every creature. No living creature, no elder on his throne, no angel, no saint, had virtue enough to open the book.

4. "And I wept much, because no man was found worthy," &c. It has been supposed that St. John wept because of the contents of the roll, which in some unexplained way he was supposed to know before the book was unrolled; but it cannot be so. He wept because the mystery of God's dealings was apparently not capable of being disclosed. Amongst creatures in heaven, in earth, and under the earth, there was no one who could unfold the Divine secrets.

5. "And one of the elders saith unto me, Weep not." Was St. John then permitted to be close to the throne of God, in the very circle of the elders, so that one of the elders could speak to him, as to one standing close to him? We are to remember that in such a vision of God as this, the Apostle is raised above the limitations or conditions of space and time. All that appeared before him was vast and illimitable, and yet he was close to all.

[CHAP. V.] THE ROOT OF DAVID. 65

ᵈ the Lion of the tribe of Juda, ᵉ the Root of David, hath prevailed to open the book, ᶠ and to loose the seven seals thereof.

6 And I beheld, and, lo, in the midst of the throne and of the four beasts, and in the midst of the elders, stood ᵍ a Lamb as it had been slain,

ᵈ Gen. xlix. 9, 10. Heb. vii. 14.
ᵉ Isa. xi. 1, 10. Rom. xv. 12. ch. xxii. 16.
ᶠ ver. 1. ch. vi. 1.
ᵍ Isa. liii. 7. John i. 29, 36. 1 Pet. i. 19. ch. xiii. 8. ver. 9, 12.

---

5. "To loose" omitted by A., B., P., fifty Cursives, Vulg. (Amiat.), &c.; retained only by ℵ.
6. "Stood a Lamb as it had been slain." Lit., "a Lamb standing as slain."

"The Lion of the tribe of Juda, the Root of David." The figure of the lion is taken from Jacob's prophecy respecting Judah in Gen. xlix. 9: "Judah is a lion's whelp: from the prey, my son, thou art gone up: he stooped down, he couched as a lion, and as an old lion who shall rouse him up?" The lion represents the force, the activity, the courage of the Messiah, whilst the root ("Root of David") signifies the source of life—the all-sustaining grace—the richness of the Second Adam. "The name Root of David proclaims that Christ is more than a Branch or Rod from out of the stem of Jesse (Isaiah xi. 1); it declares that He is the origin of David; He is the Rod or Branch because He is man; He is the Root because He is God" (Wordsworth).

"Hath prevailed to open the book, and to loose the seven seals thereof." How did He prevail? What was His weapon? He prevailed by weakness. His weapon was submission to death, and so the Evangelist goes on:

6. "And I beheld, and, lo, in the midst of the throne and of the four beasts, and in the midst of the elders, stood a Lamb as it had been slain" (or, a Lamb standing as though it had been slain). "Standing," as being alive, and "as it had been slain," with all the marks of death. Standing as the great High Priest, as it had been slain, as the all-sufficient Victim; standing as ready to open the books, and as slain, to sanctify and bless with His all-prevailing Atonement; standing as life-giving, slain as reconciling. The most wonderful association—one might almost say identification—of life and death conceivable. There seems to me that there is no such figure embodying the two great opposites in all Scripture.

The "Lamb" (diminutive, little Lamb) is the Lord Jesus—"as it

having seven horns and ʰ seven eyes, which are ⁱ the seven Spirits of God sent forth into all the earth.

ʰ Zech. iii. 9. & iv. 10.
ⁱ ch. iv. 5.

had been slain" refers to the wounds in His adorable Body, from which the blood flowed which redeemed the world, purchased the Church, and washes from sin each soul who applies for its cleansing virtue.

During the remainder of this book the usual name given to the Redeemer is the Lamb.

Now may it be permitted to us to ask why the Redeemer is presented to us under the figure of a Lamb? He appeared, after His Resurrection, to His disciples as a man. They recognized His form and features. They were sure that He was not a spirit because of the wounds in His hands and feet and side. Why should not St. John have seen Him and described Him as when he saw Him on the day of His Resurrection? It must be because He mediates through His past Death. His Sacrifice, though once for all endured, is eternal in its Divine Efficacy. We have to look upon Him as our Passover; His Sacrifice is not a thing of the past. It was endured but once, and cannot be repeated; but it abideth ever, as His Priesthood abideth ever. In heaven He presents it because He presents Himself a Lamb standing as slain, and this corresponds to His memorial on earth. Both in heaven and in earth His Sacrificial memorial is not a whole Body, but a broken Body, a wounded Body.

"Having seven horns and seven eyes." The horn of a living creature denotes its strength just as the eye signifies its observation and consequent knowledge. That the Lamb has seven horns implies the perfection of His power—in fact, that He is Almighty; and the seven eyes the perfection of His knowledge, which He has through the operation of the Divine Spirit Who is first in Him, and these proceed from Him conveying to Him the truth of all that exists and takes place.

The question now presents itself—did St. John see the Lord under this figure under which he describes Him here, or did he see the Lord as he saw Him on the first Easter Day, as the Risen Jesus with wounds in His hands and His side? Unquestionably the former: because it was the will of God that His Church throughout all ages should look upon His Son not as the Eternal Word

7 And he came and took the book out of the right hand ᵏ of him that sat upon the throne.   ᵏ ch. iv. 2.

8 And when he had taken the book, ˡ the four beasts and four *and* twenty elders fell down before the Lamb, having every one of them ᵐ harps, and golden vials full of ‖ odours, ⁿ which are the prayers of saints.

    ˡ ch. iv. 8, 10.
    ᵐ ch. xiv. 2. & xv. 2.
    ‖ Or, *incense*
    ⁿ Ps. cxli. 2. ch. viii. 3, 4.

---

only, nor as the Mediator simply, but as the Mediator through His Past Death, the power of which Death is never separated from Him, and abides with Him as if it were a part of His Essence.

If it be objected that it is impossible thus to represent the Lord, we answer that it may be impossible to us thus to represent the Lord in picture or in marble, but that does not undo the fact that St. John, for God's purposes, saw the Lord under this appearance, and though we may not be able to represent the Lord thus, or even to imagine Him like this Lamb, yet being in the midst of the throne it must have been an image of surpassing glory and beauty, just as the four living ones are of inconceivable grandeur, and yet unimaginable by us who are not in the Spirit. The figure combines innocence, patience, sacrifice, life in death, death in life, omnipotence and omniscence all combining in One Person to unfold the counsels of God.

7. "And he came and took the book out of the right hand," &c.

8. "And when he had taken the book, the four living ones, and four and twenty elders." He took the book, it was not given to Him by the hands of Him that sat on the throne. He took it out of the open hand as being worthy to take it, as if it were His own.

As soon as He had done this He received the worship of the highest existences in heaven; they fell down before Him as they would before God; they took their harps wherewith to accompany their hymn of praise, and they took golden censers full of incense; an act of worship offered to God in the most holy place.

They could not go beyond these things in worship, for they prostrate themselves, they sing His praise to Himself with the music of harps, and they burn incense to Him.

"Which are the prayers of saints." Does this mean that the

o Ps. xl. 3.
ch. xiv. 3.
p ch. iv. 11.
q ver. 6.
r Acts xx. 28.
Rom. iii. 24.
1 Cor. vi. 20.
& vii. 23. Eph.
i. 7. Col. i. 14.
Heb. ix. 12.
1 Pet. i. 18, 19.
2 Pet. ii. 1.
1 John i. 7.
ch. xiv. 4.
s Dan. iv. 1.
& vi. 25. ch.
vii. 9. & xi. 9.
& xiv. 6.

9 And ºthey sung a new song, saying, ᴾThou art worthy to take the book, and to open the seals thereof: ᑫfor thou wast slain, and ʳhast redeemed us to God by thy blood ˢout of every kindred, and tongue, and people, and nation;

---

9. "Redeemed us to God." "Us" omitted by A., but retained by ℵ, B., P., and most Cursives.

incense actually is, or that it signifies, the prayers of saints? We cannot say absolutely. The prostration, the hymnody, the instruments of music must be taken literally, and it would seem that the incense must be also. How could the actual prayers of saints be burnt as incense? but the heavenly incense might be taken to represent the prayers of saints in two particulars—their sweetness and their acceptableness to God.

We must remember that there is a revelation of heavenly things throughout this book, but how far this revelation of such things as the living creatures, the elders, the songs, the incense is, so to speak, objective or material we cannot say. I think we must accept it, if possible, in the sense in which St. John discloses it, for in most of these things no two human expositors are agreed as to what their inner or spiritual significance is.

9. "And they sung a new song, saying, Thou art worthy, ... for thou wast slain, and hast redeemed (us) to God." "A new song," for whereas the old song of iv. 11 only contemplates the glories of creation, this is a song of praise to the Lamb for the Redemption wrought by His Sufferings and Death.

There is a remarkable difference of reading in this and the next verse, for whereas the Authorized Version reads, "And hast redeemed us unto God by thy blood," the Revised reads, "Thou hast redeemed (men) unto God by thy blood out of every kindred," &c., and in the next verse, instead of "hast made us .... kings and priests," it is read "and hast made them unto God .... and they shall reign." ℵ and B., however, support "redeemed us" in verse 9. The difficulty is that if the four living ones are angelic, or super-angelic natures, they should join in the song of those redeemed by the Blood of Christ; but we are to remember the words of the Apostle where he says that God "has by Christ reconciled all things to

CHAP. V.] WORTHY IS THE LAMB. 69

10 'And hast made us unto our God kings and priests: and we shall reign on the earth.

11 And I beheld, and I heard the voice of many angels ᵘround about the throne and the beasts and the elders: and the number of them was ˣ ten thousand times ten thousand, and thousands of thousands;

12 Saying with a loud voice, ʸ Worthy is the Lamb that was slain to receive power, and riches, and wisdom, and strength, and honour, and glory, and blessing.

ᵗ Ex. xix. 6.
1 Pet. ii. 5, 9.
ch. i. 6. & xx. 6. & xxii. 5.
ᵘ ch. iv. 4, 6.
ˣ Ps. lxviii. 17. Dan. vii. 10. Heb. xii. 22.
ʸ ch. iv. 11.

---

10. "Us." The preponderance of authority by far is for reading 'them.' So ℵ, A., B., most Cursives, Vulg. (Amiat.).
"Kings and priests." "A kingdom and priests." So ℵ, A., Vulg., Copt.

himself, whether things on earth, or things in heaven" (Coloss. i. 20, also Ephes. i. 10). So that in some way not fully revealed all creation participates in the Atonement.

10. "And hast made us [them] unto our God kings and priests." Rather, "a kingdom and priests." The elders seem to have exercised the office of priests, for they were clothed in the white sacerdotal garment, but how we are not told. It must be by the priestly act of intercession, for such sacrifices as those of the law cannot be thought of, and the Eucharist seems only to be till the Lord comes (1 Cor. xi. 26).

"And we shall reign [or they shall reign] upon the earth." This seems to refer to the millennial reign. It is said by some that it should rather be translated "over the earth"—their place of reigning being not on earth, but in heaven. Pious attempts are made to get rid of this. It is said, for instance, that they shall reign over themselves which, it is added, is the best of all rules—but can the writer of this believe that such is the meaning of these words of the song?

11. "And I beheld, and I heard the voice of many angels round about the throne and [round about] the four living ones and the elders."

12. "Saying with a loud voice, Worthy is the Lamb that was slain." Here is the whole angelic host joining in the worship of

13 And ᵃ every creature which is in heaven, and on the earth, and under the earth, and such as are in the sea, and all that are in them, heard I saying, ᵃ Blessing, and honour, and glory, and power, *be* unto him ᵇ that sitteth upon the throne, and unto the Lamb for ever and ever.

14 ᶜ And the four beasts said, Amen. And the four *and* twenty elders fell down and worshipped him ᵈ that liveth for ever and ever.

ᵃ Phil. ii. 10. ver. 3.
ᵃ 1 Chr. xxix. 11. Rom. ix. 5. & xvi. 27. 1 Tim. vi. 16. 1 Pet. iv. 11. & v. 11. ch. i. 6.
ᵇ ch. vi. 16. & vii. 10.
ᶜ ch. xix. 4.
ᵈ ch. iv. 9, 10.

---

14. "Him that liveth for ever and ever" omitted by ℵ, A., B., C., P., most Cursives, most Versions. No authority for retaining these words.

the Lamb, but, it is to be remarked, not on the ground of His essential Godhead, but on the ground that in the human nature which He had assumed He had suffered an All-atoning Death. So that He is worshipped as man, as the Sinless Sufferer as well as the Son of God. God and man is one Christ Who thus receives the worship of angels.

13. "And every creature which is in heaven, and on the earth," &c. This is the song of all creation—in heaven, *i.e.*, the angels; on the earth, *i.e.*, men; under the earth, *i.e.*, in Hades, or the unseen place; in the sea, *i.e.*, whose bodies are in the deep, or it may be in ships, for it is *on* the sea.

"Blessing, and honour, and glory, and power, to him that sitteth upon the throne." That is, God the Father, and to the Lamb, Who here receives the same united praise which all creation renders, betokening His essential equality in Nature with the Father.

14. "And the four living creatures said, So be it." Some MSS. have the article—the Amen—as if it were a recognized part of the ritual of both heaven and earth.

"And the four and twenty elders fell down and worshipped." The concluding words, "him that liveth for ever and ever," have no Greek authority. The more sublime ending is "fell down and worshipped," leaving it to be inferred that they prostrated themselves before God and the Lamb.

CHAP. VI.

We now enter upon that part of the Revelation which has been called the historical (vi.-xx.). It is supposed by the preterists (see Introduction) to describe the events immediately following upon the Coming of Christ, or the imprisonment of St. John in Patmos. By those who hold to the continuous interpretation all this part is supposed to be a series of visions describing the continuous fortunes of the Church from the New Testament times to the Second Coming, and by the futurists it is held to be events which are yet future, and which will immediately precede the Second Advent. Before entering upon the exposition of this part—if that may be called an exposition of a book, or large portion of a book, of which I verily believe that God has not given to any man the key to its interpretation—I desire to put on record the enunciation of a great principle, which is this: that from the departure of our Lord at the moment of His Ascension to the moment of His Second Advent, it is not lawful for us to assume that any definite lapse of time intervenes. At the moment after our Lord's disappearance at His Ascension, two angels in white apparel appeared to the Apostles, who were straining their eyes heavenward, with this message from God: " Ye men of Galilee, why stand ye gazing up into heaven, this same Jesus which is taken up from you into heaven, shall so come in like manner as ye have seen him go into heaven." If we did not know the history of the Apostolic Church we should, I think, gather from this that the return of the Lord was to be expected in the life-time of the Apostles. And this the Lord Himself assumes when He bids the Apostles watch and wait for His second appearance: thus in Mark xiii. 33: "Take ye heed, watch and pray: for ye know not when the time is. For the Son of man is as a man taking a far journey, who left his house and gave authority to his servants, and to every man his work, and commanded the porter to watch. Watch ye therefore: for ye know not when the master of the house cometh, at even or at midnight, or at the cock crowing, or in the morning: lest coming suddenly he find you sleeping." Now reading this it is impossible to suppose that more than 1,800 years were to be counted upon by the Church as intervening between the disappearance of the Lord and His reappearance. We know that such time has intervened, but it was not to be counted upon. On the contrary, any day between the Ascension and the Second Coming might, as far as man could know, be the last. All through this long series of ages the Judge was standing at the door as He is now, and it is a part of our probation to be watching and waiting for His appearance.

But are we not compelled by the succession of visions in the Revelation to suppose that a long time must intervene? No, we are not; for it is a most noticeable fact that in these apparently successive visions there are no less than seven visions of the end, or of the consummation, and they are these:

1. At the end of the vision of the opening of the seals, at the opening of the sixth seal there is a catastrophe which from the description of it, compared with the description of the Last Day by the Lord Himself, can only be that of the end. The sun becomes "black as sackcloth of hair, and the moon as blood" (Matt. xxiv.), the stars of heaven fall, and all the wicked of every degree call on the mountains to fall on them, and the rocks to cover them (Rev. vi.).

2. At the end of the next chapter there is a vision of the glories and beatification of the elect, as occurring then, which is precisely parallel to the visions of the end in the last chapter, see particularly xxi. 4.

3. At the sounding of the seventh trumpet in chap. xi. we read: "Thou hast taken to thee thy great power, and hast reigned .... and the time of the dead, that they should be judged," &c. (xi. 18).

4. At the end of chap. xiv. there is a vision of the last judgment under the image of the Son of man seated on a white cloud reaping the earth, and immediately succeeding it a vision of the reaping of the vine of the earth.

5. In xvi. 17 there is another vision of the end at the pouring out of the seventh vial, where a great voice out of the temple of God says, "It is done" ($\gamma\acute{\epsilon}\gamma o\nu\epsilon$), and every island fled away, and the mountains were not found.

6. In xix. 11 the Son of man appears again on the white horse and ushers in what, from the judgments on the beast, and the false

prophet, and on all the people of the world who fought against God, we cannot but account to be a vision of the end.

7. And the final vision, after the millennial period as it is called, when the great white throne appears, and the dead were judged out of those things which were written in the books.

So that these visions from chap. vi. to chap. xix. cannot form one continuous history, for the Lord cannot come seven times to such final judgments as are here described.

CHAP. VI.

AND ^aI saw when the Lamb opened one of the seals, and I heard, as it were the noise of thunder, ^bone of the four beasts saying, Come and see.

2 And I saw, and behold ^ca white horse: ^dand

^a ch. v. 5, 6, 7.
^b ch. iv. 7.
^c Zech. vi. 3. ch. xix. 11.
^d Ps. xlv. 4, 5. LXX.

---

1. "One of the seals." ℵ, A., B., C., and most Cursives, Vulg., Syr. Æth., read, "one of the seven seals."

"Come and see." "And see" omitted by A., C., P., Vulg. (Amiat.), Arm., &c.; retained by ℵ, B., and many Cursives.

1. "And I saw when the Lamb opened one of the seals, and I heard, as it were .... Come." It is not said which of the four living ones thus cried, so that it is beyond measure futile to guess that it must have been the one with the face of the lion or of the man.

The preponderance of authorities is in favour of reading simply "Come," and omitting "see." In this case the living creature must be supposed to address, not the Evangelist, but the horse-rider, bidding him come, for all is ready for His work.

2. "And I saw, and behold a white horse: and he that sat on him had a bow." It is difficult to believe how any commentator, unless he has some continuous system to maintain, can fail to interpret this as the Son of God riding forth in the power of His Gospel. The colour of the horse, which in each of these visions of the horse-riders is especially noticed, is the same as that on which the Word

he that sat on him had a bow; ᵉand a crown was given unto him: and he went forth conquering, and to conquer.

3 And when he had opened the second seal, ᶠI heard the second beast say, Come and see.

4 ᵍAnd there went out another horse *that was*

ᵉ Zech. vi. 11.
ch. xiv. 14.

ᶠ ch. iv. 7.

ᵍ Zech. vi. 2.

---

3. "Come and see." "And see" doubtful, as before.

of God—the King of Kings and Lord of Lords—appears in chap. xix. It is always throughout this book considered as the emblem of purity and holiness. The bow is the instrument of the warfare of the Messiah, as in Ps. xlv.: "In thy majesty ride prosperously because of truth and meekness and righteousness; and thy right hand shall teach thee terrible things. Thine arrows are sharp in the heart of the king's enemies; whereby the people fall under thee." This exactly describes the conquests of Christ: the arrows of His Word reach first one and then another; it is not so much a warfare of one mighty host against another, but as one in which a single warrior picks out first one and then another from amongst his enemies, and by his sharp wound, piercing each one's heart, subdues him to Himself.

"A crown was given to him." This is given to Him in token that He shall rule over those whom He has subdued. So far from their being destroyed, a new life is given to them, even an eternal one.

"And he went forth conquering and to conquer." There will be no cessation of His conquering progress till He has put all enemies under His feet. He is going forth conquering, and to conquer now not in the same parts as those in which He first won His conquests, but in other regions where He displays His subduing powers quite as conspicuously. Now if this be so, seeing that He has begun His career of victory, must there not be a reign of universal blessedness. If the Prince of Peace has set forth on His career of spiritual conquest what place can there be in future for war and its attendant miseries? We shall see.

3. "And when he had opened the second seal .... Come." The words "and see" are doubtful as in verse 1.

4. "And there went out another horse that was red: and power was given to him that sat," &c. We are not to suppose for a

red: and *power* was given to him that sat thereon to take peace from the earth, and that they should kill one another: and there was given unto him a great sword.

---

moment that the rider of the first horse had finished His career of conquest ere the second horse rider had begun to ride. On the contrary, the interpretation which I shall present is that all the four ride simultaneously.

Now this vision of the second—the blood-red horse—corrects the idea which we might have entertained from the fact that the Prince of Peace had begun His reign. We should have supposed that the progress and triumphs of the Gospel would at least have assured to the earth a deliverance from the miseries of war, but it is not so. Since the time of the first preaching of the Gospel to the present moment there has not been twenty years of continued peace amongst the nations and people with which, as we suppose, the various visions in this book have to do. And this history of war is not occupied with the wars of Christians against heathen, but with the wars of professing Christians against one another. Before the so-called Reformation, when all the Christians of Europe professed to belong to one Church, there was a constant state of warfare amongst them. Since then the state of war has been quite as continuous—not Protestants with Papists only, but Protestants among themselves. Thus in this country on the murder of Charles I. an ultra-Protestant republic was established, and the very first thing it did was to go to war with the only Protestant republic then existing—the Dutch. In our own time also we have seen the most powerful republic in the world, a republic more Protestant or Evangelical than any other, engaged in a long and sanguinary civil war. So that we have before us this most remarkable fact, that for 1,800 years the Gospel of Christ and the Demon of War have ridden side by side.

For the rider on the red horse does not himself war or fight. He is apparently engaged in stirring up strife in which he personally takes no part. He is no human tyrant or general, but, as it were, the embodiment of the Spirit of War, who has power given to him to take peace from the earth, and that they should kill one another.

5 And when he had opened the third seal, ^h I heard the third beast say, Come and see. And I beheld, and lo ⁱ a black horse; and he that sat on him had a pair of balances in his hand.

^h ch. iv. 7.
ⁱ Zech. vi. 2.

6 And I heard a voice in the midst of the four

---

5. "And when he had opened the third seal, I heard the third living one say, Come. And I beheld, and lo a black horse; and he that sat on him had a pair of balances in his hand." The black horse rider is universally taken as betokening scarcity. The balance in his hand is for the purpose of weighing corn.

Now corn, *i.e.*, wheat and barley, would even in times of only moderate plenty be measured by the bushel, but in times of very great scarcity, verging on famine, it would be measured by weight as if it were a drug; thus in Ezekiel iv. 16: "Son of man, behold, I will break the staff of bread in Jerusalem: and they shall eat bread by weight and with care," &c.; and so in the next verse,

6. "And I heard a voice in the midst of the four living ones saying, A measure of wheat for a penny, and three measures of barley for a penny." The measure of wheat mentioned here is that which would just suffice for the daily sustenance of a common labourer; and the penny (the denarius), ranging between 9*d.* and 11*d.*, would be his day's wages, so that the whole of his day's wages would be taken up in procuring one day's food. This would be severe scarcity, almost reaching famine, but if the lower price of the *chœnix* of barley be taken into account matters would be much altered for the better, for he would get three times the amount of food though of a coarser quality. The barley bread would be that which vast numbers of the poor fed upon (witness the miracle of the five barley loaves and two fishes), so that this horse-rider would by no means betoken famine, but rather poverty, and, as far as I can judge, not grinding unendurable poverty either.

The vision has been explained in two ways, naturally and spiritually, and either yields a tolerably good signification.

Both explanations are consonant with what we gather from the rest of the seals, which is, that much in the time of the Messiah's triumphal progress is not such as we should have expected.

beasts say, ‖ A measure of wheat for a penny, ‖ *The word chœnix signifieth a measure containing one wine quart, and the twelfth part of a quart.*

For instance, we should have expected that the times of the Gospel would have been times of almost universal prosperity. It was prophesied that in the future thus it should so be. Thus Ezek. xxxvi. 30: "And I will multiply the fruit of the tree and the increase of the field, that ye shall receive no more reproach of famine among the heathen." Thus Hosea ii. 22: "And the earth shall hear the corn, and the wine, and the oil," &c. And Joel ii. 19: "Behold, I will send you corn, and wine, and oil, and ye shall be satisfied therewith."

And we should the rather have expected this because the preaching of the Gospel does much to discourage many vices which occasion distress and ruin in this world, such as intemperance, drunkenness, wastefulness (John vi. 12), gambling, immorality, and such things. But it has not been so. From the first preaching of the Gospel there has been just the same hard struggle for sustenance as there was before. Of course there have been countries in which the poor have not suffered from comparative scarcity, as in newly-planted colonies, but the tendency of things has been always to bring about, sooner or later, the universal struggle for a bare subsistence.

But the riding of this horse-rider has been interpreted spiritually to mean this, that in the day of Christ's power there has not been, nor will be, that plentiful supply of the wholesome and nourishing Word of God which we should have expected. The more thoroughly we examine the history of religion, I do not mean of the Church, but of individual religion, the more we shall discover the truth of this.

For, for wellnigh 1,500 years the Word of God — meaning the Book — has been altogether out of the reach of the vast majority of Christians. Till the invention of printing each copy of the Word of God had to be written fully and fairly out. And look also at the comparative fewness of those who if by chance they possessed a copy could read it.

But we must not for a moment limit this scarcity of the wholesome nourishing Word to the scarcity of Bibles. The nourishment of the vast body of the Church is through teaching and preaching, and there may be a vast circulation of Bibles, and yet these Bibles

and three measures of barley for a penny; and ᵏ *see* thou hurt not the oil and the wine.

ᵏ ch. ix. 4.

---

remain unread and their contents undigested. Now it is the first duty of the ministers of the Church "rightly to divide" the Word of Truth. If the bread of life is what God intends it to be it is very multiform. There is first of all the life and example of the Lord Himself; His teaching, His parables, His miracles, each one an acted parable. There is the teaching respecting the mystical body of which the Epistles of the blessed Paul are so full—there is the teaching of grace—and the responsibility laid upon us for using that grace and growing in it. There is the doctrinal teaching respecting the Incarnation and the Atoning Death, and the teaching of Sacramental truth so intimately connected with it. There is the teaching of good works, what they are and the Spirit which they spring from. Now all these must have their places if the bread of life is to be the good wheaten flour, and not the barley chaff, husky and unnourishing. So that very seldom indeed has the pure Word been doled out compared to the unnourishing, unwholesome teaching. Preaching may be so-called Catholic and yet devoid of almost all the leading features of Catholic truth. Preaching may be so-called Evangelical and yet devoid of some of the leading good tidings which God designs for the edification and consolation of believers.

"And see thou hurt not the oil and the wine." On either principle of interpretation, the natural or the spiritual, this is a very difficult clause.

If interpreted naturally it would seem to signify that the same supernatural power which condemned mankind to "eat their bread by weight," still kept the wine and the oil from being injured, so that all through the dark years of scarcity the vineyards and the oliveyards yielded their wonted crops.

We are to remember that oil and wine are necessaries, or at least bordering thereon; thus God gives "wine that maketh glad the heart of man, and oil to make him a cheerful countenance, and bread to strengthen man's heart," and the widow who was commissioned to sustain Elijah had a handful of meal in a barrel, and a little oil in a cruse wherewith to bake the bread.

The voice from amidst the four living ones appears to have

CHAP. VI.] A PALE HORSE. 79

7 And when he had opened the fourth seal, ¹I heard the voice of the fourth beast say, Come and see.   ᶦ ch. iv. 7.

8 ᵐ And I looked, and behold a pale horse: ᵐ Zech. vi. 3. and his name that sat on him was Death, and

---

spoken in mercy when it said, "A chœnix of wheat for a penny, and three chœnices of barley for a penny." It was a restraining voice, restraining the evil genius of hunger and scarcity within bounds, and so God did not add to the miseries which afflicted the earth by diminishing that which contributes to the gladness and cheerfulness of man.

If, however, this place is to be taken spiritually, it may point to a very remarkable fact in the history of spiritual things, which is this, that the consolations of religion have been [in the darkest times preserved to the (true) people of God. Thus in what we call the dark ages, that which is the most comforting doctrine to the (true) people of God, that God has chosen them to be His servants, and will uphold them in the ways of true religion, was proclaimed by men like Thomas Aquinas, Anselm, Peter Lombard, Bradwardine, St. Bernard, and many others, and no doubt was extensively preached to those who could not read by the friars, who in their early days, before they become corrupted, were the evangelical preachers of those times. Then some of our sweetest hymns came from those ages, or were used all through them, and such a work of devotion as the "Imitatio Christi" comes from a time when the barley-meal, rather than the nourishing wheaten bread, was the food of the multitude.

This may sound fanciful, but there must be some adequate interpretation of "See thou hurt not the oil and the wine," and if any one can suggest one more likely, by all means let him do so.

7. "And when he had opened the fourth seal, I heard the voice of the fourth living one saying, Come (and see)."

8. "And I looked, and behold a pale horse : and his name that sat upon him was Death, and Hell [Hades] followed with him. And power was given unto them over the fourth part of the earth, to kill with sword, and with hunger . . . death . . . . beasts of the earth." The great difficulty to me in the interpretation of this seal is this, that under the second and third seals men are slain with the sword and (as is supposed) by famine, and here the two

Hell followed with him. And power was given ‖ unto them over the fourth part of the earth, ⁿ to kill with sword, and with hunger, and with death, ᵖ and with the beasts of the earth.

‖ Or, *to him.*
ⁿ Ezek. xiv. 21.
ᵖ Lev. xxvi. 22.

---

first evils are repeated, and the fourth horse-rider slays with the sword, and with hunger, and added to these with death, in all probability meaning pestilence, and with the beasts of the field. The latter seems to be the effect of the want of population occasioned by the former three, the land becomes uncultivated, and is covered with jungle or brushwood, the haunt of wild beasts. Now in the destruction or desolation occasioned by the united effects of these four plagues, it appears to me, is the interpretation of the fourth horse rider. It cannot be through accident that the means by which the fourth horse rider destroys men are the same exactly as the four sore judgments which God threatens by the mouth of Ezekiel (xiv. 2), which teach us that the holiness of great saints, such as Noah, Daniel, and Job, will not exempt the sinners in the Church from the severest judgments which God can inflict. It will be true of the greatest saints of apostate Christian times that such holy men shall deliver neither son nor daughter, they shall only deliver their own souls in their righteousness. So that the famines and plagues and pestilences and desolating wars of a fallen Christendom are not due to mere natural causes, but to the anger of Almighty God upon those who break the new and the better covenant.

And if the threatening of Almighty God in bringing upon Christendom these desolating plagues is to be received and accepted by His faithful ones, so is the consolation in the very words of the old prophet: "Yet behold therein, in these darkest times of terror and desolation, shall be left a remnant that shall be brought forth, both sons and daughters: behold they shall come forth unto you, and ye shall see their ways and their doings, and ye shall be comforted concerning the evil that I have brought upon Jerusalem, even concerning all that I have brought upon it. And they shall comfort you when ye see their ways and their doings, and ye shall know that I have not done without cause all that I have done in it, saith the Lord God."

Death shall mow down his victims as if he had a commission to destroy mankind, and Hades shall follow him as his hearse, or

9 And when he had opened the fifth seal, I saw under ^q^ the altar ^r^ the souls of them that were slain ^s^ for the word of God, and for ^t^ the testimony which they held:

q ch. viii. 3. & ix. 13. & xiv. 18.
r ch. xx. 4.
s ch. i. 9.
t 2 Tim. i. 8. ch. xii. 17. & xix. 10.

---

death cart, wherein to receive the slain, but the gates of hell shall not prevail against the Church; on the contrary, "when thy judgments are in the earth, the inhabitants of the world will learn righteousness" (Isaiah xxvi. 9).

9. "And when he had opened the fifth seal, I saw under the altar the souls of them that were slain for the word of God, and for the testimony," &c. What is this altar, and what is the meaning of the souls of the martyrs being under it? It has been said that the altar is the altar of burnt-offering, and that by the souls under it we must understand the "blood which is the life" of these martyrs which is poured out at the bottom of this heavenly altar, just as in the Jewish tabernacle the blood of the creatures which were slain was poured out at the foot of the earthly altar. It is just possible that there may be some allusion to the blood of Abel, the first martyr, crying for vengeance, but we must endeavour to see whether there cannot be an interpretation consonant with that of the first four seals, which is this: the first seal betokened the triumphant progress of the Gospel. From this we should have anticipated a millennium of peace and plenty, both temporal and spiritual, but it has not been so. The progress of the Gospel has been accompanied with a state of almost continuous war, and a scarcity of the means of subsistence, and even at times the four sore judgments of the prophet seem to be let loose upon the earth, and now under this seal the just vengeance of God upon those who have persecuted His Church, and poured out like water the blood of His saints, is suspended till the time of the end.

The key to the interpretation of this seal seems to be the Lord's words in Luke xviii. 7, 8: "Shall not God avenge his own elect, which cry day and night unto him, though he bear long with them? I tell you that he will avenge them speedily." We should have thought that the blood of the martyrs would have been avenged on the ungodly at once, seeing that the rider on the white horse has gone forth conquering and to conquer; but it is not so. The triumphant progress of the Gospel seems to be the occasion of

10 And they cried with a loud voice, saying, ᵘ How long, O Lord, ˣ holy and true, ʸ dost thou not judge and avenge our blood on them that dwell on the earth?

ᵘ See Zech. i. 12.
ˣ ch. iii. 7.
ʸ ch xi. 18. & xix. 2.

---

fresh martyrdoms, for each martyr in his sufferings and death is a most acceptable offering to God.

The triumph of the Gospel then has not done away with martyrdom. On the contrary, in every age of the Church there have been martyrs as true to Christ, and as heroic in their endurance for His Name, as in the first ages. In our own day—and late in our own day, even as it were as yesterday—there have been men like Bishop Pattison and Bishop Hannington, and Romanist martyrs in Cochin-China, and Congregationalist martyrs in Madagascar, and many who have lived martyrs' lives, as well as those who attained to a martyr's death, as Father Damien amongst the lepers; so that every age from the first to the nineteenth has contributed some martyrs to the noble army.

10. "And they cried with a loud voice, saying, How long, O Lord, holy and true, dost thou not judge and avenge our blood," &c. The Prince of martyrs when He was nailed to the Cross prayed for His enemies. His protomartyr prayed with his last breath: "Lord, lay not this sin to their charge." How is it that the souls of the martyrs call for vengeance? We are to remember that there are two ways of looking at a martyrdom. It is the greatest triumph of Divine grace, and yet it is the greatest of crimes in those who inflict this death. If any crime deserves to be punished this does, for they who put the martyrs to a cruel death, inflicted this death because of their goodness. The goodness and holiness of their lives was never, I think, taken into any account by way of mitigation. Their persecutors hated goodness itself, so far as it could be embodied amongst men, as the Lord said: "Now have they both seen and hated both me and my Father."

Then there is another way of looking at this. They who are in the unseen world throw themselves into the mind of God, so that they say their Amen to every intimation of His will. When His will is for an extension of mercy they pray accordingly, but when His time for vengeance has come they acquiesce. Venerable Bede has an admirable comment on this place. "The great cry of the

11 And *white robes were given unto every one of them; and it was said unto them, ªthat they should rest yet for a little season, until their fellowservants also and their brethren, that should be killed as they *were*, should be fulfilled.

12 And I beheld when he had opened the sixth

* ch. iii. 4, 5. & vii. 9, 14.
ª Heb. xi. 40. ch. xiv. 13.

---

souls is their great desire for those things which they know that the Lord wills to do. For it is not right to suppose that they wish for anything against the good pleasure of God when their desires are dependent upon His will. They ask not 'How long?' in hatred of their enemies, for whom they made supplication in this life, but in a love of justice in which, as they who are placed near to the Judge Himself, they agree with Him; they pray for the coming of the day of judgment when the reign of sin will be destroyed, and the resurrection of their lifeless bodies will ensue. For we also in the present time, when we are commanded to pray for our enemies say, nevertheless, when we pray to the Lord, 'Thy kingdom come.'"

11. "And white robes were given unto every one of them; and it was said unto them." What signify these white robes? Some commentators who say that these martyrs lived and suffered only in the Old Dispensation, say that this signifies a fuller and more perfect justification than that which was accorded to sinners under the Old Law, but we have no warrant for restricting the sufferings of these souls to Jewish times. The white robes are probably robes of priesthood, and betokened that they would do far more than call down vengeance on their enemies, but would intercede for the Church, and the progress of the cause of God.

"Rest yet for a little season." This seems to me to set forth the significance of the opening of this seal. Some of these martyred brethren are not called upon to suffer till near the time of the consummation, and till these be perfected they are to rest and wait. It may be a long time, and yet it is but a little season compared with the eternity of bliss in store for them.

12. "And I beheld when he had opened the sixth seal, and, lo, there was a great earthquake." There seems to be but one interpretation possible of the opening of this seal, which is that it is a

seal, ^b and, lo, there was a great earthquake; and ^c the sun became black as sackcloth of hair, and the moon became as blood;

^b ch. xvi. 18.
^c Joel ii. 10, 31. & iii. 15. Matt. xxiv. 29. Acts ii. 20.

---

prophecy of the Second Coming of Christ to judgment. Thus Christ Himself describes it: "Immediately after the tribulation of those days shall the sun be darkened, and the moon shall not give her light, and the stars shall fall from heaven . . . And then shall appear the sign of the Son of man in heaven: and then shall all the tribes of the earth mourn" (Matt. xxiv. 30).

It has been said by interpreters of opposite views, some of whom (the preterists) desire to make out that all the Apocalypse was fulfilled 1,800 years ago; and others, as Mr. Elliot, that it is now being fulfilled in the present course of things—that we need not understand these signs as precursors of the Second Advent. Thus one says, "There is not one of these metaphors which is not found in the Old Testament prophets, and in them they refer in every instance to the destruction of cities, and the establishment of new covenants, or to other earthly revolutions;" and another says that we cannot understand this of the Second Advent because many things which will certainly occur then are not mentioned here. But, in answer to the latter, we can only say that there are seven references to the Advent and final consummation in this book, in not one of which do we find collected together all the great and terrible things which will accompany it, and with respect to the former, the Second Advent will gather up into itself a number of partial fulfilments. It will be the day of days. Other days may have been days of judgment, of wrath, of vengeance on God's enemies, of triumphs to those on His side, but all these were but small, partial, and insignificant, compared to the terrors of the great day.

This expression, " calling on the mountains to fall upon them, and the rocks to cover them," was, no doubt, proverbial, and really meant that the destruction which accompanies the wrath of the Lamb will be so great and terrible, that every other form of destruction will be welcomed by the wicked in comparison of it. They would rather be crushed to death than that He should look them in the face.

" There was a great earthquake." See xvi. 19, which identifies the latter as revealing the time of the end, or its very near approach.

CHAP. VI.] THE STARS OF HEAVEN FELL.   85

13 ᵈ And the stars of heaven fell unto the earth, even as a fig tree casteth her ‖ untimely figs, when she is shaken of a mighty wind.

14 ᵉ And the heaven departed as a scroll when it is rolled together; and ᶠ every mountain and island were moved out of their places.

15 And the kings of the earth, and the great men, and the rich men, and the chief captains, and the mighty men, and every bondman, and every free man, ᵍ hid themselves in the dens and in the rocks of the mountains;

ᵈ ch. viii. 10. & ix. 1.
‖ Or, *green figs.*
ᵉ Ps. cii. 26. Isa. xxxiv. 4. Heb. i. 12, 13.
ᶠ Jer. iii. 23. & iv. 24. ch. xvi. 20.
ᵍ Isa. ii. 19.

"And the moon." According to the best MSS. "the whole moon became as blood," which she would do if she were partially deprived of the light of the sun.

13. "And the stars of heaven fell unto the earth." Which they would appear to do if the earth were suddenly stopped in her orbit round the sun.

14. "And the heaven departed as a scroll when it is rolled together." This seems (looked at from a human point of view) to be a reproduction of Isaiah xxxiv. 4.

"And every mountain and island were moved out of their places." Alford here has a most suggestive remark. "The whole earth is broken up by a change as total as any of those previous ones which have prepared it for its present inhabitants. If geology teaches us any one fact it teaches us that there have been catastrophes on the surface of our globe which have extinguished all animal forms then existing, and the earth has been re-peopled with new forms of life, none of them exactly of the old types."

15. "And the kings of the earth, and the great men, ... every bond man, and every free man." Pains are taken by the writer of the Apocalypse to include all classes of men unreconciled to God; the kings, the powerful magnates, the generals, the rich, the powerful, and every slave, and every free labourer, all will be overwhelmed with terror, all will call for annihilation. Death in its most terrible form will be chosen rather than a life of punishment in which they will be rewarded according to their deeds.

16 ʰ And said to the mountains and rocks, Fall on us, and hide us from the face of him that sitteth on the throne, and from the wrath of the Lamb:

17 ⁱ For the great day of his wrath is come; ᵏ and who shall be able to stand?

ʰ Hos. x. 8.
Luke xxiii. 30.
ch. ix. 6.
ⁱ Isa. xiii. 6,
&c. Zeph. i.
14, &c. ch.
xvi. 14.
ᵏ Ps. lxxvi. 7.

16. "The wrath of the Lamb." This is, perhaps, the most fearful saying in all Scripture. "The wrath of the Lamb" is the wrath of Incarnate Mercy. "He is our only refuge in heaven and on earth against all other wrath. Be it either the wrath of evil spirits lying in wait to destroy us, or of good and holy beings, drawing back from us; or of the Most Holy God Who is of purer eyes than to behold and bear with our iniquity; Christ crucified for us, and joining us to Himself, is the one only shelter and help against it. He binds the devil and his angels that they may not tear us to pieces, as they long to do every moment. He fills the angels and saints in heaven, and all good Christians here in His Church on earth, with tender, anxious care for His sinful creatures, causing them to pray for us more and more earnestly, and obtain for us those blessings which in a mysterious and wonderful manner He has made to depend on their prayers. And what is more than all He in His Own Person intercedes with the Father for us. He stands at the right hand of God to succour all who mourn earnestly for their sins" (Pusey).

CHAP. VII.

AND after these things I saw four angels standing on the four corners of the earth, ᵃ holding the four

ᵃ Dan. vii. 2.

1. "And after these things I saw four angels standing," &c. "After these things" may have one of two meanings. It may mean after the events which are signified by these visions, or it may mean "after these visions had been displayed before me I saw other visions," which he proceeds to describe. I believe the latter to be the true meaning, because the last vision is evidently a vision

winds of the earth, ᵇ that the wind should not blow on the earth, nor on the sea, nor on any tree. ᵇ ch. ix. 4.

2 And I saw another angel ascending from the east, having

---

of the end. Only at the time of the end will it be said, "Hide us from the face of him that sitteth on the throne, and from the wrath of the Lamb: for the great day of his wrath is come."

I believe that there is no time allotted to the world or to the Church between the disappearance of Christ on Mount Olivet and His return. During the whole of these 1,800 years and more He might have been expected at any moment; so that I think that it is not permitted to us to make the history of the events which have occurred since the visions of the Apocalypse to be the subject of these visions, so that so many centuries should elapse between the time in which St. John saw them and the present time. Where there appears to be visions of successive events it is only in appearance. This I have shown to be the interpretation of the seal-openings; the four horse-riders do not succeed one another, but ride together. All the time during which the first rider rides conquering and to conquer, the second rider pursues his career of bloodshed, and the third his career of scarcity or famine. It is to be remembered that but one such vision can appear at one time to any human being, so that if St. John is bidden to recount such visions he must recount them as coming into his horizon successively, though they are in reality simultaneous.

"I saw four angels standing on the four corners of the earth." That is, at the four points of the compass, north, south, east and west.

"Holding the four winds of the earth." That is, a destructive storm, it may be of human opinion, threatening the entire desolation and destruction of society, or it may be of causes issuing in desolating wars, or it may be even of physical calamities which God treasures up in the store-house of His vengeance with which to overwhelm a world which has braved His wrath to the uttermost.

"That the wind should not blow on the earth, nor on the sea,. nor on any tree." This looks to the perfect restraint under which these powers of vengeance are kept. So far from overwhelming the earth they do not even lash into fury the sea, they do not even agitate the trees.

2. "And I saw another angel ascending from the east," *i.e.*, from

the seal of the living God: and he cried with a loud voice to the four angels, to whom it was given to hurt the earth and the sea,

^c ch. vi. 6. & ix. 4.
^d Ezek. ix. 4. ch. xiv. 1.
^e ch. xxii. 4.
^f ch. ix. 16.

3 Saying, ^c Hurt not the earth, neither the sea, nor the trees, till we have ^d sealed the servants of our God ^e in their foreheads.

4 ^f And I heard the number of them which

---

the quarter from which light comes, *i.e.*, the most glorious quarter of the heavens.

"Having the seal of the living God." Who is this angel and what is his seal? Some say that it can be no other than the Lord Jesus Himself; some the Holy Spirit. But it cannot be the latter, for He is the seal which is impressed upon the souls of Christians; according to the words of the Apostle, "Grieve not the holy Spirit of God, whereby ye are sealed unto the day of redemption" (Ephes. iv. 30). Neither, according to the teaching of this book, can it well be the Lord Himself: for the characteristic of this book is that God works all the workings of His providence through His servants the angels. It seems to me to be one of the main designs of this book to bring out the universality of angelic ministrations. If men are commissioned to seal their brethren either in Baptism or in Confirmation with the Holy Spirit, and yet it is God alone Who baptizes, and God alone Who confirms, why should He not, if he chooses, seal through the ministration of angels? Whatever the means which this angel or his fellows employ, it is God Who uses their hands and directs them in making every single impression of the Divine Seal.

3. "Saying, Hurt not the earth, neither the sea, nor the trees," &c. Why is the loosing of the four winds and their all-destroying influence postponed till after the sealing of the elect? We cannot tell. Perhaps the calamities will be such that it requires a special putting forth of the power of God in each individual case to preserve the faith of the elect from being in danger.

4. "And I heard the number of them which were sealed: and there were sealed an hundred and forty and four thousand of all the tribes," &c. A large number of questions arise out of this to which I ask the reader's devout and prayerful attention.

were sealed: *and there were* sealed ⁵ an hundred *and* forty *and* four thousand of all the tribes of the chil- dren of Israel.

⁵ ch. xiv. 1.

5 Of the tribe of Juda *were* sealed twelve thousand. Of the tribe of Reuben *were* sealed twelve thousand. Of the tribe of Gad *were* sealed twelve thousand.

Were these the whole number of the sealed? It is not said to be so by any means, only that these were sealed (out) "of all the tribes of the children of Israel."

When, as related in verse 9, the Apostle saw a great multitude, which no man could number, out of all nations, had these been sealed in the same way as the one hundred and forty-four thousand? surely this must have been if they were amongst the number of the saved, if they had made their calling and election sure, if they had washed their robes and made them white in the blood of the Lamb.

"Of the tribe of Juda were sealed twelve thousand. Of the tribe of Reuben were sealed twelve thousand." Who then were these one hundred and forty-four thousand? Were they actual Jews, or were they of the spiritual seed of Jacob only according to the words of this Apostle respecting some who said that they were Jews and were not, and as another Apostle witnesses, "He is not a Jew which is one outwardly"?

Now it is quite possible that, no matter what the seeming improbability, they might be Jews by birth. The difficulty is that so many belong to what are called the lost tribes. But though these tribes are lost to us are they lost to God; can we limit the knowledge of God? cannot He keep in His eye every soul of the descendants of the Patriarchs, and preserve him or his posterity till the sound of the Gospel comes to him with power?

Let the reader remember that this sealing of each one may be a profound secret, known only to God and the soul whom He seals.

The reasons given why we are to understand this one hundred and forty-four thousand as being the spiritual Israel seem to me very absurd. One is because the tribe of Dan is omitted; but we have abundant reason to believe that this tribe had become extinct; another that Levi is included; another that the tribe of Ephraim j

6 Of the tribe of Aser *were* sealed twelve thousand. Of the tribe of Nepthalim *were* sealed twelve thousand. Of the tribe of Manasses *were* sealed twelve thousand.

7 Of the tribe of Simeon *were* sealed twelve thousand. Of the tribe of Levi *were* sealed twelve thousand. Of the tribe of Issachar *were* sealed twelve thousand.

---

put down as the tribe of Joseph, but why should not this be, for God gave Ephraim the right of primogeniture?

I do not, however, say that these were actual Jews by descent, but that it is quite possible they may be such; we know that in the Prophets there are many predictions of the restoration of the tribes of Israel as distinguished from Judah. The subject is of course mysterious, but nothing like so mysterious as many others of God's providential dealings.

Two other matters require a very short notice.

If this one hundred and forty-four thousand signify the spiritual seed of Abraham, why should they be classed under the names of the twelve tribes? Simply to emphasize the fact that the spiritual seed, the seed of faith, enters into the inheritance of all the promises.

If, however, they signify Israelites by descent then it may be that they are specifically mentioned here in order to console the remnant of Jacob by assuring them through the mouth of the Apostle that God has not cast away His people " whom he foreknew."

And now we ask, when did this sealing take place, and what was it in its reality? It is impossible to suppose that such a thing as the sealing of the elect body takes place at but one definite period, for it pertains to each faithful soul in every age that he should be sealed. It appears to me that the two things represented in these two visions, these sealed ones and the palm-bearers, describe what is taking place throughout the whole time covered by the opening of the seals. Notwithstanding the judgments with which God will afflict the world by wars, famines, and pestilences, there will go on without intermission the sealing of the elect and their gathering into paradise. The horse-rider judgments will in no respect hinder this. During the centuries of woe and judgment, of war,

8 Of the tribe of Zabulon *were* sealed twelve thousand. Of the tribe of Joseph *were* sealed twelve thousand. Of the tribe of Benjamin *were* sealed twelve thousand.

---

famine, and pestilence, God has been accomplishing the number of His elect, and after they are fully prepared they are drafted one by one into paradise, and take their place amongst the spirits of just men made perfect.

But what *is* the actual sealing? It is, of course, the work of the Holy Spirit, perhaps rather a work of God by the Holy Spirit; but what is it, what does it accomplish in the soul? I am thankful that other words which I have found, and which I will give to the reader, will express this far better than any of my own, " On whom did St. John see the angel impress the seal of the elect? on the servants of God; that is, on those which were found faithful, each one in his place fulfilling his Master's work. The parable of the talents is a key to the name 'servant.' It is the title of those who having received the grace of their Lord to lay out in His service, use what is entrusted to them with care and diligence; it describes the state of the regenerate, and the law of their probation."

After years well spent in faithful service, when the will and heart are ripened by trial into steadfast faith and love, then, in His mercy, God bestows a crowning gift upon His servants, the gift of perseverance.

There is an interior ministry of the Spirit, ever working, sealing by an inward and Divine Seal the proved servants of Christ, not by a capricious or mechanical predestination, but by an election founded on the moral attributes of God, and on the moral nature of man. What is the seal of the living God but the image of God renewed in the soul by the power of the Holy Ghost; the likeness and the mind of Christ stamped upon us by a perfect regeneration; the inward reality of a saintly spirit wrought in us, either by a life of steadfast obedience or by a true repentance, by a persevering grace, or by a perfect conversion?

This work of grace is now, by the ministry of the Church, fulfilling all around, and will work on unseen unto the end. Then, when the mystical number is accomplished, and every soul foreknown has received the seal of God, the seventh and last seal of the book

9 After this I beheld, and, lo, [h] a great multitude, which no man could number, [i] of all nations, and kindreds, and people, and tongues, stood before the throne, and before the Lamb, [k] clothed with white robes, and palms in their hands;

[h] Rom. xi. 25.
[i] ch. v. 9.
[k] ch. iii. 5, 18. & iv. 4. & vi. 11. ver. 14.

---

shall be opened, and the scourges of God, long pent up, come down upon the world. Ask yourselves, therefore, whether or no you are of this secret number, or whether or no you have received the seal of God.

What else is worth living for? Though you should have all and not this what shall it profit in the day of judgment? Though you have nothing else but this alone, what shall you then desire?"

9. "After this." I think immediately following it, because in some of its principal features in strong contrast to it.

"I beheld, and, lo, a great multitude, which no man could number." Mark the contrast. The number of the sealed was a great number, but it could be numbered; it was quite within the power of man to count it though multiplied many times over, but this was innumerable; only within the ken of that God Who numbers the grains of sand and the drops of dew.

"Of all nations, and kindreds, and people, and tongues." Mark the contrast here also. The former vision was of one nation, the people of Israel; one tongue, the Hebrew, though they might speak different dialects all holding one language to be their mother, their national, their sacred tongue.

"Stood before the throne, and before the Lamb." Are these supposed to be in paradise or in heaven? It is no matter. If they have not yet attained to the highest bliss—that of the Resurrection state—they are sealed for it and are as certain of its possession as if they had passed the judgment.

"Clothed with white robes." That is, white robes signifying spotless innocence: not natural innocence, of course, but innocence in the twofold sense that no former sin which they may have committed shall be imputed to them. It is all forgotten through their repentance, and their true faith in the atoning power of the Blood of Christ. And innocence in another sense, that no stain is left on their souls; the memory of past sin only remains to keep alive in them the sense

10 And cried with a loud voice, saying, ¹ Salvation to our God ᵐ which sitteth upon the throne, and unto the Lamb.

11 ⁿ And all the angels stood round about the throne, and *about* the elders and the four beasts, and fell before the throne on their faces, and worshipped God,

12 ᵒ Saying, Amen: Blessing, and glory, and wisdom, and thanksgiving, and honour, and power, and might, *be* unto our God for ever and ever. Amen.

13 And one of the elders answered, saying unto me, What

¹ Ps. iii. 8.
Isa. xliii. 11.
Jer. iii. 23.
Hos. xiii. 4.
ch. xix. 1.
ᵐ ch. v. 13.
ⁿ ch. iv. 6

ᵒ ch. v. 13, 14

---

10. "And cried with a loud voice." "And they cry with," &c. So ℵ, A., B. C., &c.

of the greatness and thoroughness of their redemption. They are not tormented with the evil lusts which it has left in them.

"And palms in their hands." In token of victory which they have achieved (John xii. 13), not because they are keeping the feast of tabernacles, which they are not.

10. "And cried with a loud voice, saying, Salvation to our God which sitteth upon the throne, and unto the Lamb." "Salvation to our God," Who orders all things, and brings about all that is in the council of His will.

"And unto the Lamb." As the Instrument, the Victim, the High Priest, the Mediator. That salvation should be thus ascribed to God and the Lamb, shows how the Lamb fully shares in the glory and honour of God.

11, 12. "And all the angels stood round about the throne . . . and fell before the throne on their faces . . . . and might, be unto our God for ever and ever. Amen." The angels are our fellow-worshippers, and in some sense partake of the blessings of Christ's Redemption, for it is written, "by him to reconcile all things unto himself; by him, I say, whether they be things in earth, or things in heaven" (Coloss. i. 20).

13. "And one of the elders answered, saying unto me." It may be that he read the thoughts of the Seer respecting whom these

are these which are arrayed in ᵖ white robes? and whence came they?

ᵖ ver. 9.

14 And I said unto him, Sir, thou knowest. And he said to me, ᑫ These are they which came out of great tribulation, and have ʳ washed their robes, and made them white in the blood of the Lamb.

ᑫ ch. vi. 9. & xvii. 6.
ʳ Isa. i. 18. Heb. ix. 14. 1 John i. 7. ch. i. 5. See Zech. iii. 3, 4, 5

15 Therefore are they before the throne of God, and serve him day and night in his temple: and

---

14. "Sir, thou knowest." Rather, "My Lord, thou knowest."

white-robed ones might be, and so gave him an opportunity of asking the question: anyhow the repetition of the account of the vision shows its importance.

14. "These are they which came out of great tribulation." Literally out of "the tribulation the great one." Does this mean out of some specific tribulation, or that the whole period in which Christians have suffered from the enmity of the world is from the time of St. John to the present one of great tribulation, as it is said in the Acts, " that we must through much tribulation enter into the kingdom of heaven." The great and last tribulation is that of the last days—the time of the end—foretold by our Lord in Matt. xxiv. 21, " Then shall there be great tribulation, such as was not since the beginning of the world."

It is impossible to say. The words in the Greek seem to imply a particular tribulation, to the time and circumstances of which we have no clue, but all Christians should remember that all suffering borne patiently for the sake of Christ is accounted to be suffering with Him, and it is a faithful saying, " If we suffer with him, we shall also reign with him " (2 Tim. ii. 12).

" And have washed their robes, and made them white in the blood," &c. See on verse 9.

15. " Therefore are they before the throne of God, and serve him day and night," &c. " Therefore," *i.e.*, because they have endured patiently, and in the power of Christ, the great tribulation, and have been cleansed and quickened with the Blood of Christ.

" And serve him day and night in his temple," *i.e.*, as His

he that sitteth on the throne shall ᵃdwell among them.   ˢ Isa. iv. 5, 6. ch. xxi. 3.

16 ᵗ They shall hunger no more, neither thirst any more; ᵘneither shall the sun light on them, nor any heat.   ᵗ Isa. xlix. 10. ᵘ Ps. cxxi. 6. ch. xxi. 4.

17 For the Lamb which is in the midst of the throne ˣ shall feed them, and shall lead them   ˣ Ps. xxiii. 1. & xxxvi. 8. John x. 11, 14.

---

priests. How is it that they are said to "serve God in his temple" and yet in the final vision St. John sees no temple in the New Jerusalem? Because the temple of God is everywhere. Where God and the Lamb are there is the temple.

"He that sitteth on the throne shall dwell among them." Properly shall tabernacle them, shall spread His tabernacle over them. He shall be so visibly overshadowing them that they shall not need a temple.

16. "They shall hunger no more, neither thirst any more." This implies a totally different condition to that in their present state. The fear of hunger is now the incentive to industry. Men labour for their bread, and by that labour are kept from almost infinite moral evils. Then the curse will be removed and other motives will keep them in the most incessant and yet the most blessed employment.

"Neither shall the sun light on them, nor any heat." This is taken almost verbatim from Isaiah xlix. 10, "They shall not hunger nor thirst; neither shall the heat nor sun smite them: for he that hath mercy on them shall lead them, even by the springs of water shall he guide them."

17. "For the Lamb which is in the midst of the throne shall feed them." Is this a reason why they shall neither hunger nor thirst? We must look somewhat higher. Apparently all finite creatures require food; and that with which the Lamb supplies these blessed ones abundantly, is suited to their glorified frames or to their intellectual nature.

Mark, it is the Lamb which does this, and yet throughout the Old Testament it is God Who is the One Feeder of the people, "I the Lord will feed them."

unto living fountains of waters: ʸ and God shall wipe away all tears from their eyes.

ʸ Isa. xxv. 8.
ch. xxi. 4.

"And God shall wipe away all tears from their eyes." The memory of past grief shall not be painful. They shall only remember what they have passed through in order evermore to glorify God for having brought them through all.

CHAP. VIII.

AND ᵃ when he had opened the seventh seal, there was silence in heaven about the space of half an hour. 2 ᵇ And I saw the seven angels which stood

ᵃ ch. vi. 1.
ᵇ Matt. xviii. 10. Luke i. 19.

1. "And when he had opened the seventh seal, there was silence in heaven about the space of half an hour." What is this silence? who is silent? The last sounds we have heard is the cry with a loud voice of the great multitude, "Salvation to our God," and the worship of the angels. "Amen: Blessing and glory .... be unto our God." Can it be that these are hushed, and the voices of the living ones which cry incessantly, "Holy, holy, holy."

I think it must rather mean the silence of expectation. The breathlessness of the creatures in expectation of the fearful judgments that are impending; or, inasmuch as there is to be an incense-offering in the sight of all heaven, it may be a silence answering to that of the worshippers when the priest was offering his incense before the veil, and the people were all in prayer till he came and gave the blessing, when the full choir of the Temple burst out into song and music. Some have even thought this silence was what fulfilled the opening of the seventh seal, but this cannot be, almost all (as Williams says) speak of it as an awful interval, the dead silence which precedes the thunderclap.

2. "And I saw the seven angels which stood before God." "I am Gabriel," says one of these angels at the time of the Incarnation,

before God; ᵉ and to them were given seven trumpets.   ᶜ 2 Chron. xxix. 25-28.

3 And another angel came and stood at the altar, having a golden censer; and there was given unto him much incense, that he should ∥ offer *it* with ᵈ the prayers of all saints upon ᵉ the golden altar which was before the throne.

∥ Or, *add it to the prayers.*
ᵈ ch. v. 8.
ᵉ Exod. xxx. 1. ch. vi. 9.

"that stand in the presence of God." Almost all commentators without exception refer to certain words in the Apocryphal book of Tobit, "I am Raphael, one of the seven holy angels which present the prayers of the saints." Why should there not be mighty angels before God, and why should they not be seven in number, and why should not God Who made them and placed them where they are, employ them when He sees it fit so to do?

"And to them were given seven trumpets." Trumpets sound to the battle and must signify something very different to the opening of the seals of a book. Almost all expositors explain the visions which succeed the sounding of these trumpets as betokening some outpouring of the wrath of God upon His enemies. They cannot well signify the use of trumpets in calling to solemn assemblies or festivals, for the visions which take place are the opposite of these.

3. "And another angel came and stood at the altar." Literally, above, or over it, so that his form appeared above it; but the Vulgate translates *ante*, before it.

"Having a golden censer; and there was given unto him," &c. "Golden," corresponding with the golden altar of incense.

"That he should offer it with." Rather, taken literally, give it to, that is, I suppose, add it to. Incense is not prayer, but is assumed to be added to prayer to make it acceptable: so that, if any thing earthly can do, it typifies the merits of Jesus Christ.

It is not improbable that this offering of incense with the prayers is the principal thing for which we have this particular vision vouchsafed to us. There must be something along with our prayers to make them acceptable. "No man cometh unto the Father but by me." What are these prayers—what is their subject matter? It would seem that we must go back to chap. vi. 10, "They cried with a loud voice, How long, O Lord, holy and true?"

4 And ᶠthe smoke of the incense, *which came* with the prayers of the saints, ascended up before God out of the angel's hand.

5 And the angel took the censer, and filled it with fire of the altar, and cast *it* ‖ into the earth: and ᵍthere were voices, and thunderings, and lightnings, ʰ and an earthquake.

ᶠ Ps. cxli. 2. Luke i. 10.
‖ Or, *upon*.
ᵍ ch. xvi. 18.
ʰ 2 Sam. xxii. 8. 1 Kings xix. 11. Acts iv. 31.

Is then the sounding of these trumpets and the consequent judgments an answer to their calls for vengeance? It would seem so; but we must remember that God's vengeance is not only for punishment, but as a call to repentance (ch. ix. 21).

4. "And the smoke of the incense, which came with the prayers of the saints, ascended up before God out of the angel's hand." Implying that on account of the incense mingled with it the prayers of the saints ascended because accepted. The incense of course contained no element of merit in itself, but typified that which has abounding merit.

5. "And the angel took the censer, and filled it with fire of the altar." It has been made a matter of dispute whether there were two altars, that of burnt-offering and that of incense. I believe there could be but one; the function of the altar of burnt-offerings—which was the showing forth of the One all-sufficient Atonement by bleeding and dead victims—was over and out of place in the presence of the all-atoning Victim; whereas the function of the altar of incense—the perfuming of the prayers with the incense of the infinite merits of the Mediator—was always necessary.

"Filled it with fire of the altar [*i.e.*, of incense] and cast it into the earth: and there were voices, and thunderings, and lightnings," &c. Of what was this casting of fire upon the earth a figure? It seems to be one of coming vengeance, not postponed, as in chap. vi. 11, but close at hand.

May it be permitted to say a word respecting the sacerdotal action of this angel. He conducts or presides over the ritual of heaven. Now, allowing to the utmost that what he does in this sublime worship is spiritual or figurative, unquestionably the outward form of it is very distinctly ritual. He does not content himself with standing or kneeling and offering up silent prayer.

6 And the seven angels which had the seven trumpets prepared themselves to sound.

7 The first angel sounded, [i] and there followed hail and fire mingled with blood, and they were cast [k] upon the earth: and the third part [l] of trees was burnt up, and all green grass was burnt up.

[i] Ezek. xxxviii. 22.
[k] ch. xvi. 2.
[l] Isa. ii. 13. ch. ix. 4.

---

7. "The first angel." "Angel" omitted by ℵ, A., B., P., four Cursives, Syriac. "Mingled with blood." "In blood" in ℵ, A., B., P., forty Cursives, Vulg., &c. "And the third part of the earth was burnt up." So ℵ, A., B., &c.

He uses, in the face of the inhabitants of heaven itself, symbolic ritual. Would he have been permitted to do this if outward forms, such as the use of an altar, standing at that altar and mingling incense with what betokens prayer, were abominable in the sight of God and were indications of the worship of Antichrist or of the beast rather than of the worship of God. The whole principle of ritual worship seems to me to be involved in such action of heavenly beings in the presence and before the throne of God.

6. "And the seven angels which had the seven trumpets prepared themselves to sound." As if they waited for the signal from the Almighty, knowing well that on the sounding of their trumpets terrible judgments would fall upon the earth.

7. "The first angel sounded, and there followed hail and fire mingled with blood, and they were cast upon the earth: and the third part of trees was burnt up." I confess that I write upon these plagues following on these first four sounding of trumpets with much reluctance. I had hoped to have found something analogous to the opening of the first four seals which seem to usher in influences or states of the world not successive, but contemporaneous. Thus the first seal, introducing the Rider of the white horse, sets forth the preaching of the Gospel of the Prince of Peace; and the second, introducing the rider of the blood-red horse, a continuous state of war side by side with the proclamation of the Gospel—thus preparing the Church for what it would not naturally have expected. I cannot find, however, anything in human history which can with any probability be identified with the four visions at the sounding of the first four trumpets, so I must content myself with giving the

8 And the second angel sounded, ᵐ and as it were a great mountain burning with fire was cast into the sea: ⁿ and the third part of the sea ᵒ became blood;

ᵐ Jer. li. 25. Amos vii. 4.
ⁿ ch. xvi. 3.
ᵒ Ezek. xiv. 19

interpretation of various expositors, not one of which I can accept as the undoubtedly true meaning.

Expositors of such opposite views on Church questions as Elliot and Wordsworth consider that these four first visions (or at least the two first), were fulfilled in the breaking up of the Roman Empire under successive incursions of the Goths, Huns, and Vandals at the beginning of the fifth century. Elliot interprets the first trumpet vision as the invasion of Italy, and taking and sacking of Rome by Alaric; the second, the conquest of the maritime provinces and the islands by the Vandal Genseric, "Invited by Count Boniface, governor of the province of Africa, he transported thither his Vandals from Spain across the African sea." But the correspondence between Genseric and his Vandal hordes, and such an infliction upon the sea as could be symbolized by a burning mountain cast into the sea, and a third of it becoming blood, and a third part of the creatures which were in the sea, and had life, dying, is, to me, beyond measure slight and unsatisfactory. Now this third part consists of the whole of the Mediterranean between Italy and Spain. Were the whole of the fish destroyed in it? Let the reader notice that the creatures in the sea *and* the ships, as distinguished from the creatures inhabiting the sea, are destroyed. The only account of destruction of ships is that of the Roman navies in the harbours of Carthagena and Bona, which were set on fire by fire-ships driven in amongst them. With all this is mixed up an eruption of the mountains of Auvergne, very far from the sea, in the middle of France; and in a note the account of an eruption of Etna which covered the sea near that part of Sicily with small ashes, not a thousandth part of the area of the west of the Mediterranean.

I will reserve remarks on Elliot's third and fourth trumpet vision till I have noticed Bishop Wordsworth on the first two seals.

He makes them both to refer to the Gothic or Hunnic invasions from the north, without taking, apparently, any notice of the extraordinary difference between a hailstorm mingled with blood destroying the land, and a burning mountain cast into the sea and turning it into blood. He makes the mountain cast into the

9 ᵖ And the third part of the creatures which were in the sea, and had life, died; and the third part of the ships were destroyed.   ᵖ ch. xvi. 3.

---

sea and turning it into blood to be the uprooting of Rome, "the great imperial mountain," by the assaults of the Goths, Vandals, and Huns, and "the mighty empire dismembered and decomposed, and its solid mass dissolved and melted away into a swelling sea which was long agitated by the winds and waves of revolutionary storms and political hurricanes."

Mede also explains these two first trumpet visions of the incursions of barbarians breaking up the Roman Empire, the first trumpet vision relating to Alaric; the second of Goths and Vandals to Genseric.

Bengel says, "The trumpet of the first angel befittingly assails the Jews, and comprises the Jewish wars under Trajan and Adrian," and of the second trumpet vision he writes, "A mass of barbarian nations is meant, concerning the migration and irruption of which, attended with the greatest injuries from the third century, history is so full that it is needless to quote particular authors."

The above remarks will suffice for the historical interpetations.

Alford, Williams, Bishop Boyd-Carpenter, Lee, in "Speaker's Commentary," and Milligan, deprecate our understanding any historical fulfilments, but none of them seem to be agreed what mystical, or allegorical, or symbolical, or spiritual, or moral fulfilment is to be given to any one vision.

Cornelius à Lapide cites Irenæus and Lactantius as agreeing with Aretas and Ribera that these predictions are to be understood literally, but that they will only be fulfilled at the end, "inchoabunt et fieri incipiunt ante judicium et ante Antichristum." I have not been able, however, to verify the reference to Irenæus.

Archdeacon Farrar, as representing the preterists, says, "The language is obviously that of daring symbolism. Taken literally, the fall of the burning mountain resembles no event ever seen or known in the history of the world. Taken metaphorically, it may be meant to depict great calamities connected with the sea and ships, deaths by drowning and massacre which 'incarnadine the multitudinous seas.' The times of Nero furnished abundant instances. Such were the inundations which devastated the

10 And the third angel sounded, ⁹ and there fell a great star from heaven, burning as it were a lamp, ʳ and it fell upon the third part of the rivers, and upon the fountains of waters;

11 ˢ And the name of the star is called Worm-

ᵠ Isa. xiv. 12. ch. ix. 1.
ʳ ch. xvi. 4.
ˢ Ruth i. 20.

---

coasts of Lydia, and the destruction of fleets, and the waves reddening with the blood of men, as at Joppa and on the coasts of the Dead Sea, and on the lake of Galilee." "At Joppa the sea was bloody a long way, and the maritime parts were full of dead bodies, and the number of dead bodies that were thus thrown out of the sea was four thousand two hundred." A large number, it is true, but scarcely enough to warrant the third part of the sea as turned into blood and all the fish dying.

With respect to this third part which is referred to in each trumpet vision, Elliot understands it of the western part of the Roman Empire and its adjacent seas, and gives a map describing exactly what he means by the third part, which comprises Britain, Gaul, Spain, Italy, and the parts of Africa opposite to Spain and Italy. But Alford responds that all special interpretations seem to him utterly to have failed, and of these none so signally as that of Mr. Elliot, as he says, and apparently rightly, that it is not said that the hail, &c., was cast upon a third part (of the earth), but that the destruction occasioned by them extended to a third part of the earth on which they were cast, and he would take the third part (τό τρίτον) as signifying "that though the judgment is undoubtedly, as to extent, fearful and sweeping, yet that God in inflicting it spares more than He smites—two-thirds escaping in each case."

10-11. "And the third angel sounded, and there fell a great star from heaven, burning as it were a lamp, ... and the name of the star is called Wormwood: and the third part of the waters became wormwood." This is interpreted historically by Elliot, Mede and Wordsworth. Elliot considers it to have been fulfilled in Attila, whose campaigns were principally by the banks of rivers. "'The Huns,' says Gibbon, 'were masters of the great rivers.' But it is specially the river-frontier of the same western third of the empire, to which the other trumpets refer, that I suppose is chiefly intended in the present. Accordingly, about A.D. 450, in fulfilment of a

wood: 'and the third part of the waters became wood:^t   ^t Exod. xv. 23. Jer. ix. 15. & xxiii. 15.

treaty with Genseric, he moved against the western provinces along the upper Danube, reached and crossed the Rhine at Basle, and thence tracing the same great frontier stream of the west down to Belgium, made its valley one scene of desolation and woe, burning the cities (of which Strasburg, Spires, Worms, Mentz, Andernach, Treves, Tongres, Maestricht, are specially particularized), massacring the inhabitants and laying the country waste. After sustaining a severe defeat at Châlons, he fell on another destined scene of ravage, the European *fountains* of waters, in the Alpine heights and Alpine valleys of Italy. Then Aquileia, Pavia, Verona, Mantua, Milan, Turin felt his vengeance. 'From the Alps to the Apennines,' says Segovius, 'all was flight, depopulation, slaughter, slavery, and despair.' But what of his course of devastation. Surely with all Italy defenceless before him one might have expected that, like his predecessor, Alaric, it would have continued on to Rome. Instead of this, behold an embassy from the Western Emperor Valentinian, accompanied by the venerable Romish Bishop Leo I., was successful in deprecating his wrath, and having granted them peace, he repassed the Alps and retired.' Wherefore a result, humanly speaking, so unlikely? Methinks we see the reason. The prediction had expressly marked the term of Attila's devastating progress. Already Attila had made bitter the river line of the upper Danube and Rhine and the Alpine fountains of waters." But surely all this is very unsatisfactory; to massacre the inhabitants and burn the cities on the banks of a river is not, I should think, to make the waters bitter; to sack Pavia, Verona, Mantua, Milan, is not to make bitter the fountains of their rivers in the far off Alpine heights.

Mede interprets the third trumpet of Odoacer, but, unlike Elliot, with little or no attempt to account for the connection of the vision with fountains of waters becoming bitter.

Wordsworth interprets the falling star and the embittering of the waters as being heresies; and certainly if the Scriptures be the fountains of the water of life, then, in a sense, the reception of heresies makes bitter the very fountains of life, for he who has received the heresy turns the Scriptures themselves into bitterness. Instead of receiving them submissively he puts his own interpre-

wormwood; and many men died of the waters, because they were made bitter.

---

tation upon every place which does not suit his views. This is particularly the case with the first of the great heresies, the Arian. The man who holds it goes through the New Testament, systematically giving a low and inadequate interpretation to every place which sets forth the Divine Nature and Attributes of the Eternal Son.

I cannot help saying that this appears to me far more consonant with the figures in this vision than the interpretation connecting it with the ravages of Attila by the banks of certain rivers.

Bengel also interprets it of heresy. "The name of the star is called Wormwood"—Arianism, "full of bitterness."

Williams, "The star may include Arius, Eutyches, Apollonaris, Sabellius, Nestorius.

Bishop Boyd-Carpenter seemingly interprets it of the fall of the great ones of the earth before the advance of the Gospel, but he adds, "their fall will bring misery to mankind."

Alford avoids any particular or historical interpretation, but as an illustration notices the evils arising from the use of ardent spirits.

So also apparently Cornelius à Lapide, "Vocatur absinthium: quia amaricabit aquas, idque in pœnam sceleratæ voluptatis ac præsertim gulæ et crapulæ impiorum, ut qui biberunt vina dulcissima et sapidissima iisque ventrem ingurgitarunt, jam bibant absinthium, eoque crucientur et enecentur."

Milligan interprets it spiritually. "They represent the bitterness of that water with which, instead of the water of life, the world seeks to quench the thirst of its votaries."

Archdeacon Farrar, as representing the preterists, "As stars are the images of rulers, and fallen stars of rulers flung down from heaven, the symbol may dimly express the bitterness and terror caused by the overthrow of Nero, and the ominous failure of the Julian line. The details of the image may have been suggested by the wicked habit of poisoning the waters of which an enemy was to drink. The Romans excused their cruelty at Jerusalem by asserting that the springs and fountains had been poisoned by the Jews."

12 ᵘ"And the fourth angel sounded, and the third part of the sun was smitten, and the third part of the ᵘ Isa. xiii. 10.
Amos viii. 9.

---

12. "And the fourth angel sounded, and the third part of the sun was smitten, and the third part of the moon, and the third part of the stars .... and the day shone not for a third part of it, and the night likewise." The sun, moon, and stars constantly in the language of prophecy are taken to represent sovereign princes, emperors, and kings. In accordance with this Elliot interprets this as the extinction of the Roman emperor in the west, *i.e.*, in the third part of the Roman empire (according to the boundaries traced out in the map to which I have before alluded). "The glory of Rome had long departed .... little remained to it but the vain titles and insignia of sovereignty; and now the time was come when these, too, should be withdrawn. Some twenty years or more from the death of Attila .... Odoacer, chief of the Heruli—a barbarian remnant of the host of Attila left on the Alpine frontiers of Italy—interposed with his command that the name and office of Roman emperor of the west should be abolished: the authorities bowed in submission to him. The last phantom of an emperor, whose name Romulus Augustus (or Augustulus) was singularly calculated to bring in contrast the past glories of Rome and its present degradation, abdicated. . . . Thus of the Roman imperial sun that third which appertained to the western empire was eclipsed and shone no more. The senate, however, still continued to assemble; the consuls were appointed yearly. Odoacer himself governed Italy under a title (that of Patrician) conferred on him by the eastern emperor: and as regards the more distant western provinces, or at least considerable districts of them, the tie which united them to the Roman Empire was not altogether severed. There was still a certain, though often faint, recognition of the supreme imperial authority. The moon and the stars might still seem to shine in the west with a dim reflected light. In the course of the events, however, which rapidly followed one on the other in the next half century, these, too, were extinguished. Theodore the Ostrogoth, on destroying the Heruli and their kingdom at Rome and Ravenna, ruled in Italy from A.D. 493 to 526 as an independent sovereign. Soon after the senate and consulship were abolished."

moon, and the third part of the stars; so as the third part of them was darkened, and the day shone not for a third part of it, and the night likewise.

^x ch. xiv. 6. & xix. 17.

13 And I beheld, ^x and heard an angel flying

---

13. "An angel." ℵ, A., B., thirty-five Cursives, Vulg., Copt., Syr., Æth. read, "eagle." Only P. and a few Cursives read, "angel."

Mede considers that the fourth trumpet vision was fulfilled in the ravages of Totilas, whereby Rome received its last desolations.

Bengel has a very short note: "That [the smiting of the sun, moon, &c.] was done in the fifth century, when Italy and Rome, the seat of empire, were occupied and obscured by foreign nations."

Wordsworth remarks: "Here we see a prophecy of a great prevalence of errors, defections, apostasies, and confusions in Christendom such as abounded in the seventh century."

Of non-historical interpreters Alford gives us not the least hint of what he thinks it means.

Bishop Boyd-Carpenter suggests the chaos which precedes the new creation.

Milligan gives no word of definite meaning.

Williams remarks: "These emblems [sun, moon, stars] under the sixth seal betokened the fall of Jerusalem, but now the defection of the Christian Church; yet only partial, in eclipse, not fallen, for they are still in heaven."

Archdeacon Farrar, representing the preterists: "In accordance with the recognized imagery of Apocalypse and Prophecy, ruler after ruler, chieftain after chieftain of the Roman Empire and the Jewish nation was assassinated and ruined. Caius (Caligula), Claudius Nero, Galba, Otho, Vitellius all died by murder or suicide. Herod the Great, Herod Antipas, Herod Agrippa and most of the Herodian princes, with not a few of the leading high priests of Jerusalem perished in disgrace, or in exile, or by violent hands. All these were quenched suns and darkened stars."

Cornelius à Lapide, citing Ribera, refers to the Lord's prediction that at the end "the sun shall be darkened and the moon shall not give her light, and the stars shall fall from heaven," &c., but the Lord seems to set forth a far more terrible infliction of darkness than is here signified.

13. "And I beheld, and heard an angel [one single eagle] flying

through the midst of heaven, saying with a loud voice, "Woe, woe, woe, to the inhabiters of the earth by reason of the other voices of the trumpet of the three angels, which are yet to sound!

^r ch. ix. 12. & xi. 14.

---

through the midst of heaven, saying with a loud voice, Woe, woe, woe," &c. I cannot help thinking that this angel or eagle makes a marked difference between the preceding and the succeeding visions, and seems to indicate that compared to the inflictions impending under the three last trumpets, the past inflictions were as nothing. Now taking these four trumpet visions to signify the breaking up of the old Roman Empire by various incursions of Goths and others, it is quite certain that though certain parts of Italy were rendered desolate, yet the remainder must have been pretty nearly the same as they always were. Supposing that an immense invading army crossed over a large country, France, Spain, Germany, it could, as far as I can see, ravage or render desolate a comparatively small part, and in the remainder the operations of agriculture must go on as usual. And then an effete empire would be displaced by several strong smaller kingdoms which, even taking into account fierce wars between them, must have been an immense advantage to the western Roman world.

CHAP. IX.

AND the fifth angel sounded, ^a and I saw a star fall from heaven unto the earth: and

^a Luke x. 18. ch. viii. 10.

---

1. "And the fifth angel sounded, and I saw a star fall from heaven unto the earth: and to him was given the key of the bottomless pit." Respecting the interpretation of what took place under this fifth trumpet there is unanimity among expositors who usually do not agree with one another. Mede, and after him Elliot, Bishop Wordsworth, Williams, explain it of the rise and

^b Luke viii. 31. ch. xvii. 8. & xx. 1. ver. 2, 11. to him was given the key of ^bthe bottomless pit.

---

early progress of Mahomedanism; Elliot devotes to it above eighty pages; Mede more space than he gives to apparently far more important visions; Wordsworth one of his longest notes.

I will first take the twelve verses seriatim.

"I saw a star fall from heaven." Rather, "fallen ($\pi\epsilon\pi\tau\omega\kappa\acute{o}\tau\alpha$) from heaven." This more grammatical interpretation is far more difficult. Was the star lying on the ground? The Lord says, "I saw Satan like lightning fall from heaven."

"Star" by some is interpreted as a ruler dethroned; by others as a Christian teacher fallen from the true faith into heresy, and those who uphold this opinion say that it was through the divisions of Christendom, occasioned by the heresies, that Mahomedanism as a military power was able to make such rapid progress. Elliot, however, shows that Mahomet was by birth of the noblest tribe in Arabia. "Mahomet was by birth of the princely house of the Koreish, governors of Mecca. Originally the principality had been in the hands of another tribe. But one of the Koreish had bought from them the keys of the Caaba, and that which went with the keys, the principality of Mecca, which from him descended lineally to Mahomet's grandfather, and was in fact in his hands at the time of the grandson's birth. Now this principality and government was one of no small eminence among the Arabs."

Some, however (as Mede) seem to think that this star was Satan himself, and no doubt both the errors of Mahomedanism and its ferocity were alike the work of the enemy of mankind.

"And to him was given the key of the bottomless pit." By whom we are not told, and, in fact, it is idle to inquire, for the pit was not, of course, a local pit existing somewhere on the surface of the earth; but the vision teaches us that an evil influence from hell, which had before been restrained, burst out now on the earth. Mahomedanism is from beneath: its denial of the essential Fatherhood of God alone would prove this. The bottomless pit is literally the well of the abyss—the abyss is the abode of the powers of evil—in which the devils cast out by our Lord prayed Him that they should not be shut (Luke viii. 31).

2. "And he opened the bottomless pit; and there arose a smoke

2 And he opened the bottomless pit; ᶜ and there arose a smoke out of the pit, as the smoke of a great furnace; and the sun and the air were darkened by reason of the smoke of the pit.

3 And there came out of the smoke ᵈ locusts upon the earth: and unto them was given power, ᵉ as the scorpions of the earth have power.

4 And it was commanded them ᶠ that they

ᶜ Joel ii. 2, 10.

ᵈ Exod. x. 4. Judg. vii. 12.

ᵉ ver. 10.
ᶠ ch. vi. 6. & vii. 3.

---

out of the pit, as the smoke of a great furnace; and the sun and the air were darkened." This betokens some evil teaching darkening the light of heaven. It could not have been any natural darkness, for any obscuration of the natural heavens such as this has never taken place in the world's history, though we are assured on the authority of Christ Himself that there will be such before the final catastrophe.

3. "And there came out of the smoke locusts upon the earth." Assuming for the time that this trumpet vision refers to Mahomedanism, then the imagery is parallel to that in the book of Joel, where immense armies desolating all in their progress are compared to flights of locusts. The spread of the Gospel and of Islamism are in the greatest possible contrast; the one was by the preaching of the Gospel, and the conquests of its soldiers were by preaching; the other was by the sword, for there was, comparatively speaking, little or no proselytism by word of mouth.

It has been noticed that the locusts did not come out of the abyss itself, but out of the smoke which arose from it. This was what engendered them, as it were. In the case of every other irruption of destroying men, it only need be said that they came out of some region or other at the instigation of their own bloodthirstiness or love of plunder, but not so with the Mahomedan Arab hosts. They came out of the obscuring smoke of false doctrine, which itself came from hell. Without it they would have had no impelling, no overpowering fanaticism, which was the real secret of their success.

"And unto them was given power, as the scorpions of the earth have power."

4. "And it was commanded them that they should not hurt the

should not hurt ᵍthe grass of the earth, neither any green thing, neither any tree; but only those men which have not ʰthe seal of God in their foreheads.

ᵍ ch. viii. 7.
ʰ ch vii. 3. See Exod. xii. 23. Ezek ix. 4.

---

grass of the earth, neither any green thing." They have power, not as the natural locusts, whose power is to ravage the crops and green fields, but as the scorpions of the earth; that is, they have power of poisoning by their stings. As Williams writes: "They are 'as scorpions,' not merely as an armed multitude, but leaving behind the insidious poison of the second death in that ever-enduring part of man, the soul. . . . Not devouring only, but they had tails like unto scorpions, and stings in their tails, planting after their devastations a sting worse than death, as found in the undying spirit of man, which in vain, when bitten by that serpent, wishes to die; for this scorpion again is no scorpion, but partakes of the undying worm. Thus clear it is that this plague cannot be merely of devastating armies, nor of any spread of infidelity alone, but must be of both combined, and that too under very peculiar circumstances, such as attended the progress of the prophet-conqueror of Islam."

"But only those men which have not the seal of God in their foreheads." A question arises upon this, "What is the signification of this hurting?" It would seem that it is injury in a moral or religious point of view, for such is the hurting which is ascribed to these scorpion locusts. Their hurting as locusts, *i.e.*, by ravages of the countries which they conquer and overrun, is very subsidiary indeed to their hurting as scorpions. It is clear that this scorpion injury must be taken as symbolical of soul-poisoning, and if so, then the sealed of God were preserved from it by the impression of the Divine Seal. But such irruptions as those of the Saracens must have been attended with much human physical misery, and were the elect of God preserved from this? Alford lays it down that they could not have been so preserved, and he adduces this as the reason why we are not to understand the fifth trumpet vision of the irruptions of the Saracens, which he assumes to have been perfectly general in their injurious ravages—affecting good and bad alike. But surely God, Who could preserve His own from the evil represented by the scorpion stings, could equally preserve them

5 And to them it was given that they should not kill them, ¹but that they should be tormented five months: and their torment *was* as the torment of a scorpion, when he striketh a man.

¹ ch. xi. 7. ver. 10.

---

from the evils signified by their mouths armed with formidable teeth.

5. "And to them it was given that they should not kill them, but that they should be tormented five months: and their torment was as the torment of a scorpion, when he striketh a man." This has been interpreted, with some show of reason, that the Christians were not to be massacred, but put under tribute, and if they submitted to this and some other signs of subjection they should have the free use of their religion.

The following were, according to Elliot, the degrading conditions under which they were granted life. "Deprived of the use of arms, like the Helots of old, and with tribute enforced as their annual life-redemption tax; with a different dress enjoined them from their masters, and a more humble mode of riding; an obligation to rise up deferentially in the presence of the meanest Moslem, and to receive and gratuitously entertain for a certain time whosoever (Moslem) of them when on a journey might require it. They were prohibited from building new churches, or chiming the bells in those retained by them, and to refuse no admittance into them to the scoffing Moslem." I can scarcely think that such conditions can be described as men seeking death and not finding it.

"That they should be tormented five months." This place has given much difficulty to expositors. Taking the interpretation of the vision to be the Saracenic inroads, it would seem that the infliction on each person stung would be five months of acute pain, because this five months' torment is evidently contrasted with death. Those punished were not to be killed, but to be tormented five months.

What were these five months? Were they five months' pain to individual persons under the wrath of God, or was the duration of the plague from first to last five months? It could not be so short a time or it would scarcely have been worthy of such a place in this book of prophecy, and so it has been explained, as by Elliot, on the year-day principle, *i.e.*, three times five prophetic days, or one hundred and fifty years.

6 And in those days ᵏ shall men seek death, and shall not find it; and shall desire to die, and death shall flee from them.

7 And ˡ the shapes of the locusts *were* like unto horses prepared unto battle; ᵐ and on their heads

ᵏ Job iii. 21.
Isa. ii. 19.
Jer. viii. 3.
ch. vi. 16.
ˡ Joel ii. 4.
ᵐ Nahum iii. 17.

---

6. "Shall flee." So B. and most Cursives. A. P. read, "fleeth."

But the baleful ascendancy of Mahomedanism must have been longer than this. In fact, when can it be said really to have ended? The degradation and persecution of the Christians was carried on by the Turks professing the same religion.

It has been said that the "five months" is to be explained by the fact that the period of locusts is five months, and after that they perish, but this is no explanation whatsoever, though each expositor duly records it. The fact that a natural locust only exists five months does not undo the fact that every year they are renewed, and fresh myriads succeed them in their depredations.

6. "And in these days shall men seek death, and shall not find it; and shall desire to die, and death shall flee from them." Notice is drawn by many to the article, *the* "men shall seek death," &c., *i.e.*, the men who have not the seal of God on their foreheads, but inasmuch as such have been in all ages, to all appearance, the great majority, it seems that it is best to understand this of men in general, the plague will be almost universal on the godless world.

7. "And the shapes of the locusts were like unto horses prepared unto battle." Elliot gives an ingenious picture illustrative of the appearance of these locusts, which, however, can by no means be made to agree with the account given by the Evangelist. He draws a locust with a man's head and a scorpion's tail, but the two most salient points, the appearance of the horse ready to battle and the lion's teeth do not appear. A single glance at the picture and at the Apocalyptic description is sufficient to prove the futility of any such attempt. Every part of the description must be taken as symbolical. The horse prepared unto battle betokens vast armies of cavalry such as would be furnished by Arabia—said by naturalists to be the native country of the horse.

"And on their heads were as it were crowns of gold." This has

were as it were crowns like gold, ⁿ and their faces *were* as the faces of men.

ⁿ Dan. vii. 8.

8 And they had hair as the hair of women, and ^o their teeth were as *the teeth* of lions.

^o Joel i. 6.

9 And they had breastplates, as it were breastplates of iron; and the sound of their wings *was* ^p as the sound of chariots of many horses running to battle.

^p Joel ii. 5, 6, 7.

---

been said by Mr. Elliot to be the turbans of the Arabs, but a turban cannot possibly be put for a crown. Wordsworth, with more likelihood, understands these crowns as betokening victory. They were not kingly diadems.

"And their faces were as the faces of men." That is, they were not unreasoning creatures, whether locusts or horses, but had all human intelligence which is expressed by the human countenance. It may also mean that, though warlike and rapacious, they were not devoid of human feelings, they did not destroy or massacre indiscriminately.

8. "And they had hair as the hair of women." This may imply effeminacy. It is, however, actually true of the Arabs. The Arabians and Saracens are described by ancient writers as wearing their hair "long and flowing, and sometimes plaited, like women" (Ammian., Marcellin., xxxi. 18), where Valesius says "such was the costume of the Saracens, wearing their hair long and braided, hanging down on their backs, 'crinitis vittatisque capitibus'" (note in Bishop Wordsworth).

"And their teeth were as the teeth of lions." It might have been supposed that having been likened to locusts they would devour the crops, as do locusts, but, on the contrary, they have teeth wherewith to ravage and destroy all living things. They are withheld, it is true, from hurting those who are sealed with the seal of God, but all others which are not thus miraculously protected they may slay without mercy.

9. "And they had breastplates, as it were breastplates of iron." That is, they were fully armed with defensive armour as well as with offensive weapons.

"And the sound of their wings was as the sound of chariots of

10 And they had tails like unto scorpions, and there were stings in their tails: ⁹and their power *was* to hurt men five months.

⁹ ver. 5.

11 ʳAnd they had a king over them, *which is* ˢthe angel of the bottomless pit, whose name in

ʳ Eph. ii. 2.
ˢ ver. 1.

---

10. "And there were stings in their tails." Perhaps, "And stings, and in their tails is their power," ℵ, A., B.

many horses running to battle." This is a reminiscence of Joel ii. 5, "Like the noise of chariots on the tops of mountains shall they leap." It seems another indication of the hosts of cavalry on which this scourge of man would mainly rely.

10. "And they had tails like unto scorpions, and there were stings," &c. They not only slew and ravaged, but they left a poison behind them. This must have been some infidelity or heresy, for there is nothing in the outward or physical world that at all resembles it. Now in this the Saracenic irruptions were in contrast with others. The ravages of the Goths, for instance, were those of professing Christians, or who shortly became such, but the Saracens imposed their false religion on those whom they conquered (always excepting those who had been sealed by God). And their spiritual venom was the denial of the Divine Nature and Sonship of Jesus, and the Fatherhood of God. Worse errors could not be ; Christ as a prophet was, in their eyes, very inferior to Mahomet, and the future hopes of men were fixed on a sensual paradise.

"And their power was to hurt men five months." Here again we have the five months' injury. I confess I have seen no explanation in the least degree satisfactory.

11. "And they had a king over them, which is the angel of the bottomless pit, whose name in the Hebrew tongue is Abaddon. . . . Apollyon." In contrast with the natural locusts these multitudinous hordes have a king, and the king has the name of an evil angel. This is not said, as far as I can remember, of any other marauding hosts; showing that these hosts are not simply plunderers, but under demoniacal control, agents of the evil one, Antichrists, supernatural in their evil work, for that work is, if Mahomedanism, the denial of the Son of God.

"Whose name in the Hebrew tongue is Abaddon." In the Greek

the Hebrew tongue *is* Abaddon, but in the Greek tongue hath *his* name ‖ Apollyon.

‖ That is to say, *A destroyer.*

"Apollyon." This seems to fix his personality as one well known. If, as we gather from the book of Daniel, various angels of God have committed to them the guardianship of different kingdoms, it seems only natural that so marked an agency of evil as Mahomedanism should have its directing and informing evil spirit.

With respect to other interpretations Bishop Boyd-Carpenter, without speaking confidently, seems to lean to the same interpretation as that of Elliot, and Mede, and Wordsworth.

Alford seems to consider these locusts as something in the future: "The most that we can say of their import is that they belong to a series of judgments on the ungodly which will immediately precede the Second Advent of our Lord: that the various and mysterious particulars of the vision will no doubt clear themselves up to the Church when the time of its fulfilment arrives: but that no such clearing up has as yet taken place a very few hours of research among histories of Apocalyptic interpretation will serve to convince any reader who is not himself the servant of a preconceived system."

Milligan writes: "All application to the host of the Mahomedans may be at once dismissed. The woe fell upon the whole world, not merely upon a part of it, and it is not permitted to affect the redeemed Church. At the same time it cannot find its fulfilment in mere war, or in the calamities which war brings. The woe is obviously spiritual. It issues from the abyss of hell; the smoke of it darkens the air; the torment which accompanies it is not one that brings death, but that makes the soul weary of life. These circumstances point to a great outburst of spiritual evil which shall aggravate the sorrows of the world; make it learn how bitter is the bondage of Satan, and teach it to feel, even in the midst of enjoyment, that it were better to die than to live."

Archdeacon Farrar, as representing the preterists, is very vague as to whether in this general picture of the hosts of hell swarming out of the abyss there is any direct allusion to the Idumeans, Zealots, and Sicarii stinging themselves to death with untold anguish, like scorpions encircled by a ring of fire; or again, in the tumults, bloodshed and agonies of Rome, the frequency of suicide, and the many

12 'One woe is past; *and*, behold, there come two woes more hereafter.

ᵇ ch. viii. 13.

13 And the sixth angel sounded, and I heard a voice from the four horns of the golden altar which is before God,

---

13. "Four." So B.; but omitted by אᶜ, A.

tales of those who seemed to long for death in vain, cannot be affirmed. "The description of the scorpion-locusts evidently recalls the Egyptian plague, and the language of Joel, and the fanciful allusions to locusts which abound in the songs and proverbs of the East. The five months may point to the summer period, which is the time of locust plagues. But two circumstances seem to show that we are here dealing not with human avengers but with invisible demons of the air. One is, that the leader is the Demon Destroyer; the other is, that Christians, and Christians only, are expressly exempted from their power to hurt."

12. "One woe is past; and, behold, there come two woes more hereafter." By these words there seems to be signified that the incursions of the Arabs and their devastations have come to an end; but there is this difficulty about this interpretation, that though the Arab or Saracen conquests have come to an end, their tyranny over the subject races continues as before.

13. "And the sixth angel sounded, and I heard a voice from the four horns of the golden altar which is before God, saying to the sixth angel which had the trumpet, Loose the four angels," &c. There is a great contrast between the first effects of this sixth trumpet and that of the fifth. In the fifth a star falls from heaven, to whom is given the key of the abyss. This seems altogether an evil agent, whereas here the voice from the four horns of the altar which is before God must be holy and good.

And it commands the angel which sounded the sixth trumpet to "Loose the four angels which are bound." Mede, and after him Elliot, explains this as the Turkish woe following close upon the Saracenic.

Mede considers that the four angels are four Turkish sultanies, Bagdad, Cæsarea, Aleppo, and Damascus, between which the Turcoman power was at first divided. Elliot, however, holds that there was no such fourfold division acting for evil on the Greek

14 Saying to the sixth angel which had the trumpet, Loose the four angels which are bound ᵘ in the   ᵘ ch. xvi. 12. great river Euphrates.

15 And the four angels were loosed, which were prepared ‖ for an hour, and a day, and a   ‖ Or, *at.* month, and a year, for to slay the third part of men.

Empire, but that the action of the angel in loosing these four is to be considered as one; no reason being assigned for the angels loosed being numbered as four except, perhaps, as representing the four quarters of the globe, north, south, east, and west.

He considers that the Turcoman power dated its commencement from the time that the Caliph of Bagdad called Togrul Bey to his assistance in quelling some intestine factions, and from this time the Turcomans took the lead as the head of Mahomedan powers, superseding altogether the Arabians or Saracens. He endeavours to show that from this time to the taking of Constantinople the Turks may well be represented as one people, united in one paramount design of humbling Christendom.

15. "And the four angels were loosed, which were prepared for an [the] hour, and a day, and a month, and a year, for to slay the third part of men." This hour, day, month, and year are calculated on the year-day system (a year for a day, 365 years + 30 years) to constitute a period of about 395 years (roughly); I say roughly, because there is a difference amongst expositors whether we are to take the year to be 360 or $365\frac{1}{4}$; and the period between this assumed commencement of the Turkish power and the taking of Constantinople is about 395 years. The siege began on January 18th, A.D. 1453, and the city was taken May 29th of the same year.

"To slay the third part of men." This seems to me to upset, or to render beyond measure uncertain, the whole of the preceding calculation; for how could the taking of Constantinople, even if every human being in it was massacred, be the destruction of the third part of men. Elliot falls back upon the division I have before alluded to, of the Roman Empire being divided into three parts, the Eastern empire constituting one of them; but surely one must ask, "Was Constantinople inhabited by a third of the whole Greek

16 And the ˣnumber of the army ʸof the horsemen *were* two hundred thousand thousand: ᶻand I heard the number of them.

17 And thus I saw the horses in the vision, and them that sat on them, having breastplates of fire, and of jacinth, and brimstone: ᵃand the

ˣ Ps. lxviii. 17.
Dan. vii. 10.
ʸ Eze. xxxviii. 4.
ᶻ ch. vii. 4.
ᵃ 1 Chr. xii. 8.
Isa. v. 28, 29.

---

part of the Roman Empire?" We have no right to say or to assume anything of the sort.

16. "And the number of the army of the horsemen were two hundred thousand thousand: and I heard the number of them." Two hundred thousand thousand would be two hundred millions. There is now not an army in the world, except, perhaps, the Russian, that reaches a million. There must be some mistake in the figures if it is a human army whose numbers are asserted to be so great, for the population of the world was far less then than it is now.[1]

17. "And thus I saw the horses in the vision, and them that sat on them, having breastplates of fire, and of jacinth, and brimstone: and the heads of the horses were as the heads of lions." Were these what is usually understood by breastplates? It would seem so from the Apostle's account; but Mede, and those who follow him, understand by these breastplates of fire, smoke, and brimstone the mouths of the huge cannon which were brought to bear upon the devoted city of Constantinople, by which breaches were made in its hitherto impregnable walls, and the Turks entered

---

[1] Elliot, citing Danbury, thinks that there may be probably an allusion also in the form of expression to the Turcoman custom of numbering by tomans or myriads. For though not unused among other nations, yet there is probably none with whom it has been from early times so prevalent as with the Turcomans and Tartars. Thus in the Seljukian age, if I remember right, the population of Samarcand was rated at seven tomans because it could send out 70,000 horsemen warriors. Again, the dignity and rank of Tamerlane's father and grandfather was thus described: "that they were the hereditary chiefs of a toman of 10,000 horse." So that it is not without his usual propriety of language that Gibbon speaks of the myriads of the Seljukian Turks; Turkish horse overspreading the Greek frontier from the Taurus to Erzeroum; or of the cavalry of the earlier Turks of Mount Altai "having both men and horses proudly computed by millions." But all this is beside the mark, for St. John says that he heard the number as 200,000,000, and afterwards repeats it as it were, "And I heard the number of them."

heads of the horses *were* as the heads of lions; and out of their mouths issued fire and smoke and brimstone.

18 By these three was the third part of men killed, by the fire, and by the smoke, and by the brimstone, which issued out of their mouths.

19 For their power is in their mouth, and in their tails:

---

19. "For their power;" or, "the power of the horses," ℵ, B, C.

through the breaches and took the city. These of course poured out of their mouths fire, smoke, and brimstone.

"And the heads of the horses were as the heads of lions." Elliot notices that some of the first Turkish leaders or generals took the very name of lions, thus "Oluf (or Olf) Arslan" signifies valiant lion; but taking such a name scarcely seems a fitting accomplishment of the prediction, "the heads of the horses were as the heads of lions," we should rather look for an analogy in the account of the preceding woe-trumpet, "their teeth were as the teeth of lions."

"And out of their mouths issued fire and smoke and brimstone." Not, as in the preceding verse, jacinth and brimstone, but smoke and brimstone; but the jacinth seems to indicate the blue flame of the sulphur.

Such is the meaning of this vision according to the historical interpreters, at least the principal, as Mede and Elliot. I cannot help regarding it as exceedingly unsatisfactory. For consider, the four angels unloose an army of two hundred millions of horsemen somewhere near Bagdad. Their mission is to take the city of Constantinople. They make use of artillery which vomits fire and brimstone at this siege, not during the four hundred years of their previous ravages. So that this figure of the horsemen and these riders is only true of the last days of their career (I mean so far as the Apocalyptic vision is concerned). They thus fulfil their commission in destroying the third part of men; but is it likely that the city of Constantinople should symbolize the third part of men?

19. "For their power is in their mouth, and in their tails: for their tails were like unto serpents, and had heads." If this refers to artillery, then the tail is that part to which the fire is applied, and the head is, of course, the orifice from which the ball is

ᵇ for their tails *were* like unto serpents, and had heads, and
with them they do hurt.

ᵇ Isa. ix. 15.

---

propelled by the fire and brimstone, but this is exceedingly unsatisfactory.

"For their tails were like unto serpents, and had heads," &c. I confess that I do not see in the least what this means. Looking to the analogy of the last plague (locusts with the poisonous stings of scorpions in their tails), it would seem to indicate some moral or religious poison; and if the Saracens diffused the poison of false religion, so would the Turks, rather much more.

I cannot gather from Bengel's "Gnomon" what are his views. The only clue that I can find is that the hour, day, month, and year is "a period of about 207 years, from A.D. 629 to 836, or from A.D. 634 to 840, that is from the last time of Abubeker to the death of Motassem."

Williams, without giving anything definite, rejects the usual historical interpretation: "Indeed the mere number (two hundred millions) would preclude any private interpretation, for it could neither be the early persecutors, with Berengardus, nor the Roman army, with Dr. Hammond, nor the Turkish, with Mede. 'I heard their number,' says St. John, as he had also that of the Redeemed, but that number is put for what is almost without number, two myriads of myriads."

Bishop Boyd-Carpenter makes some good, but very general remarks: "We have these horses, which are mighty, malicious, and relentless, and which are bidden forth against mankind for their sins and worldliness (see verses 20-21). It is not once only in the history of the world that such powers have been let loose. The desolations wrought by invading hordes; the force and ferocity of Turkish power establishing itself in Europe, and threatening the powers of Christendom; the widespread terror and slaughter promoted by the outbreak of the spirit of unrestrained violence in France, followed by reckless war, may illustrate such a vision as the present; but the main teaching of it is the never-failing truth that the spirit of worldliness provokes its own punishment, wherever it may exist; and its retribution is in a form which serves to reveal what latent power of destruction lurks behind every sin, and what hidden spiritual foes there are to intensify human passions and to increase human misery."

There is nothing definite in the remarks of Alford or of Milligan. Todd, however, has a remark that deserves notice: "Again it must be observed that the four angels are said to have been bound at or in the river Euphrates, and we are therefore probably to look to that region as the scene of this great judgment; inasmuch as the prophecy seems distinctly to assert that from thence shall issue the great multitude of horsemen who are to be the instruments of the predicted massacre, wherein the third part of men shall be slain. This conclusion is in exact conformity with the inference to which, in a former course of lectures, we were led from a consideration of the prophecies of Daniel, namely, that the countries in the region of the Euphrates, once the seat of such mighty empires, are destined at some future period to recover their political power, and to become the scene of the last great struggle between the princes of the world and the people of God" (pp. 151, 152).

I have reserved to the last what appears to me by far the strangest exposition, and that by one of the most learned and godly of commentators, Bishop Wordsworth. Comparing this vision of the sixth trumpet with the opening of the fifth, he says that the comparison necessitates that this trumpet-vision should be from God, not in the same way in which all things are from God, the good directly from Him, and the evil controlled by Him so as to bring about the fulfilment of His purposes, but from God in the sense in which the preaching of the Gospel itself is from God. He compares the fifth woe-trumpet as involving evil, or, indeed, diabolical agency, being a star fallen from heaven, and opening the mouth of the bottomless pit with this trumpet-vision, which is inaugurated by a voice from between the four horns of the golden altar which is before God commanding these angels to be loosed. The angels which were bound he considers to be the Word of God (represented by the four Gospels), each angel representing a Gospel, which was bound by being shut up in dead languages. He holds the unloosing to be the translation of the Scriptures into all the languages of the known world, and its diffusion (as it might be by the agency of the Bible Society, though he does not mention such an agency). He answers the objection that an army from God could not be represented as killing men by fire, and smoke,

20 And the rest of the men which were not killed by these plagues ᶜyet repented not of the works of their hands, that they should not worship ᵈdevils, ᵉand idols of gold, and silver, and brass, and stone, and of wood: which neither can see, nor hear, nor walk:

ᶜ Deut. xxxi. 29.
ᵈ Lev. xvii. 7. Deut. xxxii. 17. Ps. cvi. 37. 1 Cor. x. 20.
ᵉ Ps. cxv. 4. & cxxxv. 15. Dan. v. 23.

---

and brimstone proceeding out of their mouths to destroy men, by citing the words of Ps. xviii.: "There went up a smoke out of his nostrils, and fire out of his mouth devoured: coals were kindled by it." When it is objected that the Word of God could not well be compared to a serpent, he appeals to the fact that Moses's rod—which might well be taken to represent the Bible, Moses having written its first five books—was changed into a serpent: "The very badge of office of the Hebrew legislator, the instrument by which Moses wrought his miracles, by which God punished His enemies and delivered His people, was changed into a serpent. This was its first appearance, and it is added 'Moses fled from before it' (Exod. iv. 3). But God commanded him to take hold of it by its *tail* [the italics are Bishop Wordsworth's], in which is the serpent's sting (? ?), and which is noted in this vision as noxious to God's enemies (v. 19); and Moses 'put forth his hand, and caught it, and it became a rod in his hand.' Thus it was shown that God's faithful servants (Heb. iii. 2-5, 'Moses was faithful in all his house') can take hold of and handle that which is destructive to his adversaries, and that they can work wonders with it. This was a very significant emblem of Holy Scripture, the first books of which were written by him who bore the rod of power which became a serpent."

And with respect to the trumpet being a woe-trumpet, he adds, "This vision inculcates an important religious and moral truth. It reminds us that the present diffusion of the Scriptures may be a terrible woe to those who do not attend to them."

20, 21. "And the rest of the men .... nor of their thefts." These verses show that this second woe must take place before the time of the end, because after it had been inflicted there was time for repentance, which, however, was not acted upon: those plagued continuing as impenitent as ever. This woe of the

21 Neither repented they of their murders, 'nor of their sorceries, nor of their fornication, nor of their thefts. ᶠ ch. xxii. 15.

Turkish invasion was one inflicted on the East, and yet Mr. Elliot considers that it was intended for the West, because the thefts were the robbing of men by religious delusions such as the supposed sanctity of the bones of saints, and the miracles falsely supposed to be performed by their means.

CHAP. X.

AND I saw another mighty angel come down from heaven, clothed with a cloud: ᵃ and a rainbow *was* ᵃ Ezek. i. 28.

---

1. "And a rainbow." א, A., B., C. read, "And the rainbow."

We are yet under the sixth trumpet, as the account of the seventh trumpet sounding is in verse 15 of the eleventh chapter; but the tenth and the first part of the eleventh chapter contain two episodes, as they have been called, rather they should have been designated intermediate visions—the mighty angel holding the little book, and the two witnesses.

The first of these has been described as the inauguration of St. John to deliver prophecies of a (supposed) more sacred character, having to do more especially with the fortunes and conflicts of the Church, and not judgments on the outer world.

1. "And I saw another mighty angel come down from heaven, clothed with a cloud: and a rainbow was upon his head." Very many expositors (perhaps the majority) consider this angel to be the vision of the Lord Jesus Himself. They say how can such glories as are here ascribed to Him be said without blasphemy of any creature.

"Clothed with a cloud." Reference is made to the cloud of the Shechinah; to the words of the Psalmist, "clouds and darkness are round about him;" to the Lord appearing to the Israelites under

upon his head, and ᵇhis face *was* as it were the sun, and ᶜhis feet as pillars of fire:

ᵇ Matt. xvii. 2. ch. i. 16.
ᶜ ch. i. 15.

---

a pillar of cloud by day; to the Lord on His Ascension being received by a cloud out of the sight of the Apostles.

"And a rainbow was upon his head." "Can any created angel," they ask, "have such a thing about his head seeing that the throne of God is said to be encompassed with a rainbow like unto an emerald?" (iv. 3).

And again, "His face was as it were the sun." They remind us of the Transfiguration, when the Lord's face shone as the sun, but they forget what the Lord said of the glorious appearance of His people in the future state, "Then shall the righteous shine forth as the sun in the kingdom of their Father" (Matt. xiii. 43).

"And his feet as pillars of fire." We are reminded of Rev. i. 15, "And his feet like unto fine brass, as if they burned in a furnace."

But, notwithstanding all this, I cannot conceive that this is a vision of the Lord, for could He possibly be designated as *another* mighty angel. It may be conceivable that He should be designated as an angel in the words, "The angel of the covenant," but not as another angel—one out of many. Then there is, to me, another overwhelming reason. When St. John in the first vision of this book saw the Lord, it is said that "he fell at his feet as dead" (i. 17), though he had lain in His bosom, but nothing of this extreme awe is hinted at here. Without the least intimation of fear the Apostle goes up to this angel and asks him for the book in his hand, which is given him to eat. Alford rightly, I think, says, "Such a supposition (that the Lord Himself was the angel) entirely breaks through the consistency of Apocalyptic analogy. Throughout the book . . . angels are the ministers of the Divine purposes, and the carriers out of the Apocalyptic course of procedure, but are everywhere distinct from the Divine Persons themselves. In order to this their ministry with such symbols and such delegated attributes as beseem in each case the particular object in view; but no apparent fitness of such symbolic investiture to the Divine character should induce us to break through the distinction. When St. John means to indicate the Son of God he indicates Him plainly, none more so."

There is, however, much to be learnt from what is said of this

2 And he had in his hand a little book open: ᵈ and he set his right foot upon the sea, and *his* left *foot* on the earth,

ᵈ Matt. xxviii. 18.

3 And cried with a loud voice, as *when* a lion roareth: and when he had cried, ᵉ seven thunders uttered their voices.

ᵉ ch. viii. 5.

---

angel. His appearance and attributes seem to be Divine, but after all he is but a creature, and, as other holy creatures do, he swears by his Creator. In such a vision as this we learn the power of God. What creatures He can make to serve His purposes. In the almost seeming Divine attributes of this exalted being there is but a faint reflection of the attributes of God. No matter how Divine all about him seems, he is at an infinite distance from God.

2. "And he had in his hand a little book." Why a little book? This book is a little one (so many hold) as compared with the sealed roll in the hand of Him Who sat on the throne. It contains only a part of what is written therein, which St. John had now to make known (verse 11).

"And he set his right foot upon the sea, and his left foot on the earth." That is, as one taking possession of the whole globe—sea and land. Bishop Wordsworth writes: "His feet are fully planted in the sea, the third element, denoting nations in a state of turbulence and agitation, for He will tread beneath His feet the swelling surge of human pride and passion as He walked on the waves of the sea of Galilee in the storm; and His feet are set on the earth, the emblem of worldly power opposed to the kingdom of God."

3. "And cried with a loud voice, as when a lion roareth." As it is not recorded what the purport of this loud cry was, it has been supposed, with some appearance of reason, that his cry, like the sound of the trumpet, was a summons to the thunders to utter their voices.

The thunders seem to utter their voices in response to the voice of this mighty angel.

The article should be translated, "The seven thunders uttered their voices," as if they were seven well-known thunders, or as if they were part of the consecutive visions of this book (seven seals,

4 And when the seven thunders had uttered their voices, I was about to write: and I heard a voice from heaven saying unto me, ᶠSeal up those things which the seven thunders uttered, and write them not.

5 And the angel which I saw stand upon the sea and upon the earth ᵍlifted up his hand to heaven,

ᶠ Dan. viii. 26. & xii. 4, 9.

ᵍ Exod. vi. 8. Dan. xii. 7.

---

4. "Their voices" omitted by ℵ, A., B., C., P., Cursives, and most versions.
5. "His hand." ℵ, B., C., P., most Cursives, &c., read, "his right hand."

seven trumpets, seven vials), only what they uttered is not recorded.

4. "And when the seven thunders had uttered their voices, I was about to write: and I heard a voice from heaven saying unto me, Seal up those things," &c. That these thunders were not like ordinary thunders, but voices uttering articulate sounds, and communicating to the Apostle a revelation, which was perhaps a necessary part of his preparation for the prophetic office, is evident from his having been about to write what they made known unto him, and from the voice which said unto him, "Seal up those things which the seven thunders uttered, and write them not."

They were intelligible because St. John was on the point of writing them, but he was forbidden by a voice from heaven to write them because men were not prepared to receive them. And yet they are not lost. They are sealed up now, but the seal will be broken in God's good time, and they will then be revealed.

It seems incredible to think what a devout Christian man has written about these thunders: that they were the anathema of the Pope Leo X. in Luther's time; that they were sevenfold because Rome is the city built upon the seven hills, and he even draws attention to the seven thunders uttering their own voices (τὰς ἑαυτῶν φωνάς) as being their own and not God's. It seems wonderful to me that any man should have written such an interpretation, then having written it should have corrected the impression, and then published five or six editions of it.

5, 6. "And the angel which I saw stand upon the sea and upon the earth lifted up his hand to heaven, and sware by him that liveth for ever and ever, who created heaven, and the things that therein are,"

6 And sware by him that liveth for ever and ever, [b] who created heaven, and the things that therein are, and the earth, and the things that therein are, and the sea, and the things which are therein, [i] that there should be time no longer:

7 But [k] in the days of the voice of the seventh angel, when he shall begin to sound, the mystery of God should be finished, as he hath declared to his servants the prophets.

[b] Neh. ix. 6. ch. iv. 11. & xiv. 7.

[i] Dan. xii. 7. ch. xvi. 17.

[k] ch. xi. 15.

---

7. "The mystery of God should be finished." Rather, "Then is finished the mystery of God."

&c. This oath has been supposed to refer to what was said to the souls of the martyrs, that they should "rest for a little season" (vi. 11). But why should it be given to the angel to take this solemn oath? Perhaps for this reason, that the consummation had been long delayed, but now it was near at hand; an end was to be put at last to the weary conflict between sin and evil on the one side, and between righteousness and truth on the other.

The angel seems to swear as the representative of the Divine Being. He recounts the mighty empire of that Being, heaven and all that is therein, angels, principalities, and powers; the earth and all that is therein, its kings, generals, armies, senates, every bondman and every free; the sea which seems to swallow up all that are engulfed in it, but they are all known to God, and the sea shall give up its dead.

"That there should be time no longer."

7. "But in the days of the voice of the seventh angel." This has been explained by some as if he sware that time was coming to an end, and eternity now beginning to set in; but we should rather understand it as if there should be no more delay, but in the days of the seventh angel the mystery of God should be finished. The account of the sounding of the seventh trumpet is undoubtedly the account (or rather one account, for there are seven in this book) of the final consummation (see xi. 15).

"The mystery of God." Everything that God is, not only His existence as a Trinity in Unity, but His Omnipotence, Omniscience, His Omnipresence, and all His doings, His plans, His toleration of

8 And ¹ the voice which I heard from heaven spake unto me again, and said, Go *and* take the little book which is open in the hand of the angel which standeth upon the sea and upon the earth.

9 And I went unto the angel, and said unto him, Give me the little book. And he said unto me, ᵐ Take *it*, and eat it up; and it shall make thy belly bitter, but it shall be in thy mouth sweet as honey.

¹ ver. 4.

ᵐ Jer. xv. 16.
Ezek. ii. 8. &
iii. 1, 2, 3.

---

evil, His making evil which He hates work out His own purposes of grace—all are mysteries; but inasmuch as it is said here that when the seventh angel sounds the mystery of God shall be finished, it is more than probable that the mystery of God here is His toleration of evil, and His making it subservient to His purposes.

As He hath declared unto His servants the prophets, particularly we may say in Daniel xii., where the "man clothed in linen . . . . held up his right hand and his left unto heaven, and sware by him that liveth for ever, that it shall be for a time, times, and an half," &c.

8. "And the voice which I heard from heaven spake unto me again, and said, Go and take the little book which is open in the hand of the angel," &c. This little book is open, not sealed, as was the roll of ch. v. 1, which seems to show that its contents were known to the Apostle. We shall afterwards have to consider what it contained.

9, 10. "And I went unto the angel, and said unto him, Give me the little book. And he said unto me, Take it, and eat it up; and it shall make thy belly bitter . . . . my belly was bitter." There is but one place in Scripture parallel to this, Ezekiel iii. 1, but there is this seeming difference, that in Ezekiel the prophet, as he is commanded, eats the roll, and tastes only its extreme sweetness, but here the Apostle finds it sweet in his mouth but bitter in his belly, but it has been noticed that when the prophet went forth to fulfil his commission he went "in bitterness, in the heat of his spirit" (Ezek. iii. 14).

It seems agreed upon by most commentators that the contents

10 And I took the little book out of the angel's hand, and ate it up; ⁿ and it was in my mouth sweet as honey: and as soon as I had eaten it, ᵒ my belly was bitter.

ⁿ Ezek. iii. 3.

ᵒ Ezek. ii. 10.

---

of this little roll in the angel's hand are the succeeding prophecies. St. John is commanded to eat them; that is, to make them his own, to thoroughly digest them, to assimilate them, as the modern expression is.

But how is it that the after-effect of the words eaten is bitter, though at first sweet. Bishop Boyd-Carpenter seems well to express this. "The flaming zeal to emancipate mankind from thraldoms to other and ruinous sins may stir the soul with a holy joy, but there come moments when men are almost tempted to turn back, and to think that they have undertaken a hopeless task, when they find how slow is their progress, and what new and unexpected difficulties arise. Such was the bitterness which Moses felt. 'Why is it that thou hast sent me, for since I came to Pharaoh to speak in thy name, he hath done evil to this people, neither hast thou delivered thy people at all.' The most enthusiastic souls, who love their fellow-men, and who feel how sacred and high is their calling, perhaps feel most of this bitterness. Their very love makes all failures bitter to them, yet it is through this martyrdom of failure that the noblest victories are won."

We have now to consider an interpretation of this vision widely differing from any I have mentioned—which is that of Mr. Elliot. He interprets this vision of the mighty angel as predicting the Lord Himself appearing at the time of the Reformation to make, as it were, a new beginning of Christianity. He considers the little book in His hand to be the Bible, or, at least, the New Testament, which began then, as he (Mr. Elliot) supposes, to be studied for the first time. He considers the Apostle St. John to represent the Reformed Ministry, especially Martin Luther, the head of it all. He looks upon Luther in prison in a lonesome castle of the Wartzburg forest as the fulfilment, as it were, of St. John's imprisonment in Patmos. "Indeed, Luther himself has unconsciously, and in a somewhat singular manner, marked the resemblance. In his correspondence, the appellation by which he was wont to designate this his place of imprisonment and exile was that of his Patmos."

K

11 And he said unto me, Thou must prophesy again before many peoples, and nations, and tongues, and kings.

---

11. "He said." ℵ, A., B. read, "they said" (λέγουσίν).

It follows, "'And the voice said, Go, take the little book out of the angel's hand.' This signifies that the chief occupation of Luther during his year of exile was the translation of the New Testament into the vernacular German."

But, further than this, Mr. Elliot considers that the angel having the little book in his hand, and giving it to St. John, was a sort of presentiment of the change made in the Office of Ordination at the period of the Reformation. He allows that in the pre-Reformation rite the volume of the four Gospels was given in the Ordination of Deacons, but this seems to be undone by the delivery at the Ordination of Priests of the chalice and paten into the hands of the person ordained. This being now superseded in the Reformed bodies by the delivery of the Bible, marks the significance of the change between the Old and the New Ordination. Christ personally, under the appearance of the angel, sets aside all mere Apostolic succession, and now Himself ordains the Reformed ministers, just as He ordained the Apostles at the first. In fact the Reformation was not only a new departure, but a supersession by Christ Himself of all historical Christianity, everything before Luther's time having become Antichrist: not only Antichristian, but Antichrist himself.

I do not think I have misrepresented the views of Mr. Elliot. I have compressed, and I think without exaggeration, the substance of what he writes respecting this vision in vol. ii. of his "Horæ Apocalypticæ." I shall further on treat at some length the reference of the Apocalypse to mediæval Christianity.

CHAP. XI.

AND there was given me ᵃa reed like unto a rod: and the angel stood, saying, ᵇ Rise, and measure the temple of God, and the altar, and them that worship therein.

ᵃ Ezek. xl. 3, &c. Zech. ii. 1. ch. xxi. 15.
ᵇ Numb. xxiii. 18.

---

1. "And there was given me a reed like unto a rod: and the angel stood, saying, Rise, and measure the temple of God, and the altar, and them that worship therein. But the court . . . . tread under foot forty and two months." We are now entering upon what has been pronounced by many expositors, as Alford, to be the most difficult vision of this book. The details of the prophetical revelation are so circumstantial that I do not see that, having reverence for the Word of God, they are to be expounded in a general way, as if they meant general moral or evangelical truths, and yet nothing has hitherto occurred in the history of the world or of the Church which seems in the least degree to correspond to them. I will, God helping, take three expositions which make a fair attempt to particularize the various incidents in the vision, as relating to things which may occur, or have occurred, in this outward world of time and sense, and set them before the reader.

The first is that of Dr. Todd in his "Donnellan Lectures," preached before the University of Dublin.

The second that of Bishop Wordsworth in his commentary.

The third that of Mr. Elliot in his "Horæ Apocalypticæ."

Dr. Todd considers that the interpretation of this vision (xi. 1-15) lies in the future, and before I had read his lecture I had made up my mind that such a view was most probably the true one, because much in the vision indicates that its fulfilment will take place "near the end," as immediately upon the conclusion of this vision the end comes, and is said to come quickly (*i.e.* "the third woe cometh quickly").

The vision is founded upon one in the prophecy of Zechariah,

2 But ᶜthe court which is without the temple ⳨ leave out, and measure it not; ᵈfor it is given unto the Gentiles: and the holy city shall they ᵉtread under foot ᶠforty *and* two months.

ᶜ Ezek xl. 17, 20.
† Gr. *cast out*.
ᵈ Ps. lxxix. 1. Luke xxi. 24.
ᵉ Dan. viii. 10.
ᶠ ch. xiii. 5.

---

which it may be well to give in full (Zech. ii. 1), " I lifted up mine eyes again, and looked, and behold a man with a measuring line in his hand. Then said I, Whither goest thou? And he said unto me, To measure Jerusalem, to see what is the breadth thereof, and what is the length thereof. And, behold, the angel that talked with me went forth, and another angel went out to meet him. And said unto him, Run, speak to this young man, saying, Jerusalem shall be inhabited as towns without walls for the multitude of men and cattle therein. For I, saith the Lord, will be unto her a wall of fire round about, and will be the glory in the midst of her."

Now this remarkable vision teaches two things. First, that Jerusalem shall not be circumscribed by walls, that is, it shall be illimitable. There are to be no hindrances to its extending itself on every side, as a circumscribing wall would be, and yet it will be infinitely better protected without walls, for " the Lord will be unto her a wall of fire round about." If we are to be guided by this vision, then the part measured will be also immense, capable of holding all that will take refuge in it; in fact, in the highest sense Catholic, and yet, notwithstanding this, there will be a part unmeasured by the Apostle, because profane; it is given to the Gentiles. And so the holy city will be trodden under foot.

Now what is this Jerusalem, and what are the Gentiles which will tread it under foot. It has been supposed to be the Church with its two kinds of members, sincere Christians who have through faith access to the presence of God, Who dwells in the Holy of Holies between the Cherubim, and have access to the altar at which through the same faith they offer up spiritual sacrifices of praise and intercession, but who in the latter days will be afflicted by the persecutions of false apostate Christians who will be under the rule of antichrist: or it has been supposed to be the restored temple of the Jews, which we have reason to believe will be rebuilt in Jerusalem itself before the Second Advent and the con-

3 And ‖ I will give *power* unto my two [g] witnesses, [h] and they shall prophesy [i] a thousand two hundred *and* threescore days, clothed in sackcloth.

4 These are the [k] two olive trees, and the two candlesticks standing before the God of the earth.

‖ Or, *I will give unto my two witnesses that they may prophesy.*
[g] ch. xx. 4.
[h] ch. xix. 10.
[i] ch. xii. 6.
[k] Ps. lii. 8. Jer. xi. 16. Zech. iv. 3, xi. 14.

---

4. "God." ℵ, A., B., C. read, "Lord."

summation, and in this case, *i.e.*, on this explanation, the court which is without, which is to be left unmeasured, will be the court of the restored temple, which will be under the power of Antichrist.

If the vision had ended with verse 2, I think we should have unhesitatingly classed this description of the temple and its measuring with those many intimations of Scripture which speak of the divided state of the visible Church, but the difficulty is in the remainder of this vision, beginning:

3. "I will give power unto my two witnesses, and they shall prophesy a thousand two hundred and threescore days, [forty and two months] clothed in sackcloth." Now these two witnesses have not been mentioned, and yet they are brought on the scene as if they were well known (τοῖς δυσὶ μάρτυσί μου). But we are immediately referred for some account of them to another part of the prophecy of Zechariah: "These are the two olive trees and the two candlesticks standing before the God of the earth." When we turn to Zechariah iv., we find that he sees a "candlestick all of gold, with a bowl upon the top of it, and his seven lamps thereon, and seven pipes to the seven lamps, which are upon the top thereof. And two olive trees by it, one upon the right side of the bowl, and the other upon the left side thereof." And, when he asks the meaning, a message is sent to Zerubbabel, "Not by might, nor by power, but by my Spirit, saith the Lord of hosts." And when he further asks the meaning of the two olive trees, and the two olive branches which through the two golden pipes empty the golden oil out of themselves, he is answered, "These are the two anointed ones, that stand by the Lord of the whole earth" (Zech. iv. 14).

It is clear, then, that we must look to the older prophecy in

5 And if any man will hurt them, ¹fire proceedeth out of their mouth, and devoureth their enemies: ᵐand if any man will hurt them, he must in this manner be killed.

6 These ⁿ have power to shut heaven, that it rain not in the days of their prophecy: and ᵒ have power over waters to turn them to blood, and to smite the earth with all plagues, as often as they will.

¹ 2 Kings i. 10, 12. Jer. i. 10. & v. 14. Ezek. xliii. 3. Hos. vi. 5.
ᵐ Numb. xvi. 29.
ⁿ 1 Kings xvii. 1. James v. 16, 17.
ᵒ Exod. vii. 19.

Zechariah, and we get no assistance from it to enable us to identify the persons, if they are persons, here mentioned; but we are taught this, that these two witnesses are not two earthly witnesses, but two heavenly ones which enlighten the innermost Church with supernatural light. The olive trees which stand alongside of these two candlesticks are evidently supernatural beings. They supply the candlestick which lights the sanctuary of God with a never-failing supply of that which by means of the candlestick gives light—evidently enlightening grace. And they do this in a way evidently miraculous. Who ever heard of an olive tree yielding its oil without the intervention of the olive press. So that the power by which these witnesses instruct, or enlighten, or edify the Church, is in the highest sphere of the supernatural.

In this respect they are not ordinary witnesses, even such as St. John the Baptist, or an Apostle might be.

But we now proceed to what more distinctly witnesses to their supernatural place as instruments of God.

5. "If any man will hurt them, fire proceedeth out of their mouth, and devoureth their enemies: and if any man will hurt them, he must," &c. We are here, of course, reminded of Elijah, whose voice called down fire from heaven, and destroyed the messengers of the idolatrous king.

6. "These have power to shut heaven, that it rain not in the days of their prophecy: and have power over waters to turn them to blood." Here we have another power which Elijah exercised—the power of stopping the rain from heaven, and bringing on a long and grievous famine; and another power exercised by Moses,

7 And when they ᵖ shall have finished their testimony, ᑫ the beast that ascendeth ʳ out of the bottomless pit ˢ shall make war against them, and shall overcome them, and kill them.

ᵖ Luke xiii. 32.
ᑫ ch. xiii. 1, 11. & xvii. 8.
ʳ ch. ix. 2.
ˢ Dan. vii. 21. Zech xiv. 2.

---

the greatest of Jewish prophets, over waters, to turn them into blood, "and to smite the earth with all plagues, as often as they will."

No prophets since the times of Moses and Elias have so acted in the power of God. These were works of protection or of vengeance, but the mighty works done by the Apostles were not of this kind, or done with this intent. They were all done for the purpose of commending the Gospel to men's notice by mighty deeds exemplifying the power of the Gospel to heal and restore rather than to destroy its enemies, or to deliver its preachers out of the hands of those that sought their lives.

I repeat, no witnesses of God have had such powers for such purposes, and the explanations given of the exercise of these powers have been utterly inadequate. They have been more or less rationalistic. When it is said, for instance, in the Apocalypse, that "fire proceedeth out of their mouths and destroyeth their enemies," and that this only means that God will visit with the fire of His anger those who neglect His word by *whomsoever* spoken, it is clear that there is nothing peculiar in the enforcement of this threat more than what accompanies any threat against those who disobey the Word, written or preached. All men, everywhere, who resist the Gospel, do it at the peril of their eternal well-being. We proceed:

7. "And when they shall have finished their testimony." This surely cannot mean their testimony to the truth of the ordinary Gospel proclaimed by its thousands upon thousands of preachers. It must, I think, be some message peculiar to these two prophets. Hitherto their lives have been by God's special power preserved in the midst of a society or kingdom very hostile. Now they seem to be deprived of the special miraculous protection, and take their place for a very short time amongst the ordinary servants of God.

"The beast that ascendeth out of the bottomless pit shall make

> 8 And their dead bodies *shall lie* in the street of ᵗthe great city, which spiritually is called Sodom and Egypt, ᵘwhere also our Lord was crucified.

ᵗ ch. xiv. 8. & xvii. 1, 5. & xviii. 10.
ᵘ Heb. xiii. 12. ch. xviii. 24.

---

war against them, and shall overcome them, and kill them." That so fearful an evil power as the wild beast—the "therion"—should make war against these two witnesses, as if they were two mighty kingdoms, shows their extremely high place in the spiritual world.

8. "And their dead bodies shall lie in the street of the great city, which spiritually is called Sodom and Egypt, where also our Lord was crucified." What is signified by the "dead bodies" of these witnesses? It must be that which was once instinct with life—a life worthy of being the life of two such witnesses for God—but now deprived of it. In this they are in contrast with the first martyrs, whose remains were eagerly sought and treasured up, and perhaps in later times entombed in the altars of churches. No explanation has been given of all this but that which is utterly inadequate, as we shall see when we come to the two other expositions which I have promised.

"In the street of the great city," *i.e.*, in the broad street or broadway.

"The great city, which spiritually is called Sodom and Egypt." Sodom on account of its debasing wickedness, and Egypt because of its oppression of the true people of God.

"Where also our Lord was crucified." This seems to identify the city with Jerusalem. If the crucifixion is the literal crucifixion, then, of course, no other place can be meant; if, however, we are to interpret this place in the light of that saying of St. Paul where he says of fallen Christians, "that they crucify the Son of God afresh," then, wherever in the whole world there are churches which contain mere nominal Christians as well as true ones, our Lord is there crucified. It is in this sense quite as true of London as it is of Rome, or any Jerusalem which may be built on the site of the old one.

9. "And they of the people and kindreds and tongues and nations shall see their dead bodies." This enumeration of "people

9 ˣ And they of the people and kindreds and tongues and nations shall see their dead bodies three days and an half, ʸ and shall not suffer their dead bodies to be put in graves.

10 ᶻ And they that dwell upon the earth shall rejoice over them, and make merry, ᵃ and shall send gifts one to another; ᵇ because these two prophets tormented them that dwelt on the earth.

11 ᶜ And after three days and an half ᵈ the Spirit of life from God entered into them, and they stood upon their feet; and great fear fell upon them which saw them.

ˣ ch. xvii. 15.
ʸ Ps. lxxix. 2, 3.
ᶻ ch. xii. 12. & xiii. 8.
ᵃ Esth. ix. 19, 22.
ᵇ ch. xvi. 10.
ᶜ ver. 9.
ᵈ Ezek. xxxvii. 5, 9, 10, 14.

---

9. "Shall see"—"shall not suffer." ℵ, A., C. read in the present tense—"see"—"do not suffer"—"rejoice"—"send gifts."
"Three days." "The three days," A., B., C.

and kindreds and nations" looking upon these dead bodies seems to imply more than the dwellers in a single city, but we must remember that the great city of the prophecy may be a sort of metropolis, and that if the fulfilment of this prophecy is in the future, and that the means of transit go on improving, one city may contain representatives of all tribes of the earth.

"And shall not suffer their dead bodies to be put in graves." This was done evidently by the special providence of God, that the actual death and resurrection of these witnesses might be known by all their enemies.

10. "And they that dwell upon the earth shall rejoice over them . . . . and shall send gifts one to another; because these two prophets tormented," &c. They spoke so plainly to the consciences of ungodly men, and foretold such terrible things of their future doom, that they could not abide their presence and warnings.

11. "And after three days and an half the Spirit of life from God entered into them, and they stood upon their feet." These three days and a half could not be a time of great length, for, if so, the greater part of those who had seen these prophets would have died or been dispersed, and it seems a part of the teaching of the vision that their death and resurrection should be seen at once by all; for

e Isa. xiv. 13.
ch. xii. 5.
f Isa. lx. 8.
Acts i. 9.
g 2 Kings ii.
1, 5, 7.

12 And they heard a great voice from heaven saying unto them, Come up hither. ᵉ And they ascended up to heaven ᶠ in a cloud; ᵍ and their enemies beheld them.

---

it is said "great fear fell upon them which saw them," and that this fear was beneficial and so inspired by God for purposes of mercy is evident from the last clause of verse 13, "and the remnant . . . gave glory to the God of heaven."

12. "And they heard a great voice from heaven saying unto them, Come up hither. And they ascended up to heaven in a cloud; and their enemies beheld them." In these witnesses we see a fulfilment—if so it may be called—of what happened to the Lord Himself. As He was crucified, killed, raised again, and called up to heaven, so were they, but there is this difference between their resurrection and that of the Lord, that the Lord's Resurrection was seen by no one, and His Ascension only by His friends and faithful followers, and the ascension of these witnesses is seen by all, especially by their enemies.

I will now give Dr. Todd's futurist explanation. "The act of measuring the temple denotes its restoration to the worship of God and to the offices of Divine service. The testimony which this prophecy, literally understood, has given us is clearly this, that, at the time predicted, Jerusalem shall be inhabited again, and the temple rebuilt; that after this restoration the city shall be taken and sacked by the Gentiles, the outer court also of the temple seized and profaned, but the sanctuary itself and a remnant of them that worship therein graciously preserved in the midst of the surrounding desolation, which desolation shall be of very limited duration, three years and a half."

Now it is to be remembered that all this may be if God continues in the future to take an interest (to use a very inadequate expression) in Jerusalem as He has done in the past. As Dr. Todd says "There is nothing impossible, nothing inconsistent with faith or reason, nothing which can furnish the smallest justification to us for departing from the natural meaning of the words."

And now we turn to the prophecy of the two witnesses. These have been supposed or pronounced to be the resuscitation of Enoch and Elijah, or of Moses and Elijah. The explanation of our Lord in answer to the Apostle's question ("How say the scribes, that Elias must first come?") by no means limits the reappearance of Elijah to the mission or person of the Baptist as His forerunner. We must remember that the Second Coming much more naturally accords with the words "the great and terrible day of the Lord" than the First Coming, and that if before the First Coming there was an antitypical forerunner, much more before the Second Coming may there be a forerunner who may fulfil to the letter the very last words of the Old Testament.

With respect to the other witness it has been supposed to be Enoch, because he was "translated without seeing death;" but it appears much more likely to have been Moses, for the miracles which one of the witnesses performed were those which Moses alone performed—he turned the water into blood, and he smote the earth with all plagues—which is more true of Moses than of Enoch or Elias. Dr. Todd writes: "There is therefore nothing impossible, nothing inconsistent with faith or reason in supposing that, under the great affliction which is foretold, the same miraculous powers will be committed to the two witnesses: that, like Elijah when the Jewish Church was groaning under the tyranny of her idolatrous kings, and like Moses when Israel was bowed under the bondage of Egypt, they shall be sent for the support of the Church in that bitter day of trial in which the Holy People shall be delivered over into the hand of him who shall speak great words against the Most High, and shall wear out the saints of the Most High" (p. 186).

"In the ancient Church the opinion was almost universal . . . . that in the times of Antichrist two prophets should appear with miraculous powers. . . . . On a subordinate question, viz., who the two prophets will be who are foretold under the name of the witnesses, some discrepancy certainly prevailed. Many thought that Moses and Elias would again be sent. . . . . But by far the greatest number of the ancient Christians were of the opinion that the witnesses are Enoch and Elijah, who having both been received into heaven without tasting death were believed to be reserved for this very purpose, that they may come again in the end of the world to prepare the Church for the Second Advent, and being now, and ever since their translation, in the presence of God, they may fitly be described as the two olive trees and the two candlesticks which stand before the God of the earth." With respect to what

140 TENTH PART OF THE CITY FELL. [REVELATION.

ʰ ch. vi. 12.
ⁱ ch. xvi. 19.
† Gr. *names of men*, ch. iii. 4.
ᵏ Josh. vii. 19. ch. xiv. 7. & xv. 4.

13 And the same hour ʰ was there a great earthquake, ⁱ and the tenth part of the city fell, and in the earthquake were slain † of men seven thousand : and the remnant were affrighted, ᵏ and gave glory to the God of heaven.

---

is alleged respecting the difference between Enoch and Moses in that Enoch was translated without seeing death, and Moses actually dying and being buried by God Himself, it is to be remembered that we are led to infer that because Moses appeared with Elijah his body was in the same condition as that of Elijah in order that he might be seen by mortal eyes on the Mount of Transfiguration.

And now a word or two respecting the resurrection and ascension of these witnesses. We gather from the whole passage that it occurs at a time when God will have resumed that supernatural or miraculous action of His which has been long suspended. During the periods in which He has thus acted He has raised the dead at the prayers of His servants, and more particularly at the time of His Son's First Advent, when He raised Him from the dead and called Him up to sit at His Right Hand.

If these events, the measuring of the temple and the testimony of the two witnesses, occur just before the Second Advent, at which everyone will be raised again in his body, then it is only an anticipatory miracle of what will occur to all mankind, and may be intended to prepare them for it in a way that no mere preaching or teaching could possibly do.

13. "And the same hour was there a great earthquake, and the tenth part of the city fell, and in the earthquake were slain of men seven thousand." God in His judgments remembers mercy. Of this great and apparently wicked city only a tenth part was destroyed, and only seven thousand perished.

2. Bishop Wordsworth explains the vision of the measuring and the witnessing as signifying what is now and always going on in the Church. The rod or measuring reed is the canon of Holy Scripture, and the two witnesses are the Old and New Testament. The measuring reed is put into the hands of St. John because he was the last of the Apostles, and as being such he is supposed to

close the canon of the books of the New Testament. The canon is supposed to measure the church in the sense of dividing or separating the wheat from the tares—the bad from the good—the true members of the Church from the hypocrites or false members. This is true of the contents of Scripture, but not of its canon. The canon is the list of books which are held to be canonical, but the word is, as far as I can ascertain, never applied to the contents of such books as means of measuring the faith of the members of the Church, or dividing the good from the evil. The Bishop writes, "The reed —the Hebrew Kaneh, or reed, whence the word canon is derived—represents the canon, or rule of Holy Scripture, completed and sealed by Christ. This reed is said to be like unto a rod—the rod of iron frequently mentioned in the Apocalypse. Holy Scripture, though it measures as a reed, yet is not frail and quivering as a reed. It is not shaken by the wind of vain doctrine (Matt. xi. 7; Ephes. iv. 14). It is not, as some Romish writers have ventured to call it, a Lesbian rule, or rule of lead, which may easily be bent and twisted in different ways. . . . No, it is a rod of iron, which cannot be bent or broken, but will break all its foes to pieces like a potter's vessel. And yet by this reed Christ is said, $\pi o\iota\mu a\iota\nu\epsilon\iota\nu$, to do the work of a shepherd (Rev. ii. 27; xii. 5) for by the pastoral staff or reed of His Word all faithful shepherds under him . . . . guide the sheep of His pasture."

"The court outside the sanctuary is given to the Gentiles and they will tread down the holy city forty and two months. This vision, therefore, represents a corrupt state of Christianity. The outer court of the temple is given to the Gentiles and they will tread the holy city. Many enemies of God will domineer there. And the line of demarcation between them and the true worshippers is to be drawn by the measuring reed like unto a rod. The reed of Holy Scripture measures the Church and it draws the line between true Israelites and those who in the Divine Eye are like heathen men and publicans."

Bishop Wordsworth explains the two witnesses as being the two divisions of the Word of God—the Old and New Testament. This seems scarcely feasible, for the reed is, according to him, Holy Scripture. It seems not right to explain the reed and the two witnesses as being the same thing.

He explains the fact of fire coming out of their mouths and destroying their enemies as the woes that fall upon all who despise the Scriptures. "They can shut heaven, like Elias, and exclude all who reject them. The dews of Divine Grace are withheld from all who scorn them. The heavens are brass and the earth is iron under their feet. The waters of salvation become blood to revilers or scoffers of Scripture. To them the blessing is a bane, the Scriptures a scourge, preaching a plague, the Word a woe."

Now it is to be remembered that the Scriptures are a book, and so cannot act personally. Persons, *i.e.*, personal preachers, may denounce woe against those who do not believe the Scriptures and obey the words contained in them, but even they can do nothing in carrying out these threats. God must do it in all cases according to His good pleasure. But the words of the Apocalypse have to do with persons who themselves (of course by the power of God) shut heaven and turn the waters into blood. Bishop Wordsworth entirely ignores the signs of distinct personal action inherent in this vision. Then it is said that the beast out of the bottomless pit shall make war upon them, but has he not always done so in the sense of instilling infidelity into the minds of men so that they should not believe the testimony of the Scriptures.

And what meaning can possibly be attached to the dead bodies of the Scriptures lying unburied in the broad street of the city; but only for the very limited period of three days and a half. Have not the Scriptures in the very nature of things always been a dead letter to unbelievers, and a living life-giving thing to believers?

Then, has there ever occurred anything in the history of the world answering to the dwellers in the earth rejoicing over the death of Scripture, and the Spirit of God, after a very brief space of time,[1] entering into the dead body, or bodies, of Scripture again, and making it in the sight of the whole unbelieving world stand on its feet, and then being called to ascend into heaven in the sight of their enemies: so that by the very fact of this removal the two Testaments cease to bear witness in the world where they are most wanted.

As far as I can see, the good Bishop gives no explanation of the murder of the witnesses or of their dead bodies lying exposed

---

[1] I say a very brief space of time as compared with other periods of time mentioned in the Apocalypse. This three days and a half must, if words have any meaning, be very short compared to the forty and two months of verse 2 of this chapter, and the thousand two hundred and threescore days of verse 3.

in the street, or of their resurrection, or of their ascension. The only reference that I can find is the following: "Something of the Spirit described in this vision is seen in those of the Church of Rome who, on the plea of obscurity in Holy Scripture, withhold it from the people, and so virtually kill it, and when they have done so will not allow it to be committed to those enduring *monuments* of literature, such as editions and vernacular translations by which its words may be engraved on the memory of man 'in perpetuam rei memoriam.'"

But the excellent and learned Bishop seems to have some doubts of the soundness of his exposition of this vision when he writes the words: "The complete accomplishment of this part of the prophecy seems to be reserved till the last days of the world, for it is said, 'When they shall have finished their witness' (v. 7) which will not be till the eve of the end, and this prophecy is immediately succeeded by the third woe or Last Trumpet, the Trumpet which will call all men to judgment."

Mr. Elliot explains the measuring of the naos of the temple and the non-measurement of the outer court to be when "Luther and his fellow reformers would, as the sequel of their resumption of prophesying or Gospel preaching, be directed to the regular constitution of the *Reformed* Church (that which might now alone be rightly deemed Christ's Church visible, for the measuring implies the edification and constitution of what is measured" (vol. ii. p. 517). "The difficulty of providing for the instruction and edification of the Lutheran Churches began to be more and more apparent. It was not possible that public worship, and the administration of the Sacrament could be conducted decently and in order without some plan of ecclesiastical discipline. The great personal authority of Luther seemed to be the only cement among those that loved the Gospel" (p. 519). "The accounts follow in history of the execution of this most important commission assigned them, of measuring or ecclesiastically constituting what was called the Evangelic Church, the mystic temple; of the authorization and introduction throughout the Saxon Churches of new formularies of public worship drawn on Evangelic principles by Luther and Melancthon; of the removal from the Church and Church worship of Romish images and superstitions; of the appropriation of the ecclesiastical revenues of the Electorate to the support of the Reformed parochial clergy and schools; and of the ordination, independently altogether of the Romish Hierarchy, of a fresh supply of ministers of the Gospel. All this was effected in the autumn of 1525" (p. 521).

Strange interpretation indeed, and altogether unlike what the measuring line of Ezekiel or Zechariah can possibly mean (Ezek. xl. 3; Zech. ii. 1, 2). "The reed like unto a rod," Mr. Elliot makes to signify the temporal power of the German princes on the side of the Reformer, and the Reformers themselves exalted to high positions as magistrates in the civil government. Now when one reads the history of these times it is absurd, indeed, worse than absurd, to identify the measuring of the temple of God and the altar, " and them that worship therein," with the favour or protection of God accorded to Lutherans as the true saints of God. I mean as a body, for there was from the first the same difference to be found in them as in all other professing Christian bodies. The many, the bulk, were but nominal Christians. Luther himself bewails the fearful spread of immorality from the very first amongst those professing his doctrines, and no wonder, when we read his Epistle to the Galatians. For in his earnest zeal to commend the atoning merits of Christ, he preaches at times the grossest Antinomianism, and this, notwithstanding his protests, was taken to the letter by his hearers, " Pecca fortiter " was taken in fearful earnest.

And now we pass to his (Elliot's) exposition of the meaning of the two witnesses. There was a large number of sects who, in the times before the Reformation, protested against the prevailing superstitions of the dominant Church. Mr. Elliot classes these under two heads. He is bound to make *two*, because the Apostle says, speaking in the Name of Christ, " I will give power unto my two witnesses." And how does he make out the two? Why by taking certain as of Eastern, and certain others as of Western origin. He takes the origin of the Eastern witnesses to be the Paulicians who were the disciples of an Armenian named Constantine, who named his followers Paulicians because they professed to derive their teaching wholly from St. Paul's Epistles. They were afterwards headed by a teacher named Sergius, and in the year 970 they were removed in a body by the Eastern emperor across the Bosphorus, and their history from that time, as Mr. Elliot tells us, is European. He traces the sect down the middle ages to their persecution at the Council of Orleans, when two of the canons of Orleans were converted by them and afterwards burnt alive. He connects the celebrated name of Berenger with them, and Peter de Bruys, whose followers were known as Petrobrussians. He considers that some reputed heretics who were discovered and burnt at Cologne in 1147 were their successors.

He considers that the witnesses of Western origin, the Waldenses, though they are named after Peter Waldo, a merchant of Lyons, A.D. 1160, had existed, as protesters against the dominant superstition, long before in the remote valleys of Dauphiné and Piedmont, and so there were from very early times Protestant sects in the valleys of the Cottian Alps who derived their evangelical teaching from the disciples of Augustine. He takes great pains to prove that the Waldensian protest existed from very ancient times, because unless it did there could scarcely be accounted *two* lines of witness existing through the middle ages till the time of the Reformation. Mr. Elliot's account of the testimony of these two lines of witnesses is exceedingly interesting. Nothing can be conceived more heroic than their endurance in the face of massacre, imprisonment, and the stake; but what I want the reader to understand is, that it altogether fails in the matter of its likeness to this Apostolical prophecy in the most conspicuous feature of that prophecy, which I am sure every one will agree with me to be that "fire proceedeth out of their mouths and devoureth their enemies: and if any man will hurt them, he must in this manner be killed." In this these witnesses differ from all other martyrs, that they have supernatural power given them by God wherewith to defend themselves and slay their enemies; but this was not the case with Mr. Elliot's two witnesses (or lines of witnesses) during the period of their testimony. They suffered death under the same forms of persecution as the martyrs of New Testament times and of the succeeding ages underwent. Mr. Elliot in the whole 220 pages and more of his account does not attempt to give even the most far-fetched fulfilment of this part of the prophecy. In p. 698 he speaks of Saxons and Lombards, Saracens and Seljukian Turks; but in no way were these connected with the mouths of the witnesses, nor in fact were they scourges inflicted on the men living in the neighbourhood of those witnesses, but upon those living at a vast distance. No instance is given of God withholding rain from heaven at the word of these witnesses, and it surely is impossible to suppose for a moment that the servants of God, as these witnesses were, would pray that God would withhold the rain of His Spirit from those who had hitherto rejected their testimony.

The death of these witnesses Mr. Elliot accounts to be the entire cessation of all witness for Christ during the few years preceding the Reformation; their bodies lying unburied he holds to be the denial of Christian burial in later Papal times to heretics; and their resurrection to be the revival of Gospel preaching by Luther and his associates.

But the most marvellous of all is Mr. Elliot's exposition of the ascension of these witnesses. The heaven of Mr. Elliot is not the holy heaven of God into which Christ ascended but (what does the reader suppose?) why the heaven of political power! I will give his explanation in his own words. "After the defeat of the Protestants at Mühlberg the Protestant cause was itself in jeopardy throughout Germany. But in this case, as so often in others, through God's gracious overruling, the epoch of depression did only precede and introduce that of more conspicuous elevation. New and unexpected agencies were now brought into operation. The betrayer of the Protestant cause in the war just ended, Prince Maurice, was led to espouse it (let it be remembered that it is with the political bearing of the subject that I am now dealing). Then followed the surprise of the Emperor Charles at Innspruck, and the consequent Peace of Passau, concluded August 12th, 1552, that celebrated peace confirmed in 1555 at Augsburg, whereby in the fullest measure toleration was accorded to Protestantism; and Protestants, equally as Romanists, admitted to sit as judges in the Supreme Imperial Chamber. In short it was the fulfilment of the Apocalyptic figuration of the witnesses' ascent into the political heaven in Germany— Germany the originating locality, under God, of the great revolution .... 'And their enemies beheld them.' This pre-intimated the presence of enemies, on occasion of the witnesses' ascension, just as before of their resurrection: as if the result would be accomplished in the face of their enemies, and in spite of them. And so it was. At the passing of each decree by which the Protestants rose into ascendancy their enemies were present in the Diets and Councils " (page 141).

13. "And the same hour was there a great earthquake." This predicted the great schism occasioned by the preaching of the Reformed doctrine by Luther and others.

"And the tenth part of the city fell." This is interpreted by Mr. Elliot as the falling away of England from the Papacy.

"And in the earthquake were slain of men seven thousand." This is interpreted of the falling away from the Papacy of the seven united Provinces, *i.e.*, Holland.

"And the remnant were affrighted, and gave glory to the God of heaven." "Penal enactments were passed against the Romanists not in Spain, Italy, France, and Austria, but in the very limited part which includes England and Scotland, and (I suppose) Holland."

I would conclude the account of the exposition of Mr. Elliot with two remarks:

1. I have hitherto not noticed that the witnesses for God, at least the Eastern branch of them, undoubtedly were deeply tainted with the Manichean heresy—the error of holding two co-equal principles, one light and the other darkness. The reader will see ample proof of this in a pamphlet written in 1845 by the late Rev. T. K. Arnold, in which he quotes largely in proof of this from Giessler, a Lutheran ecclesiastical historian. I have not noticed this for this reason, that granting that the Paulicians were as good and holy and orthodox men as Mr. Elliot would have them to be, this does not in the least degree undo the fact that they in no respect correspond to the most characteristic feature of these two witnesses, which is, that they were supernaturally protected by God from being slain—which, on Mr. Elliot's own showing, they were not. All through their career they suffered as ordinary martyrs for the truth till the beast made war upon them, and then their dead bodies were exposed unburied for a comparatively short time.

2. The second remark shall be this: that the key to the Apocalypse is not to be found in its protest against Romish corruption. No matter how gross such corruptions are, the Apocalypse was not written specially to oppose them, but other forms of evil as well.

18. "And the same hour there was a great earthquake, and the tenth part of the city fell. . . . The second woe is past; and, behold, the third woe cometh quickly." The 13th verse, then, evidently relates what is supposed to be an awful calamity, as an earthquake in all circumstances must be, but if the tenth part of the city falling, and the seven thousand men perishing means the passing

14 ¹ The second woe is past; *and*, behold, the third woe cometh quickly.

15 And ᵐ the seventh angel sounded; ⁿ and there were great voices in heaven, saying, ᵒ The kingdoms of this world are become *the kingdoms* of our Lord, and of his Christ; ᵖ and he shall reign for ever and ever.

16 And ᵠ the four and twenty elders, which sat

ˡ ch. viii. 13. & ix. 12. & xv. 1.
ᵐ ch. x. 7.
ⁿ Isa. xxvii. 13. ch. xvi. 17. & xix. 6.
ᵒ ch. xii. 10.
ᵖ Dan. ii. 44. & vii. 14, 18, 27.
ᵠ ch. iv. 4. & v. 8. & xix. 4.

---

15. "The kingdoms of this world." ℵ, A., B., C. read, "The kingdom" in the singular.

over of England and the seven united Provinces to the side of the Reformation, then, according to the ultra-Protestant view, the being shaken to pieces by this earthquake and the consequent destruction was the best thing that could possibly have happened to those that were involved in the ruins. In such absurdities does the anti-papal historical view land us.

"The third woe cometh quickly." For the woeful nature of this woe we must look to chap. vi. 15, 16, where the fearful side of the Second Advent appears. Here, as we shall see, it is described only on its glorious and happy side—as it will be experienced by the righteous.

15. "And the seventh angel sounded; and there were great voices in heaven, saying, The kingdoms of this world are become the kingdoms of our Lord and of His Christ." This is no doubt the general judgment and the consummation ("He shall reign for ever and ever"). As I have said, there are no less than seven accounts of the general judgment in this book. The account in chap. vi. 12-17 describes it as the exhibition of the wrath of the Lamb. Here it only appears as the Advent of His glory, and the final deliverance of His elect ones. Its terrific side being passed over at present.

He shall reign in every kingdom, in every family, in every heart.

16. "And the four and twenty elders, which sat before God . . . . fell upon their faces . . . . Saying, we give thee thanks, O Lord God Almighty . . . . because thou hast taken to thee thy

before God on their seats, fell upon their faces, and worshipped God,

17 Saying, We give thee thanks, O Lord God Almighty, ʳ which art, and wast, and art to come; because thou hast taken to thee thy great power, ˢ and hast reigned.

18 ᵗ And the nations were angry, and thy wrath is come, ᵘ and the time of the dead, that they should be judged, and that thou shouldest give reward unto thy servants the prophets, and to the

ʳ ch. i. 4, 8. & iv. 8. & xvi. 5.
ˢ ch. xix. 6.
ᵗ ver. 2, 9.
ᵘ Dan. vii. 9, 10. ch. vi. 10.

---

17. "And art to come" omitted by ℵ, A., B., C.

great power." They thank God that he has put an end to the weary warfare between sin and holiness. The mystery of God (as the great angel swore it would be at the blast of the seventh angel) is finished. "Thou hast taken (to thee) thy great power," that is, to exercise it in the restraint or abolition of evil, and the establishment of truth and righteousness. "We give thanks to thee" reminds us of the words in the Gloria in Excelsis, "We give thanks to thee for thy great glory."

"And hast reigned." This is put in the past tense, as if it were already accomplished. What God has begun may be considered as already done.

18. "And the nations were angry, and thy wrath is come." It is unfortunate that the translation of "anger" is not the same in both clauses. "The nations were angry, and *thine* anger is come," or "the nations were wrath and *thy* wrath is come." The two wraths are in contrast—the one, that of the nations, impotent; the other, that of God, irresistible.

"And the time of the dead, that they should be judged." Not only the living, but the dead—those in Hades. This shows us very plainly that this is the time of no inferior, but the general judgment. "I saw the dead, small and great, stand before God" (xx. 12).

"And that thou shouldest give reward unto thy servants the prophets, and to the saints, and them that fear thy name, small

saints, and them that fear thy name, ˣ small and great; ʸ and shouldest destroy them which ‖ destroy the earth.

19 And ᶻ the temple of God was opened in heaven, and there was seen in his temple the ark of his testament: and ᵃ there were lightnings, and voices, and thunderings, and an earthquake, ᵇ and great hail.

ˣ ch. xix. 5.
ʸ ch. xiii. 10. & xviii. 6.
‖ Or, *corrupt*.
ᶻ ch. xv. 5, 8.
ᵃ ch. viii. 5. & xvi. 18.
ᵇ ch. xvi. 21.

---

and great." As in Rev. vi. 12-17, under the sixth seal there was a revelation of punishment, so here of reward.

"And shouldest destroy them which destroy [or corrupt] the earth." This is the only intimation of "woe" in this vision of judgment, but it is a very terrible one. All the tribes of the earth mourn.

19. "And the temple of God was opened in heaven, and there was seen in his temple the ark of his testament." The ark of the covenant was the most remarkable type of Jesus Christ. It contained the tables of the Law—in Him is the law of perfect righteousness. It originally contained the pot of manna—in Him is the true manna. It contained Aaron's rod of the priesthood—in Him is the succession of the true priesthood. Perhaps it may mean what Hengstenberg says: "The ark of the covenant is made visible in order to signify that the covenant has received its most signal accomplishment. God has now remembered His holy covenant, and His people may now serve Him without fear."

"And there were lightnings, and voices, and thunderings, and an earthquake, and great hail." This, in substance, occurs twice in this book, once in chap. viii. 5, when "the angel took the censer and cast it into the earth," and once in xvi. 18, when the seventh angel poured his vial into the air, "and there were voices, and thunders, and lightnings, and there was a great earthquake." As Alford writes, "The solemn salvos, so to speak, of the artillery of heaven, with which each series of visions is concluded."

CHAP. XII.

In this chapter we seem to have an account of the great warfare between good and evil in the world. The key of it seems to be the primeval prophecy, "I will put enmity between thee and the woman, and between thy seed and her seed." All the visions in this book of the great struggle between the two antagonistic forces have their root in this original enmity. They are not natural developments of evil so much as the actual conflict between the author of evil and the good which has been introduced into the race by the coming amongst us of the Son of God.

1. "And there appeared a great wonder in heaven; a woman clothed with the sun, and the moon under her feet, and upon her head a crown of twelve stars: And she being with child cried, travailing in birth, and pained to be delivered.... And she brought forth a man child, who was to rule all nations with a rod of iron: and her child was caught up unto God, and to his throne." Who was this child thus brought forth, thus destined to rule all nations, and caught up unto God, and to His throne. It seems blasphemy to suggest any name but One, and that the Name of Jesus. But who then is the woman? He had but one mother, and that a lowly virgin, but richly endowed with the highest grace which God can bestow—that which shone most conspicuously in His own Son—the grace of humility. It was a great thing for her to be clad with the sun, to have the moon under her, and to be crowned with twelve stars; but what was all this, multiplied ten thousand times over, to what God brought about in her that she should have the unspeakable glory of being the bearer in her womb, as being His mother, of the Only Begotten Son of God. In her that took place to which the creation of the brightest sun was as nothing. In her the Word was made flesh. In her sin and evil were already conquered, for if God had begun in her so wondrous a mystery of grace He would bring all to a glorious conclusion. It is a great thing to be clothed with the sun; but is it not said of all the righteous, that they shall shine forth as the sun in the glory of their Father? But does this agree with a later part of the

vision; for after her Son is raised to the throne of God she seems to disappear, and her place—not only her place, but her very person to be taken by the Church. Well, this is the fulfilment of the prophecy, " I will put enmity between thee and the woman, *and between thy seed and her seed.*" The enmity was not to cease when the woman was delivered, neither was the enmity to cease when the woman was removed by death. It was then to be directed against the Church. Now what is the Church? It is called the body of Christ. It is called the bride of Christ. It is the Lamb's wife. But is the Church anything to the Virgin? Is the Virgin anything to the Church? The answer is, that if the Incarnation had not taken place in this blessed woman, the Church would have been non-existent. The Church was not an offshoot of the Law nor of the Jewish Church—which, in comparison with Christ's, was no Church at all—but the Church was the offshoot of the Incarnation. All the good in the Church which God regards with unspeakable favour is the product of the new nature of the second Adam, which began to exist in the womb of this blessed woman, and which came forth when He was born, and which was renewed when He received life again from the dead that He might communicate it to us. But is not the Church the creation of the Holy Spirit? Certainly; but that Holy Spirit uses means for the diffusion of the new Nature of the Virgin-born. He works not only in the written or preached Word, but in the Sacraments, which have rightly been called extensions of the Incarnation.

There are multitudes of good men, good women—true children of God, true followers of Christ—but where does all this goodness come forth? From Him Who was born of the Virgin Mary. If it had not been for the Incarnation there would have been no holiness, no goodness in the Church. But was there not true holiness and goodness in the elder Church? Yes, but it pleased God that there should be a new beginning in the Second Man, "conceived by the Holy Ghost, born of the Virgin Mary."

But does not the supposition that this woman is thus crowned with glory, and resplendent with light tempt us to worship her. Only those I answer who are "inexpressibly foolish." In this vision not only the woman but the dragon are represented as they are in the moral and spiritual universe; the one all resplendent with grace, the other all fearful and hideous, because the author and sustainer of all evil, all enmity to God, all hatred to the image of

God in man. The Virgin, then, rightly represents the Church in its origin as founded in the Incarnation, but she does not continue to do so, because she does not continue in the world. And so the Church, which is in a sense derived from her, takes her place and flees into the wilderness.

We shall know at some time or other that the enmity of the dragon to the woman is because of the Incarnation—because of the infinite grace of God displayed in it and communicated to us through it; so that the enmity of the dragon to the woman is enmity to God in the highest form of His grace, and so the persecution of the woman is continued to the Church, to those in it who bear the fruits of grace. Now, these as long as they are in the world are always in the wilderness, and in them is fulfilled the Apostolic word, "All that will live godly in Christ Jesus must suffer persecution." Such are the true brethren of Christ, born again not of corruptible seed, but of incorruptible.

CHAP. XII.

AND there appeared a great || wonder in heaven; a woman clothed with the sun, || Or, *sign*.

---

1. "And there appeared a great wonder in heaven; a woman clothed with the sun, and the moon under her feet." In the introductory remarks I showed that it was but right to understand this literally of the most favoured of the human race, even of her in whom "the manhood was taken unto God." The glory surrounding her is beyond measure transcendent, but it is far below that which took place in her. If we only try to realize how God magnified her by making her the human channel and means in which the Eternal Word was made flesh, we shall not think it strange that she was arrayed in such splendour.

"In heaven." It has been said by those who consider this woman to represent primarily the Church (excluding all thought of the Virgin) that she is seen in heaven because heaven is the home of

and the moon under her feet, and upon her head a crown of twelve stars:

^a Isa. lxvi. 7.
Gal. iv. 19.

2 And she being with child cried, ^a travailing in birth, and pained to be delivered.

‖ Or, *sign*.

3 And there appeared another ‖ wonder in

---

the Church, but when the woman is persecuted by the dragon she evidently is seen on earth. Why should she be represented as descending to earth to be persecuted? Must we not rather understand that St. John being in the spirit sees all things in heaven. Heaven is the scene before him in which all takes place. Thus in the fifth chapter he sees what goes on in heaven, and in the sixth he sees what goes on on earth at the opening of each seal, without the least hint of any change of point of view.

"And the moon under her feet." It has been explained as if the woman were above the changes in this sublunary state, but may it not be by way of addition to her glory?

"And upon her head a crown of twelve stars." By those (and there are such) who explain the woman to be the Jewish Church, the stars are the twelve patriarchs or twelve tribes. By those who represent her as signifying the Christian Church, they are of course the twelve Apostles. But may they not be simply additions to her glory.

2. "And she being with child cried, travailing in birth, and pained to be delivered." This has been applied to the Jewish Church, which existed in constant expectation of the coming of the Messiah. It cannot be referred, except in a most circuitous way, to the Christian Church after the time of Christ. It can only be primarily so applied by a tacit ignoring of the coming of Christ into the world "born of a woman." To say that the Church is the mother of Christ, and bears Christ, is only true in a very secondary sense, and there must be an antecedent mystery, which is that the Son of God is born of a Virgin. Unless Christ had been thus born no human being could have had Him within him either mystically or spiritually.

3. "And there appeared another wonder in heaven; and behold a great red dragon, having seven heads and ten horns, and seven crowns upon his heads." This is the old serpent who deceived

heaven; and behold ᵇ a great red dragon, ᶜ having seven heads and ten horns, ᵈ and seven crowns upon his heads.

4 And ᵉ his tail drew the third part ᶠ of the stars of heaven, ᵍ and did cast them to the earth: and the dragon stood ʰ before the woman which was ready to be delivered, ⁱ for to devour her child as soon as it was born.

5 And she brought forth a man child, ᵏ who

ᵇ ch. xvii. 3.
ᶜ ch. xvii. 9, 10.
ᵈ ch. xiii. 1.
ᵉ ch. ix. 10, 19.
ᶠ ch. xvii. 18.
ᵍ Dan. viii. 10.
ʰ ver. 2.
ⁱ Ex. i. 16.
ᵏ Ps. ii. 9. ch. ii. 27. & xix. 15.

Eve, and to whom God said, "I will put enmity between thee and the woman, and between thy seed and her seed."

"Having seven heads." Seven being the number of perfection denoted his almost superhuman, infinite intelligence.

"And ten horns." Denoting the greatness of his power.

"And seven crowns upon his heads." Denoting his almost universal dominion as the prince of this world. I am well aware, of course, that the wild beast of the next chapter has seven heads and ten horns, and seven crowns, but these heads and horns, and crowns cannot have, it appears to me, the same significance as they had when attached to the therion. Satan could not have had them originally, because if they were dynasties or monarchies he existed long before them.

4. "And his tail drew the third part of the stars of heaven, and did cast them to the earth." Williams (and many others) suggests that "the third part of the stars" are the angels whom Satan drew down with himself into perdition. In fact it seems by far the most likely interpretation.

"And the dragon stood before the woman which was ready to be delivered." Almost all, even those who ignore the reference in the star-crowned woman to the Virgin, interpret this part of the vision as of Herod endeavouring to destroy the Lord as soon as He was born; and certainly no act of wicked men was ever more fiendish, more worthy of the direct inspiration of Satan, than this.

5. "And she brought forth a man child, who was to rule all nations with a rod of iron: and her child was caught up unto God, and to his throne." This can be only true of the Lord: for though

was to rule all nations with a rod of iron: and her child was caught up unto God, and *to* his throne.

^l ver. 4.

6 And ^l the woman fled into the wilderness, where she hath a place prepared of God, that they should feed her there ^m a thousand two hundred *and* threescore days.

^m ch. xi. 3.

ⁿ Dan. x. 13, 21. & xii. 1.

7 And there was war in heaven: ⁿ Michael and

---

the Lord promises that to him that overcometh He will give power over the nations to rule them with a rod of iron, yet this would only be true of His people who should overcome, because it was true of Him, and no one was received up to *God's* throne but Himself.

6. "And the woman fled into the wilderness, where she hath a place prepared of God." Does this in any way signify or allude to the flight of Mary into Egypt, which, compared with the worship of the true God in Jerusalem, might be called a wilderness. It took place at the time when Herod, at the instigation of Satan, attempted to destroy the life of Jesus; and the flight, and the place to which the Holy Family fled, was prepared by God: but there is this against it, that according to the received chronology the sojourn of the Holy Family in Egypt was only a few months, not three years and a half; and this also, that the flight of the woman into the wilderness is assumed to be posterior to the Ascension.

7. "And there was war in heaven: Michael and his angels fought against the dragon; and the dragon fought and his angels." When did this take place? Under the guidance of Milton (a very unsafe guide indeed) we are to imagine it took place before the creation of the world, but according to our Lord's words it seems not to have taken place till immediately before the Crucifixion (John xii. 31). And, according to St. Paul, Satan and his hosts had in some sense access to heaven many years afterwards (Ephes. vi. 12, "wicked spirits in heavenly places").

It may be that it was a part of the triumph of the Divine Intercessor that about the time of His Ascension the accusers were cast out.

"Michael and his angels fought against the dragon," &c. Who

CHAP. XII.] THE GREAT DRAGON WAS CAST OUT. 157

his angels fought °against the dragon; and the dragon fought and his angels,

8 And prevailed not; neither was their place found any more in heaven.

9 And ᵖthe great dragon was cast out, ᵠthat old serpent, called the Devil, and Satan, ʳwhich deceiveth the whole world: ˢhe was cast out into the earth, and his angels were cast out with him.

° ver. 3.
ch. xx. 2.
ᵖ Luke x. 18.
John xii. 31.
ᵠ Gen. iii. 1, 4. ch. xx. 2.
ʳ ch. xx. 3.
ˢ ch. ix. 1.

---

8. "Neither was their place found." "And not so much as their place was found." So ℵ, A., B., C.

is Michael? He is assuredly only the archangel, he is not the Son of God. The Son of God not having taken upon Him the angelic nature would certainly not be called angel or archangel. How could there be war in heaven? If there were two characters in heaven; if there were in heaven good and evil spirits, then assuredly there would be war. Would this war be physical or spiritual only? If the good spirits have physical power, and if the evil ones lost not their physical power when they fell, then there assuredly would be war something like the war which men wage one with another in any place in which they could meet with one another.

8. "Neither was their place found any more in heaven." Alford renders, "nor was ever their place found any more in heaven." This implies that they had access before to heaven which they now ceased to have. Thus Job i. 6 and 1 Kings xxii. 21.

9. "And the great dragon was cast out, that old serpent, called the Devil, and Satan." What old serpent? that ancient serpent, so designated because at the beginning of the human race he deceived Eve; called "the devil," *i.e.*, the accuser; and "Satan," *i.e.*, the adversary.

"Which deceiveth the whole world." Which he did once for all in our first parents, and which he has done ever since in his attacks on the faith of individual souls.

"He was cast out into the earth, and his angels were cast out with him." Whatever the reality of this was it certainly signifies that through the Incarnation and Ascension of Jesus Christ the devil lost the place of power which he once possessed. Thus St.

10 And I heard a loud voice saying in heaven, ᵗNow is come salvation, and strength, and the kingdom of our God, and the power of his Christ: for the accuser of our brethren is cast down, ᵘwhich accused them before our God day and night.

11 And ˣ they overcame him by the blood of the Lamb, and by the word of their testimony; ʸ and they loved not their lives unto the death.

12 Therefore ᶻ rejoice, *ye* heavens, and ye that dwell in them. ᵃ Woe to the inhabiters of the earth and of the sea! for the devil is come down

ᵗ ch. xi. 15. & xix. 1.
ᵘ Job i. 9. & ii. 5. Zech. iii. 1.
ˣ Rom. viii. 33, 34, 37. & xvi. 20.
ʸ Luke xiv. 26.
ᶻ Ps. xcvi. 11. Isa. xlix. 13. ch. xviii. 20.
ᵃ ch. viii. 13. & xi. 10.

---

12. "To the inhabiters." ℵ, A., B., C. omit.

Paul speaks of a great triumph of Christ at His Ascension over Satan, "Having spoiled principalities and powers, he made a show of them openly, triumphing over them" (Coloss. ii. 15).

10. "And I heard a loud voice saying in heaven, Now is come salvation, and strength, and the kingdom of our God, and the power of his Christ." We should have thought that a single word from God would have annihilated all the power of Satan, but it is not so. The free will of man must be respected. Men must use their own will and the means which God has given them. The Blood of the Lamb must be pleaded by them, and the power of His Word received by them must be manifested in their holding not their lives dear unto them. We cannot say how all this actually took place. It would seem as if the war in heaven depended not merely on the prowess of the angels, but on this being followed up by the pleading of the Cross by men and the manifestation of God's Word in the life of men. Perhaps these two things went before the angelic warfare and victory.

12. "Therefore rejoice, ye heavens, and ye that dwell in them." It seems as if the inhabitants of heaven receive an addition to their bliss by the casting out of Satan, and consequently there is greater danger to the inhabitants of the earth and of the sea (we should think those who dwell in the isles of the sea) because,

"The devil is come down unto you, having great wrath, because he knoweth that he hath but a short time." In what way does he

unto you, having great wrath, ᵇ because he knoweth that he hath but a short time.

ᵇ ch. x. 6.

13 And when the dragon saw that he was cast unto the earth, he persecuted ᶜ the woman which brought forth the man *child*.

ᶜ ver. 5.

14 ᵈ And to the woman were given two wings of a great eagle, ᵉ that she might fly ᶠ into the

ᵈ Ex. xix. 4.
ᵉ ver. 6.
ᶠ ch. xvii. 3.

---

14. "Two wings." A. and C. read, "the two wings."

show his wrath? Is it by the greater violence and subtlety of his temptations? This can scarcely be, because he has always from the first been able to tempt men. May it not be because he has now more power to persecute? thus he acts now through the beast revealed in the next chapter, giving him "his power, and his seat, and great authority." It appears, both from our Lord's words and other intimations of Scripture, that the persecutions and woes when the end is approaching will be far more bitter than ever before.

13. "And when the dragon saw that he was cast unto the earth, he persecuted the woman which brought forth the man child." Here the original woman, whose Child was caught up to the throne of God, seems to disappear. Is then all between verses 7 and 12 by way of episode, and does the action of the 13th verse follow on that of the 7th? Is the account of the war in heaven interjected, as it were, to account for the further fury and violence of the dragon? I think so. The woman now appears as the Church, and properly so, if, as we all believe, the Church is the product of the Incarnation. It is not mere virtue which Satan hates and would destroy, but the holiness which results from the New Nature. The dragon at first would destroy the New Nature itself; now, as he cannot do that, he seeks to destroy that Church which communicates it.

14. "And to the woman were given two wings of a great eagle, that she might fly into the wilderness." I think that there is here a manifest allusion to Exod. xix. 4, "Ye have seen what I did unto the Egyptians, and how I bare you on eagles' wings, and brought you unto myself." We are not to look into any circumstances of history to explain the meaning of these eagle's wings, but simply to see in them the power of God in bringing His Church into a

wilderness, into her place, where she is nourished ᵍ for a time, and times, and half a time, from the face of the serpent.

ᵍ Dan. vii. 25. & xii. 7.

ʰ Isa. lix. 19.

15 And the serpent ʰ cast out of his mouth water as a flood after the woman, that he might cause her to be carried away of the flood.

16 And the earth helped the woman, and the earth opened her mouth, and swallowed up the flood which the dragon cast out of his mouth.

---

state of safety. To convince us of this we have only to look at some of the explanations of expositors. Wordsworth, for instance, considering them to be the two Testaments; Mede explaining them as the Roman Empire under its two successions of Cæsars, Eastern and Western, protecting the Church; Elliot as the two wings of the Roman Empire united under Theodosius.

"Unto her place," *i.e.*, not so much a local place as a state of comparative safety.

"A time, and times, and half a time." This is the same period as the thousand, two hundred, and threescore days of verse 6. I shall advert to these and other periods in my introduction.

In no case do we know at present when these periods begin.

15. "And the serpent cast out of his mouth water as a flood [or river] after the woman, that he might cause her to be carried away of the flood." There has been considerable unanimity among commentators that the river or flood signifies the incursions of hostile nations, which, in some cases heathen (as the Assyrians or Babylonians), or, in later ages, the Goths and Vandals, threatened the existence of the Church. This shows that the dragon had power not only to tempt men to heresy and sin, but to stir up strife among nations, excited, of course, by the love of plunder and desire to enlarge their territories.

16. "And the earth helped the woman, and the earth opened her mouth," &c. This is remarkably true of the incursions of the barbarians at the time of the extinction of the Western Empire, for the invading Gothic hordes, instead of uprooting Christianity were themselves with marvellous rapidity converted to the religion of those whom they subdued.

17 And the dragon was wroth with the woman, ⁱ and went to make war with the remnant of her

ⁱ Gen. iii. 15; ch. xi. 7. & xiii. 7.

Thus Lange (quoted in Lee), "The earth, *i.e.*, consolidated ecclesiastical and political orders, devoured the stream (of the German nations) and amalgamated with itself the wild tribes."

17. "And the dragon was wroth with the woman, and went to make war," &c. Hitherto the dragon had persecuted the woman only. Now, for the first time, her seed appears in fulfilment of the original prophecy, "between thy seed and her seed." Apparently the woman is now in safety and her seed only is exposed to the wrath of the dragon. I cannot give any explanation in the least degree satisfactory of the woman being safe, or disappearing from view, and her seed being exposed to the fury of the dragon. Owing to the earth helping the woman she undoubtedly appears now to be in safety, and yet her best and truest children, "the *remnant* of her seed which keep the commandments of God" are made war upon by the dragon. Here, apparently, the true believers are considered as separate from, *i.e.*, as not identical with, the Church.

Alford has a singular way of getting over the difficulty. He considers that the woman represents the true *visible* Church, which in the contentions and declensions and false doctrine of the middle ages disappears from view. What then is the seed of the woman—to what body do they belong? I am afraid that Alford would have said that this is quite a secondary matter—if worth attention at all. My own opinion respecting the difficulties of this place is that they will be greatly minimized if we look upon the whole as given to us to impress upon us that the whole conflict, from beginning to end, in the Church itself as well as in the world, arises out of the original enmity which reaches its culminating point in the attempted destruction of Jesus Christ, as soon as He was born, by Herod, the instrument as well as impersonation of the dragon; and in the latter part of the vision the seed of the woman takes the place of the Virgin and of the Church, which she represents, and culminates with the godly seed only suffering the brunt of the enmity.

Why is the woman, the Virgin, brought in at all? Because she was the means by which God brought about the Incarnation. Why does she afterwards appear as the Church, or rather disappear in her offspring? Because the enmity continues to the end, and will

seed, [k] which keep the commandments of God, and have [l] the testimony of Jesus Christ.

[k] ch. xiv. 12.
[l] 1 Cor. ii. 1.
1 John v. 10.
ch. i. 2, 9. &
vi. 9. & xx. 4.

be found at the last to be an enmity not against human virtue but against the true reconciliation to God, and the diffusion of His grace by the renewal of His image in mankind which was in Christ in virtue of His having been " conceived by the Holy Ghost and born of the Virgin Mary."

CHAP. XIII.

AND I stood upon the sand of the sea, and saw [a] a beast rise up out of the sea,

[a] Dan. vii. 2, 7.

---

1. "And I stood." So B., P., and most Cursives; but ℵ, A., C., two Cursives, Vulg., Syriac, Arm. read, " he stood."

1. " And I stood upon the sand of the sea, and saw a beast rise up out of the sea, having seven heads and ten horns, and upon his horns ten crowns, and upon his heads the name of blasphemy." We now enter upon by far the most difficult vision of the Apocalypse—the vision of the beast having seven heads and ten horns (usually called the first beast). But with this beast is inseparably joined by the Apostle a second beast, of a somewhat different character in appearance, " another beast coming out of the earth " (the first comes out of the sea) verse 11 ; the second had " two horns like a lamb," but he was in fact of the same evil character as the first beast, for " he spake as a dragon." This second beast is never alone, but always acts with reference to, and in the sight of, the first.

The interpretations which it will be necessary to take notice of are three or perhaps four, and are the following :

1st. The historical—these of Bishop Wordsworth and Mr. Elliot —that the first beast is the Roman persecuting or anti-Christian power, at first heathen, then transformed into nominal Christian, under the ecclesiastical rule of the Popes. The second or lamblike

[Chap. XIII.] SEVEN HEADS AND TEN HORNS. 163

^bhaving seven heads and ten horns, and upon   ^b ch. xii. 3. & xvii. 3, 9, 12.

---

beast being the Papal clergy as laying themselves out to uphold the authority of the Papal See.

2nd. That of Dean Alford, who considers the first beast to be the secular persecuting power, in fact heathen Rome, and then merging into secular Christendom; and the second, sacerdotalism, first in heathenism and then in Christianity.

3rd. Bishop Boyd-Carpenter, and, I think, Dr. Lee, of Dublin, explain the first beast as the brutal world-power, and the second beast as the refined, intellectual, cultured world-spirit which, just as much as the former, is antagonistic to Christ.

"I stood upon the sand of the sea." The authorities are in favour of "I stood" (ἐστάθην). Those who adopt the reading ἐστάθη suppose that this refers to the dragon of the last vision who stood on the sand summoning the first beast to whom he might give his power and authority to persecute the seed of the woman.

"The sea." According to Wordsworth, "From a confused and tumultuous element." The power of the beast is thus represented as due to a confused and restless condition of civil affairs and as emerging therefrom.

"A beast rise up out of the sea." The word for beast is θηρίον, a wild beast, savage and ferocious; an apt illustration of a kingdom regardless of human life, and advancing by sanguinary wars.

"Having seven heads and ten horns." In the explanation given of this in chap. xvii. 10, by the angel, the seven heads are seven mountains, and then immediately following, as seven kings, "five are fallen, and one is, and the other is not yet come."

These seven kings are explained by Elliot, who says that he adopts with the most entire satisfaction "that generally received Protestant interpretation which, following the authoritative statements of Livy and Tacitus, enumerates kings, consuls, dictators, decemvirs, and military tribunes as the five first constitutional ruling heads of the Roman Empire; then, as the sixth, the imperial head commencing with Octavian, better known as Augustus Cæsar." Now if the reader will turn to any Roman history written for children, or to any respectable dictionary, he will find, which probably he learned when in his grammar school, that the dictators and decemvirs were

his horns ten crowns, and upon his heads the ‖ name of blasphemy.

§ Or, *names*, ch. xvii. 3.

---

in no sense heads as the kings or consuls were, because they were only temporary governors elected for particular emergencies.

Bishop Wordsworth does not commit himself to any such a notion, but directs attention to the seven hills which, as he thinks, are absolutely decisive as to the fact that Rome is meant; but Constantinople—the new Rome, the rival of Rome—is built upon seven hills, and these hills I believe far more defined, far more conspicuous than those of old Rome. Bishop Wordsworth explains the seven heads as meaning kingdoms which the last one—the Roman—absorbed into itself: 1, the Babylonian; 2, the Medo-Persian; 3, the Greek or Macedonian; 4, the Syrian; 5, the Egyptian; 6, the Roman Heathen Imperial. This seems more likely than the former exposition.

"And ten horns." These horns are explained by the angel in chap. xvii. 12 as ten kings. Bishop Wordsworth does not say who these ten kings are but refers his readers to chap. xvii. On turning to this place, however, we find no list of these kings, only that they were Papal at the first and yet gave their power to the beast, and then turned upon the harlot and hated her and ate her flesh.

Mr. Elliot describes these horns as ten kingdoms which the Gothic invaders created, who all became the subjects or vassals of the Roman See. He gives two lists. One between A.D. 486 to 490, Anglo-Saxons, Franks, Allemans, Burgundians, Visigoths, Suevi, Vandals, Heruli, Bavarians, Ostrogoths. Then in A.D. 532, the list of kingdoms still remained ten, Anglo-Saxons, Franks of Central Alleman, Franks of Eastern, and Burgundic Franks of Southeastern France, the Visigoths, the Suevi, the Vandals, the Ostrogoths in Italy, the Bavarians, and the Lombards, ten in all, and he adds, "At certain long subsequent epochs of time . . . the number ten will be found to have been adhered to from time to time as that of the Western Roman or Papal kingdoms." Now I cannot see how with any truth this can be asserted: take the Reformation period. The kingdoms then were England, Scotland, France, Spain, Portugal, Italy, three (Naples, Roman States, Savoy), Switzerland, Netherlands, Denmark, Austria, Poland,

2 ᶜAnd the beast which I saw was like unto a leopard, ᵈand his feet were as *the feet* of a bear, ᵉand his mouth as the mouth of a lion: and ᶠthe

ᶜ Dan. vii. 6.
ᵈ Dan. vii. 5.
ᵉ Dan. vii. 4.
ᶠ ch. xii. 9.

Russia, in all fourteen. And why is Turkey to be excluded? If it was anti-Papal so were England and Scotland.

"And upon his horns ten crowns." Rather "ten diadems." Bishop Wordsworth takes no notice of the diadems on these heads, whereas Elliot makes very much of them. He asserts that the Gothic kings who divided the old Roman Empire between them received at their investiture not the crown, but the diadem which had been worn from Diocletian's time by the emperors, thereby asserting their absolute sovereignty.

"And upon his heads the name of blasphemy." Perhaps "names of blasphemy." If this describes the beast in his heathen state the name (or names) of blasphemy consist in the divine titles and consequent idolatrous worship which was accorded to the emperors, the heads of the heathen Roman state.

2. "And the beast which I saw was like unto a leopard, and his feet were as the feet of a bear, and his mouth as the mouth of a lion." This seems to identify this fourth beast as the great world-power which Daniel saw in the likeness of three beasts which are all united in this beast. The first, the Babylonian, was like a lion; the second, the Persian, like a bear; the third, the Grecian, like a leopard; but the fourth one, "dreadful and terrible and strong exceedingly," was not likened by the prophet Daniel to any particular wild beast; but the ten horns out of his head seem to betoken identity with this Apocalyptic beast.

Now it will be necessary to note that this description of St. John's therion as following so closely upon that of Daniel can only refer to a great heathen world-power, or a world-power which, though nominally Christian, was entirely heathen in its antagonism to God and Christ. We cannot for a moment suppose that this describes a nominal Christian power rising up out of the sea. We shall have then to look carefully to this, how a beast, not only originally heathen but the evident successor of certain idolatrous world-powers, becomes Christian without losing its character as a therion, becomes the successor of Daniel's three beasts, or rather four beasts. The heathen Roman Empire may be the embodiment of these four

dragon gave him his power, ᵍand his seat, ʰand great authority.

3 And I saw one of his heads ⁱas it were †wounded to death; and his deadly wound was

ᵍ ch. xvi. 10.
ʰ ch. xii. 4.
ⁱ ver. 12, 14.
† Gr. *slain*.

---

3. "I saw" omitted by ℵ, A., B., C., P., forty Cursives, most versions.

beasts of Daniel, but a Christian, or even professedly Christian power, I think, cannot. If the originally heathen beast becomes converted to Christianity, some mention would surely have been made of so surprising a change.

"And the dragon gave him his power, and his seat [throne], and great authority." The dragon (that is the devil, "that old serpent, called the Devil, and Satan") "gave him (the beast) his power, and his seat, and great authority." When did this take place? Taking the beast to be the Roman Empire, it might have taken place when the Roman state was first founded, in which case the evil one must have had some sort of prescience that the new-founded civitas would be in its whole career inimical to God; or was it given when the ten Gothic kingdoms came into being? but they came into being as kingdoms within the bounds of the old Roman Empire when they Christianized themselves: in such a case this enormous difficulty would have to be met, that when these ten kingdoms became Christian they would be fitter to be the instruments of Satan than in their heathen state.

3. "And I saw one of his heads as it were wounded to death; and his deadly wound [the wound of his death] was healed." This is explained somewhat diversely by the two historical, or anti-Papal commentators. Wordsworth represents it as signifying this: "The head that was first wounded, after the age of St. John, was the imperial head of Rome. It was wounded in A.D. 476, when Romulus Augustulus, the last Roman emperor, abdicated the imperial dignity, and the Roman Empire ceased to be. It is not said in this prophecy that the head was restored, but that the wound of the death of the beast was healed, and he lived." The Bishop considers that the life was restored, and so the wound of his death healed in the Papacy.

Elliot considers that the deadly wound was inflicted by the suppression of the heathen worship, especially by the action of the Emperor Theodosius, who would not allow even toleration for the

healed: and ᵏ all the world wondered after the   ᵏ ch. xvii. 8.
beast.

4 And they worshipped the dragon which gave power unto the beast: and they worshipped the beast, saying, ˡ Who *is* like unto the beast? who   ˡ ch. xviii. 18.
is able to make war with him?

---

4. "Which gave power unto the beast." So ℵ, A., C., P., several Cursives, Vulg. (Am.), Syriac, Æth., &c.

heathen worship. "We read that in a full meeting of the Senate the Emperor proposed, according to the form of the Republic, whether the worship of Jupiter or that of Christ should be the religion of the Romans; and that, on a regular division, Jupiter was condemned and degraded by a large majority" (Gibbon quoted in Elliot). And then we read that "the Bishops of Rome began to be a new head of empire to it, and that in the rise of the Papal superstition to supremacy the deadly wound of its last ruling pagan head was healed."

Wordsworth quotes the words of Bishop Andrews. "The seven-headed beast is the Roman power in its different successive forms, first as it was under the pagans, and next as it is under the Popes. That power received a deadly wound in the Empire, and revived under the Papacy."

"And all the world wondered after the beast."

4. "And they worshipped the dragon which gave power unto the beast: and they worshipped the beast, saying, Who is like unto the beast, who is able," &c. Bishop Wordsworth, who is anxious to show that this refers to the Papacy, quotes several passages in which προσκυνειν is used in a lower sense than as indicating the worship due to the Supreme Being amongst men (Matt. iv. 10), but it is quite evident that St. John is describing what he considers a very great sin for which no palliation or excuse can be made. It is evidently worship of the most idolatrous character which is here offered to the dragon, and knowingly and of set purpose, because "he hath given his authority to the world-power." The very words in which this worship is embodied are given: "Who is like unto the beast," reminding us of the words of Micah (vii. 18, "who is a God") and to the words of the Song of Moses in Exodus,

5 And there was given unto him ᵐa mouth speaking great things and blasphemies; and power was given unto him ‖ to continue ⁿforty *and* two months.

6 And he opened his mouth in blasphemy

ᵐ Dan. vii. 8, 11, 25. & xi. 36.
‖ Or, *to make war.*
ⁿ ch. xi. 2. & xii. 6.

"Who is like unto thee, O Lord, among the gods?" (Exod. xv. 11).

"All the world wondered after the beast .... and they worshipped the dragon," &c. No worship of the evil one has as yet occurred like this in any part of the world known to us. No men that we have ever heard of have ever worshipped the evil one because he has set up another power of evil to whom he has made over his own power and authority. It reads like a worship of evil as such, and of this the Church of Rome has not been guilty, neither has heathen Rome, whose worship, we are taught, sprung out of that of the powers of nature, as the sky, the sea, the powers of reproduction.

5. "And there was given unto him a mouth speaking great things and blasphemies; and power was given unto him to continue forty and two months."

6. "And he opened his mouth in blasphemy against God .... and his tabernacle." If these blasphemies are what are usually called blasphemies, that is, words impugning the majesty, the sovereignty, the goodness of Almighty God, and if to "blaspheme His tabernacle (and) them that dwell in heaven" be to speak evil of the departed saints and the angels, then assuredly no dynasty, or episcopal succession, or any kingdom, or any ten kingdoms, singly, or united, or divided, have done this. The Turks who took Constantinople, and put an end to the Greek Empire, may have done something like this with respect to Jesus Christ, when they affirm, as all Mahomedans do, there is no God but the one God (Allah, the representative of the Hebrew Elohim) and Mahomet is his prophet: but there was no blasphemy of the name of the Supreme Being as such till the time of the French Revolution. If the beast represents the pagan Roman Empire then, as I said, the Name of Jesus may have been blasphemed, in comparison with Gods supposed to represent the various functions of nature, but after this,

against God, to blaspheme his name, º and his tabernacle, and them that dwell in heaven.

º John i. 14.
Col. ii. 9.

---

when the Empire became Christian, there was no blaspheming of the name of the Trinity, or of any Person in the Trinity; but the words of St. John imply with certainty that there was. Bishop Wordsworth attempts to draw a distinction between βλασφημεῖν πρὸς τὸν Θεόν and βλασφημεῖν τὸν Θεόν, but both are used in this very passage.

What can be blasphemy against the *name* of God, but blasphemy against Him as the Author of good, or the Father of the Son, or the Judge of all. Mr. Elliot accuses the Bishop of Rome of blasphemy because he claims to be the Vicar of Christ. But surely if we read the New Testament we shall see that Christ evidently desires very strongly that His ministers should consider themselves as representatives of Himself. "He that heareth you heareth me, and he that despiseth you despiseth me." "As my Father sent me, so send I you." Now the Bishop of Rome in assuming to be the perpetual representative of Christ may be very wrong, but exaggerating certain features of Christ's own Christianity is not blasphemy. In page 362 of his third volume of "Horæ Apocalypticæ," note 3, Mr. Elliot gives us a specimen of the blasphemy of certain atheists at the time of the French Revolution. "Three of the leaders of the municipality," says Alison (ii. 18) " publicly expressed their determination to dethrone the King of Heaven, as well as the monarchs of the earth. The comedian Monort cried in the Church of St. Roque: 'God, if you exist, avenge your injured name. I bid you defiance. You remain silent. You dare not launch your thunders. Who after this will believe in your existence?'" Now if it be blasphemy for a man to assume to represent Christ, even as a perpetual Apostle, what name can be given to this?

It appears to me that St. John in his words in verse 6, desires to express no modified form of blasphemy, but the very extremity of it.

"And power was given to him to continue forty and two months." If forty and two months be actual months, *i.e.*, three years and a half, then, in God's infinite mercy, such a scourge of men has but a comparatively short time, but if it means, on the year-day system,

7 And it was given unto him ᵖ to make war with the saints, and to overcome them : ᑫ and power was given him over all kindreds, and tongues, and nations.

ᵖ Dan. vii. 21.
ch. xi. 7. &
xii. 17.
ᑫ ch. xi. 18.
& xvii. 15.

1,260 years, then the history of European religion, at least of Western Europe, has been, at least during the greater part of it, one continued blasphemy against the name of God and His saints and His angels, if the body followed at all the leading of the head. I for one do not believe this.

7. "And it was given unto him to make war with the saints, and to overcome them." Who are these saints? According to the New Testament meaning of saint they are those who are baptized into the Church of Christ, and continue in its fellowship and make a credible profession, but, according to Mr. Elliot, they are the Paulicians, the Waldenses, and Albigenses, who were destroyed as heretics. In fact it was improper, indeed sinful, to give the name of saints to any persons in communion with the Church of Rome. The most godly self-denying priest, if he was in communion with the Church of Rome, and upheld the Papal supremacy, was a follower of Antichrist. St. Thomas Aquinas, St. Anselm, St. Bernard were none of them saints of God, the adherence to the Papal system turned their religion into blasphemy. The war with the saints meant the persecutions of those who, in the middle ages, opposed the corruptions of the Church of Rome. Now I would desire to give every honour to these noble-hearted men who, even though they held some errors, and were imperfect in their Church organization, and their views of the Sacraments, protested in the name of God against the Papal tyranny, but it seems to me absurd to the last degree to confine the term "saints" to them, good men though they undoubtedly were, and cruelly treated, not for their goodness, but for their opposition to the pretensions of the Papacy.

"And to overcome them." If by "them" is meant the opponents of the Papacy, then that was by no means all through the period of its domination. At and after the Reformation, in many instances, the Protestants asserted their rights and liberties, and overcame the Papists, as in this country and in the United Provinces, and in a large portion of Germany, Switzerland, and elsewhere.

8 And all that dwell upon the earth shall worship him, ^r whose names are not written in the book of life of the Lamb slain ^s from the foundation of the world.

^r Ex. xxxii. 32. Dan. xii. 1. Phil. iv. 3. ch. iii. 5. & xx. 12, 15. & xxi. 27.
^s ch. xvii. 8.

"And power was given him over all kindreds, and tongues, and nations." Mr. Elliot is very particular in impressing upon us that the Papal domination must be sought for only in the area of the kingdoms of Western Europe, which are supposed to be represented by the ten horns of the beast. His words are: "It seems reasonable to me that we should seek the ten kingdoms on the territory not of the whole Roman Empire, but of *the Western only* [italics Mr. Elliot's]. For the separation of the Roman world into Eastern and Western—a separation first sketched out and prepared by Diocletian's formation of the beast's seventh head, and one by which the latter division came alone to be attached to the capital of the Seven Hills—I say this separation and division was effectually carried out in the interval between the first wounding of the seventh head, and the rise of the eighth, or Papal. Further it was over this part only of the Roman world that the Gothic flood swept away the old imperial government, and made room for new kingdoms to arise."

But surely it is manifestly wrong to interpret the power "over all kindreds, and tongues, and nations" as power over ten only. And from these ten we are told we must exclude Constantinople, and Ephesus, the seat of St. John's Apostleship, and Judæa, where he was born, and the great historical kingdoms of Egypt and Persia and Mesopotamia and Arabia.

8. "And all that dwell upon the earth shall worship him, whose names are not written," &c. By worship we suppose (if the allusion is to the Bishop of Rome) is meant reverence to his sacerdotal powers, but are we really to suppose that the acceptance or denial of the Papal pretensions is in every human being a test of the secret and eternal election of God. Surely no man, unless he is utterly blinded by Orange partizanship, can say such a thing.

"The Lamb slain from the foundation of the world." In the purpose of God, Who designed to save all men that would be saved by the Blood of the Lamb, slain first in type in the sacrifices ordained in the first family, and in due time immolated on the Cross.

t ch. ii. 7.	9 ᵗ If any man have an ear, let him hear.
u Is. xxxiii. 1.	10 ᵘ He that leadeth into captivity shall go into
x Gen. ix. 6. Matt. xxvi. 52. y ch. xiv. 12.	captivity : ˣ he that killeth with the sword must be killed with the sword. ʸ Here is the patience and the faith of the saints.
z ch. xi. 7.	11 And I beheld another beast ᶻ coming up out

---

10. The readings here are very confusing. Alford reads and translates, "If any is for captivity into captivity he goeth: if any to be slain with the sword he must be slain with the sword." I adhere to the sense contained in the Vulgate, "Qui in captivitatem duxerit in captivitatem vadet. Qui in gladio occiderat, oportet cum gladio occidi."

9. "If any man have an ear, let him hear." Taking up the words so often uttered by the Lord, that besides the outward ear there is a circumcised ear, the organ of an understanding heart. Is it possible, then, that a man may have his ear spiritually opened, and turn a deaf ear? It may be possible.

10. "He that leadeth into captivity shall go into captivity: he that killeth with the sword must be killed with the sword." There is a reference to, or rather quotation from, Jeremiah xv. 1, &c.: "Then said the Lord unto me, Though Moses and Samuel stood before me, yet my mind could not be toward this people: cast them out of my sight, and let them go forth. And it shall come to pass, if they say unto thee, Whither shall we go forth? then thou shalt tell them, Thus saith the Lord; Such as are for death, to death; and such as are for the sword to the sword." But this is a declaration of vengeance, and seems not to be applicable in this place. It seems to me that the key to it is in the Lord's words to Simon Peter, "Put up thy sword into its sheath, for all they that take the sword shall perish by the sword." The saints are not to resist with carnal weapons. If they take the sword they seem at this juncture to lose their patience in following the footsteps of Christ, and their faith in the protection of God (Matt. xxvi. 52).

11. "And I beheld another beast coming up out of the earth; and he had two horns like a lamb, and he spake as a dragon." This beast is called elsewhere the false prophet, thus chap. xix. 20, where he is, as here, described as doing miracles in the sight of the first beast.

of the earth; and he had two horns like a lamb, and he spake as a dragon.

12 And he exerciseth all the power of the first beast before him, and causeth the earth and them which dwell therein to worship the first beast, ª whose deadly wound was healed.

13 And ᵇ he doeth great wonders, ᶜ so that he maketh fire come down from heaven on the earth in the sight of men,

ª ver. 3.
ᵇ Deut. xiii. 1, 2, 3. Matt. xxiv. 24.
2 Thess. ii. 9. ch. xvi. 14.
ᶜ 1 Kin. xviii. 38. 2 Kin. i. 10, 12.

His horns like a lamb betoken that he does not exhibit the same ferocity as the first; but his speaking as a dragon implies that he dissembles and deceives like the old serpent, or dragon, who deceived Eve through his subtleties. It does not imply ferocity of speech so much as malignity and plausibility.

12. "And he exerciseth all the power of the first beast before him [that is, in the presence of the first beast], and causeth the earth and them that dwell therein to worship the first beast, whose deadly wound," &c. Apparently this second beast exists only for the sake of the first. There has been as yet no separate institution, or monarchy, or dynasty, in the history of the world which has acted thus, and so it has been taken by ultra-Protestant expositors, as Wordsworth and Elliot, to signify the Papal clergy, but there is to me an enormous objection to this in the very nature of things, for the Papal clergy are part and parcel of the system of the Papacy. They are an integral and necessary part of the same whole. A bishop is powerless without the clergy of his diocese. A metropolitan cannot be such without the bishops and clergy of his province. I cannot believe, then, the Apostle intended to make two institutions of what is palpably but one.

13. "And he doeth great wonders [σημεῖα μεγάλα, the words used by the Lord in Matt. xxiv. 24], so that he maketh fire to come down from heaven," &c. Are these false or true miracles? Are they mere jugglery or imposture, or are they real miracles done by evil supernatural power? The Lord's words in Matt. xxiv. 24 certainly imply that the miracles done before the time of the end will be real. They will deceive, if possible, the very elect. And I cannot help thinking that the widespread denial of the

14 And ᵈdeceiveth them that dwell on the earth ᵉby *the means of* those miracles which he

ᵈ ch. xii. 9.
& xix. 20.
ᵉ 2 Thess. ii. 9, 10.

reality of the miracles of the Bible will prepare the way for the ready acceptance of these miracles of Antichrist. Men will have given up all idea that what they call the laws, but which they should rather call the routine of nature, can be set aside or interfered with. They find that it *is* set aside, and they fall down and worship him who by the power of the evil one sets it aside, even Antichrist.

It is absurd to suppose that such miracles as we read of in the "Lives of the Saints" can be the fulfilment of such a prophecy as "He doeth great wonders, so that he maketh fire to come down from heaven on the earth in the sight of men." Mark these words, "in the sight of men." Mr. Elliot considers that this refers to Transubstantiation, which he likens to calling down fire from heaven, but how can this be said to be "in the sight of men.' Transubstantiation is a hidden thing. Though a fanatic (as Loyola) may have imagined that he saw it, no congregation has ever seen the change take place. Elliot also refers to the ceremony of an excommunication, of lighting candles and casting them down; but he must be playing with the understanding of his readers in putting such a thing in writing as the fulfilment of this prophecy. There is not, that I am aware of, any miracle of the agents of the Papacy which has found its way into history, and has been treated by respectable chroniclers as serious enough (on account of the evidences for it) to be gravely discussed.

Alford, in noticing an allusion of Victorinus to some lying wonders permitted to the pagan priests to try the faith of God's people, writes: "We cannot help, as we read, thinking of the moving images, and winking and speaking pictures so often employed for purposes by their far less excusable Papal successors." But any serious thinking upon this point would convince us that such follies cannot be mentioned as the σημεῖα μεγάλα of our Lord and St. John, or of the anomos of St. Paul, whose coming is after the energizing of Satan, 'in all power, and signs, and wonders of falsehood' (2 Thess. ii. 9).

14. "And deceiveth them that dwell on the earth." Those that dwell on the earth cannot well be only the ten kingdoms, of which three were irretrievably lost to the Papacy. Those that dwell on

had power to do in the sight of the beast; saying to them that dwell on the earth, that they should make an image to the beast, which had the wound by a sword, ᶠ and did live.   ᶠ 2 Kin. xx. 7.

15 And he had power to give † life unto the image of the beast, that the image of the beast   † Gr. *breath*.

---

the earth, are not to include, we are told, such empires as Turkey and Russia, and the enormous bodies of men in Asia, India, China.

"Saying to them that dwell on the earth, that they should make an image to the beast, which had the wound by a sword, and did live." This image is interpreted by Elliot as signifying the work of the general councils held under the Papacy. It is difficult, however, to see how this could be. The general councils when assembled upheld or asserted the doctrines of the Papacy, and initiated proceedings against heretics, but this is a very indirect way of describing the making an image of the Papacy and making men worship it. To say that the Papal councils were themselves an image of the Papacy seems still more wide of the mark.

Bishop Wordsworth has a very different interpretation. "The first beast is the Papacy, and the εἰκών or image of it, is the personification of the Papacy in the visible form of the Pontiff for the time being." But every succession of rulers, whether in Church or State, must be represented by the ruler for the time being, or it would as a power, either of the world or of the Church, cease to exist. The second beast, in Papal matters, does not make an image of the first. By election the succession is continued, and each Pope inherits the powers and prerogatives of his predecessor.

15. "And he had power to give life unto the image of the beast, that the image of the beast should both speak," &c. Wordsworth remarks on this: "The Papal hierarchy first consult together and frame decrees, or prepare rescripts, either in councils summoned by the Pope, or by some other means prescribed by him, and when this preliminary process has been gone through, then they submit their decrees to the Pope, and desire him to ratify their verdict by his authority. This is supposed to be the fulfilment of the prophecy 'that the image of the beast should speak.' Till, therefore, these formalities have been gone through he is supposed to be speechless."

should both speak, ᵍand cause that as many as would not worship the image of the beast should be killed.

16 And he causeth all, both small and great, rich and poor, free and bond, ʰ† to receive a mark in their right hand, or in their foreheads:

17 And that no man might buy or sell, save he that had the mark, or ⁱthe name of the beast, ᵏ or the number of his name.

18 ¹Here is wisdom. Let him that hath under-

ᵍ ch. xvi. 2. & xix. 20. & xx. 4.
ʰ ch. xiv. 9. & xix. 20. & xx. 4.
¹† Gr. *to give them.*
ch. xiv. 11.
ᵏ ch. xv. 2.
ˡ ch. xvii. 9.

---

16. "To receive a mark"—"that they give to them."

"And cause that as many as would not worship the image of the beast should be killed." This implies an almost universal massacre of those who, if this second beast is the Papal clergy, do not acknowledge the Papacy.

16. "And he causeth all, both small and great, rich and poor, free and bond, to receive a mark in their right hand, or in their foreheads." Bishop Wordsworth explains this mark as the profession of the Papal Creed, particularly the articles appended at the Council of Trent to the Nicene Creed. Mr. Elliot applies it to the cross which Crusaders against heretics were to wear on their vesture. He also explains it as the sign of the cross on their foreheads received at confirmation, as well as attendance at mass, &c.

17. "And that no man might buy or sell, save he that had the mark, or the name of the beast, or the number of his name." If this is to be taken literally, then in the domain of the Papacy it has been very laxly observed indeed. Mr. Elliot cites the decrees of but two or three councils or synods, one the third Lateran, a synod at Tours, and a decree of the Constance Council. Certainly it has made no mark in the commercial history of this country. If it is to be taken spiritually that no one is to teach or to administer the Sacraments but those who have received the Apostolical succession, then it is true of all countries possessing the Roman obedience, but I need scarcely say that buying and selling is a very unlikely way of describing spiritual intercourse.

18. "Here is wisdom. Let him that hath understanding count the number of the beast: for it is the number of a man; and his

CHAP. XIII.] THE NUMBER OF THE BEAST. 177

standing count ᵐthe number of the beast: ⁿfor it is the number of a man; and his number *is* Six hun-dred threescore *and* six.

ᵐ ch. xv. 2.
ⁿ ch. xxi. 17.

---

number is Six hundred threescore and six." An immense number of conjectures have been hazarded as to the significance of this. All readers capable of understanding a treatise on the Apocalypse know that in Greek and Roman times the letters of the alphabet had each a numerical value, and these values of the letters of any particular name when added together make the number of the name. A number of names have been expressed in Greek letters, and their letters added up, Mahomet, for instance, Napoleon Buonaparte, and even Luther. A Father of the Church (Irenæus), living within one hundred years after the writing of the Apocalypse, mentions three names. He says: "The name Evanthas (Ευανθας) contains the required number, but I make no allegation regarding it. Then also Lateinos (Λατεινος) has the number six hundred and sixty-six, and it is a very probable solution, this being the name of the last kingdom (of the four seen by Daniel). For the Latins are they who at present bear rule." He gives, however, but hesitatingly, the preference to the word Teitan. Taking the Roman Empire to be the fourth beast of Daniel, this name Lateinos is by far the most likely of all. The solution is as follows:

$$\lambda = 30$$
$$\alpha = 1$$
$$\tau = 300$$
$$\varepsilon = 5$$
$$\iota = 10$$
$$\nu = 50$$
$$o = 70$$
$$\varsigma = 200$$
$$\overline{666}$$

It will now be necessary for me to recapitulate my reasons for not believing that these two beasts are two different aspects of the Papacy: the one, the first, the individual for the time being holding the Papal See, and the other, his clergy.

In order to this let us go back to the former vision (in chap. xii.)

the vision of the woman bringing forth the man child, then this woman, as representing the Church, fleeing into the wilderness, and there being persecuted by the dragon who casts out of his mouth floods of water to destroy her.

In this is described the origin of the Church. The Church of the New Testament has its origin in the Incarnation, at least so far as this, that it would not have existed unless the Son of God " for us men and for our salvation had come down from heaven, and had been incarnate by the Holy Ghost of the Virgin Mary and had been made man."

The origin of the Church was not out of the sea. It did not come into existence because " the four winds of the heaven strove upon the great sea." Nor, as Bishop Wordsworth says, "From a confused and tumultuous element—a confused and restless condition of civil affairs." It was the kingdom of heaven upon earth. Its birthday was the day of Pentecost when the Holy Ghost worked in men the new nature of the God-man. When it established itself upon earth it attracted to itself the fiercest enmity of the evil one. When it existed only in its Head he stood ready to devour it, and when it had increased and multiplied, and had subdued to itself the great world-power by Christianizing the Empire, there was a second crisis brought on by the dragon which (humanly speaking) wellnigh annihilated it. The dragon cast out of his mouth floods of water, which almost all interpreters agree as signifying the incursions of northern barbarians which overwhelmed as by a flood the western part of the Roman Empire. It did not destroy Christianity, however, as it threatened to do, for the barbarians were absorbed in the populations of the various countries which they overran, and became Christians and even orthodox Christians.[1]

---

[1] "But God had his own means of preserving the Church visible, and within it His true Church—the Christian. The Trinitarian faith had been so inwrought into the national minds and habits, as well as institutions and laws, especially from the effects of Theodosius' reign, that to sweep Christianity away it needed to sweep away the Roman population itself.... Superstitious and earthly though the Roman population had become, yet thus far they did service to Christ's Church in her present exigency. In those continuous and bloody wars, of which the Western world had been the theatre, the barbarous invading population was so thinned, so absorbed as it were into the land they had invaded, that it needed their incorporation as one people with the conquered to make up the necessary constituency of kingdoms.... At first indeed it was for the most part *Arian* pseudo-Christianity. Such was their profession in France, Spain, and Africa. But after a century or

CHAP. XIII.] THE BLASPHEMY OF THE BEAST. 179

These Gothic conquests became the ten kingdoms into which we learn the Romano-Gothic Empire subsided. Now these (according to the anti-Papal interpreters) constituted the body of the first beast. We are told very expressly that we are to look for them in Western Europe, and we are expressly told nowhere else. But if this be so, then unquestionably the bringing forth the body of the beast out of the tumultuous sea of nations was the act of God. It was because these ten kingdoms adopted orthodox Christianity that the Papal beast (or beast in its Papal aspect) had existence. The Pope being considered to be the head of the Church in Western Europe would be accepted as such along with all the other parts of Latin Christianity, as the confession of the Trinity, and the Incarnation; so that it is astounding to think that the greatest misfortune to the Church was the conversion of these nations to Christianity, for if they had continued either heathen or Arian, the greatest evil that ever befell Christianity, the rise of Antichrist, would not have been.

Verse 4. There has been hitherto no such thing in history as this united worship of the evil one and of the beast. All men, by a sort of straining of words, may be said to worship the author of evil when they commit any sin whatsoever, but this worship is described as something very different from following ordinary sinful inclinations. It is saying "Who is like unto the beast? Who is able to make war against him?" It seems as if those who said this had deliberately chosen evil to be their good. They desired in so many words the downfall of good and the future triumph of evil.

Verse 6. "And he opened his mouth in blasphemies against God." What would be blasphemy against the name of God? Surely it could only be to deny His Attributes, His Eternity, His Goodness, His Justice, His Eternal Fatherhood, as being the Father from all eternity of one Eternal Son. The pretensions of the Bishop of Rome have been quite different from this. They have been, in so far as they or some of them are evil, in a different sphere of evil so to speak.

Verse 7. "And power was given him over all kindreds, and

---

more of the flux and reflux of the invading flood, this too was abandoned for the more orthodox Trinitarian Christianity. The influence of the Roman See, which was gradually more and more operative with the barbarians, powerfully tended to this result."—Elliot, vol. iii. p. 63. The candid reader will readily acknowledge that this was a good work for the See of Rome to do, on the very eve of its becoming Antichrist.

tongues," &c. No words can more fully describe the aggregate of all human beings inhabiting the surface of the earth, and yet we are strictly enjoined (by Mr. Elliot) to limit this expression to the inhabitants of ten kingdoms—some of them very small ones; the sphere of the ministrations of the Apostle not being among them, but 500 miles away from the nearest.

Verse 8. "All that dwell upon the earth," &c. So that there is, according to this statement, no elect Christian amongst those who accept the Papacy. Every evil man will sooner or later adore him.

Verse 12. "And causeth the earth and them that dwell therein to worship." This can only have even a semblance of fulfilment in history by making one institution into two, and accounting the Church or Bishop of Rome to be the first beast, and its clergy the second. The worship here, too, is not worship as used in verse 4 of this chapter, but simply an acknowledgment of Papal infallibility in matter of doctrine.

Verse 13. "And he doeth great wonders," &c. No one since the Apostle's time has performed the *semeia* here described. The supposed miracles, such as the liquefaction of the blood of St. Januarius, have been obstacles in the way of the hearty reception of Papal pretensions rather than commendations of them.

We have now shortly to consider what anti-Papal interpreters consider the strongest point in the proof of the identification of the Papacy with the Antichrist. They lay down that the beast of Revelation xiii. is the man of sin of St. Paul, and one of their main points is this, that there is a certain let or hindrance, foretold by St. Paul, to the appearance of the man of sin which must be taken away before he is permitted to appear, and this they affirm to be the Roman Empire, which in its western phase disappeared with the last emperor, Romulus Augustulus, when the Western Empire fell to pieces and the Gothic kingdoms, Franks, Burgundians, and others took its place. The Fathers almost universally understood that this hindrance (τὸ κατέχον) was the Roman Empire, and that when that Empire would be destroyed they conceived that the hindrance to the development of the *anomos* (lawless one or man of sin) would be removed, and that he would immediately be revealed.

Now what was the hindering principle in the Roman Empire,

and when was it removed? This is important, because upon the answer to this depends whether the restraint exercised by the hindering power was an arbitrary matter, as if, for instance, a certain dynasty continued in the world till another dynasty of much the same character as itself took its place, or whether the restraining power embodied a principle which naturally, as it were, restrained the outbreak or revelation of a contrary principle. No doubt the latter. If the man of sin, the Antichrist, be the lawless one, what must restrain him except law (*nomos*). Now this was the spirit of the Roman power. It was law—cruel, iron, inflexible law, but still law so far good that the Apostle could speak of those who ministered it, even though they persecuted him and his fellow-Christians, as the minister of God to men for good (Rom. xiii. 4).

And the due consideration of this will serve to show that the cessation of any Roman dynasty need not at all be the cessation of Roman rule, considered as a principle.

"When was that which 'let,' or 'hindered,' or 'restrained,' taken out of the way? If this restrainer be any dynastic succession of Roman emperors, it must have been removed at one of two times. The Roman Empire in the east collapsed in 1453, and the Empire in the west nominally ceased under Romulus Augustulus in 476, and was succeeded in part by such an empire as that of Charlemagne, which was afterwards divided into the German and French Empires. Now I have nothing to do with the history of these or any other divisions of the great Roman Empire except this, that these empires and kingdoms maintained law. None of them for a moment attempted to act the part of an Anomos—least of all that bishop whom so large a portion of the Protestant world has united in dignifying with this title. Granting fully that during this period, whilst the old Roman Empire was breaking up, the Bishops of Rome gained temporal sovereignty over the middle of Italy, and consolidated a system of ecclesiastical supremacy over the Western Church, this may have been very tyrannical and bad, but to say that such a Papal system was the fulfilment of the prophecy of the Apostle, that it was the revelation of the man of sin who opposeth and exalteth himself above all that is called God, or worshipped, and who is to be revealed suddenly, not by a gradual progress of growth, and is to be destroyed, not by a lingering atrophy, but as in a moment by the brightness of the Lord's Coming, seems to me an interpretation of a prophecy as opposite to the terms of the prophecy itself as any two things can be."

The above is taken with but little alteration from an excursus on the Anomos, or Man of Sin, at the end of my remarks on the Second Epistle to the Thessalonians. Alford makes some good observations: "The κατέχον and κατέχων, the one the general hindrance, the other the person in whom that hindrance is summed up, are in this view very plain. All the Fathers understood them of the Roman Empire and Emperor, standing and ruling in their time, repressing the outbreak of sin and enormity; so have we been taught by history to widen this view, and understand them of the *fabric of human polity*, and those who rule that polity, by which the great upbursting of ungodliness is kept down and hindered. I say we have been taught this by history; seeing that as often as these outbursts have taken place their course and devastations have been checked by the knitting up again of the fabric of temporal power; seeing that this power, wherever the seeds of evil are most plentiful, is strictly a coercive power, and that there only is its restraining hand able to be relaxed where the light and liberty of the Gospel are shed abroad; seeing that especially has this temporal power ever been in conflict with the Papacy, restraining its pretensions, modifying its course of action, witnessing more or less against its tyranny and its lies" (Alford, "Prolegomena to 2 Thessalonians").

CHAP. XIV.

^a ch. v. 6.
^b ch. vii. 4.

AND I looked, and, lo, ^a a Lamb stood on the mount Sion, and with him ^b an hundred

---

1. "And I looked, and, lo, a [the] Lamb stood on the mount Sion, and with him an hundred forty and four thousand, having his Father's Name [His and His Father's Name] written in their foreheads." I think we may safely give to this vision an exposition analogous to that of the 144,000 who were sealed, of which we read in chap. vii. 4-8. We explained this as referring to the fact that

forty *and* four thousand, ᶜ having his Father's name written in their foreheads.

2 And I heard a voice from heaven, ᵈ as the voice of many waters, and as the voice of a great thunder: and I heard the voice of ᵉ harpers harping with their harps:

3 And ᶠ they sung as it were a new song before the throne, and before the four beasts, and

ᶜ ch. vii. 3 & xiii. 16.
ᵈ ch. i. 15. & xix. 6.
ᵉ ch. v. 8.
ᶠ ch. v. 9. & xv. 3.

---

1. "His Father's name." Rather, "His and his Father's," ℵ, A., B., C.

during all the troubles indicated by the vision at the opening of each seal, the work of the sealing of the elect would be going on without intermission. During these ages of war, famine, persecution, and pestilence, the work of God in perfecting the number of his elect would not be intermitted; and so with this vision. Notwithstanding the tyranny of these two wild beasts, and their massacre of all who would not worship the image of the beast, the work of God would proceed. Whilst the beast was impressing his name and mark on the children of the world, the Lamb was impressing His on the children of the kingdom.

The Lamb was standing on the mount Sion, not sitting to receive worship, but standing to help and defend.

"The mount Sion." As the writer of the Epistle to the Hebrews says: "Ye are come unto the mount Sion." The mount Sion is the Church of the Living God, the Heavenly Jerusalem. It signifies the Church in its heavenly aspect, and these 144,000 have not only come to it, but are abiding in it.

"Having his Father's name." The best MSS. read, "His name and his Father's."

"And I heard a voice from heaven, as the voice of many waters." Whose is this voice? From chap. i. 15 we should judge it to be that of the Lamb Himself.

"And I heard the voice of harpers harping with their harps." These were inhabitants of the mount Sion who accompanied the song of the 144,000.

3. "And they sung as it were a new song before the throne, and before the four living ones." A new song, because of the victory over Satan, and over the wild beast to whom he had

the elders: and no man could learn that song ᵍ but the hundred *and* forty *and* four thousand, which were redeemed from the earth.

ᵍ ver. 1.

4 These are they which were not defiled with women; ʰ for they are virgins. These are they ⁱ which follow the Lamb whithersoever he goeth. These †ᵏ were redeemed from among men, ˡ *being* the firstfruits unto God and to the Lamb.

ʰ 2 Cor. xi. 2.
ⁱ ch. iii. 4. & vii. 15, 17. & xvii. 14.
† Gr. *were bought.*
ᵏ ch. v. 9.
ˡ James i. 18.

---

given his power and authority. The new song is new because of the new deliverance.

"And no man could learn that song but the hundred and forty," &c. Does this signify that they were the most holy souls of the whole company of the redeemed, or that they had had a special conflict with the evil one, and had achieved a special victory. I cannot help thinking that it means the latter.

4. "These are they which were not defiled with women; for they are virgins." Is this to be taken literally, that they are in the actual sense virgins, or are they pure and holy though they are or have been in the holy estate of matrimony? I think the fact that they are specifically mentioned as virgins indicates that they were like the Apostle, and had continued unmarried (1 Cor. vii. 8). If they lived in chaste wedlock there would be no need to mention them, for all Christians, by the mere fact of their being true Christians, are assumed to have their hearts "purified by faith."

Bishop Wordsworth explains the fact of their not being defiled with women as meaning that they were not corrupted by the spiritual harlotries of Babylon, the false Church which is seated on the beast, *i.e.*, the Church of Rome. They have not defiled themselves with any spiritual fornications, such as that of the woman Jezebel, the false teacher already described (Rev. ii. 20-22). But such an interpretation should be energetically protested against.

"These are they which follow the Lamb whithersoever he goeth." "If he goes to Gethsemane they follow him thither; if he goes to Calvary they take up their cross and follow Him thither; and, therefore, since He is gone to heaven, they will be with Him there also."

"These were redeemed from among men, being the firstfruits unto

5 And ᵐ in their mouth was found no guile: for ⁿ they are without fault before the throne of God.

ᵐ Ps. xxxii. 2.
Zeph. iii. 13.
ⁿ Eph. v. 27.
Jude 24.

6 And I saw another angel ᵒ fly in the midst of heaven, ᵖ having the everlasting gospel to preach unto them that dwell on the earth, ᑫ and to every nation, and kindred, and tongue, and people,

ᵒ ch. viii. 13.
ᵖ Eph. iii. 9, 10, 11. Tit. i. 2.
ᑫ ch. xiii. 7.

---

5. "No guile." "No lies," ℵ, A., B., C.
"For" omitted in some MSS.

God and to the Lamb." These were redeemed, not to be ordinary followers, but *as* firstfruits. This does not mean, of course, that they were the first converted, but they were redeemed to be the choicest of the fruits of redemption.

5. "And in their mouth was found no guile: for they are without fault (before the throne of God)." The Apostle has here in his mind the words of Psalm xv. These 144,000 were on the mount Sion, and the Psalmist describes the character of those who shall sojourn in God's tabernacle, and shall dwell in His holy mountain. "He that walks blameless, who hath not spoken craftily with his tongue" (Πορευόμενος ἄμωμος Ὃς οὔκ ἐδόλωσαν ἐν γλώσσῃ αὐτοῦ).

6. "And I saw another angel fly in the midst of heaven, ... and tongue, and people." Here it may be asked what is the significance of these three angels, one proclaiming the everlasting Gospel, the second the fall of Babylon, and the third the judgment of those who have the mark of the beast? We are to remember that at the conclusion of this chapter there is another revelation of the end, and before that "end" comes the Gospel must be preached to all nations. "This Gospel of the kingdom shall be preached in all the world for a witness unto all nations; and then shall the end come" (Matt. xxiv. 14). Before the end, immediately before, is the fall of Babylon (xviii. 2 and 21), and immediately after is the judgment on the beast and the false prophet (xix. 20).

Elliot supposes that this was fulfilled somewhere at the beginning of this century, when the Church Missionary Society, the Wesleyan Missionary Society, the London Missionary Society, and the Bible Society took their beginning, and older societies, as the Society for the Propagation of the Gospel, received new life; but it

^r ch. xi. 18.
& xv. 4.
^s Neh. ix. 6.
Ps. xxxiii. 6.
& cxxiv. 8. &
cxlvi. 5, 6.
Acts xiv. 15.
& xvii. 24.
^t Isa. xxi. 9.
Jer. li. 8.
ch. xviii. 2.
^u Jer. li. 7.
ch. xi. 8. &
xvi. 19. & xvii.
2, 5. & xviii.
3, 10, 18, 21.
& xix. 2.

7 Saying with a loud voice, ^r Fear God, and give glory to him; for the hour of his judgment is come: ^s and worship him that made heaven, and earth, and the sea, and the fountains of waters.

8 And there followed another angel, saying, ^t Babylon is fallen, is fallen, ^u that great city, because she made all nations drink of the wine of the wrath of her fornication.

---

8. "Another angel." Rather, "Another second angel." So א^c, A., B., C.
"City" omitted by א, A., B., C.
"Because she made"—"which made."

is probable that this vision points to a far more universal diffusion of the Gospel than has yet taken place.

7. "Saying with a loud voice, Fear God, and give glory to him." Remarkable this proclamation of the angel, "Fear God," as if there could be no proclamation of the true Gospel which would not result in the fear of God.

"And give glory to him." The acceptance of the true Gospel must give glory to God in the life and conversation of all who embrace it.

"And worship him that made heaven, and earth, and the sea, and the fountains of waters." This is a call upon all men to worship God as the Creator Who has made all things at the first to be "very good," and will, on the completion of His redeeming work, restore them to their original goodness. It has been noticed that the seas, and the rivers, and the fountains of waters are distinguished. Peculiar judgments or plagues have been inflicted upon them, and now every curse shall be removed, and all God's works shall glorify Him.

8. "And there followed another angel, saying, Babylon is fallen, is fallen, that great city, because she made all nations drink of the wine," &c. We shall see what this Babylon is when we come to chap. xvii. I would notice that there is nothing whatsoever said of the punishment of her inhabitants, or of her citizens, or of those connected with her.

9 And the third angel followed them, saying with a loud voice, ˣ If any man worship the beast and his image, and received *his* mark in his forehead, or in his hand,

ˣ ch. xiii. 14, 15, 16.

---

9. "And the third angel." "Another third," אᶜ, A., B., C.

9-11. "And the third angel followed them, saying with a loud voice, If any man worship the beast and his image .... The same shall drink of the wine of the wrath of God .... and he shall be tormented with fire and brimstone in the presence of the holy angels .... And the smoke of their torment ascendeth up for ever and ever," &c. I said that there is no punishment said to be inflicted on those who are seduced by the harlot, that is by Babylon, but here the most tremendous punishment which God can inflict is pronounced not only against the beast, but against those who have anything to do with him in the way of receiving his mark. It seems to me clear from this that they who have received the mark of the beast have committed the sin against the Holy Ghost. And a little consideration will make this clear, so far as it can be made clear. The sin against the Holy Ghost is ascribing the works of God, or Christ, to Satan. It can scarcely be committed in its fulness except by those who are not what are commonly called infidels, for these do not believe in Satan, but by those who knowing what Satan is, the author and director of moral evil, choose Satan to be their God, who say to evil, "Evil be thou my good." Now it is said in chap. xiii. 4, that all the world who wondered after the beast "*worshipped the dragon which gave power unto the beast.*" What is this but a part of the same intensely evil mind which ascribes the adorable works of Christ to Satan. The worshipping, then, of the beast is worshipping him because he is evil, and the active representation of him who is the author of evil (xiii. 2). If it can be asked how can such things take place in this world of God's, we answer that that is the very thing against which the Book of the Revelation is written to warn us. Not against some form of evil which can be held with some acknowledgment of the Incarnation and Atonement, but against an incarnation of the evil one to which all other powers of evil are as nothing.

Another word upon this. The second of these angels proclaims the fall of Babylon, and the third the punishment of those who

10 The same ʸ shall drink of the wine of the wrath of God, which is ᶻ poured out without mixture into ᵃ the cup of his indignation; and ᵇ he shall be tormented with ᶜ fire and brimstone in the presence of the holy angels, and in the presence of the Lamb:

11 And ᵈ the smoke of their torment ascendeth up for ever and ever: and they have no rest day nor night, who worship the beast and his image, and whosoever receiveth the mark of his name.

12 ᵉ Here is the patience of the saints: ᶠ here *are* they that keep the commandments of God, and the faith of Jesus.

ʸ Ps. lxxv. 8.
Isa. li. 17.
Jer. xxv. 15.
ᶻ ch. xviii. 6.
ᵃ ch. xvi. 19.
ᵇ ch. xx. 10.
ᶜ ch. xix. 20.

ᵈ Isa. xxxiv. 10. ch. xix. 3.

ᵉ ch. xiii. 10.
ᶠ ch. xii. 17.

---

12. "Here are they" to be omitted with ℵ, A., B., C. "Here is the patience of the saints who keep," &c.

worship the beast and receive his mark. Now taking it for granted that the Babylon is the harlot sitting upon the scarlet beast, the harlot and the scarlet beast cannot both be Romanism, because the rider and the animal ridden cannot possibly be the same. Ultra-Protestant commentators, as Wordsworth and Elliot, and to a great extent Alford, take no notice of this extraordinary incongruity. They all interpret the beast, and the two-horned beast, and the harlot as Romanism. One of them also (Elliot) interprets one of three frogs as the Romanist spirit. Well, if the Apocalypse is written with one purpose, to warn men against the errors or delusions of the Church of Rome, then they are right; but if it be written to warn men against a far more stupendous evil which is yet to come, then they fail utterly in making a corrupt church to be the Antichrist, and those who listen to them are not warned.

12. "Here is the patience of the saints: here are they that keep the commandments of God, and the faith of Jesus." "He that endureth to the end the same shall be saved." "Companions of those who through faith and patience inherit the promises." The patience of the saints is their patience under temptation and in tribulation.

There are two marks of their perseverance. They keep the

13 And I heard a voice from heaven saying unto me, Write, ᵍ Blessed *are* the dead ʰ which die in the Lord ‖ from henceforth: Yea, saith the Spirit, ⁱ that they may rest from their labours; and their works do follow them.

ᵍ Eccles. iv. 1, 2. ch. xx. 6.
ʰ 1 Cor. xv. 18. 1 Thess. iv. 16.
‖ Or, *from henceforth saith the Spirit, Yea.*
ⁱ 2 Thess. i. 7. Heb. iv. 9, 10. ch. vi. 11.

---

13. "And their works." ℵ, A., C. read, "for their works."

commandments of God, as for instance, that under no pressure of persecution they should worship the beast—that under no temptation should they swerve from the faith once for all delivered unto the saints.

The saints have two marks—not one only—they keep the commandments of God, and keep the faith of Jesus.

13. "And I heard a voice from heaven saying unto me, Write, Blessed are the dead which die in the Lord from henceforth: Yea saith" &c. Nothing can be plainer than this enunciation, nothing more comforting, and yet scarcely any commentators agree as to what is meant—what time, that is, is indicated by the words "from henceforth." Some suppose it to refer to the time of judgment now about to be ushered in, but death will cease at judgment, and apparently these words seem to imply a continuance of death. The words seem to teach a change in the condition of those who now pass into the unseen world, but as to what the nature of that change of condition is we are told nothing. Some conjecture that it dates from the time when our Lord offered up His Sacrifice; but why should the fruit of that Sacrifice be represented as if it were something new?

Perhaps the words may betoken some very severe tribulation impending which would make death preferable to life. The words, however, are true of all times, and so they are embodied in our Service for the Burial of the Dead.

"In the Lord." That is in union with Him; in union with His Body.

"Even so saith the Spirit, for they rest from their labours; and their works," &c. The words "what the Spirit saith unto the churches" are frequent in the first chapters. Underlying all the words of angels in this book there is the word—the Revelation of

14 And I looked, and behold a white cloud, and upon the cloud *one* sat ᵏ like unto the Son of man, ˡ having on his head a golden crown, and in his hand a sharp sickle.

ᵏ Ezek. i. 26.
Dan. vii. 13.
ch. i. 13.
ˡ ch. vi. 2.

15 And another angel ᵐ came out of the temple, crying with a loud voice to him that sat on the

ᵐ ch. xvi. 17.

---

the Holy Ghost. They die that they may enter into rest from their labours; no more weariness, no more painfulness, no more watching against enemies, no more conflict either within or without. And yet the time spent in labour and conflict is not lost. "Their works follow them," not precede them as the ground of their justification, but follow them—not merely in memory, but as adding to their bliss. The cup of cold water only, in the name of a disciple, shall not lose its reward.

14. "And I looked, and behold a white cloud, and upon the cloud one sat like unto the Son of man." This is another of the visions of the end or last judgment, which teach us that this book is not a book of consecutive history. It is not a connected history of events from the First to the Second Coming, but the Apostle throughout it reiterates the teaching of his Master, that He is to be expected at any time. He comes at the end of the vision of the seals; at the end of the witnessings of the two witnesses; and now at the end of the times of the beast and false prophet.

"Behold a white cloud, and upon the cloud." We are constantly told that He will come in the clouds of heaven. Thus Matt. xxiv. 30: "They shall see the Son of man coming in the clouds of heaven." "Behold He cometh with clouds."

This vision, rather these two visions, set forth the judgment as an act of reaping, as the harvest of the world, just as Rev. vi. sets it forth in its aspect of terror and vengeance, and Rev. xi. 15, as the commencement of the eternal kingdom and personal rule of God.

15. "And another angel came out of the temple, ... Thrust in thy sickle and reap, for the time is come for thee to reap," &c. At first sight it seems somewhat strange that the Son of man should receive His commission to reap, that is, to judge the world through an angel, but it is in strict accordance with what we learn

cloud, ⁿ Thrust in thy sickle, and reap: for the time is come for thee to reap; for the harvest °of the earth is ‖ ripe.

16 And he that sat on the cloud thrust in his sickle on the earth; and the earth was reaped.

17 And another angel came out of the temple which is in heaven, he also having a sharp sickle.

18 And another angel came out from the altar, ᴾ which had power over fire; and cried with a loud cry to him that had the sharp sickle, saying, ᑫ Thrust in thy sharp sickle, and gather the clusters of the vine of the earth; for her grapes are fully ripe.

ⁿ Joel iii. 13. Matt. xiii. 39.
° Jer. li. 33. ch. xiii. 12.
‖ Or, *dried*.

ᴾ ch. xvi. 8.

ᑫ Joel iii. 13.

---

elsewhere, that the Son of God knows not the moment when He is to come to judge, but receives the intimation of it from His Father. As Wordsworth writes: "The angel is only the bearer of the message. The commission comes from the ναὸς of God—that is from the inner shrine of the heavenly temple—from the oracle of the heavenly Holy of Holies, in which the Godhead dwells in ineffable glory, and it comes to Christ as Son of man. 'The Father judgeth no man, but hath committed all judgment to the Son; and hath given Him authority to execute judgment also, because He is the Son of man' (John v. 22.) And the *hour* appointed for the last judgment is determined by the Father."

Because of the use of the word ἐξεράνθη (translated "is ripe") it has been supposed that both these acts of judgment are on the wicked, but inasmuch as the second act of judgment is upon the wicked, it is not likely that this is too. All grain that is fully ripe is withered in appearance. If it had any green colouring it would not be fully ripe.

17, 18. "And another angel came out of the temple which is in heaven, he also having a sharp sickle. And another angel came out from the altar, which had power over [the] fire .... Thrust in thy sharp sickle," &c. There is a remarkable difference between this second vision of judgment and the former one. In the former

19 And the angel thrust in his sickle into the earth, and gathered the vine of the earth, and cast *it* into ʳ the great winepress of the wrath of God.

20 And ˢ the winepress was trodden ᵗ without the city, and blood came out of the winepress,

ʳ ch. xix. 15.
ˢ Isa. lxiii. 3. Lam. i. 15.
ᵗ Heb. xiii. 12. ch. xi. 8.

---

one the Son of man only performs the function of judgment. In the latter He does not appear personally, but an angel having, as He had, a sharp sickle, seems to take His place. In our Lord's explanation of the procedure at the general judgment, in Matt. xiii. 39, He says distinctly that the reapers are the angels. As then in the first vision the Son of man alone seems to reap, yet this is not to exclude the subordinate agency of the angels, so here angels alone are mentioned, though the Son is all the while sitting on the throne of His glory. None of the visions of this book describe the whole procedure of what is going on, only certain features which God requires us to take notice of.

The angel which had power over the fire seems to be the same as the one in chap. viii. 5, which filled his censer " with fire from the altar and cast it upon the earth." He was the angel of vengeance, and so here he takes part in the judgment of wrath.

19. "And the angel thrust in his sickle into the earth, and gathered the vine of the earth, and cast it into the great winepress of the wrath of God." The treading of a winepress is in one of the most remarkable of Messianic prophecies associated with the vengeance of the Redeemer: " Wherefore art thou red in thine apparel, and thy garments like him that treadeth in the winefat? I have trodden the winepress alone; and of the people there was none with me: for I will tread them in mine anger, and trample them in my fury, and their blood shall be sprinkled upon my garments, and I will stain all my raiment" (Isaiah lxiii. 2, 3).

By the " vine of the earth " one cannot help being reminded of the true vine, Jesus Christ, of John xv., which bears fruit not to sin or to Satan, or to the world, or to self, but to God.

20. "And the winepress was trodden without the city, and blood came out of the winepress, even unto the horse bridles, by the space," &c. This is an exceedingly difficult place, both theologically and otherwise. It seems to be a vision of the final

ᵘ even unto the horse bridles, by the space of a thousand *and* six hundred furlongs.　　　　　　ᵘ ch. xix. 14.

---

judgment and condemnation of the wicked, and answering to the gathering in of the righteous into the garner of God of the former vision; but there are two features of this last vision which almost forbid us to think that it indicates an eternal recompense of woe. First the winepress is trodden without "the city." No place could well be mentioned by St. John as "the city," except as meaning Jerusalem, the earthly rather than the heavenly. And, secondly, the vengeance seems to be confined to the slaying of the bodies of those judged, so that their blood should be shed in appalling profusion. Now this, though very terrible, seems very different to being shut up for ever in the lake of fire. We have the same difference in the account of the judgment on the beast and on the false prophet and their followers in chap. xix. 20, 21, "And the beast was taken, and with him the false prophet that wrought miracles before him, with which he deceived them that had received the mark of the beast, and them that worshipped his image. These both were cast alive into a lake of fire burning with brimstone. And the remnant were slain with the sword of him that sat upon the horse, which sword proceeded out of his mouth, and all the fowls were filled with their flesh." This last, inflicted on the followers or army of the beast, is very different indeed from that inflicted on the beast himself, and is strictly analogous to that inflicted in this second vision of judgment.

Scarcely any commentators agree upon the meaning of these furlongs or stadia. Some, as Bishop Wordsworth, take it as emblematical of all space. Others, who have respect to the city being Jerusalem, consider it to be approaching to the length of the Holy Land; others, having respect to Rome as *the* city, notice that it is about the breadth of Italy.

CHAP. XV.

^a ch. xii. 1, 3.
^b ch. xvi. 1. & xxi. 9.
^c ch. xiv. 10.

AND ^a I saw another sign in heaven, great and marvellous, ^b seven angels having the seven last plagues; ^c for in them is filled up the wrath of God.

^d ch. iv. 6. & xxi. 18.
^e Matt. iii. 11.

2 And I saw as it were ^d a sea of glass ^e mingled with fire: and them that had gotten the victory

---

1. "And I saw another sign in heaven great and marvellous." As the former chapter ended with two visions of the last judgment, one the reaping of the good, the other of the wicked, it is clear that the Apostle here goes back to some former point, and commences afresh with judgments affecting the whole earth, concluding with another vision of the time of the end (xvi. 20).

"Another sign in heaven great and marvellous," &c. There was something which we are not told which must have constituted the marvellousness of this vision. Perhaps it was the majesty of these ministering spirits; perhaps the severity of their appearance; perhaps that, on beholding them, the fearful nature of the infliction of which they were about to be the instruments was manifest.

"Having the seven last plagues." This should rather be rendered the "seven plagues, the last ones," for in them, as being the last, is finished (because filled up) the wrath of God.

2. "And I saw as it were a sea of glass mingled with fire." This has been taken by most expositors as betokening mingled mercy and judgment: mercy signified by the beautifully clear sea, unruffled by any agitating winds, and yet mingled with fire, as betokening the wrath of God as yet not finished.

Mr. Elliot's explanation is very singular. He supposes that "Rome will be destroyed by a volcanic outburst from beneath—that the glassy sea, mingled as it were with fire, which was presented to John's eye in vision, being a flood of vitrified rock and lava, spreading in destructive inundation over the territory of the anti-Christian beast, and with the fire that fused it breaking forth conover the beast, ᶠ and over his image, and over his mark, *and* over the number of his name, stand on the sea of glass, ᵍ having the harps of God.

3 And they sing ʰ the song of Moses the servant of God, and the song of the Lamb, saying, ⁱ Great

ᶠ ch. xiii. 15, 16, 17.
ᵍ ch. v. 8. xiv. 2.
ʰ Ex. xv. Deut. xxxi. 30. ch. xiv. 3.
ⁱ Deut. xxxii. 4. Ps. cxi. 2. & cxxxix. 14.

---

2. "And over his mark" omitted by ℵ, A., B., C., &c.

tinually from the mass, as from the glowing lava of Vesuvius, whilst the harpers, escaped triumphantly from out of his Egyptian domination, stood with their harps unharmed upon its edge" (p. 471, 3rd vol.).

"And them that had gotten the victory over the beast, and over his image, and over his mark, and over the number of his name." If the beast is the embodiment of infidelity, or of superstition, we can understand what is meant by getting the victory over him; but what is meant by getting the victory over his image, and over his mark, and over the number of his name? God has not as yet revealed it to us.

"Having the harps of God," the harps consecrated to the praise of God, and of Him alone.

3. "And they sing the song of Moses the servant of God, and the song of the Lamb, saying." The song of Moses is doubtless that which was sung by the Israelites on the shores of the Red Sea when they saw their enemies overwhelmed in the sea. It has been asked whether they sang the very words. Why should they not? The words, understood spiritually, are appropriate enough. They lend themselves to the glorification of a greater deliverance than that of the passage of the Red Sea. In fact, a very large portion of the Psalms are used by us Christians in a higher sense than that in which they were first composed. When we repeat them we understand by David the Spiritual David; by the enemies with which He contends, and over which God gives Him the victory, our spiritual enemies; by Mount Zion, the city of the living God, the Jerusalem which is above, which is the mother of all believers.

"And the song of the Lamb." What is this song of the Lamb? Must it not be that of chap. v. 9, "Thou art worthy to take the book and to open the seals thereof, for thou wast slain, and hast redeemed us unto God by thy blood out of every kindred and

and marvellous *are* thy works, Lord God Almighty; ᵏjust and true *are* thy ways, thou King of ‖ saints.

4 ˡWho shall not fear thee, O Lord, and glorify thy name? for *thou* only *art* holy: for ᵐ all nations

ᵏ Ps. cxlv. 17.
Hos. xiv. 9.
ch. xvi. 7.
‖ Or, *nations*, or, *ages*.
ˡ Ex. xv. 14, 15, 16. Jer. x. 7.
ᵐ Isa. lxvi. 23.

---

3. "King of saints," or "of nations," or "of the ages," ℵ*, C.

tongue and people and nation. And hast made us unto our God Kings and Priests, and we shall reign upon the earth."

"Saying, Great and marvellous are thy works, Lord God Almighty; just and true are thy ways, thou King of saints" (or, thou King of the nations or of the ages). These words do not exclude the words of such a song as that of the four living ones and of the elders to the Lamb; they rather supplement them. One writes: "The song is one and the same, and the expression which characterizes it betokens, as do so many other notices and symbols in this book, the unity of the Old and New Testament Churches." All very well, but why should not Redemption by the infinitely precious Blood be particularly mentioned? And it is if we consider that by the song of the Lamb is meant the song sung by the living ones and elders when He took the book and began to open the seals.

4. "Who shall not fear thee, O Lord?" This question is asked in Jeremiah x. 7, in a similar context.

"For thou only art holy." This is not to be taken as denying holiness in the creature, but such holiness is derived, whereas the holiness of God is one of His essential attributes. In the "Gloria in excelsis" the Church ascribes this to Christ: "Thou only art holy: Thou only art the Lord."

"For all nations shall come and worship before thee, O Lord." This is also taken from the Old Testament, from Isaiah lxvi. 23, and from Psalm lxxxvi. 9. It seems as if before the infliction of the plagues there is a declaration that, though the plagues will be very terrible, they will be partial in their operation: "All the ends of the world shall remember themselves, and be turned unto the Lord, and all the kindreds of the nations shall worship before him" (Ps. xxii).

shall come and worship before thee; for thy judgments are made manifest.

5 And after that I looked, and, behold, ⁿ the temple of the tabernacle of the testimony in heaven was opened:

6 ᵒAnd the seven angels came out of the temple, having the seven plagues, ᵖclothed in pure and white linen, and having their breasts girded with golden girdles.

7 ᑫAnd one of the four beasts gave unto the

ⁿ ch. xi. 19. See Num. i. 50.

ᵒ ver. 1.

ᵖ Ex. xxviii. 6, 8. Ezek. xliv. 17, 18. ch. i. 13.

ᑫ ch. iv. 6.

---

6. "Clothed in pure and white linen." Some (A., C.) read, "stone," λιθον, instead of λινον, "linen."

"For thy judgments are made manifest." This may be said in anticipation of the effect produced by the pouring forth of the vials, or by the preaching of the gospel to every nation and kindred and tongue and people (xiv. 6).

5. "And after that I looked, and, behold, the temple of the tabernacle of the testimony," &c. The temple here is *naos*, and signifies that the monument, shrine, or dwelling-place of God ("Thou that dwellest between the cherubims") was opened. This was not as betokening very full access to God for all, but rather that the impending judgments came direct from God,—more so, perhaps, than any previous judgments.

6. "And the seven angels came out of the temple, having the seven plagues, clothed in pure and white linen, and having their breasts girded," &c. This is not said of the angels which bore the trumpets, nor indeed of any of the heavenly ministering spirits except these, and it is much emphasized if we adopt the reading of A. and C., stone, λιθον, *i.e.*, their garments were arrayed, ornamented, with stones most costly, adding to the shining and glistening nature of their appearance.

"And having their breasts girded with golden girdles," as our Lord Himself was when St. John saw Him in the opening vision of this book.

7. "And one of the four living ones gave unto the seven angels seven golden vials full of the wrath of God, who liveth for ever and

seven angels seven golden vials full of the wrath of God,
^r who liveth for ever and ever.

8 And ^s the temple was filled with smoke ^t from the glory of God, and from his power; and no man was able to enter into the temple, till the seven plagues of the seven angels were fulfilled.

^r 1 Thess. i. 9. ch. iv. 9. & x. 6.
^s Ex. xl. 34. 1 Kin. viii. 10. 2 Chr. v. 14. Isa. vi. 4.
^t 2 Thess. i. 9.

---

ever." This plainly indicates that the Zoa were not impersonations, but real beings instinct with life. They were nearer to God than the seven angels, and so they gave the vials from God to these angels.

"Seven golden vials full of the wrath of God, who liveth for ever and ever." These vials were not what we commonly call vials, but rather censers in which incense was burnt; but now instead of incense they were full of its opposite, for with respect to those on whom their contents were to be poured the time of acceptance denoted by the sweet-smelling savour of the incense was over, and the time of judgment was come.

8. "And the temple was filled with smoke from the glory of God, and from his power; and no man was able," &c. This is evidently a reminiscence of Exod. xl. 34: "Then a cloud covered the tent of the congregation, and the glory of the Lord filled the tabernacle. And Moses was not able to enter into the tent of the congregation because the cloud abode thereon." Also 1 Kings viii. 11. So also: "Clouds and darkness are round about him, righteousness and judgment are the habitation of his seat." Wordsworth remarks, "The vials are to the empire of the beast what the trumpets are to the whole body of God's enemies, with this difference, that the trumpets announce judgments, the vials execute them."

CHAP. XVI

AND I heard a great voice out of the temple saying [a] to the seven angels, Go your ways, and pour out the vials [b] of the wrath of God upon the earth.

2 And the first went, and poured out his vial [c] upon the earth; and [d] there fell a noisome and grievous sore upon the men [e] which had the mark of the beast, and *upon* them [f] which worshipped his image.

[a] ch. xv. 1.
[b] ch. xiv. 10. & xv. 7.
[c] ch. viii. 7.
[d] Ex. ix. 9, 10, 11.
[e] ch. xiii. 16, 17.
[f] ch. xiii. 14.

---

1. "And I heard a great voice out of the temple saying to the seven angels, Go your ways, and pour out the vials of the wrath of God upon the earth." As no one, *i.e.*, no living being, was able to enter into the temple because of the smoke of God's wrath, this must have been the voice of God Himself, and such is in accordance with all the awful circumstances of these visions as coming more directly from God Himself than any previous inflictions.

2. "And the first went, and poured out his vial upon the earth." As I believe that the fulfilment of these visions are all in the future I will not attempt to explain them. The explanations of other commentators will serve to convince the reader of the futility of suggesting guesses, some of which, I am afraid, bring the book itself into contempt.

"And there fell a noisome and grievous sore upon the men which had the mark of the beast, and upon them which worshipped his image." Taking, as all the anti-papal historical commentators do, these that had the mark of the beast to be Roman Catholics, no plague or infliction has ever come from God by which they have been smitten, and from which the Protestants living along with them or among them have escaped uninjured. Elliot considers that this sore or boil (ἕλκος) was the spread of infidelity among the Romanists in Spain, France, and Italy; but surely the men who continued Romanists escaped this, and the people who disavowed Romanism were thus punished.

3 And the second angel poured out his vial ᵍ upon the sea; and ʰ it became as the blood of a dead *man*: ⁱ and every living soul died in the sea.

4 And the third angel poured out his vial ᵏ upon the rivers and fountains of waters; ˡ and they became blood.

5 And I heard the angel of the waters say, ᵐ Thou art righteous, O Lord, ⁿ which art, and wast, and shalt be, because thou hast judged thus.

ᵍ ch. viii. 8.
ʰ Ex. vii. 17, 20.
ⁱ ch. viii. 9.
ᵏ ch. viii. 10.
ˡ Ex. vii. 20.
ᵐ ch. xv. 3.
ⁿ ch. i. 4, 8. & iv. 8. & xi. 17.

---

5. "O Lord" omitted by ℵ, A., B., C., P.
"And shalt be." ℵ, B., C., read "holy."

3. "And the second angel poured out his vial upon the sea; and it became as the blood of a dead man: and every living soul died in the sea." In interpretation of the plagues of this vial, Wordsworth writes: "The sea in the Apocalypse represents nations in a restless state, tossed about by winds and storms of passion like the sea to which the wicked are compared by Isaiah: 'The wicked are like the troubled sea when it cannot rest, whose waters cast up mire and dirt,'" &c. (lvii. 20); but this is universally the case, and what we want is some direction as to the time when this particular instance of judgment occurred. Alford believes that these vial plagues will occur shortly before the final consummation, and so does not profess to give any explanation. Elliot explains the sea turned into blood of the naval victories of England under Lord Nelson, by which the maritime power of the nations continuing attached to the Papacy—Spain, Portugal, and France—was utterly destroyed. It is hard to see how such victories as Trafalgar brought about that every living soul should die in the sea. Wordsworth takes the word soul ($\psi\upsilon\chi\eta$) to designate the carnal mind, and the word living is added to show that while alive in name they are in fact dead. He quotes the saying of Christ to the Church of Sardis: "Thou hast a name that thou livest, and art dead" (iii. 1).

4-6. "And the third angel poured out his vial upon the rivers and fountains of waters; and they became blood. And I heard the angel of the waters say, Thou art righteous, O Lord, ... because thou hast judged thus. For they have shed the blood of

6 For ᵒ they have shed the blood ᵖ of saints and prophets, ᵑ and thou hast given them blood to drink; for they are worthy.

ᵒ Matt. xxiii. 34, 35. ch. xiii. 15.
ᵖ ch. xi. 18. & xviii. 20.
ᵑ Isa. xlix. 26.

---

6. "For (they are worthy)." "For" omitted by A., B., C., P., forty Cursives.

saints and prophets," &c. Alford, considering the fulfilment of this vision as yet in the future, gives no explanation. Wordsworth writes: "The rivers and wells are the channels and springs of the prosperity and health of the power which is here punished. The prophecy contained in this vial has also already been in part fulfilled. It foretold calamities to be inflicted on the resources of the Papacy, and announced that those very things which were once tributary to it, and supplied it with the means of greatness, would be turned against it, and become occasions and instruments of its suffering and shame."

Elliot refers back to his explanation of the fulfilment of the third trumpet. He supposes that the third trumpet was fulfilled in the ravages of the Goths and Huns on the banks of certain rivers, notably the Upper Danube and Rhine, and that the embittering of those waters by the ravages predicted under the star Wormwood was the desolations on the banks of these rivers by the barbarian forces, and that afterwards Attila desolated the mountain valley from which the rivers of the valley of the Po took their rise. Now under this vial poured on the rivers he sees "the commencement of the judgment of war and bloodshed on the countriés watered by the Rhine and Danube, and on the sub-Alpine provinces also of Piedmont and Lombardy." He says that on consulting the chronicles of the French revolutionary wars we shall not fail to discover the fulfilment of the prediction, which fulfilment he supposes begun by the declaration of war by the French National Assembly against the German Emperor; on the September following against the King of Sardinia; and ere the close of that year it resulted that both the Rhine began to be noted as one fateful scene of the outpouring of this vial of blood, and that advance was made by the French towards a second scene destined to suffer under it, the Alpine streams of Piedmont and Lombardy. Three pages are taken up with notices of the desolating wars on the banks of the Rhine and Danube, and two more (386 and

7 And I heard another out of the altar say, Even so, ^r Lord God Almighty, ^s true and righteous *are* thy judgments.

8 And the fourth angel poured out his vial ^t upon the sun; ^u and power was given unto him to scorch men with fire.

^r ch. xv. 3.
^s ch. xiii. 10. & xiv. 10. & xix. 2.
^t ch. viii. 12.
^u ch. ix. 17, 18. & xiv. 18.

---

387) with the reasons for these desolations, in the horrible massacres and cruelties inflicted on the Protestants, or rather upon all those who denied or resisted the extreme claims of the Church of Rome. To these the angel of the waters and the voice of the altar are supposed to allude when one said, "They have shed the blood of saints and prophets, and thou hast given them blood to drink;" and when the other said, "Even so, Lord God Almighty, true and righteous are thy judgments."

This may have been so. We are to remember that the profession of an imperfect form of Christianity does not put men out of the pale of humanity; that if a Protestant holding low views of the ministry and sacraments is murdered, God will most assuredly, sooner or later, require his blood at the hand, not of the generation perhaps, but at the hand of the nation which murdered and tortured him.

I have not the least belief that the ravages of Napoleon on the banks of the Rhine and Danube were, as Elliot thinks, the fulfilment of the pouring out of this vial on the rivers and fountains, but it may have been, notwithstanding, the judgment of God on a guilty people who had murdered in times long past their fellow-citizens.

8. "And the fourth angel poured out his vial upon the sun; and power was given unto him to scorch men with fire." This is the exact contrary to the painful effect of the sounding of the fourth trumpet. By it men were deprived of the third part of the light of the sun. Here, under the fourth vial, whilst nothing is said of the light, the heat is intensified so as to become insufferable. Alford, as was to be expected, gives no suggestion. Wordsworth writes that this has been already partly accomplished: "The temporal splendour of the Papacy has already had an effect similar to that which is here described. The earthly grandeur of the Romish

9 And men were ‖ scorched with great heat, and ˣ blasphemed the name of God, which hath power over these plagues: ʸ and they repented not ᶻ to give him glory.

10 And the fifth angel poured out his vial

‖ Or, *burned*.
ˣ ver. 11, 21.
ʸ Dan. v. 22, 23. ch. ix. 20.
ᶻ ch. xi. 13. & xiv. 7.

---

hierarchy, its profuse expenditure in pompous pageantries and in sumptuous edifices, its prodigal profusion in the aggrandizement of Papal families, and in their luxurious affluence of palaces, equipages, pictures, statues, demesnes, and gardens, have made themselves felt by those under its sway in galling exactions and oppressive burdens entailed upon them for the maintenance of the solar splendour of that brilliant magnificence. The meridian glory of this spiritual empire has scorched the people of the Romagna and of Italy by the glare of its rays."

Elliot, still more anti-papal, takes a different view. He holds the Emperor of Austria, as the inheritor of the glories of the old Roman empire, to be the sun, and he looks upon the total eclipse of that sun to be the despoiling of the Emperor of Austria of his prestige as the heir of the dignities of the old Roman empire by Napoleon. In 1806, the year after the battle of Austerlitz, we read of the German Emperor's solemn renunciation, on Napoleon necessitating it, of his title of Emperor of the Holy Roman Empire and of Germany. But how an empire which was, if one may use the expression, snuffed out, was empowered to scorch men we are not told. Later on, however, it appears that Mr. Elliot considers it not unlikely that the scorching men as with fire is an allusion to the artillery used by the French Emperor to an extent beyond all former example in military annals. So that the sun on whom the vial is poured has nothing to do with the scorching of men, but they are scorched by an altogether different agent raised up for the purpose.

9. "And they repented not to give him glory." This is the first intimation which we have that these plagues were not designed for vengeance only, but to bring men to repentance.

10. "And the fifth angel poured out his vial upon the seat of the beast; and his kingdom was full of darkness; and they gnawed their tongues," &c. The last angel, the fourth, had poured his vial on the sun, but instead of being darkened, his rays were made more

204   THEY GNAWED THEIR TONGUES. [REVELATION.

^a ch. xiii. 2.
^b ch. ix. 2.
^c ch. xi. 10.

^a upon the seat of the beast; ^b and his kingdom was full of darkness; ^c and they gnawed their tongues for pain.

^d ver. 9, 21.

11 And ^d blasphemed the God of heaven because of their pains and ^e their sores, ^f and repented not of their deeds.

^e ver. 2.
^f ver. 9.

^g ch. ix. 14.
^h See Jer. l. 38. & li. 36.
ⁱ Isa. xli. 2, 25.

12 And the sixth angel poured out his vial ^g upon the great river Euphrates; ^h and the water thereof was dried up, ⁱ that the way of the kings of the east might be prepared.

---

12. "The kings of the east," literally, "the kings which are from the rising of the sun."

insupportable. Here, however, under the fifth angel, there is darkness upon the throne of the beast, which seems to imply the withdrawal of the sun's rays.

Now what is this darkness? It may be either a natural or a spiritual. There is a precedent, as it were, for a natural darkness in God's dealing with Egypt, when there was a thick darkness in all the land of Egypt three days (Exod. x. 22). A spiritual darkness would not occasion pain, it would rather be the benumbing of men's spiritual faculties.

Elliot explains this darkness of the spoliation of the Popedom of all its temporal power under Napoleon, but how can this be prophesied of as an infliction of *darkness*. The teaching of Catholic doctrine, with little intermission, went on in each diocese, one may say in each parish, much the same as ever. No one single act of Napoleon made the Church in the least degree more or less scriptural or more or less evangelical, *i.e.*, according to Mr. Elliot's view of matters.

12. "And the sixth angel poured out his vial upon the great river Euphrates; and the water thereof was dried up, that the way of the kings of the east," &c. There is here a manifest reference to the taking of Babylon by Cyrus, when the waters of the Euphrates, which passed through it, were diverted by canals and the Persian army entered under the gates. It is impossible to say what this manifestly unfulfilled prophecy refers to; and the same may be said

13 And I saw three unclean [k] spirits like frogs *come* out of the mouth of [l] the dragon, and out of the mouth of the beast, and out of the mouth of [m] the false prophet.

[k] 1 John iv. 1, 2, 3.
[l] ch. xii. 3, 9.
[m] ch. xix. 20. & xx. 10.

---

of the remainder of this chapter. The most opposite opinions are entertained by expositors.

Thus, Bishop Wordsworth considers the kings from the sun-rising to be the army of Christ. Bishop Boyd Carpenter, on the contrary, explains "the kings of the east" or of the sun-rising, as the forces of rude and open evil which have been long restrained. As the four barbarian tyrant kings (Gen. xiv. 1-24) from the east invaded the land of promise in Abraham's days, so the leaders of open and violent hate of right, purity, and Christ have the way of their advance prepared.

Alford also considers it a prophecy of evil. "To suppose the conversion of eastern nations, or the gathering together of Christian princes to be meant, or to regard the words as relating to any auspicious event, is to introduce a totally incongruous feature into the series of vials, which confessedly represent the 'seven last plagues.'"

Elliot considers the drying up of the Euphrates to be the wasting away of the Turkish power in the former part of this century.

13, 14. And I saw three unclean spirits like frogs come out of the mouth of the dragon .... For they are the spirits of devils, working miracles which go forth unto the kings," &c. What these spirits are it is utterly impossible to say. Alford writes: "We can only explain the similitude from the uncleanness and the pertinacious noise of the frog." Bishop Wordsworth: "They are called frogs and unclean spirits. They are strangers to the clear light and fresh streams of divine truth, and dwell in the slime and quagmire of sordid cogitations, loving the slough of debasing lusts, or the misty glimmerings of false philosophy and worldly policy, and yet are puffed up with pride, and speak swelling words, and come forth in the evening of the world's existence and make it ring with their shrill discord." Bishop Boyd Carpenter writes: "We must consider their origin. The world-power would have us worship the things seen. It sends forth the spirit of earthliness; the spirit

14 ⁿ For they are the spirits of devils, ᵒ working miracles, *which* go forth unto the kings of the earth ᵖ and of the whole world, to gather them to ᑫ the battle of that great day of God Almighty.

15 ʳ Behold, I come as a thief. Blessed *is* he that watcheth, and keepeth his garments, ˢ lest he walk naked, and they see his shame.

ⁿ 1 Tim. iv. 1. James iii. 15.
ᵒ 2 Thess. ii. 9. ch. xiii. 13, 14. & xix. 20.
ᵖ Luke ii. 1.
ᑫ ch. xvii. 14. & xix. 19. & xx. 8.
ʳ Matt. xxiv. 43. 1 Thess. v. 2. 2 Pet. iii. 10. ch. iii. 3.
ˢ 2 Cor. v. 3. ch. iii. 4, 18.

---

14. "Of the earth and of the whole," omitted by ℵ, A., B., &c.
" That great day," " the great day," ℵ, A.

which works in the voluptuous, the ambitious, and the avaricious; 'the spirit which makes earthly things its end' (Phil. iii. 19). The world culture (lamb-like beast) sends forth its spirit of intellectualism, which denies the spiritual nature of man, and substitutes taste and culture for spirituality. The dragon sends forth the spirit of egoism, of proud self-sufficient independence, which culminates in an utter hatred of the Creator."

"Spirits of devils, working miracles." No doubt the miracles of the latter days effected by the power of Satan, "so as to deceive, if possible, the very elect." Many prophecies converge to assure us that, before the second coming, Satan will be permitted to put forth all his power as the prince of evil spirits.

It is to be remembered that these evil beings come forth, not to reign over men, but to gather them against the good and the right in the final conflict.

Elliot, who alone gives or attempts an historical explanation, holds that this going forth of evil spirits took place in the former part of this century, and considers them to be the spirit of revived infidelity, of revived Romanism, and of sacerdotalism, having its origin in the Tractarian movement.

15. "Behold, I come as a thief. Blessed is he that watcheth," &c. This interjection by our Lord Himself of the suddenness of His second Coming, and how it will find the world, nay even the Church, unprepared, is in remarkable accordance with all the rest of this book, in which, in the midst of its visions, there are so many intimations of the sudden Coming of the Lord. The second Coming —at least, the intimation of its very near approach—is not to be

16 ᵗ And he gathered them together into a   ᵗ ch. xix. 19.
place called in the Hebrew tongue Armageddon.

17 And the seventh angel poured out his vial into the air; and there came a great voice out of

---

found once at the end of the whole series of visions, but all through them, so that the student of the book never knows how close he may be to the consummation (see particularly page 72, where these intimations are enumerated). It is to be remarked and remembered that six times does our Saviour say that He will (when He comes again) come as a thief (Matt. xxiv. 43; Luke xii. 39; 2 Thess. v. 2; 2 Pet. iii. 10; Rev. iii. 3, xvi. 15).

16. "And he gathered them together into a place called in the Hebrew," &c. This place is celebrated in the Old Testament as the scene of various conflicts and defeats. It is the place where Gideon and Barak conquered the enemies of Israel. At Megiddo two kings of Judah, Ahaziah and Josiah, were slain. It has been questioned whether this Armageddon is a locality. Whether the war or battle waged here was not a war of principles. "The progress of the spiritual struggle in individual men must lead us the same way to a mountain of decision, where the long wavering heart must take sides and the set of the character may be determined. But may it not be both together? The principles are good and evil, and at this last period of the world they do not fight only and merely by harangues and debating, but by actual warfare. Why may not a war of principles issue in fierce and bloody engagements? It has been so—witness the wars of the French Revolution—and it will be so again."

17. "And the seventh angel poured out his vial into the air." This has been supposed to have taken place, because Satan is called "the prince of the power of the air" (Ephes. ii. 2).

It may, as some have supposed, be because the air encompasses every thing, and so the vial which is poured upon it is not local in its infliction, but affects everything, and so it is immediately followed by a great earthquake which shakes to pieces every city.

"And there came a great voice out of the temple of heaven, from the throne, saying, It is done."

the temple of heaven, from the throne, saying, ᵘ It is done.

18 And ˣ there were voices, and thunders, and lightnings; ʸ and there was a great earthquake, ᶻ such as was not since men were upon the earth, so mighty an earthquake, *and* so great.

19 And ᵃ the great city was divided into three parts, and the cities of the nations fell: and great Babylon ᵇ came in remembrance before God, ᶜ to

ᵘ ch. xxi. 6.

ˣ ch. iv. 5. & viii. 5. & xi. 19.
ʸ ch. xi. 13.
ᶻ Dan. xii. 1.

ᵃ ch. xiv. 8. & xvii. 18.
ᵇ ch. xviii. 5.
ᶜ Isa. li. 17, 22. Jer. xxv. 15, 16. ch. xiv. 10.

---

17. "Of heaven," omitted by ℵ, A., &c.

"It is done." It is doubtful to what these words—evidently spoken by God Himself—refer. They may be an anticipation of the end of all things, which is certainly imminent: or they may refer to the conclusion of the seven plagues. I cannot help thinking the latter. The word is again spoken by God in chap. xxi. 6, where it refers to the conclusion of the great contest.

18. "And there were voices, and thunders, and lightnings; and there was a great earthquake, such as was not since men," &c. Was this an actual earthquake, or a shaking to pieces of the foundations of human society? We are tempted to explain it as the latter; but we are to remember that we gather from our Lord's predictions of His second coming, that external nature itself will give evidence of the near approach of the personal presence of its Creator. The earth will be moved, the heavens will be rolled up as a scroll, and, as we read (v. 24), "the very islands will be as if they took to themselves wings. The mountains will disappear and will not be found."

19. "And the great city was divided into three parts." What city this is we are not distinctly told, but the last verse of the next chapter seems to imply that it is the harlot—the mystical Babylon. It may allude to some great centre of human society, and not a city of walls and towers. At the first French Revolution all the bulwarks and foundations of human society were, as it were, razed to the ground.

"And great Babylon came in remembrance before God to give unto her." This would seem as if great Babylon were an actual city; but it is clear that she will incur punishment, not as a mere

give unto her the cup of the wine of the fierceness of his wrath.

20 And ᵈ every island fled away, and the mountains were not found.   ᵈ ch. vi. 14.

21 ᵉ And there fell upon men a great hail out of heaven, *every stone* about the weight of a talent: and ᶠ men blasphemed God because of ᵍ the plague of the hail; for the plague thereof was exceeding great.   ᵉ ch. xi. 19.   ᶠ ver. 9, 11.   ᵍ See Exod. ix. 23, 24, 25.

---

city of walls and stones, but as an active centre of evil diffused throughout the world, or that part of it which is the scene of the Apocalyptic visions.

21. "And there fell upon men a great hail out of heaven, every stone about the weight of a talent," &c. A plague of hail similar to this occurred at Beth-horon, when the children of Israel were warring at Gilgal (Josh. x. 11).

It seems also that this last of the plagues of the seven vials was sent, if possible, to reclaim sinful men, but without effect, for, instead of turning to God Who manifested Himself in so terrible an infliction, they blasphemed God. So that this crowning judgment was ineffectual. It seems rather to have hardened those who survived. So that no judgment, no matter how severe, will cause men to repent unless God bruises and breaks the heart with the sense of sin.

CHAP. XVII.

AND there came ᵃ one of the seven angels which had the seven vials, and talked with me, saying unto me, Come hither; ᵇ I will shew   ᵃ ch. xxi. 9.   ᵇ ch. xvi. 19. & xviii. 16, 17, 19.

---

1. "And there came one of the seven angels which had the seven vials," &c. This chapter and the next form one episode, and should be taken as one. For this angel says to the Apostle

unto thee the judgment of ᶜthe great whore ᵈthat sitteth upon many waters:

2 ᵉWith whom the kings of the earth have committed fornication, and ᶠthe inhabitants of the

ᶜ Nahum iii. 4. ch. xix. 2.
ᵈ Jer. li. 13. ver. 15.
ᵉ ch. xviii. 3.
ᶠ Jer. li. 7. ch. xiv. 8. & xviii. 3.

"(Come) hither; I will shew unto thee the judgment of the great harlot." But the judgment of God inflicted upon her because of her sins forms the subject of the eighteenth chapter, to which the seventeenth is preliminary. The question arises, when did the things described in this vision take place? We are told that *one* of the angels which had the seven vials called the Apostle aside— δεῦρο, hither, come hither. Which of the angels it was we are not told, and it is evidently not intended for us to know. We cannot but gather, however, that he had poured out his vial, whichever it was, and was now standing ready to fulfil any behest of God, and he could hardly have given such an account to the Apostle except at the express command of God.

The great harlot had been mentioned twice before as Babylon; once in xiv. 8, "And there followed another angel saying, Babylon is fallen, is fallen, that great city, because she made all nations drink of the wine of the wrath of her fornication," and again xvi. 19, "And great Babylon came in remembrance before God."

"That sitteth upon many waters." This is the first description of the harlot—that she sitteth upon many waters. *The* many waters. These can scarcely be explained as meaning about five or six kingdoms, two of them small ones.

2. "With whom the kings of the earth have committed fornication." This seems to forbid us to interpret the harlot as pagan Rome—the Rome of St. John's time—for there were no kings then existing, except at Parthia, reigning at the outskirts of the Empire.

"Have committed fornication," *i.e.*, they must have been seduced by her into some idolatry, or some other form of declension from God. This can scarcely mean that they "fell away of their own lusts and were enticed." It must mean something which involved their religious belief or practice.

"And the inhabitants of the earth have been made drunk." In ancient Rome there was a remarkable connection between

earth have been made drunk with the wine of her fornication.

3 So he carried me away in the spirit ᵍ into the wilderness: and I saw a woman sit ʰ upon a scarlet coloured beast, full of ⁱ names of blasphemy, ᵏ having seven heads and ˡ ten horns.

ᵍ ch. xii. 6, 14.
ʰ ch. xii. 3.
ⁱ ch. xiii. 1.
ᵏ ver. 9.
ˡ ver. 12.

---

drunkenness and fornication; the low pothouses were in very many cases kept by depraved women, to which no doubt there is here (as well as in verse 4) a covert allusion.

3. "So he carried me away in the spirit into the wilderness." What wilderness is this? The only wilderness which has as yet been mentioned in this book is that into which the woman of chap. xii., when pursued by the dragon, fled. Now it is not impossible that these wildernesses may be the same; for if the woman, though at the first representing pure religion, declines from God, then, in the language of the prophets, she becomes an harlot. Thus Isaiah i. 21, "How is the faithful city become an harlot! it was full of judgment; righteousness lodged in it; but now murderers" (also Jerem. ii. 21).

"I saw a woman sit upon a scarlet coloured beast, full of names of blasphemy." This is, no doubt, the first beast of chap. xiii., for though this one is distinguished by his colour, scarlet, yet there is not likely to be in one book of visions *two* beasts each with seven heads and ten horns. He is supposed to be coloured scarlet because of the blood which he has shed.

"Full of names of blasphemy." Of the beast of chap. xiii. it is said, "upon his heads the name of blasphemy." Here he seems to be covered with these names. What are they? They would seem to be blasphemous titles, by the use of which he arrogates to himself the names and attributes of God. Alford gives as specimens of this blasphemy such names as "most Christian and most faithful king," given to Louis XIV. and Philip II., or "defender of the faith," given to Charles II. and James II.; but surely this is trifling with a most serious matter. It is to be remarked, and we shall have more than once to repeat the remark, that these names of blasphemy are not upon the woman, but upon the beast on which she rides.

"Having seven heads and ten horns." This the angel explains

4 And the woman ᵐ was arrayed in purple and scarlet colour, ⁿ and † decked with gold and precious stones and pearls, ᵒ having a golden cup in her hand ᵖ full of abominations and filthiness of her fornication:

5 And upon her forehead *was* a name written, ᑫ MYSTERY, BABYLON ʳ THE GREAT, ˢ THE

<small>ᵐ ch. xviii. 12, 16.
ⁿ Dan. xi. 38.
† Gr. *gilded.*
ᵒ Jer. li. 7. ch. xviii. 6.
ᵖ ch. xiv. 8.
ᑫ 2 Thess. ii. 7.
ʳ ch. xi. 8. & xiv. 8. & xvi. 19. & xviii. 2, 10, 21.
ˢ ch. xviii. 9. & xix. 2.</small>

in verses 9, 10, and 11. We shall reserve our remarks till we come to these verses.

4. "And the woman was arrayed in purple and scarlet colour, and decked with gold and precious stones and pearls." Assuming that the woman represents a fallen Church, are these—this purple and scarlet and gold—to be accounted parts of her fall. Are they, that is, unlawful, and constitute the Church which uses them, unfaithful to Christ? Why, we find that they were enjoined in the ritual of the Old Testament (not to mention a vast number of other things) that they should be in the breastplate of the high priest. It is impossible to suppose that, if devoutly used, they could help to make the Church which so uses them a filthy harlot. Then, too, as has been noticed, the foundations of the walls of the New Jerusalem were of precious stones, so that their sacred use is claimed for God, and if it is lawful to use any ornament in the service of God, such should be as rare and costly and beautiful as can be procured. We may be sure that the Lord who accepted costly offerings from the Magi would not spurn such things, however He might inspire His servants the prophets to warn men lest they put the slightest trust in them.

"Having a golden cup in her hand full of abominations and filthiness," &c. This, as I said before, alludes to the brothels being kept by abandoned women who sold wine. They were, in fact, low taverns as well as what are now designated as houses of ill-fame. What was the abominable mixture in the cup? It may have been the worship of saints and angels; and it may equally have been Antinomianism, or denial of the Incarnation, or some aspect of infidelity.

5. "And upon her forehead was a name written, Mystery. Babylon the great." Here there seems an allusion to the words

MOTHER OF ‖ HARLOTS AND ABOMINA- ‖ Or, *fornica-*
TIONS OF THE EARTH.   *tions.*

written on the plate on the forehead of the high priest, which was, "Holiness to the Lord," but here it is "Babylon the great, the mother of harlots," &c.

"Mystery." "The name is 'mystery.' Not a mere figure or allegory, but some deep device of Satan, that cannot be understood or explained, in corrupting the Church of God" (Williams, p. 325).

"Mystery." As someone has well said, this seems to forbid us to explain this woman of heathen Rome, for wickedness was, as it were, natural to her, being a heathen city. It was only natural to her to inherit the name of the great heathen city which preceded her in ruling the world and persecuting the people of God.

"Babylon the great." As I go on I shall answer, or at least take notice of, questions which are suggested by the text. Now here with respect to Babylon. It is very remarkable that the term harlot in the Old Testament is not applied to heathen cities, but to such cities as Jerusalem and Samaria, once worshipping the true God, and then fallen from Him into idolatry. Thus Babylon is actually called in one place a virgin, "Come down, and sit in the dust, O virgin daughter of Babylon" (Isaiah xlvii. 1).

"The mother of harlots and abominations of the earth." "Harlots." Are these harlot churches, or are they actual harlots? If harlot churches, which are they? Are they the national churches of France, Spain, Portugal, Italy, and Austria, which invoke in worship the mother of the Lord, and His foster-father, and St. Peter and St. Paul? But take the eastern churches. They are involved in the same saint-worship, and yet they are not usually accounted part of Antichrist, and the Church of Rome can scarcely be said to be the mother of them, for they invoked saints at least as early as she had done. But the Apostle may allude to a totally different state of things, not a religious one, which most certainly, from the luxury which it has caused, may be the mother of those vices which luxury never fails to engender.

Again, as Williams remarks, "The generation [His own generation] against which our Lord testified as 'adulterous,' had no idol worship, but was worse in His sight than that of their forefathers,

> t ch. xviii. 24.
> u ch. xiii. 15.
> & xvi. 6.
> x ch. vi. 9, 10.
> & xii. 11.
>
> 6 And I saw ᵗthe woman drunken ᵘwith the blood of the saints, and with the blood of ˣthe

which had been called adulterous by the prophets on account of actual idolatry."

6. "And I saw the woman drunken with the blood of the saints, and with the blood of the martyrs of Jesus." No church or body of Christians has persecuted with such rancour, with such bitterness, on such a scale, with such determination to stamp out all that she characterizes as heresy, as the Church of Rome. Now in what I say I trust that it will not be taken in palliation, for there cannot be the shadow of palliation for such an institution as the Inquisition, but the question must be asked, how is it that the Church of Rome stands out amongst all churches as the persecuting church? I answer, simply because she has had the power. She has been, in time past, the directress of certain despotic governments who have regarded all differences of opinion in religious matters as dangerous to the state, as dividing it, and so weakening it. Besides this, absolute monarchs, such as those of France and Spain, regarded those who differed from the established religion as differing from themselves, and this of course they would not tolerate; but it is to be remembered that every body of Christians has persecuted when it has had the power. The religious history of this country has, for a century and a half, if not more, been a history of persecution. The Church persecuting Puritans, then when they got the power, Puritans persecuting the Church.

Let the reader get any biographical dictionary and glance over the lives of Calvin, Servetus, and Grotius, and he will get some faint idea of how Protestants could persecute one another.

With respect to this matter of religious persecution, especially at the hands of the Inquisition, Llorente, who wrote with calmness, and had access to the archives of the tribunal, gives an approximate estimate of the number executed under each inquisitor-general, from which it results that the total amount in Spain is about 32,000 persons burnt, either alive or after being strangled, 17,000 burnt in effigy, and 291,000 condemned to various terms of imprisonment, to the galleys, or subjected to other penalties. During the eighteen years of Torquemada's inquisitorship alone, about 8,800 persons were burnt. This calculation does not include the Spanish colonies,

martyrs of Jesus: and when I saw her, I wondered with great admiration.

---

nor the Islands of Sicily and Sardinia which were long subject to the Spanish Inquisition.

It is to be remembered, however, that by far the most cruel tribunals were those of Spain, and it is to be remembered also that in many cases the atrocities perpetrated were not done by the authority of the Pope, but even against his will.[1]

---

[1] A very remarkable instance of this is to be found in the famous trial of Carranza, Archbishop of Toledo, in the reign of Philip II., who had attended Charles V. in his last moments, and whom neither the briefs of the Pope, Pius IV., nor the remonstrances of the prelates assembled at the Council of Trent, could save from being confined in the prisons of the Spanish Inquisition for more than seven years without a termination of his trial; and when at last the Pope, Pius V., demanded of the Spanish inquisitor and of the king, under pain of excommunication, that the archbishop and the papers of his trial should be sent to Rome, all sorts of obstacles were thrown in the way of his departure and his final acquittal by the Pope. After the death of Pius V. new proceedings were set on foot in Spain to prove him guilty of heresy; and on the information being transmitted to Rome, Gregory XIII., who had succeeded Pius V., was, though with evident reluctance, induced to declare on the 14th of April, 1576, that the Archbishop of Toledo was strongly suspected of believing sixteen propositions qualified as Lutheran. He was then sentenced to five years confinement in a Dominican convent and other canonical penances. A few days after this sentence the archbishop, who was then seventy-two years of age, was taken dangerously ill, and before receiving the sacrament, on the 30th of April, he solemnly declared, in presence of several witnesses, "that he had never fallen into the errors with which he had been charged; that his expressions had been distorted to express meanings totally different from his own; that he, however, humbly submitted to the judgment pronounced by the sovereign pontiff, and heartily forgave all those who had taken part against him in the trial, and would pray for them before the throne of grace." On the 2nd of the following May the archbishop died in the convent of La Minerva at Rome, in which he was detained and where he was buried. An inscription was placed over his tomb by order of Gregory XIII., in which he was described as "a prelate illustrious for his birth, his life, his doctrine, his preaching, and his charity." Llorente gives a copious account of this celebrated trial in chapters xxxii., xxxiii., and xxxiv. of his "History of the Inquisition."

The above is from an article entitled "The Holy Office," in Knight's (Penny) "Cyclopædia." I give another short extract from the same article showing that the early Church till the end of the fourth century was exceedingly adverse to temporal punishments for heresy. "The first person on record who was juridically condemned and put to death for heresy is Priscillianus, the leader of a sect in Spain in the latter part of the fourth century. Two Spanish bishops, one of whom was called Idacius, accused Priscillianus, with two other priests or bishops, before a Council held at Bordeaux, A.D. 385. Priscillianus appealed to the Emperor Maximus, who had assumed the imperial purple in Gaul, and who was then residing at Treves, whither Priscillianus and his friends were taken, being followed by their persecutor,

7 And the angel said unto me, Wherefore didst thou marvel? I will tell thee the mystery of the woman, and of the beast that carrieth her, which hath the seven heads and ten horns.

8 The beast that thou sawest was, and is not; and ʸ shall ascend out of the bottomless pit, and ᶻ go into perdition: and they that dwell on the

---

But the question arises, could the cruelties and murders on behalf of Catholicism be said to be a fulfilment of the words, "drunken with the blood of the saints, and with the blood of the martyrs of Jesus?" Were the multitudes condemned by the Inquisition and other tribunals martyrs in the sense in which the original Apostles were martyrs? They might not have been; but their deaths were certainly foul and cruel murders, and have to be repented of and confessed; and, if not, the wrath of a just God must abide on any system which vindicates and upholds them, no matter on what plea.

It is said that when St. John saw the harlot drunk with the blood of saints and martyrs, he was astonished with a great astonishment. He could not have wondered at the blood of saints shed by Domitian, for he was accustomed to that, but to see a Christian Church shedding blood so as to be drunk with it, that was so contrary to all his ideas of the institution of Christ, that his astonishment was unbounded.

7. "And the angel said unto me, Wherefore didst thou marvel? I will tell thee the mystery of the woman, and of the beast that carrieth her.... The beast that thou sawest was, and is not; and shall ascend out of the bottomless pit, and go into perdition." Why does the angel apparently reprove the Apostle for marvelling? It may be because the Apostle marvelled at what was plainly a mystery, which, though human nature prompts us to marvel at it, yet is to be accepted at the mere word of God.

Idacius. Martin, Bishop of Tours, interceded on their behalf, but after his departure from Treves, Maximus entrusted Evodius, the prefect of the Prætorium, with the trial of the accused, and upon his report Maximus condemned them to be beheaded. This cruelty was generally censured, and Ambrose and Martin of Tours strongly reprobated the part which Idacius had acted, and which they characterized as unbecoming the episcopal character. The consequence was that Idacius was excommunicated, and died in exile.

earth ᵃ shall wonder, ᵇ whose names were not written in the book of life from the foundation of the world, when they behold the beast that was, and is not, and yet is.

ᵃ ch. xiii. 3.
ᵇ ch. xiii. 8.

8. "The beast that thou sawest was, and is not; and shall ascend out of the bottomless pit." The only plausible interpretation which is given by commentators is this: "The beast is not so much the Roman Empire as the world-power underlying and acting through all the succession of empires which have in turn dominated in the world and oppressed the people of God. This world-power first was unloosed in Egypt, then in Assyria, then in Babylon, then in Persia and Greece, and lastly in Rome."

But when Rome became Christian, then as a world-power contrary to God it became as if it were not. "Its peculiar power and essence seem suspended while the empire is Christian by profession. The beast (though he is not) is not actually put out of existence, but has only received a deadly wound which shall be again healed." This is the only plausible explanation of the "was, and is not," but the reader will observe that this Christian phase of the beast takes place at least two hundred years after St. John's time, two hundred years after the angel has told him that the beast *is not*. So that the "is not" is in the comparatively far future. This, to me, is exceedingly unsatisfactory, but I have no other explanation to give.

Some explain as if the deadly wound which was healed was the destruction of the beast's power by the Death and Resurrection of Jesus Christ. Thus the Lord says, "of judgment because the prince of this world is judged," and again, "now is the judgment of this world; now shall the prince of this world be cast out."

"And shall ascend out of the abyss." This may be when, as we read in chap. xiii, the beast rises out of the sea, and apparently there and then the dragon "gave him his power, and his seat, and great authority."

"And they that dwell on the earth shall wonder, whose names were not written in the book of life," &c. This wonder means the wonder of admiration. They are, in the great warfare between sin and holiness, secretly on the side of the beast, and their wonder is

9 And ᶜhere *is* the mind which hath wisdom. ᵈThe seven heads are seven mountains, on which the woman sitteth.

ᶜ ch. xiii. 18.
ᵈ ch. xiii. 1.

10 And there are seven kings: five are fallen,

---

aptly expressed in the words of chap. xiii. 4, "Who is like unto the beast? who is able to make war with him?"

9. "And here is the mind which hath wisdom. The seven heads are seven mountains, on which the woman sitteth." Almost all expositors of this book consider this passage as undoubtedly identifying the city (verse 18) with Rome. Thus Horace is quoted, "De quibus septem placuere colles;" and Propertius (iii. 10), "Septem urbs alta jugis, quæ toti praesidet orbi." Another writer, "No one acquainted in the slightest degree with ancient literature can doubt that Rome is the place to which this description points. The seven heads of the beast denote, with regard to the woman, that her capital is the city of the seven hills" (Dean of Llandaff *in loco*). But may I, notwithstanding such confident assertions, be permitted humbly to ask this question: If it undoubtedly fixes the beast to the city of Rome, why should St. John have prefaced what he is about to say with the words, "Here is the mind which hath wisdom," whereas it requires no divine wisdom to see the city of Rome on the seven hills, for it is described as such in some of the best-known heathen authors, as will be seen in such commentaries as those of Alford and Wordsworth?

Evidently by the words, "here is the mind which hath wisdom," the Apostle must allude to something more secret and more mysterious. Now the numeral seven is itself a deeply mysterious one, and may signify here divine completion and may indicate something far more extensive than Rome. The "many waters" are not literal waters, but, as explained in verse 15, "peoples, and multitudes, and nations, and tongues," and so the seven hills (mountains they are not, but mere elevations) may signify something more approaching to the signification of very widespread dominion than we have been led to suppose. Thus, in Isaiah ii. 2, "It shall come to pass in the last days, that the mountain of the Lord's house shall be established in the top of the mountains," &c.

10. "And there are seven kings: five are fallen, and one is, and the other is not yet come." These kings are explained as not indi-

and one is, *and* the other is not yet come; and when he cometh, he must continue a short space.

11 And the beast that was, and is not, even he is the eighth, and is of the seven, ᵉand goeth into perdition.

12 And ᶠthe ten horns which thou sawest are

ᵉ ver. 8.
ᶠ Dan. vii. 20. Zech. i. 18, 19, 21. ch. xiii. 1.

---

vidual kings, but seven empires in which the wild beast (representing the power of the world as opposed to Christ and God) is, as it were, incarnated. The first, by Alford and others, is supposed to be Egypt, the second Assyria, the third Babylon, the fourth Persia, the fifth Greece—these five have fallen, fallen from their high estate as leading kingdoms of the world-power—one, that is Imperial Rome, *is*, and the other is not yet come. When he comes he will not be one kingdom, but ten, which will exercise a sort of joint dominion, but all as one world-power opposed to Christ.

"And when he cometh, he must continue a short space." Short, that is, compared to the duration of the whole world-power, though, in reality, perhaps many centuries. If, however, this king is Antichrist, then he may continue but an actual short space; being destroyed by the appearance of Christ, Who shall destroy him with the spirit of His mouth.

11. "And the beast that was, and is not, even he is the eighth, and is of the seven, and goeth into perdition." He is not the seventh, but the eighth, coming after the reign or power of the seventh is finished. This seems as if the world-power in its last stage would not act through some empire, but directly through Antichrist himself.

"And is of the seven." Meaning not one of the seven, for he is expressly declared to be the eighth, but "of" in the sense of from them—derived from them—concentrating in himself all their power and all their evil.

"And goeth into perdition." He does not simply fall like Egypt or Babylon fell, by losing power and place among the nations, but his perdition is described in chap. xix. 20, "And the beast was taken, and with him the false prophet that wrought miracles before him. . . . . These both were cast alive into a lake of fire burning with brimstone."

12. "And the ten horns which thou sawest are ten kings, which

ten kings, which have received no kingdom as yet; but receive power as kings one hour with the beast.

13 These have one mind, and shall give their power and strength unto the beast.

---

13. "Shall give;" rather, "give," אׄ, A., B.

have received no kingdom as yet." These, taken roughly, seem to be the ten kingdoms into which, so far as western Europe is concerned, the western Roman Empire was broken up by the incursions of the barbarians. The exact number of ten, as I have noticed, cannot be made out. If we take them to be independent kingdoms there are more than ten, in fact nearly double that number.[1]

"No kingdom as yet," *i.e.*, in St. John's time, had appeared, much less ten.

"But receive power as kings one hour with the beast." If this refers to the modern kingdoms of Europe into which the Roman Empire was divided, it is a very awful prophecy respecting them. They share power with him to whom Satan has given "his power, and his seat, and great authority." Are they then utterly godless? Apparently in the eyes of God they are. Is England one of them? Well, we must remember that her amazing works, missionary, philanthropic, Christian, these are not the works of the nation, but of a very small minority of the nation. When God looks down upon London, and regards the mind of that enormous multitude of human beings, can He regard them as on His side? What is the spirit of the vast mass? Is it holy, just, and good, or is it money-making, pleasure-seeking, carnal, sensual, earthly? We cannot answer: He only knows.

13. "These have one mind, and shall give their power and strength," &c. What is this mind? what is the meaning of their having one mind? Is it one mind upon Romanism or Protestantism; upon the rule of faith and the ministry and the Sacraments? or is it one mind upon self-interest, upon the accumulation of wealth,

---

[1] Take the time of the Reformation: 1. England; 2. Scotland; 3. France; 4. Spain; 5. Portugal (always distinct from Spain); 6, 7, 8. Italy (Turin, the States of the Church, South Italy and Sicily); 9. Switzerland; 10. The United Provinces; 11. Germany; 12. Austria; 13. Poland; 14. Hungary; 15. Turkey; 16. Russia, then beginning to be a power; 17. Scandinavia and Denmark.

14 ⁸ These shall make war with the Lamb, and the Lamb shall overcome them: ʰ for he is Lord of lords, and King of kings: ⁱ and they that are with him *are* called, and chosen, and faithful.

15 And he saith unto me, ᵏ The waters which thou sawest, where the whore sitteth, ˡ are peoples, and multitudes, and nations, and tongues.

⁸ ch. xvi. 14. & xix. 19.
ʰ Deut. x. 17. 1 Tim. vi. 15. ch. xix. 16.
ⁱ Jer. l. 44, 45. ch. xiv. 4.
ᵏ Isa. viii. 7. ver. 1.
ˡ ch. xiii. 7.

---

above all upon the permanency, may we not say on the eternity, of the present course of things? Have they not all one mind, or are getting to have one mind upon such things as a superintending Divine Providence; upon the Second Coming, and upon the judgment of all men according to the deeds done in the body? On these things they have one mind, they believe in the world. And so naturally they give their power and strength to the world-power, *i.e.*, to the therion.

14. "These shall make war with the Lamb, and the Lamb shall overcome." What the nature of this warfare is we cannot tell. There is always a state of war between Christ and the world, between Christ and Satan, and He always overcomes, because all power is given unto him in heaven and in earth. Even when his forces receive a reverse or a check, it conduces to the ultimate victory of the truth.

It seems incredible that men should gather themselves together and fight against Christ Himself appearing personally; but men opposed Him when He came the first time. He gave them every proof, consistent with His continuing in a state of humiliation, that He was the Christ, and yet they rejected Him and crucified Him. Why may they not go a step further and fight against Him when He rides on the white horse leading the armies of the saints?

"And they that are with him are called, and chosen, and faithful." He does not conquer without allies. In whatever warfare He is engaged, whether simply spiritual or more outward and visible, He will have His saints with Him and will lead them to victory.

We are called, and chosen, let us see to it that we are faithful. Let it be our one business to make our calling and election sure.

15. "And he saith unto me, The waters which thou sawest,

16 And the ten horns which thou sawest upon the beast, ^m these shall hate the whore, and shall make her desolate ⁿ and naked, and shall eat her flesh, and ^o burn her with fire.

17 ^p For God hath put in their hearts to fulfil his will, and to agree, and give their kingdom

^m Jer. l. 41, 42. ch. xvi. 12.
ⁿ Ezek. xvi. 37-44. ch. xviii. 16.
^o ch. xviii. 8.
^p 2 Thess. ii. 11.

---

16. "Upon the beast." ℵ, A., B., &c., read, "and the beast."

where the whore sitteth." These seem to comprise the multitudinous inhabitants of the whole world. It seems to me next to impossible to understand them of the four or five nations which have hitherto supported the pretensions of the Papacy. Can Italy, Italy which has made Rome the capital of its secular kingdom: and can France be reckoned amongst these people, and nations, and tongues? hardly, for a whole century past. The thread which seems to bind her to the Church of Rome is of the slenderest.

Connected with this prophecy there are questions which I cannot answer. Thus the harlot is said (verse 3) to sit upon the scarlet beast, and yet she sits upon the waters. Has the beast thrown her off? The seven mountains are, in verse 9, expressly said to be the seat of the woman, but here she sits upon the waters of peoples and tongues. Her original seat seems to be on the waters. Then she apparently temporarily sits on the beast, then she sits on the seven hills, but five of these are fallen. It is clear that God has not yet revealed the key to all this.

16. "And the ten horns which thou sawest upon the beast, these shall hate the whore, and shall make her desolate and naked, and shall eat," &c. By anti-papal interpreters, such as Wordsworth, this is said to mean the despoiling of the papacy of her temporal possessions. But the words of the prophecy require a more severe interpretation by far, "shall eat her flesh," followed by "burn her with fire," imply her utter destruction. This destruction seems to be at the hand of man, though it undoubtedly takes place through the providence of God, Who, as we read in the next verse, puts it into the hearts of these kings to fulfil *His* will, whilst they imagine they are carrying out their own or rather the will of the therion, to whom they have surrendered their own individual wills.

CHAP. XVIII.] THAT GREAT CITY. 223

unto the beast, ᑫ until the words of God shall be fulfilled.   ᑫ ch. x. 7.

18 And the woman which thou sawest ʳ is that great city, ˢ which reigneth over the kings of the earth.   ʳ ch. xvi. 19. ˢ ch. xii. 4.

---

17. "Until the words of God shall be fulfilled." This may mean the whole purpose of God with reference to the world which is given to us in part in this book of visions, or it may mean His special prophecies respecting the harlot and the doom awaiting her.

18. "And the woman which thou sawest is that great city, which reigneth over the kings of the earth." This is all in the present—is (ἐστίν) that great city which hath dominion (ἔχουσα βασιλείαν). Does the harlot mean the then existing city of Rome, or does it mean that Rome which will be converted to Christianity, and which, in course of time, will fall from her purity and become unfaithful to God, and so of whom it may be said, as of Jerusalem of old, "How has the faithful city become an harlot" (Isaiah i.)? Or does it signify not one particular city, or the Church of one particular city, but the Church universal which in each and all its branches has declined from God. This we shall be better able to see when we have come to the end of the next chapter.

CHAP. XVIII.

AND ᵃ after these things I saw another angel come down from heaven, having great power; ᵇ and the earth was lightened with his glory.   ᵃ ch. xvii. 1. ᵇ Ezek. xliii. 2.

---

1. "And after these things I saw another angel come down from heaven, having great power; and the earth was lightened with his glory." This is previous to the actual destruction of Babylon. The fall or destruction is represented as already taken place, whereas its actual place in the Apocalyptic series or events is after the end of this chapter and the beginning of the next. In

2 And he cried mightily with a strong voice, saying, ^cBabylon the great is fallen, is fallen, and ^d is become the habitation of devils, and the hold of every foul spirit, and ^ea cage of every unclean and hateful bird.

^c Isa. xiii. 19. & xxi. 9. Jer. li. 8. ch. xiv. 8.
^d Isa. xiii. 21. & xxi. 8. & xxxiv. 14. Jer. l. 39. & li. 37.
^e Is. xiv. 23. & xxxiv. 11. Mark v. 2, 3.

chap. xiv. the same angel is represented as appearing in heaven, and uttering the same prediction of the fall of Babylon.

2. "And he cried mightily with a strong voice .... and is become the habitation of devils, and the hold of every foul spirit, and a cage of every unclean and hateful bird." This account of her debased and degraded state is taken from the prophets Isaiah and Jeremiah. In Isaiah xxxiv. 14, 15, it occurs in a prophecy of Idumæa, "The satyr shall cry to his fellow; the screech owl also shall rest there and .... the great owl make her nest .... there shall the vultures also be gathered," &c. And in Jeremiah xli. 39, the same is predicted respecting Babylon.

What is the reality of this? It was fulfilled literally in the case of Idumæa and also of Babylon. With respect to the city of Rome it never has been fulfilled literally. Rome (the city) never has been rendered desolate as Edom was. The history of Rome ecclesiastical was this. About two centuries after the death of St. John it became Christian. Then, though it retained every article of the faith, its Christianity became corrupted by Mariolatry and saint-invocation, and unwarrantable assumption of supremacy on the part of its bishops over all other bishops. Then at the time of the Reformation it, in a certain measure, reformed itself. Then it passed through the tremendous crisis of the first French Revolution, and emerged from it in much the same state as before. As far as we can gather from history it has never so fallen from the faith or the morality of the Gospel as that its leading bishops or priests could be characterized as "unclean and hateful birds," *i.e.*, of course, so far as the eye of man can see. The present Bishop of Rome could not well be so named; neither, notwithstanding his wrong-headedness, could the last. Two of its late cardinals, brought up in the English Church, were particularly holy men: so that it seems difficult to pronounce this prophecy as anything but an hitherto unfulfilled one. Isaac Williams remarks on this: "('These

3 For all nations ᶠ have drunk of the wine of the wrath of her fornication, and the kings of the earth have committed fornication with her, ᵍ and the merchants of the earth are waxed rich through the ‖ abundance of her delicacies.

4 And I heard another voice from heaven, saying, ʰ Come out of her, my people, that ye be

ᶠ ch. xiv. 8. & xvii. 2.
ᵍ ver. 11, 15 Is. xlvii. 15.
‖ Or, *power*.
ʰ Is. xlviii. 20. & lii. 11. Jer. l. 8. & li. 6, 45. 2 Cor. vi. 17.

---

words) are doubtless to be accomplished in spiritual senses. It is even now seen in places where an adulterous church has been, and is removed: we see infidelity, licentiousness, and ' the unclean and hateful bird ' of heresies—' unclean,' as external to God's Church ; ' hateful,' for our Lord says the ' doctrine of the Nicolaitanes which I hate.'" "The woman," says Aretas, " does not mean any particular city, but the time of Antichrist."

3. "For all nations have drunk .... and the kings of the earth .... and the merchants of the earth are waxed rich through the abundance of her delicacies." "All nations" and "the kings of the earth" have been mentioned previously, but the mention of the merchants of the earth imports a new feature into the whole matter, which we shall have carefully to consider. It infuses, as we shall see, an element of extraordinary difficulty into the reasoning of those who would have us look upon this whole prophecy as fulfilled in Rome, Papal or ecclesiastical, and in nothing else.

4. "And I heard another voice from heaven, saying, Come out of her, my people." This, of course, will not come as an audible voice from heaven but it will be a secret, yet universal intimation to all that are in the mystical Babylon, that they are to leave her society, her fellowship, and it may be, as of course it was in the case of the Babylon of old, to leave the city, if it is Rome or any other city.

Now assuming for a moment the truth of the anti-Papal interpretation, it is perfectly clear that this voice has not as yet come to the ears of God's elect dwelling in the mystic Babylon, for if God's voice were now to sound within their ears, "Come out," we ask it with all reverence, where are they to go ? God would not call them out unless He had provided a place for them. Now, one of the most remarkable things in the history of Christianity has

not partakers of her sins, and that ye receive not of her plagues.

ⁱ Gen. xviii. 20, 21. Jer. li. 9. Jonah i. 2.
^k ch. xvi. 19.
^l Ps. cxxxvii. 8. Jer. l. 15, 29. & li. 24, 49. 2 Tim. iv. 14. ch. xiii. 10.

5 ⁱ For her sins have reached unto heaven, and ^k God hath remembered her iniquities.

6 ^l Reward her even as she rewarded you, and double unto her double according to her works:

6. " Rewarded you." " You," omitted by א, A., B., C.
" Double unto her," omitted by א, A., B., C.

been the utter failure, on the part of the various Protestant bodies which have existed since the time of the Reformation, to provide a home for the true people of God. The Protestantism of Germany and Holland and France and Switzerland has become honeycombed with Rationalism. They have no daily service, no creeds in which the fundamental mystery of Christianity—the Incarnation —occupies its proper place. They disclaim one of the chief features of the Catholic Church—continuity of orders and ministry from the first. Their view of the sacraments, at least that of the most of them, is essentially Zwinglian. It is true we of the Church of England can offer them a Church formed on the primitive model, but those of the Roman communion dwelling here are the merest handful. When this voice of God, then, reaches the ears of devout and faithful Romanists He will have provided a suitable place of shelter for them, and He has certainly not done so as yet.

4, 5. "That ye be not partakers of her sins, and that ye receive not of her plagues. For her sins have reached unto heaven, and God hath remembered," &c. Those who belong to any organization or city or kingdom or state which God regards with just anger on account of its sins will, if they have neglected the warning to leave her, be accounted as if they belonged to her —they will have cast in their lot with her and must take the consequences.

6. " Reward her even as she rewarded you, and double unto her double according," &c. This seems to be said to the people of God who are commanded to come out of her. There is a fearful phase of God's dealings revealed in the Scriptures, in which the righteous are said to be the executioners of God's wrath, and even to rejoice in their work of vengeance. Thus Psalm lviii. 10, " The righteous

[m] in the cup which she hath filled [n] fill to her double.   [m] ch. xiv. 10. [n] ch. xvi. 19.

7 [o] How much she hath glorified herself, and lived deliciously, so much torment and sorrow give her: for she saith in her heart, I sit a [p] queen, and am no widow, and shall see no sorrow.   [o] Ezek. xxviii. 2, &c.   [p] Is. xlvii. 7, 8. Zeph. ii. 15.

8 Therefore shall her plagues come [q] in one   [q] Is. xlvii. 9. ver. 10.

---

shall rejoice when he seeth the vengeance: he shall wash his footsteps in the blood of the ungodly." The sentiment in the text is taken from Jeremiah iv. 15, "Take vengeance upon her, as she hath done do unto her," and in verse 29, "Recompense her according to her work, according to all that she hath done do unto her." This was also said to the harlot Jerusalem, "I will even deal with thee as thou hast done."

"In the cup which she hath filled, fill to her double." So in the thanksgiving of the third vial, "They have shed blood, and thou hast given them blood to drink."

But who are the ministers of this vengeance? We should gather from xvii. 12, that it is the ten horns of the therion who hate the harlot and shall make her desolate, but from this chapter the kings of the earth bewail her and lament for her (verses 9 and 10). Evidently the key is not yet given.

7. "How much she hath glorified herself, and lived deliciously, ... she saith in her heart, I sit a queen, and am no widow." Williams has a beautiful comment. "'She hath glorified herself,' whereas the faithful Church says, God forbid that I should glory, save in the cross of our Lord Jesus Christ. 'And lived deliciously,' but she that liveth in pleasure is dead while she liveth. In the expressive account of the Babylon of old, 'I shall be a lady for ever, I shall not sit as a widow, neither shall I know the loss of children.' She feels not herself a widow from the absence of her Lord, nor fasts on the days wherein the bridegroom is taken away, whereas 'she that is a widow indeed, and desolate, trusteth in God, and continueth in supplications and prayers night and day' (1 Tim. v. 5, 6)."

8. "Therefore shall her plagues come in one day, death, and

day, death, and mourning, and famine; and ʳ she shall be utterly burned with fire: ˢ for strong *is* the Lord God who judgeth her.

9 And ᵗ the kings of the earth, who have committed fornication and lived deliciously with her, ᵘ shall bewail her, and lament for her, ˣ when they shall see the smoke of her burning,

10 Standing afar off for the fear of her torment, saying, ʸ Alas, alas that great city Babylon, that mighty city! ᶻ for in one hour is thy judgment come.

ʳ ch. xvii. 16.
ˢ Jer. l. 34. ch. xi. 17.
ᵗ Ezek. xxvi. 16, 17. ch. xvii. 2. ver. 3.
ᵘ Jer. l. 46.
ˣ ver. 18. ch. xix. 3.
ʸ Is. xxi. 9. ch. xiv. 8.
ᶻ ver. 17, 19.

---

mourning, and famine; and she shall be utterly burned with fire," &c. The fall of old Babylon came suddenly in one night, whilst they were impiously feasting, and drinking wine to the honour of their gods from the sacred vessels of the Temple. The enemy having diverted the course of the river came suddenly under the river gates, and in the graphic words of the prophet, "One post shall run to meet another, and one messenger to meet another, to show the king of Babylon that his city is taken" (Jer. li. 31).

8-10. "And she shall be utterly burned with fire: for strong is the Lord God who judgeth her. And the kings of the earth who have committed fornication and lived deliciously with her. .... Standing afar off for the fear of her torment." Elliot has a very ingenious suggestion here. Looking to the situation of Rome as built on volcanic soil, he supposes that at the bidding of the Almighty the pent up internal flames will break out again and consume the city, and so her paramours, the kings and merchant princes, shall stand afar off when they see the smoke of her conflagration, which they could scarcely be represented as doing if they themselves, or the armies of their neighbours, had kindled it by the ordinary means used in war for the destruction of hostile cities, " Were the mere burning of Rome by human agency the thing intended, whence all the terror and standing afar off of the kings, merchants, and shipmasters?"

He supposes that this fire will never be quenched, but continue eternally burning, and so in this destruction of the Papal

11 And ᵃ the merchants of the earth shall weep and mourn over her; for no man buyeth their merchandise any more: ^{ᵃ Ezek. xxvii. 27-36. ver. 3.}

12 ᵇ The merchandise of gold, and silver, and precious stones, and of pearls, and fine linen, and purple, and silk, and scarlet, and all ‖ thyine wood, and all manner vessels of ivory, and all manner vessels of most precious wood, and of brass, and iron, and marble. ^{ᵇ ch. xvii. 4.} ‖ Or, *sweet*.

13 And cinnamon, and odours, and ointments, and frankincense, and wine, and oil, and fine flour, and wheat, and beasts, and sheep, and horses, and chariots, and ‖ slaves, and ᶜ souls of men. ‖ Or, *bodies*. ᶜ Ezek. xxvii. 13.

---

city there will be at least a partial fulfilment of Isaiah lxvi. 24, "And they shall go forth, and look upon the carcases of the men that have transgressed against me: for their worm shall not die, neither shall their fire be quenched; and they shall be an abhorring unto all flesh."

"And the merchants of the earth shall weep and mourn over her; for no man buyeth their merchandise any more." Can this be true of any inland city—having no trade worth speaking of, no ships, no commerce, no manufactures, no colonies? We must surely look in some other direction than that of Rome for the interpretation. And this becomes still more certain as we proceed.

12, 13. "The merchandise of gold, and silver, and precious stones, and of pearls. ... And cinnamon, and odours, and ointments, and frankincense ... souls of men." Not one of these commodities can be connected particularly with any ecclesiastical state of things. It is impossible, as regards the greater part of them, to interpret them spiritually. And it is to be remembered that they are not merchandise in which the city (or supposed city) traffics, but which she buys. She does not purchase them to sell them again, but to enjoy them, so we cannot but gather from verse 14, the next verse.

14 And the fruits that thy soul lusted after are departed from thee, and all things which were dainty and goodly are departed from thee, and thou shalt find them no more at all.

^d ver. 3, 11.

15 ^d The merchants of these things, which were made rich by her, shall stand afar off for the fear of her torment, weeping and wailing,

^e ch. xvii. 4.

16 And saying, Alas, alas that great city, ^e that was clothed in fine linen, and purple, and scarlet, and decked with gold, and precious stones, and pearls!

^f ver. 10.

^g Is. xxiii. 14. Ezek. xxvii. 29.

17 ^f For in one hour so great riches is come to nought. And ^g every shipmaster, and all the company in ships, and sailors, and as many as trade by sea, stood afar off,

---

17. "And all the company in ships." "Everyone who saileth to a place," so ℵ, A., B., C., &c.

Now there happens to be one iniquitous species of traffic with which the history of Rome is associated—that which nearly four centuries ago was on the eve of bringing about the destruction of her whole system, the sale of indulgencies—but by no possibility can any one of the species of merchandise recounted here with such particularity be imagined to typify or signify spiritually any such traffic. They are each and all the sort of commodities which would be gathered for sale in any great port of some great luxurious empire, and nothing else. The cinnamon, and odours, and incense, and ointments are necessary articles of oriental luxury, as are the precious stones and the vessels of ivory, and to say that the destruction of an inland city would make all the merchants of the earth lament (evidently as a body) because no man buyeth their merchandise any more, seems as inapplicable to a city of priests and monks as any perversion of prophecy can well be.

And yet this is nothing to what is coming in the 17th verse.

17, 19. "And every shipmaster, and all the company in ships, and sailors, and as many as trade by sea, stood afar off. . . . And they cast dust on their heads, and cried, weeping and wailing, saying,

18 ʰ And cried when they saw the smoke of her burning, saying, ⁱ What *city is* like unto this great city!

19 And ᵏ they cast dust on their heads, and cried, weeping and wailing, saying, Alas, alas that great city, wherein were made rich all that had ships in the sea by reason of her costliness! ˡ for in one hour is she made desolate.

ʰ Ezek. xxvii. 30, 31. ver. 9.
ⁱ ch. xiii. 4.
ᵏ Josh. vii. 6. 1 Sam. iv. 12. Job ii. 12. Ezek. xxvii. 30.
ˡ ver. 8.

Alas, alas that great city wherein were made rich all that had ships," &c. Now we would ask, with all reverence, what is the purpose of Almighty God with respect to prophecy? Is it not to warn His people respecting coming judgments which they are to be aware of, and so "flee from the wrath to come." But if this be so the prophecy must present features which are recognizable. The traffic of Papal Rome has been in the sale of indulgencies, in fees at institution to bishoprics and other dignities, in mortuary masses, in exactions, in exemptions—not in anything which can enrich merchants, shipowners, sailors, and such like. There are features, as for instance, the sitting on the seven hills, which would seem to lead us to believe that the Church of Rome is intended, and when one comes to look at her unwarrantable pretensions, based upon gross frauds, her persecution by torture and burning of all who differ from her, her saint worship and Mariolatry—such things have made men like Isaac Williams say, "It must be allowed that the prophecy does in some awful manner hover, as with boding raven wing, over Rome." And even when deprecating the reference to Rome he writes: "There would be no reason, according to the analogy of the Apocalypse, to conclude that Rome is here literally intended, were it not from the fact of there being a Church there of so wonderful and mysterious a character."

I agree with all this, but it seems to me that these references to cargoes (γομον), to freights, to ships, shipowners, &c., must be intended to lead us to look in another direction—in fact to a collapse of a great commercial system—not of a political, or of a social, or least of all, of an ecclesiastical, but of a commercial system, and apparently, to me, of nothing else. It is as if London and Liverpool and Glasgow and New York were all amalgamated

20 ᵐRejoice over her, *thou* heaven, and *ye* holy apostles and prophets ; for ⁿGod hath avenged you on her.

21 And a mighty angel took up a stone like a great millstone, and cast *it* into the sea, saying, °Thus with violence shall that great city Babylon be thrown down, and ᵖshall be found no more at all.

ᵐ Is. xliv. 23. & xlix. 13. Jer. li. 48.
ⁿ Luke xi. 49, 50. ch. xix. 2.
° Jer. li. 64.
ᵖ ch. xii. 8. & xvi. 20.

---

20. "And ye holy apostles and prophets." "Ye holy ones and ye apostles," א, A., B., &c.

together and involved, as in a moment, in one common and irreversible ruin.

If it be asked, can a commercial system be so evil in the sight of God as that He should prophecy that its overthrow should delight the angels in heaven? I answer, has anything else revived in the cities of Christian Europe the worst sins of heathenism? Look at the vice, the misery, the prostitution, the fraud, the overreaching, the gambling, the drunkenness which is rife among the populations of the huge cities of Europe and America; the direct result of their commercial prosperity, which seems to suck up as in a vortex the iniquity and misery of the world.

If the Almighty had intended (primarily) to put us on our guard against a great ecclesiastical centre, would He have made the collapse and ruin of such a metropolis the occasion of wailing to shipowners, because no persons could be found any more to buy their cargoes? Impossible. As Alford has written, "The details of this mercantile lamentation far more nearly suit London than Rome at any assignable period of her history."

20. "Rejoice over her, thou heaven, and ye holy apostles and prophets." The Rome of old, heathen Rome, actually destroyed such holy Apostles as Peter and Paul by putting them to death. Rome Papal can only be said to persecute them by corrupting their teaching.

21. "And a mighty angel took up a stone like a great millstone, and cast it into the sea, saying, Thus with violence." As we should say, "Thus with a rush." It combines the idea of violence and suddenness or swiftness.

THE VOICE OF HARPERS.

22 ᵠAnd the voice of harpers, and musicians, and of pipers, and trumpeters, shall be heard no more at all in thee; and no craftsman, of whatsoever craft *he be*, shall be found any more in thee; and the sound of a millstone shall be heard no more at all in thee;

23 ʳAnd the light of a candle shall shine no more at all in thee; ˢand the voice of the bridegroom and of the bride shall be heard no more at all in thee: for ᵗthy merchants were the great men of the earth; ᵘfor by thy sorceries were all nations deceived.

24 And ˣin her was found the blood of prophets, and of saints, and of all that ʸ were slain upon the earth.

ᵠ Is. xxiv. 8.
Jer. vii. 34.
& xvi. 9. &
xxv. 10.
Ezek. xxvi. 13.

ʳ Jer. xxv. 10.
ˢ Jer. vii. 34.
& xvi. 9. &
xxv. 10. &
xxxiii. 11.
ᵗ Is. xxiii. 8.
ᵘ 2 Kings ix. 22. Nah. iii. 4. ch. xvii. 2, 5.
ˣ ch. xvii. 6.
ʸ Jer. li. 49

22, 23. " And the voice of harpers, and musicians, and of pipers .... and no craftsman .... sound of a millstone .... light of a candle .... voice of the bridegroom and the bride." None of these are specially connected with such a capital as Rome. It has not had in its ecclesiastical times the reputation of being a joyous and light-hearted city, as Paris or Naples. Not a city of craftsmen, if we except the copying of pictures, nor a city of bridegrooms and brides. That the light of candles should not be seen there, and the sound of millstone should not be heard, seems to point to a ruined city, not one destroyed from the foundations in a moment by such natural causes as are suggested by Mr. Elliot.

No one can read these verses over without being struck with their extraordinary sublimity and beauty. It is as if the Apocalyptic seer lamented with all his heart the desolation which it was laid upon him to foretell.

EXCURSUS ON THE APPLICATION OF THE PROPHECY TO ROME.

What then are we to understand by the great harlot. It has been said:

1. That it means the Church and city of Rome; or that
2. It signifies not Rome only, but universal Christendom, every part and branch of which has been guilty of compromising more or less with the world, and so has been guilty of spiritual fornication; or
3. That it means heathen Rome, and not Christian Rome or a Christian system at all.

(1.) With respect to the first it has been till some years past the almost universal opinion of Protestant interpreters, and so has got thoroughly rooted in not only our religious prejudices, but almost, one might say, in our literature.

That the figure of a harlot represents an apostate Church we gather from the Old Testament, "How is the faithful city become an harlot! it was full of judgment; righteousness lodged in it; but now murderers" (Isaiah, i. 21); so also Jeremiah ii. 20, 21; Ezekiel, xxiii. (Aholah and Aholibah); Hosea ii. 2.

Now for men who regarded the Apocalypse as an historical sketch of the fortunes or vicissitudes of the Church from St. John's time till the second Advent, and who were intensely embittered against the Church of Rome for her persecutions of all who opposed her pretensions, it was only natural to regard this church as exclusively the harlot. "Not a few of the darkest traits of 'Babylon' apply to her with a closeness of application which may not unnaturally lead us to think that the picture of these chapters has been drawn from nothing so much as her. Her idolatries, her outward carnal splendour, her oppression of God's saints, her merciless cruelties with torture, the dungeon and the stake, the tears and agonies and blood with which she has filled so many centuries, these and a thousand circumstances of a similar kind may well be our excuse if in Babylon we read Christian Rome. Yet this interpretation is false" (Milligan).

Now in looking over the counts of accusation against her, there is, first of all, her enormous pretensions—pretensions which simply amount to this, that to have fellowship with Christ men must have fellowship with the Bishop of Rome; and these pretensions based partly upon such absurdities as Rome being the burial place of the Apostles Peter and Paul, and partly upon the most impudent and baseless forgeries. This pretension is expressed in Rev. xviii. 7, "how much she hath glorified herself... she saith in her heart, I sit a queen, and am no widow, and shall see no sorrow." It would take me far too long to go over, even very summarily, the history of these pretensions; suffice it to say, that in their present state they mainly depend on what are called the false decretals, the forged letters of Popes from Clement of Rome to the middle of the eighth century. They were first published by one Isidore Mercator, about the year 850, and were at once accepted by Rome, *i.e.*, by the Bishop of Rome, though he must have known that there were no such letters or decretals in the archives of Rome, where, of course, they would have been if they were genuine. The reader, if he chooses, will see the account of these letters in a note on them at the end of Dr. Littledale's "Petrine Claims." Now considering that the late origin of these forgeries is allowed on all hands, is it not due to the truth of God, rather, to the God of truth, to disclaim them, and to acknowledge that the present Papal pretensions as set forth at the last Vatican council are based upon falsehoods. Without asserting that the putting forth of such claims, based on such untruths, of itself constitutes her to be the harlot, it most certainly makes her a rebel against the truth of God, and will sooner or later bring her under the judgment denounced against every one who "loveth and maketh a lie."

(2.) Then, in the next place, men have naturally held her to be the harlot because of her idolatrous invocation of the Blessed Virgin and saints. I subjoin the following from a well-known writer, the Rev. R. F. Littledale, who cannot be accused of the smallest leaning to ultra-Protestantism. "It is not true, as is often alleged in defence [of prayers to the Virgin and saints] that the prayers of the departed saints are asked only in the same sense as those of living ones, with the added thought that they are now more able to pray effectually for us. The petitions are not at all limited to a mere 'Pray for us,' but are constantly of exactly the same kind and wording as those addressed to Almighty God, and are offered kneeling and in the course of Divine Service, which is not how we ever ask the prayers of living friends. A few specimens are here set down from the 'Raccolta' (Engl. Translation, Burns and Oats, 1873), a collection of prayers specially indulgenced by the Popes, and therefore of indisputable authority in the Roman Church.

"' Hail, Mary, Queen, Mother of Mercy, our Life, Sweetness, and Hope, all hail! To thee we cry, banished sons of Eve, to thee we sigh, groaning and weeping in this vale of tears. Turn then, O our Advocate, thy merciful eyes to us, and after this our exile show us Jesus, the blessed fruit of thy womb. O merciful, O loving, O sweet Virgin Mary.'

V. "' Make me worthy to praise thee, O sacred Virgin.'

R. "' Give me strength against mine enemies.'

2. "' We fly beneath thy shelter, O holy Mother of God, despise not our petitions in our necessities, and deliver us always from all perils, O glorious and blessed Virgin.'

3. "' Heart of Mary, Mother of God . . . . worthy of all the veneration of angels and men. . . . . Heart full of goodness, ever compassionate towards our sufferings, vouchsafe to thaw our icy hearts. . . . . In thee let the Holy Church find safety, shelter; protect it and be its sweet asylum, its tower of strength. . . . . Be thou our help in need, our comfort in trouble, our strength in temptation, our refuge in persecution, our aid in all dangers. . . . .'

4. "' Sweet heart of Mary, be my salvation.'

5. "' Leave me not, my Mother, in my own hands, or I am lost. Let me but cling to thee. Save me, my hope; save me from hell.'

6. "' Michael, glorious prince, chief and champion of the heavenly host . . . . vouchsafe to free us from all evil, who with full confidence have recourse to thee.'

7. "' Benign Joseph, our guide, protect us and the holy Church.'

8. "' Guardian of virgins, and holy father Joseph, to whose faithful keeping Christ Jesus, innocence itself, and Mary, virgin of virgins, were committed, I pray and beseech thee by these two dear pledges, Jesus and Mary, that, being preserved from all uncleanness, I may, with spotless mind, pure heart, and chaste body, ever most faithfully serve Jesus and Mary. Amen.'

"It may, perhaps, be argued, that expressions of devotion, even if somewhat unguarded, are not to be rigidly weighed and judged. Some extracts from a formal theological work, Liguori's 'Glories of Mary,' are therefore added here: 'Queen Mother and Spouse of the King, to her belong dominion and power over all creatures.

She is Queen of Mercy, as Jesus is King of Justice.' 'In the Franciscan chronicles it is related that brother Leo saw a red ladder, on the top of which was Jesus Christ; and a white one, on the top of which was His most holy Mother; and he saw some who tried to ascend the red ladder, and they mounted a few steps and *fell*; they tried again, and again *fell*. They were then advised to go and try the white ladder, and by that one they easily ascended; for our Blessed Lady stretched out her hands and helped them, and so they got safely to heaven.'"

If this (as observes Dr. Littledale) which Liguori twice uses as proof of the tenet it involves, be not blasphemy against the Lord Jesus, and a formal denial of His power to save, and His being the way to heaven, there are no such sins possible.

I might have filled this whole volume with such instances, but I take these from Dr. Littledale's book because of his known High Church opinions. They are not taken from Orange tracts against Romanism, but from the writings of a learned man who would carefully weigh every word that he wrote on such a subject.

Then a third count against her has been her diabolical persecutions. I have entered fully upon this in my notes on chap. xvii. 6, and must direct my reader back to this. Suffice it now to refer to authorized documents asserting her right to extirpate heresy. Thus in the catechism of the Council of Trent: "It is not to be denied that heretics and schismatics are within the power of the Church, and may be called to trial by her, be punished, and condemned by anathema;" and, by the third canon of the fourth council of Lateran, accounted a general council by the Roman Church, it is ordered that "all secular princes do extirpate every heretic in their states; and in the event of failure to comply with this injunction, such princes are to be excommunicated, their subjects released from their oath of allegiance, and their territories to be given to Catholics, who are to destroy the heretics and possess the country as their reward."

And this was so faithfully carried out that in Spain alone 32,000 persons were burnt, either alive or after being strangled, 17,000 burnt in effigy, and 291,000 condemned to various forms of imprisonment, to the galleys, or subjected to other penalty. It is appalling to think of the amount of misery represented by these statements, and that in one Roman Catholic country alone.

One would think that these three counts alone, her pretensions based on gross misconception and fraud, her creature worship and her persecutions by fire, stake, and steel, would have been sufficient to brand her as the harlot, and yet there is much in history that is overwhelmingly (I may say) against it.

For first of all this (so-called) harlot Church has been the pillar of the truth of our Blessed Lord's Incarnation, or at least of His Godhead. This is very fully acknowledged by such a prejudiced writer as Mr. Elliot. In speaking of the Gothic invasions under the figure of the river cast out of the dragon's mouth: "The successive tribes, whether of Visigoths, Ostrogoths, Heruli, Huns, &c., abandoned their Paganism for Christianity. At first sight indeed it was for the most part *Arian*—pseudo-Christianity. Such was their profession in France, Spain, and Africa. But after a century or more of the flux and reflux of the invading flood, this, too, was abandoned for the more orthodox Trinitarian Christian faith. The influence of the Roman See, which was gradually more and more operative with the barbarians, powerfully tended to this result."

Now this defence and promulgation of the true faith on the part of the Church of Rome was done by her when, according to ultra-Protestant interpreters, she was fast becoming Antichrist. By the years 600 or 700 she had become Antichrist, and this flood of the barbarians took place at different times in the two preceding centuries. But did she continue to hold this faith? Let us take her at the time in which she was supposed to be at her worst, the time, say, of the Council of Trent. In the catechism of the Council of Trent Question Fourteen is, "What advantages and blessings are chiefly bestowed upon the human race through the Passion of Christ?" Answer: "It alone remains that the blessing and advantages which flow to the human race from the Passion of Christ be accurately explained by the pastor. In the first place, then, the Passion of our Lord was our deliverance from sin; for as St. John says, 'He hath loved us and washed us from our sins in His own Blood.' 'He hath quickened you together with Him,' says the Apostle, 'having forgiven you all trespasses,' &c. In the next place, it hath rescued us from the tyranny of the devil, for our Lord Himself says, 'Now is the judgment of this world: now shall the prince of this world be cast out. And I, if I be lifted up from the earth will draw all unto me.' He hath also discharged the punishment due to our sins. And next, as no sacrifice more grateful and acceptable could have been offered to God, He hath reconciled us to the Father, appeased His wrath, and propitiated His Justice. Finally, by taking away our sins, He opened unto us heaven, which was closed by the common sin of the human race, as the Apostle doth signify in these words, 'Having therefore, brethren, a boldness to enter into the holiest by the Blood of Jesus.' Nor is there wanting some type and figure of this mystery under the Old Law, for those who were prohibited to return into their native country before the death of the high-priest, typified that until that Supreme and Eternal High-priest, Christ Jesus, had died, and by dying had opened the gates of heaven to those who, purified by the Sacraments, and gifted with faith, hope, and love, become partakers of His Passion, no one, however just and pious his life, could have gained admission into the heavenly country."

Anyone who knows anything of Roman devotional writing will confess that, no matter what their errors in other respects, God has not withheld from them the faith and the confession of Christ crucified.

Then, in the next place, more than any Western Church, or Christian body in Western Europe, the Roman Church has set forth the Apostolic life of self-denial and absolute poverty. There have been numerous bodies of men, Dominicans, Franciscans, Passionists, &c., who have given up all worldly goods and devoted themselves to missionary work, in preaching, teaching the young, tending the sick in hospitals, visiting the poorest of the poor, reclaiming criminals, shutting themselves up among lepers, in fact, devoting themselves to every conceivable work of mercy and religion.

Then, in the next place, she has nourished a number of saints who have exhibited to men the highest types of unworldliness and devotion. Amongst a multitude of others we name Aquinas, Bernard, Anselm, Charles Borromeo, Francis Xavier, Theresa, Francis de Sales, and in our own days, Father Damien. One brought up in Presbyterianism has confessed that the Church of Rome has nurtured the noblest types of devotion that the world has ever seen (Milligan, "On Revelation," Baird Lecture, page 184).

With respect to the Roman Church being the Apocalyptic harlot, it is to be remembered that every church or body of professing Christians has, in some very important particular, fallen from God. Thus the Greek Communion has been equally tainted with creature worship, especially in respect of Mariolatry, as the

Roman. Then look at the declension of the continental Protestant bodies in France, Holland, Switzerland, and Germany from the confession of the Godhead of Christ. Which, if it may be allowable to suggest such a comparison, must be the worst error in the sight of God, an undue honour of the Virgin, so as even to worship her, because of her having been ordained by God as the instrument of His Son's Incarnation; or a scornful denial, through Rationalistic principles, of any Incarnation at all: and then if the decline of the Romish Church be owing to worldliness, what could exceed the secularity of the Church of England in the last century? Considerations like these have made many good men think that the harlot represents not a fallen Church, but a fallen Christendom.

Some, however, as Dean Vaughan, have interpreted the harlot of heathen Rome, and not Christian (*i.e.* Papal) Rome at all: "Against the Empire of Rome St. John was instructed to lift up the voice of prophecy: that was the foe then predominant; the foe which invaded the sanctuaries, and desolated the homes of the Church. Cold and scanty had been the comfort for those days if St. John, as some have dreamed, had been directed to keep silent on the present, and to promise deliverance from an enemy not yet arisen. Prophecy would have been wanting to her chief duty, and neglectful of her noblest office, if she had overleaped the Empire and sought out the Papacy; if she had disregarded the calamity that was, and spoken only of a corruption not yet operative. Those who interpret the mystic Babylon as descriptive of the errors and vices of the Papacy, forget how the same thing would have presented itself to them under Nero or under Domitian; how barren and unpersuasive would have been the word of prediction which regarded only the sufferers under a Hildebrand or a Borgia."

This reasoning does not seem to me just. It is only true if the Apocalyptic visions only refer merely to the time of the Apostle. If they have any reference to further and more distant evils, then such evils may, by the Holy Spirit, be brought within the horizon of the Seer.

But it is to be remembered that it by no means follows that if the Church of Rome be not the harlot, God will not visit her, because of her unwarranted pretensions to universal dominion based on forgeries, and also because of her gross Mariolatry and creature worship, and because of her centuries of murder and cruelty in upholding her pretensions.

If any Church, just as any Christian man or woman, has committed a sin, that sin has to be lamented and confessed, and if it be an open sin known to all mankind has to be openly confessed, ere the all-atoning Blood can be applied; or else what truth is there in the Apostolic declaration, "If we confess our sins he is faithful and just to forgive us our sins"?

And this, because of its claim of infallibility in all times and places, applies more directly to the Church of Rome than to any other Church. She claims an absolute identity throughout the ages. If so, she is bound to confess the murders and cruelties committed by her, and sanctioned by the express authority in past ages of her chief pastors. It is no excuse to say that in past times governments universally sanctioned such modes of defending the truth. Being infallible, she ought to have known better, and ought to have made her voice heard in reprobating such scandals on the religion of Christ.

CHAP. XIX.

AND after these things ᵃI heard a great voice of much people in heaven, saying, Alleluia; ᵇSalvation, and glory, and honour, and power, unto the Lord our God:

ᵃ ch. xi. 15.
ᵇ ch. iv. 11.
& vii. 10, 12.
& xii. 10.

---

1. "And honour," omitted by א, A., B., C.
"Are our Gods." א, A., B., C.

1. "And after these things I heard a great voice of much people in heaven, saying, Alleluia; Salvation, and glory, and honour, and," &c. This is in strong contrast with what we have read in the last chapter. There we had lamentation of kings and merchant princes and shipmasters and sailors over the fall of Babylon. Here we have the rejoicing of the multitudes in heaven, who see things as God sees them, over the same catastrophe. For "just and true are his judgments, for he hath judged the great whore."

Whatever secondary causes may have brought about the destruction of Babylon, it is all God's doing altogether. His arm

2 For ᶜtrue and righteous *are* his judgments: for he hath judged the great whore, which did corrupt the earth with her fornication, and ᵈhath avenged the blood of his servants at her hand.

3 And again they said, Alleluia. And ᵉher smoke rose up for ever and ever.

4 And ᶠthe four and twenty elders and the

ᶜ ch. xv. 3. & xvi. 7.
ᵈ Deut. xxxii. 43. ch. vi. 10. & xviii. 20.
ᵉ Isa. xxxiv. 10. ch. xiv. 11. & xviii. 9, 18.
ᶠ ch. iv. 4, 6, 10. & v. 14.

---

has wrought the salvation; to His power it is altogether to be ascribed.

2. "For true and righteous are his judgments: for he hath judged the great whore, which did corrupt the earth with her fornication." "True and righteous are his judgments." For He hath condemned the harlot because of her evil—because of her corrupting the earth. Again I repeat, it seems impossible to understand the earth here of a few kingdoms in the West of Europe, important though those kingdoms may have been in the history of the world and of the Church. The earth must mean far more than what remained to the Papacy of the ten kingdoms of mediæval Europe. Though the Alleluia was heard in heaven, yet if the lamentation took place upon earth, upon earth it must have been heard; but no such lamentation of kings and nobles and merchants has as yet assailed the ears of men.

If the avenging of the blood of God's servants be punishment exacted from the harlot in this world, then no such infliction has as yet taken place.

3. "And again they said, Alleluia. And her smoke rose up," &c. Is this the smoke of the everlasting burnings of lost souls, or is it to be understood of perpetual desolation as if by fire, as in the last chapter (xviii. 18), where not souls in Gehenna, but the shipmasters and all the company of sailors stood afar off when they saw the smoke of her burning, saying, "What city is like unto this great city"? And in Isaiah xxxiv. 10, which was evidently before the eye of the Seer, it is spoken of the perpetual desolation of Edom, not in the future world, but in this.

4. "And the four and twenty elders and the four living ones," &c. It is evident from this particular mention of the worship of the highest of created existences, that by the vengeance executed

four beasts fell down and worshipped God that sat on the throne, saying, ^g Amen; Alleluia.

5 And a voice came out of the throne, saying, ^h Praise our God, all ye his servants, and ye that fear him, ⁱ both small and great.

6 ^k And I heard as it were the voice of a great multitude, and as the voice of many waters, and as the voice of mighty thunderings, saying, Alleluia: for ^l the Lord God omnipotent reigneth.

7 Let us be glad and rejoice, and give honour

g 1 Chron. xvi. 36. Neh. v. 13. & viii. 6. ch. v. 14.
h Ps. cxxxiv. 1. & cxxxv. 1.
i ch. xi. 18. & xx. 12.
k Ezek. i. 24. & xliii. 2. ch. xiv. 2.
l ch. xi. 15, 17. & xii. 10. & xxi. 22.

---

5. "And ye that fear him." "And ye," omitted by א, C., but retained by A., B.

on the harlot some great way unknown to us was opened for the final glory of God and the triumph of His Church.

Amen and Alleluia are both Hebrew words, and it has been thrown out that this betokens a Jewish or Hebrew element; but this is absurd, for we learn from 1 Corinthians xiv. that the repetition of Amen formed a recognized part of the Eucharistic service. "In these days," says St. Augustine, "throughout the world the Amen and the Allelujah is sung." And Jerome also confirms this: "The Amen and Allelujah in likeness of the heavenly thunderings."

5. "And a voice came out of the throne, saying, Praise our God, all ye his servants," &c. This voice from the throne is not the voice of Christ, who in John xx. distinguishes Himself from the creatures of God, "I ascend to my God and your God," but probably is the voice of one of the living ones, or of one of the elders.

6. "And I heard as it were the voice of a great multitude . . . the Lord God omnipotent reigneth." He reigneth without a rival. Hitherto He had allowed Satan, the world power embodied in the beast and the false prophet to usurp His place, now He puts them aside, and destroys them. This is spoken in anticipation of what is brought about in verse 20 of this chapter. The Apocalyptic Seer, as is his wont, speaks of things hereafter to take place as if they were already accomplished (see xiv. 8; and xvi. 19).

7. "Let us be glad and rejoice, and give honour to him, for the

to him: for ᵐthe marriage of the Lamb is come, and his wife hath made herself ready.

8 And ⁿto her was granted that she should be arrayed in fine linen, clean and ‖ white: ᵒfor the fine linen is the righteousness of saints.

9 And he saith unto me, Write, ᵖBlessed *are* they which are called unto the marriage supper of

ᵐ Mat. xxii. 2. & xxv. 10. 2 Cor. xi. 2. Eph. v. 32. ch. xxi. 2, 9.
ⁿ Ps. xlv. 13, 14. Ezek. xvi. 10. ch. iii. 18.
‖ Or, *bright.*
ᵒ Ps. cxxxii. 9.
ᵖ Mat. xxii. 2, 3. Luke xiv. 15, 16.

---

marriage of the Lamb is come, and his wife hath made herself ready." The marriage supper of the Son of the great King is represented in the Gospels as the consummation of this dispensation (Matt. xxii. 2). At the close it is brought before us as ten virgins going forth to meet the bridegroom. From St. Paul we learn that the work of grace in the hands of Christ's ministers is an espousal to one husband, that each and all may be presented as a chaste virgin to Christ (2 Cor. xi. 2), and further and more explicitly in the Epistle to the Ephesians, the husband is the head of the wife, even as Christ is the head of the Church, and He is the Saviour of the mystical body, and we His people are not only His servants, not only His brethren, but members of His body, of His flesh and of His bones, and will, if we continue in the faith, be presented by Himself to Himself, as a glorious Church, not having spot or wrinkle, or any such thing, but holy and without blemish (Ephes. v. 25-27). This marriage of the Lamb is not described, only in a future chapter an angel says to the Apostle, "Come hither, and I will show thee the bride, the Lamb's wife," and he proceeds to show him an unspeakably great and glorious city.

8. "And to her was granted that she should be arrayed in fine linen, clean and white: for the fine linen is the righteousness of saints." Not without Christ, for they have washed their robes and made them white in the Blood of the Lamb. And yet it is their own. The whiteness of their garments corresponds with the purity of their souls. It is impossible even to imagine that amongst the realities of heaven there should be such an incongruity as a robe of righteousness thrown over a polluted soul to hide its defilement.

9. "And he saith unto me, Write, Blessed are they which are

the Lamb. And he saith unto me, ^q These are the true sayings of God.

10 And ^r I fell at his feet to worship him. And he said unto me, ^s *See thou do it* not: I am thy fellowservant, and of thy brethren ^t that have

^q ch. xxi. 5. & xxii. 6.
^r ch. xxii. 8.
^s Acts x. 26. & xiv. 14, 15. ch. xxii. 9.
^t 1 John v. 10. ch. xii. 17.

---

called unto the marriage supper," &c. What does this calling mean? Does it mean that they are effectually called, so that they cannot resist the invitation? The Lord's own parable in Matt. xxii. seems to forbid such a view. All God's calls have to be responded to and accepted and continued in. Or does it mean some calling at the last? Amongst the Jews there was a second calling. "All things are now ready, come to the marriage." This calling may be restricted to those who are known by God to be worthy.

"And he saith unto me, These are the true sayings of God." Interjected as it were, so that we may pay the more reverent attention to them. It is like the Saviour's twofold Amen before some of His more important sayings.

10. "And I fell at his feet to worship him. And he said unto me, See thou do it not." Temptations are according to the nature of the minds to which they present themselves. This was a temptation to no other than an Apostle. In order to see its force we must enter somewhat into the glory of the angelic nature and into the unspeakable greatness of the revelation set before him by the ministry of that angel. Ordinary religious minds will wonder at the Apostle being tempted, even for a moment, to do such a thing, but this wonder arises from their utter inability to realize what the Apostle saw. An angel is to them an ordinary fellow-creature, perhaps very ordinary, because they have never set before themselves the ministrations of these exalted ones, as Hooker did a little before he was called hence to join their company.

"I am thy fellowservant, and of thy brethren that have the testimony of Jesus," *i.e.*, of thy brethren the prophets, for the ability to set before our fellow-creatures the person and work of Jesus Christ is the spirit of prophecy.

The highest prophets can say nothing greater or so great as the glory and grace of Jesus.

the testimony of Jesus: worship God: for the testimony of Jesus is the spirit of prophecy.

^u ch. xv. 5.
^x ch. vi. 2.
^y ch. iii. 14.
^z Isa. xi. 4.

11 ^u And I saw heaven opened, and behold ^x a white horse; and he that sat upon him *was* called ^y Faithful and True, and ^z in righteousness he doth judge and make war.

"Worship God." He only is worthy to receive the worship of His creatures. They must not only not worship saints and angels, but they must worship Him with all concentration of mind and with all lowliness of body.

11. "And I saw heaven opened, and behold a white horse; and he that sat upon him was called Faithful and True, and in righteousness," &c. Where does all this occur, and what is the nature of this warfare? Now St. John saw heaven opened, and there is the rider on the white horse, and it is said that "the armies which were in heaven followed him on white horses." This betokens a warfare in heaven, but what is the manner of this warfare? He slays His enemies with a sharp sword proceeding out of His mouth, and it is noticed that the armies which follow Him have no arms, offensive or defensive, and yet it seems evident that His enemies are destroyed, as men are destroyed in human warfare, for all the fowls are filled with their flesh, so that this warfare is a mystery. We might have thought that, owing to the fact that the sword proceeded out of His mouth, this warfare was a spiritual warfare, and that His enemies were not actually slain, but brought over to His side by conversion effected by His word; but this seems not to be so. Again, a remarkable emphasis is laid upon His Name. He is said to have four names. He is called (verse 11) Faithful and True. Again, He has a Name written (apparently on His diadems) which no one knoweth but Himself. Again, His Name is called the Word of God; and lastly, on His vesture and on His thigh there is a Name written, "King of Kings, and Lord of Lords."

Let us take the things said of Him in their order.

"And in righteousness he doth judge and make war." This is said, apparently, with reference to his name of "Faithful and True." His judgment and his warfare is not like the judgment of man, having always much imperfection mixed up with it. He

12 ᵃHis eyes *were* as a flame of fire, ᵇ and on his head *were* many crowns; ᶜand he had a name written, that no man knew, but he himself.

13 ᵈAnd he *was* clothed with a vesture dipped in blood: and his name is called ᵉThe Word of God.

14 ᶠAnd the armies *which were* in heaven followed him upon white horses, ᵍclothed in fine linen, white and clean.

ᵃ ch. i. 14.
& ii. 18.
ᵇ ch. vi. 2.
ᶜ ch. ii. 17.
ver. 16.
ᵈ Isa. lxiii. 2, 3.
ᵉ John i. 1.
1 John v. 7.
ᶠ ch. xiv. 20.
ᵍ Mat. xxviii. 3. ch. iv. 4.
& vii. 9.

---

maketh war always in righteousness, so that He may rid the earth of those who destroy it.

12. "His eyes were as a flame of fire." Fire, because of its light, searching, piercing, before consuming. This is the account of Him in the opening of this book (chap. i. 14).

"And on his head were many crowns." In chap. vi. 2 it is said that a crown (*stephanos*), the crown of victory, was given to Him because He was to go forth conquering and to conquer. Here the crowns are the *diademata*, and, being many, betoken universal rule.

"And he had a name written, that no man knew, but he himself." This is the new name of chap. iii. 12. This name the Apostle saw written (according to Alford) but knew not its import. Some suppose that it was the "Word of God" of the next verse, of which no human understanding can fathom the deep significance, but we had better take it as unknown to any creature, and leave it in the mystery in which God has shrouded it.

13. "And he was clothed with a vesture dipped in blood." Does this signify His own Blood or the blood of His enemies? It is evidently a reference to Isaiah lxiii. 2, 3, "Wherefore art thou red in thine apparel, and thy garments like him that treadeth in the winefat? I have trodden the winepress alone: and of the people there was none with me," &c. And yet it would be most appropriate if the garment was stained with His own Blood.

"And his name is called the Word of God." Only in the Gospel of this Evangelist is this name given to the Lord. A very strong proof, amongst many others, that the two books are written by the same author.

14. "And the armies which were in heaven followed him upon

15 And ʰ out of his mouth goeth a sharp sword, that with it he should smite the nations: and ⁱ he shall rule them with a rod of iron: and ᵏ he treadeth the winepress of the fierceness and wrath of Almighty God.

16 And ˡ he hath on *his* vesture and on his thigh a name written, ᵐ KING OF KINGS, AND LORD OF LORDS.

ʰ Isa. xi. 4.
2 Thes. ii. 8.
ch. i. 16.
ver. 21.
ⁱ Ps. ii. 9.
ch. ii. 27. & xii. 5.
ᵏ Isa. lxiii. 3.
ch. xiv. 19, 20.
ˡ ver. 12.
ᵐ Dan. ii. 47.
1 Tim. vi. 15.

---

white horses," &c. Are these the angels? We should gather from chap. xii. 7 that they were, and yet from the mention of their clothing, fine linen, clean and white, they seem rather glorified saints (verse 8). Fine linen (*bussinon*), which is the righteousness of saints.

15. "And out of his mouth goeth a sharp sword, that with it he should smite the nations." We are told that we are not to connect this sword with the converting power of Christ's word, but solely with the exercise of His wrath and vengeance, and unquestionably all the other figures are of war and slaughter. Still the figure is remarkable. We cannot help thinking of the "Word of God, quick and powerful, and sharper than any two-edged sword, piercing even to the dividing asunder of soul and spirit," of Hebrews iv. 12.

"That with it he should smite the nations: and he shall rule them with a rod of iron." This is equally applicable to a rule of unswerving rectitude as well as to one of force, but the next clause seems to confine all this to His wrath and judgment.

"And he treadeth the winepress of the fierceness and wrath of Almighty God." The heaping up of words of judgment is very striking, "the winepress of the fierceness and wrath of Almighty God." He is set forth as treading the winepress in chap. xiv. 19, 20.

16. "And he hath on his vesture and on his thigh a name written, King of Kings, and Lord of Lords." This name is given in 1 Tim. vi. 15 to God the Father. That it is here given to the Son of God, the Word, is an irrefragable proof of his Godhead and equality with the Father.

Some expositors explain "upon His vesture and His thigh" as

CHAP. XIX.] AN ANGEL STANDING IN THE SUN.   249

17 And I saw an angel standing in the sun; and he cried with a loud voice, saying ⁿ to all the fowls that fly in the midst of heaven, ᵒ Come and gather yourselves together unto the supper of the great God;

18 ᵖ That ye may eat the flesh of kings, and the flesh of captains, and the flesh of mighty men, and the flesh of horses, and of them that sit on them, and the flesh of all *men, both* free and bond, both small and great.

19 ᑫ And I saw the beast, and the kings of the earth, and their armies, gathered together to make war against him that sat on the horse, and against his army.

ⁿ ver. 21.
ᵒ Ezek. xxxix. 17.
ᵖ Ezek. xxxix. 18, 20.
ᑫ ch. xvi. 16. & xvii. 13, 14.

---

17. "The supper of the great God;" perhaps, "the great supper of God." So ℵ, A., B.

the place where the sword was, but His sword proceeds out of His mouth.

17, 18. "And I saw an angel standing in the sun; and he cried with a loud voice, saying to all the fowls .... both free and bond, both small and great." This is a close reproduction of Ezekiel xxxix. 17-20, and signifies the utter destruction of those who gather themselves together against God and Christ. The call, as many other things in this book, is anticipatory. It anticipates what is said in verse 21.

19. And I saw the beast, and the kings of the earth, and their armies," &c. Is the *therion* then to be distinguished as one personal entity from the kings of the earth and their armies? It would seem so, and yet where all is so involved in mystery it is impossible to speak certainly. Many things in this book would lead us to believe that he is not a mere figure, a mere impersonation of the world power. He cannot be any kingdom, for the kings and kingdoms are distinguished from him. What is he, and what the false prophet? The latter seems to be the Antichrist. But who is this *therion* who is below Satan, for Satan gives him his

20 ʳAnd the beast was taken, and with him the false prophet that wrought miracles before him, with which he deceived them that had received the mark of the beast, and ˢthem that worshipped his image. ᵗThese both were cast alive into a lake of fire ᵘburning with brimstone.

21 And the remnant ˣwere slain with the sword of him that sat upon the horse, which *sword* proceeded out of his mouth: ʸand all the fowls ᶻwere filled with their flesh.

ʳ ch. xvi. 13.
ˢ ch. xiii. 12, 15.
ᵗ ch. xx. 10. See Dan. vii. 11.
ᵘ ch. xiv. 10. & xxi. 8.
ˣ ver. 15.
ʸ ver. 17, 18.
ᶻ ch. xvii. 16.

---

power and his seat and great authority—and yet he is above the second *therion* who causes his image to be worshipped?

20, 21. "And the beast was taken, and with him the false prophet .... And the remnant were slain with the sword of him that sat upon the horse." I desire with all humility and submission to the will of God to call attention to the different fates of the deceivers and the deceived. The deceivers were cast into Gehenna. The deceived were simply slain; their bodies were consumed by the vultures, and nothing more is said of them. I do not think it is right and in accordance with the will of God to say that their souls were irretrievably lost, and when once out of their bodies, to share the punishment of the two deceivers. God evidently makes an unspeakable difference between the two fates—the two are sentenced to Gehenna, the remnant are not. It seems just that deceivers and deceived should not be dealt with alike.

It is of very great importance in respect of our setting forth of the character of God that we should not make Him out as having but one punishment, and that an eternity of torment in the lake of fire.

CHAP. XX.

AND I saw an angel come down from heaven, ^a having the key of the bottomless pit and a great chain in his hand.

2 And he laid hold on ^b the dragon, that old serpent, which is the Devil, and Satan, and bound him a thousand years,

3 And cast him into the bottomless pit, and shut him up, and ^c set a seal upon him, ^d that he should deceive the nations no more, till the thousand years should be fulfilled: and after that he must be loosed a little season.

<small>a ch. i. 18. & ix. 1.
b ch. xii. 9. See 2 Pet. ii. 4. Jude 6.
c Dan. vi. 17.
d ch. xvi. 14, 16. ver. 8.</small>

---

1. "And I saw an angel come down from heaven, having the key of the bottomless pit, and a great chain in his hand."

2, 3. "And he laid hold on the dragon, that old serpent, which is the Devil, and Satan, and bound him a thousand years .... that he should deceive the nations no more," &c. In entering upon the consideration of this most difficult and most controverted of prophecies, we have first to consider briefly the probable time of its fulfilment. This has been said to be in the future, and it has also been said to be now in the course of accomplishment.

Now it seems to me quite clear that in respect of the binding of Satan, that he should not deceive the nations, that this is evidently in the future. Ever since the times of the Apostles to the present Satan has unceasingly deceived the people of the earth. Till the time of Constantine he deceived the great Roman world and its rulers by persuading them that Christianity was false. Immediately after the time of Constantine he deceived a large part of Christendom by the Arian heresy. Then we are told by such commentators as Bishop Wordsworth and Elliott, and multitudes of others, that for many centuries he deceived the foremost nations of the world (the ten kingdoms) by the pretensions of the Bishop

4 And I saw ᵉthrones, and they sat upon them, and ᶠjudgment was given unto them: and *I saw* ᵍthe souls of them that were beheaded for the witness

ᵉ Dan. vii. 9, 22, 27. Mat. xix. 28. Luke xxii. 30.
ᶠ 1 Cor. vi. 2, 3.
ᵍ ch. vi. 9.

---

of Rome. Then he deceived the Eastern parts of Christendom by Mahometanism, and he deceived the most populous nations of the world—the Chinese and Hindoos—by upholding their ancient unbelief and idolatry; and within this century he has perverted multitudes from the faith by Infidelity, Rationalism, Comtism, Agnosticism, and other forms of evil doctrine.

It has been said by many—amongst them Bishop Wordsworth—that the binding of Satan took place at the first, because our Lord asks, "How can one enter into a strong man's house except he first find the strong man?" but if anyone will look at the place he will see that this is a short parable simply setting forth that if the grace of God enters into a soul it first dislodges the former evil occupant. It has nothing to do with such a binding of Satan as is here described. Satan is dislodged from particular souls, but this does not prevent him going about "as a roaring lion seeking whom he may devour."

The account of the binding of Satan here is exceedingly circumstantial. He is first laid hold of, then bound, then cast into the abyss, then shut up, then sealed down, that he should deceive the nations no more till the end of a definite period.

What can be the meaning of such a series except to show that he is absolutely restrained from going about exercising his arts of deception as he had done in times past. Now let the reader remember that no matter what meaning—spiritual or literal—we give to this "sealing" and this "chain," yet, if we are to be guided by Scripture, the abyss is evidently a real, actual place (Luke viii. 31). With respect to his deceiving the nations no more, this cannot signify that sin is put an end to, because the nations have not yet risen again in their sinless bodies: so that in each person there yet remains original sin (and sin must involve deception), but there is no longer that combination on the side of evil which it is the especial prerogative of Satan to bring about.

4. "And I saw thrones, and they sat upon them, and judgment was given unto them: and (I saw) the souls of them that

of Jesus, and for the word of God, and [h] which had not worshipped the beast, [i] neither his image, neither had received *his* mark upon their foreheads, or in their hands; and they lived and [k] reigned with Christ a thousand years.

[h] ch. xiii. 12.
[i] ch. xiii. 15, 16.
[k] Rom. viii. 17. 2 Tim. ii. 12. ch. v. 10.

---

were beheaded . . . . lived and reigned with Christ a thousand years." The first inquiry respecting this prophecy of the millennium is as to what it does not contain. So much imagination arising out of former extravagances of interpretation has been brought to it, that we must consider what is not in it, and first of all it is clear that it does not imply a personal coming of Christ to this world before His coming to judge, and by consequence it does not imply a sitting of Christ in glory on a throne in this world in the midst of His saints. This is particularly noticed by that great millennial interpreter Mede. While Mede considers that the saints are to reign *on earth* with Christ during the millennium, yet he is careful to add "that he does not dare to imagine (as some of the ancients did) that Christ will Himself reign upon earth." This takes away the insuperable difficulty that Christ will come to reign visibly before the great day of His appearing, and the equally insuperable difficulty that at the end of the thousand years Christ will leave the world for a short time to Satan, for it seems unimaginable that the nations will environ the Holy City whilst He is dwelling in it in glory.

In the next place, in this account of the millennium there is nothing whatsoever said of the time of the thousand years being one of perfect felicity to all the inhabitants of the world, much less of the state of nature being changed and becoming paradisaical. If the nations of the world are yet more or less under the dominion of sin, the worst thing which could happen to them would be that they should live in unmixed prosperity.

And this leads us to consider what is meant by the reign of Christ, and what by the reign of the saints.

The reign of Christ. Surely Christ is reigning now. He began to reign when He took His seat at the right hand of God, and His reign has continued ever since. He has reigned thus all through this present state of discipline just as much as if it had been a sinless and paradisaical state—nay, more; for His power has been

5 But the rest of the dead lived not again until the thousand years were finished. This *is* the first resurrection.

---

most conspicuous in His adapting the evil of the present state of things to the perfecting of His people.

The reign of the saints. This surely must be what St. Paul alludes to when he writes to the Corinthians: "I would to God that ye did reign, that we also might reign with you" (1 Cor. iv. 8). It is quite clear that the saints will not reign in any shape or way independently of Christ: that their reign will be subordinate is manifest from its being described as the exercise of a priesthood, "they shall be priests of God and of Christ." Their office will be angelic. They will be as the angels, and will be employed as they are. Now for anything that we know they may be reigning now: not, of course, so visibly and perfectly as they may at the time indicated, but it seems to me beyond everything absurd to suppose that they have been since the time of their dissolution only employed in singing, or much less in mere resting. Our Lord speaks of the reward of the saints as the exercise of dominion, when He says that He will say to His faithful servants, "Well, thou good servant, have thou authority over ten cities," and "be thou ruler also over five cities" (Luke xix. 17-19); and "Thou hast been faithful over a few things, I will make thee ruler over many things" (Matt. xxv. 11); and He promises to the Apostles that they shall sit on twelve thrones judging the twelve tribes of Israel (judgment was given to them). When our Lord thus indicates that the reward of His servants will be the exercise of rule, He tells us in effect that it will be an employment bringing into exercise the highest faculties of intelligent creatures. Will the saints thus ruling be visible on earth? We cannot tell. An expression we find in verse 9, that besides the beloved city there was a camp ($\pi\alpha\rho\epsilon\mu\beta o\lambda\dot{\eta}$) of the saints, seems to imply that there would be a visible centre for them, but these two were, according to Alford, one and the same.

Many other questions should be noticed, though they cannot be answered with any certainty.

Who are these saints or souls sitting on thrones? It would appear that they are in the first place the souls of the martyrs, those who were beheaded for the witness of Jesus, the beheading

6 Blessed and holy *is* he that hath part in the first resurrection: on such ¹the second death hath no power, ¹ ch. ii. 11. & xxi. 8.

---

being taken to represent any form of violent death, and then those who had not worshipped the beast or his image and had not received his mark, and here the account stops. Are we to suppose these souls to be those of all real Christians who have died in the Lord ("Blessed are the dead which die in the Lord"), or only of a selection from them? The whole passage seems to imply a selection. There is not only an anastasis but an *ex*anastasis, at least, according to St. Paul, where he writes (Phil. iii. 11), "If by any means I might attain unto the resurrection out of the dead, not as though I had already attained or were already perfect."

Then are these souls clothed with their resurrection bodies? It would seem that they must be, or how could this be called the first resurrection; and yet the Apostle says that he saw the *souls*, and in the only place in which such an expression is used (Rev. vi. 9) it certainly means the disembodied souls. And yet there are some who tell us that all we are to understand by the first resurrection is a death unto sin and a new birth unto righteousness, and that the second resurrection is of the unconverted alone.

With respect to the second, or general resurrection, if it is to be, as some say, only a resurrection of the lost, what will become of those who have been born and have lived during the thousand years? They cannot partake in the first resurrection. They are born too late. Will they be all lost? Impossible.

When I said that there is nothing to lead us to consider that the state of the earth during the thousand years will be a state of paradisaical fertility and blessednesss, there is no doubt whatsoever that there is such a state in store for the earth, but whether this will take place during the time of the thousand years seems to me more than doubtful. The prophecies more probably point to the new heavens and the new earth as the scene of the restoration of the whole creation (Isaiah xi. 5, 9, and lxv. 17-25).

An immense number of questions can be raised respecting the first six verses of this chapter of which the answers can only be the merest conjectures. The difficulties of the opposing views, the literal and the (so-called) spiritual, seem equally insuperable. The greatest of all difficulties seems to me to be this, that no matter

but they shall be ᵐ priests of God and of Christ, ⁿ and shall reign with him a thousand years.

ᵐ Isa. lxi. 6.
1 Pet. ii. 9.
ch. i. 6. & v. 10.
ⁿ ver. 4.

how we understand the thousand years, a very long period is supposed to intervene between the first and the second comings of Christ. Now all the rest of Scripture, all the rest of this very book of the Apocalypse, is against this. The Lord is supposed to come suddenly, at any time, and when He does come, He comes not to reign and then to judge and then to reign again, but at once to judge and then to reign for ever without intermission. Now this difficulty is inherent, not in the reign of Christ, unless it be a visible one, of which nothing is said, nor in the reign of the saints, but in the binding of Satan, so that he should no longer deceive the nations. It is quite evident that the grossest deceptions, the most Antichristian, the most absurd, the most derogatory to the glory of God and the truth of the Gospel, have prevailed for nearly 2,000 years.

With respect to the reign of the saints, it may, for anything we know, have been going on for nearly nineteen hundred years. It may be difficult to conceive of, but surely it cannot be anything like so difficult as to imagine that men like St. Paul or St. John have been for these wellnigh two thousand years merely resting— shut up in heaven, so far as their influence in this world is concerned, as effectually as Satan was shut up in the abyss. Let us remember that the vast majority of Christians (Roman, Greek, and others) believe that the saints (some of them) are and have been for centuries reigning, only they have done to them what they have had from Holy Scripture no warrant to do, *i.e.*, invoked them and prayed to them almost as if they were reigning independently of God and of Christ. We are assured by the words of the most Apocalyptic book of the Old Testament that angels take a part, of course under God, in the direction of kingdoms (Daniel x. 6, 7, 13, 20, 21; xii. 1). They or, if not angels, at least powers of the unseen world, actually oppose one another, as if, though under the rule of the Supreme, they know not His whole will. And if angels, why not glorified saints? In the few places in which the Son of God speaks of the future state of the saints He speaks of it, as I have shown, as a state of rule, and nothing can better bring into exercise the whole intellectual, moral, and spiritual powers of redeemed man than such a state. It is the

7 And when the thousand years are expired, ᵖ Satan shall be loosed out of his prison.

8 And shall go out ᵩ to deceive the nations which are in the four quarters of the earth, ʳ Gog and Magog, ˢ to gather them together to battle: the number of whom *is* as the sand of the sea.

ᵖ ver. 2.
ᵩ ver. 3, 10.
ʳ Ezek. xxxviii. 2. & xxxix. 1.
ˢ ch. xvi. 14.

---

only one in harmony with the future state of blessedness being called a kingdom—not a temple, or a garden, or a hall of assembly, but a kingdom.

7-8. "And when the thousand years are expired, Satan shall be loosed out of his prison. And shall go out to deceive the nations which are in the four quarters of the earth," &c. Who are these nations which are in the four quarters of the earth? Evidently those who have lived under the rule of the saints, and have been outwardly restrained by them from running into the grosser forms of evil, but are not living in their renewed bodies, in which they will not be raised till the Second Coming of Christ in glory. Consequently, they are yet open to solicitations from the Evil One. However some of them may have been converted and made true Christians, the bulk of them are yet in the flesh, and so are amenable to the temptations of Satan.

We now come to the great difficulty of this prophecy. The Apostle seems very absolutely to identify the subject of this prophecy of the insurrection of the nations against Christ with the invasion of certain Scythian hordes which is said to have taken place within the years 633 and 605 B.C. This is altogether passed over in silence by the writer or writers of the Book of Kings. Ezekiel, however, devotes two chapters to the invasion of (as is supposed) a horde of Northern nations. From all that we can gather from the words of Ezekiel, the incursion was a most formidable one. It threatened the very existence of the Jewish nationality; whereas this supposed invasion of the Scythians was, according to all accounts, a matter of little or no danger to the Jews under Josiah. The Scythians, instead of threatening, much less ravaging Judæa, kept to the sea coast, and ravaged the ancient enemies of the Jews, the Philistines. They were on their way to Egypt, and were turned from their purpose by

9 ᵗ'And they went up on the breadth of the earth, and compassed the camp of the saints about, and the beloved city: and fire came down from God out of heaven, and devoured them.

10 ᵘ And the devil that deceived them was cast into the lake of fire and brimstone, ˣ where the beast and the false prophet *are*, and ʸ shall be tormented day and night for ever and ever.

ᵗ Is. viii. 8. Ezek. xxxviii. 9, 16.
ᵘ ver. 8.
ˣ ch. xix. 20.
ʸ ch. xiv. 10, 11.

---

9. "From God" omitted by A., and a few Cursives.

Psammetichus. Herodotus relates this in his second book. They went thence towards Egypt, and when they were in Palestine and Syria, Psammetichus, King of Egypt, meeting them, turned them by gifts and entreaties from going further; and when, on their return, they were in Ascalon, a city of Syria, whereas most of the Scythians passed by without harming aught, some few of them being left behind, plundered the temple of Venus Ourania. It appears that before they got back to Scythia they were destroyed at a banquet—first intoxicated, and then murdered by Cyaxares, King of the Medes—all which seems to show how utterly unlike such an invasion was to that prophesied of under Gog and Magog in Ezek. xxxvii. and xxxviii.

There can be no doubt, then, that what Ezekiel foretells is in the far future, and has had as yet no fulfilment worthy of the name, and the Rabbinical interpreters consider this prophecy to refer to the last outbreak against the rule of the Messiah. Two quotations to this effect are given by Alford. One from the Jerusalem Targum on Numb. xi. 27, in Wetstein: "At the end of the last days Gog and Magog, and their armies shall come up to Jerusalem, and by the hands of King Messiah they shall themselves fall, and seven years shall the children of Israel burn their arms." And again (from Avoda Sara, i.), "When they shall see the war of Gog and Magog, the Messiah shall say to them, 'For what purpose have ye come here?' And they shall answer, 'Against the Lord, and against his Christ.'"

A question now presents itself of much interest. It is said in the Apocalyptic account that fire came down from God out of

11 And I saw a great white throne, and him that sat on it, from whose face ᵃ the earth and the heaven fled away; ᵃ and there was found no place for them.

ᶻ 2 Pet. iii. 7, 10, 11. ch. xxi. 1.
ᵃ Dan. ii. 35.

---

heaven and devoured them. Is this fire the Spirit of the Lord's mouth, and the brightness of His coming, which shall consume and destroy the Anomos—the man of sin, the wicked one of St. Paul's second Epistle to the Thessalonians? The man of sin, or personal Antichrist, has been by many identified with the second or two-horned lamb-like therion, which "makes an image of the first therion, and compels men to worship it (xiii. 14), and this on account of his performing miracles—making fire to come down from heaven in the sight of men, and deceiving them that dwell on the earth by the means of those miracles which he had power to do." The fire which comes down from God is certainly the final catastrophe on the rebels, and it seems synchronous with the coming of the Lord as the Judge; but there is nothing said of the personal Anomos, and of the miracles by which he deceives men. The matter must be left with God. Isaac Williams has a very long note upon it, in which he considers that the three years and a half is the time of Antichrist, *i.e.*, the personal Anomos or Antichrist, so that the little season is the three years and a half, taken literally.

11. "And I saw a great white throne, and him that sat on it, from whose face the earth and the heaven fled away; and there," &c. I would have much preferred to treat this most sublime, most blessed, and yet most terrific description as Bishop Wordsworth has done—left it uncommented upon, except by the prayer from the Burial Service: "O Lord God most Holy, O Lord most mighty, O Holy and most merciful Saviour, deliver us not into the bitter pains of eternal death."

But there are features in it which require to be realized by all readers. Some such are the following.

This is an universal judgment. It is the *general* judgment. The dead, small and great, will stand before God; *all* will stand, all the righteous, as well as all the wicked, from the Apostles downwards. St. Paul is very express upon the fact that he himself will be judged, "He that judgeth me is the Lord" (1 Cor. iv. 4).

12 And I saw the dead, *b* small and great, stand before God; *c* and the books were opened: and another *d* book was opened, which is *the book* of life: and the dead were judged out of those things which were written in the books, *e* according to their works.

13 And the sea gave up the dead which were in it; *f* and death and ‖ hell delivered up the dead which were in them: *g* and they were judged every man according to their works.

b ch. xix. 5.
c Dan. vii. 10.
d Ps. lxix. 28.
Dan. xii. 1.
Phil. iv. 3.
ch. iii. 5. &
xiii. 8. & xxi. 27.
e Jer. xvii. 10.
& xxxii. 19.
Matt. xvi. 27.
Rom. ii. 6.
ch. ii. 23. &
xxii. 12. ver. 13.
f ch. vi. 8.
‖ Or, *the grave*.
g ver. 12.

"Who will render to every man according to his deeds: to them who by patient continuance in well doing seek for glory and honour and immortality, eternal life" (Rom. ii. 6, 7). "For we must all appear before the judgment seat of Christ; that every one may receive the things done in his body" (2 Cor. v. 10). Again, Rom. xiv. 10, "We shall all stand before the judgment-seat of Christ." "The Lord Jesus, who shall judge the quick and dead at his appearing, and his kingdom" (2 Tim. iv. 1).

Taking such declarations into account, it seems a monstrous thing for some in these latter days (and some of them I grieve to say dignitaries of our own Church) to say that believers are raised into a sphere above judgment. I have come across many believers, men of smooth tongues and voluble utterance, unquestionably believers, but who as unquestionably, if God is a just God, require to be judged; and no matter what is urged to the contrary, they will be. The diversity of reward asserted by the Holy Spirit— "Every man shall receive his own reward, according to his own labour" (1 Cor. iii. 8)—seems to necessitate this.

Then there is another feature of this final judgment that requires to be universally realized—that the judgment will be according to men's works. Thus in the vision of judgment in Matt. xxv., the Lord expresses it as a judgment which takes into account but one kind of works, works of benevolence, or one kind of such works, "Come ye blessed, inherit, for I was an hungred and ye gave me meat: I was thirsty, and ye gave me drink: naked, and ye clothed me, sick and in prison, and ye visited me."

14 And ʰ death and hell were cast into the lake of fire. ⁱ This is the second death.

15 And whosoever was not found written in the book of life ᵏ was cast into the lake of fire.

ʰ 1 Cor. xv. 26, 54, 55.
ⁱ ver. 6. ch. xxi. 8.
ᵏ ch. xix. 20.

---

14. To "This is the second death," add, "even the lake of fire." So ℵ, A., B., &c.

But that all works, good and bad, will be taken into account, is clear from the Word of the Lord; that a cup of cold water shall not lose its reward, and "that every idle word that men shall speak, they shall give account thereof in the day of judgment. For by thy words thou shalt be justified, and by thy words thou shalt be condemned" (Matt. xii. 36).

Again, thoughts are works. Many works, both good and evil, are acted, and so resolved upon, in the heart before they are seen in the life.

Again, Who is He on the white throne; Who is He Who judges? "The Father," it is said, "judgeth no man, but hath committed all judgment unto the Son;" and "The Son of man shall sit on the throne of his glory, and all the holy angels with him," and yet in this book of the Apocalypse, whenever the Divine Throne is mentioned, it is implied that the Father sits upon it. The two are one: as in love, as in power, as in wisdom, so in judgment.

Again, what are the books? They are the histories of souls. Each soul has its history, not only of its dealings with its fellows, but of God's dealings with it, and the account in the book of each righteous soul is a record of God's mercy and grace, and how it has responded to it; and the account in the book of each wicked soul is of God's mercy and grace, and how it has rejected it. "God is infinitely merciful to every soul; and no one has been, or ever can be, lost by surprise, or trapped in his ignorance, and as to those who may be lost, I confidently believe that our Heavenly Father threw His arms round each created spirit, and looked it full in the face with bright eyes of love, in the darkness of its mortal life, and that of its own deliberate will it would not have Him" (Faber, quoted in Dr. Pusey's "What is of Faith as regards Eternal Punishment.")

CHAP. XXI.

^a Is. lxv. 17. & lxvi. 22. 2 Pet. iii. 13.
^b ch. xx. 11.

AND ^a I saw a new heaven and a new earth: ^b for the first heaven and the first earth were passed away; and there was no more sea.

The last two chapters of the Apocalypse are upon the future of the blessed after the Day of Judgment. They contain many revelations of things to come of which it seems impossible for us to form any conception. If we understand them (or rather I should say) if we take them at all we must take them literally, for there is no other way open to us. The reader will see this clearly enough as we go on.

1. "And I saw a new heaven and a new earth: for the first heaven and the first earth were passed away; and there was no more sea." This is a very old promise. We learn it in Isaiah lxv. 17: "For behold I create new heavens and a new earth: and the former shall not be remembered, nor come into mind;" and in Isaiah lxvi. 22: "For as the new heavens and the new earth, which I will make, shall remain before me, so shall your seed and your name remain." This is taken up in the New Testament: "We, according to his promise, look for new heavens, and a new earth, wherein dwelleth righteousness" (2 Peter iii. 13). This does not mean that the planet is annihilated and another put in its place. The ancients had no idea of any earth except as to its surface. They had no idea of a globe 8,000 miles in diameter, and if the Apocalyptic writer had proceeded on any such assumption, it would have generated unbelief, or at least gross misapprehensions. All that *we* have now to do with is the mere surface. But what is the new heaven? Evidently not the angelic heaven, or the starry heaven, but that of which we have mention made at the opening of the Bible: "God made the firmament, and divided the waters which were under the firmament from the waters which were above the firmament: and it was so. And God called the firmament Heaven."

If the earth is to be renewed as to its surface, the heaven must

2 And I John saw ᶜthe holy city, new Jerusalem, coming down from God out of heaven, prepared ᵈas a bride adorned for her husband.

ᶜ Is. lii. 1.
Gal. iv. 26.
Heb. xi. 10.
& xii. 22. &
xiii. 14. ch.
iii. 12. ver. 10.
ᵈ Is. liv. 5. &
lxi. 10. 2 Cor.
xi. 2.

2. "John" omitted by ℵ, A., B.

---

also be renewed, if the earth is to be the fitting habitation of the regenerate. For a great part of our discomforts, a great part of our toil and labour, and a very great part of our diseases arise from the state of the air and the influences of the heavens. Some parts of the world are burnt up, and even uninhabitable, because there are no clouds and no rain. In other vast tracts during the greater part of the year the atmosphere is so inclement as to add very sensibly to the miseries of poverty. That God should create new heavens simply means that He will re-adapt His air, His sky, His clouds and sunshine to the new state of things: so that in the graphic words of the Psalmist, "The sun shall not strike by day, neither the moon by night," so that there shall be no more bitter cold, tempest, hurricane. Above all no more pestilential vapours breathing disease and death.

"And there was no more sea." The sea occupies above three-quarters of the surface of the globe, so that this means (whatever else is involved in it) that by far the greater part of the earth's surface shall be no longer barren and uninhabitable by man. Some divines, as Wordsworth, consider the sea here to represent the turbulent state of the nations, but the sea is mentioned as in part making up the visible surface of the globe.

2. "And I (John) saw the holy city, new Jerusalem, coming down from God out of heaven, prepared as a bride adorned," &c. How is it said that the holy city comes *down* from God *out* of heaven? Why are not the nations of men lifted up to heaven? This is but one of the extraordinary marks of difference between the idea of the future state as set forth in these two chapters and the popular ideas of the day. Some have said that she comes down from heaven because Christ ascended up to heaven to prepare a place for His people there. The glories of the new Jerusalem—her adornment for her husband—are described further on in verses 12-24 of this chapter.

3 And I heard a great voice out of heaven saying, Behold, ᵉ the tabernacle of God *is* with men, and he will dwell with them, and they shall be his people, and God himself shall be with them, *and be* their God.

ᵉ Lev. xxvi. 11, 12. Ezek. xliii. 7. 2 Cor. vi. 16. ch. vii. 15.

---

3. "Out of heaven." So B., but ℵ and A. read, "out of the throne."

3. "And I heard a great voice out of heaven [or out of the throne] saying, Behold the tabernacle of God is with men, and he," &c. This is almost a reproduction in the same words of a very old promise in Levit. xxvi. 11: "And I will set my tabernacle among you, and my soul shall not abhor you. And I will walk among you, and will be your God, and ye shall be my people;" so also in Ezek. xliii. 27. "Son of man, the place of my throne and the place of the soles of my feet when I dwell in the midst of the children of Israel for ever, and my holy name shall the house of Israel no more defile." There are four successive degrees of dwelling of the Lord God amongst His people.

First, in the tabernacle and temple. This has been called a symbolic dwelling; still, the Lord desired His people to realize that He dwelt among them, and so met them in prayer as He did in no other place on earth.

Secondly, through the Incarnation. "The Word was made flesh and tabernacled amongst us." And the Lord also said, "He that hath seen Me hath seen the Father."

Thirdly, He dwelt among men by the Holy Ghost. So mean His words, "I will not leave you comfortless, I will come to you."

But there must be a dwelling above and beyond these. The Lord Jesus Christ will then visibly manifest the presence of God, and being raised up in our resurrection bodies we shall be able to bear the sight.

"God himself shall be with them." He shall be with them not as He is with all His creatures, for all things are in Him, but He shall be with them as a father with child, a husband with wife, a friend with friend.

"And be their God." God will be to them all that He is to His

4 ᶠAnd God shall wipe away all tears from their eyes; and ᵍthere shall be no more death, ʰneither sorrow, nor crying, neither shall there be any more pain: for the former things are passed away.

5 And ⁱhe that sat upon the throne said, ᵏBehold, I make all things new. And he said unto me, Write: for ˡthese words are true and faithful.

ᶠ Is. xxv. 8. ch. vii. 17.
ᵍ 1 Cor. xv. 26, 54. ch. xx. 14.
ʰ Is. xxxv. 10. & lxi. 3. & lxv. 19.
ⁱ ch. iv. 2, 9. & v. 1. & xx. 11.
ᵏ Is. xliii. 19. 2 Cor. v. 17.
ˡ ch. xix. 9.

---

intelligent creatures: as He said to Abraham, "I am thy shield, and thy exceeding great reward."

4. "And God shall wipe away all tears," &c. So in Isaiah xxv. 8, "He will swallow up death in victory; and the Lord God will wipe away tears from off all faces." He will not only console, but console with love and tenderness, as a mother with her own hands wipes gently away the tears from her child's face.

"And there shall be no more death, neither sorrow, nor crying." Because there is no more sin, for death and sorrow and crying are the effects of sin.

"Neither shall there be any more pain." For the redemption will be completed by the bodies of the saints having been raised up, incorruptible, glorious, in eternal youth—in never-decaying strength.

"The former things are passed away." The former things—corruption, weakness, the old nature of sin and death. This corruptible shall have put on incorruption, and this mortal, immortality.

5. "And he that sat upon the throne said, Behold, I make all things new." This is the voice of the Creator Who now re-creates all things new. New heavens, new earth, new bodies and souls of men. All things now are again as they were at the first, "Very good."

"And he said unto me, Write: for these words are true and faithful." As certain as God created the first creation so certainly will He create the new. If He is faithful He will be faithful to this. This is the third time that St. John is emphatically commanded to write. In chap. xix. 9: "Write: Blessed are they which are called unto the marriage supper of the Lamb;" and xiv. 13,

6 And he said unto me, ᵐIt is done. ⁿI am Alpha and Omega, the beginning and the end. °I will give unto him that is athirst of the fountain of the water of life freely.

7 He that overcometh shall inherit ‖ all

ᵐ ch. xvi. 17.
ⁿ ch. i. 8. & xxii. 13.
° Is. xii. 3. & lv. 1. John iv. 10, 14. & vii. 37. ch. xxii. 17.
‖ Or, *these things*.

---

6. "It is done," or "They are done," "All is done" (γέγοναν).
"I am Alpha and Omega,' "the Alpha," &c. (Some omit εἰμί).

"Write, Blessed are the dead which die in the Lord." It seems as if these three commands to write were inseparably connected together. They that die in the Lord are called to the marriage supper; they that are called to the marriage supper are called to the new creation and all its blessedness.

6. "And he said unto me, It is done." This was said before at the pouring out of the seventh vial; there it seems to signify that all the vials of the wrath of God were poured forth; now that the new creation in all its parts was completed. All is come to pass—the word is probably in the plural (γέγοναν).

"I am Alpha and Omega, the beginning and the end." The latter sentence is put in as the explanation of the first. As He is the beginning from which all created things spring, so He is the end to whose glory they all converge. Isaiah wrote, "I am the first and I am the last, and beside me there is no God." This is said by the Lord—the Second Person—because it is He who has promised so emphatically to give men of the fountain of the water of life.

"I will give unto him that is athirst of the fountain of the water of life freely." This is explained by the Evangelist as signifying the Holy Spirit, "Living water." "But this spake he of the Spirit, which they that believe on him should receive: for the Spirit was not yet given; because that Jesus was not yet glorified" (John vii. 39).

"I will give unto him that is athirst." No other condition but that he should desire it and be athirst for it. This is free grace. It is the highest of all grace and yet it is given freely.

7. "He that overcometh shall inherit all things; and I will be," &c. Here, however, is a condition: "He that overcometh," *i.e.*,

things; and [p] I will be his God, and he shall be my son.

8 [q] But the fearful, and unbelieving, and the

p Zech. viii. 8. Heb. viii. 10.
q 1 Cor. vi. 9, 10. Gal. v. 19, 20, 21. Eph. v. 5. 1 Tim. i. 9. Heb. xii. 14. ch. xxii. 15.

---

that persevereth to the end. The water of life is given to refresh in the Christian conflict. The water of life—the Spirit of God—is given freely, but it is given for a purpose, and that purpose is that men should fight the good fight—should finish their course—should keep the faith.

"Inherit all things." St. Paul almost seems to go beyond this when he says: "All things are yours. . . . ye are Christ's; Christ is God's" (1 Cor. iii. 21).

"I will be his God, and he shall be my son." This is the crowning sonship. When God by His creative powers brought Adam into existence he was His son (Luke iii. 38). When one is baptized into Christ, and so puts on Christ, he becomes in a far higher way a son of God because a member of Christ. When a man is led by the Spirit then this latter sonship is perfected so far as this world is concerned; and at last when he is raised up in his glorified body he is the child of God, being the child of the resurrection (Luke xx. 36). Each of these four senses are real, they lead up one to another, but the last which is given to him that overcometh is the culminating one.

8. "But the fearful, and unbelieving," &c. Different explanations are given of these "fearful." Williams speaks of them as those that fear men rather than God. "Woe be to fearful hearts and faint hands, and the sinner that goeth two ways. This fearfulness is by the son of Sirach opposed throughout to the fear of God."

Dean Vaughan writes, "The fearful are not those who fear God; not those who have trembled at His word and served Him on earth with reverence and godly fear. It is not an excess of reverence which is here spoken of. The fearful are the opposite of him that overcometh. They are those who behave cowardly in the face of God's enemy." Similarly Alford, "But to the cowardly (the contrast to νικῶντες, the ἀποστελλόμενοι of Hebrews x. 38), those who shrank timidly from the conflict." Similarly Bishop Boyd-Carpenter, Dr. Milligan, and others.

abominable, and murderers, and whoremongers, and sorcerers, and idolaters, and all liars, shall have their part in ʳthe lake which burneth with fire and brimstone: which is the second death.

ʳ ch. xx. 14, 15.

9 And there came unto me one of ˢthe seven

ˢ ch. xv. 1, 6, 7.

"And unbelieving." Those who have had some time or other in their lives the truth in all its purity and in all its fulness presented to their minds, and have turned away from it.

"And the abominable." Alford understands these as partakers in the abomination of idolatry.

"And murderers, and whoremongers, and sorcerers, and idolaters, and all liars." Sorcerers may be those who pretend to magic or who actually have intercourse with evil spirits. Both are equally guilty. The wickedness is equally great whether there is only a pretence to a thing so wicked, or whether God permits it to be carried into effect. Let those who play with such things as spiritualism beware. They are, as far as lies in their power, laying themselves open to the most evil of all influences. All attempts at intercourse with the world of spirits is unlawful, and they who engage in it are sure to be deceived.

"All liars." They who lie in matters of religion by the circulation of false opinions, or by hypocrisy, as well as those who lie in business transactions, or in political matters, or in the matter of the character and conduct of those about them, are all liars, all workers of deceit and falsehood.

"Shall have their part in the lake which burneth with fire and brimstone: which is the second death." With this we must take the words of the Saviour and Judge, "All sins shall be forgiven unto the sons of men, and blasphemies wherewith soever they shall blaspheme" (Mark iii. 28). The Eternal Father, who regards each soul as if there were none other than Himself and that soul in the universe, will not permit any one to be lost in so terrific a gulf of agony and misery until He has tried every means to bring that soul to repentance and faith. This must be our faith in God just as much as it must be our faith that whatever punishment He inflicts is necessary for the moral order and well-being of the universe.

9. "And there came unto me one of the seven angels which had

angels which had the seven vials full of the seven last plagues, and talked with me, saying, Come hither, I will shew thee ᵗ the bride, the Lamb's wife.

10 And he carried me away ᵘ in the spirit to a great and high mountain, and shewed me ˣ that great city, the holy Jerusalem, descending out of heaven from God,

ᵗ ch. xix. 7. ver. 2.
ᵘ ch. i. 10. & xvii. 3.
ˣ Ezek. xlviii. ver. 2.

---

10. "Great" omitted by ℵ, A., B.

the seven vials," &c. Why one of these seven angels? It has been supposed because they were the last on the Apocalyptic scene, or it may be because the vials of wrath were exhausted, and now there remained only the pouring out of the love of God on a reconciled world.

"Come hither, I will shew thee the bride, the Lamb's wife." This is exactly parallel to the action of the angel who called him aside to show him the harlot. Each one is intended to illustrate the other. Both are women: but the one a virgin, the other a fallen woman. Both are cities: one is Jerusalem as contrasted with Babylon. Both are churches: but the one is corrupt and idolatrous; the other, now presented by Christ Himself, "not having spot, or wrinkle, or any such thing; but that it should be holy and without blemish" (Ephes. v. 27).

10. "And he carried me away in the spirit to a great and high mountain." When he was carried away to see the harlot, he was carried away to the wilderness: now it is to "a great and high mountain," otherwise he could have had no view of the descent of a city which covered what was equivalent to the area of a large kingdom.

"Descending out of heaven from God." He had seen something of this before—in the second verse; now he is brought more abreast of it, as it were, and is enabled to distinguish its parts and its materials.

Let the reader again notice that he is not transported to a distant heaven, but to a place on earth. We cannot but gather from this that the scene of conflict—of six thousand years of conflict in which Christ and His people have got the victory—is the scene of the glory and of the reward. The earth, on which such events as the

11 ʸ Having the glory of God: and her light *was* like unto a stone most precious, even like a jasper stone, clear as crystal;

12 And had a wall great and high, *and* had ᶻ twelve gates, and at the gates twelve angels, and

ʸ ch. xxii. 5. ver. 23.

ᶻ Ezek. xlviii. 31-34.

Incarnation and the Atonement have taken place, is not abandoned, but is continued as the place of Him Who is above all place, and the habitation of Him in whom space itself exists.

11. "Having the glory of God." Having, that is, the Shechinah within her, which illuminated her through and through: or rather, perhaps, having the Son of God within her Who shines not only with His own glory, but with that of His Father and of the Holy Ghost—the glory of the whole Godhead.

"Her light was like unto a stone most precious, even like a jasper stone, clear as crystal." This stone cannot be that which we commonly know as jasper, which is not by any means one of the most precious of stones. It is also opaque, and not clear as crystal. It has been supposed to have been the diamond, the most precious as well as the most transparent of stones: for it is to be remarked that the diamond is not mentioned amongst the other stones which contribute to the glory of this city.

12. "And had a wall great and high, and had twelve gates, and at the gates twelve angels." How is it that the city appears strongly fortified, seeing that with all other evils war will be banished from the new creation? A wall is a sign of separation, and surely there will be no separation in the future kingdom. The wall has been understood by some to surround the city in order to call to remembrance the state of warfare from which the just have emerged; but this seems unsatisfactory. May it not signify something of this sort? The city being nearly 400 miles both in breadth and in length will be enormous—larger than a great kingdom—and yet it will not be illimitable. Immense as it is it would contain, if they were crowded into it, but a small proportion of the inhabitants of the renewed earth. The city then will not be for all the saved, but for those who have won an abundant entrance. If to some of my readers this is unsatisfactory, I would put it to their common sense, what is an expositor to do who desires to deal honestly with the word of God? The locality of the blessed is not

CHAP. XXI.] THE TWELVE TRIBES. 271

names written thereon, which are *the names* of the twelve tribes of the children of Israel:

13 ᵃ On the east three gates; on the north three gates; on the south three gates; and on the west three gates.

ᵃ Ezek. xlviii. 31-34.

14 And the wall of the city had twelve foun-

---

14. "The names;" rather, "The twelve names."

described as a boundless plain, but as a circumscribed city, immense, but circumscribed—not boundless. There are walls and there are also gates which, though they are open, are made to be shut (at times at least). All such particulars must be noticed. If they cannot be explained they must be noticed if we care to deal honestly with the Bible.

"And at the gates twelve angels." Evidently as keepers of the gates. To keep them open so that no one should shut, or it may be to keep them shut so that no one should open.

"And names written thereon, which are the names of the twelve tribes," &c. The names of the Patriarchs occurring here startle us seeing that in the King and citizenship of this city there is neither Jew nor Greek—all are one in Christ, and so we should have supposed there would be in such a city no remembrance of Reuben or Simeon, or Levi or Judah, but God's thoughts are not our thoughts. In some way unknown to us, and which all will acknowledge to be just and right, there will be an association of the Israel of God with the former Israel. So that through eternal ages Abraham will be the father of the faithful, and Christ Himself will be the root and offspring of David, and the Lion of the tribe of Judah.

13. "On the east three gates; on the north three gates; on the south three gates; and on the west three gates." Mark the extraordinary circumstantiality of all this. It is as circumstantial as the description in Ezekiel xlviii., with the difference that the names of the tribes are not associated with the several gates. Isaac Williams says beautifully, "So wonderfully is the figurative pattern of the temporal Jerusalem fulfilled in the heavenly and eternal. 'I know that, whatsoever God doeth, it shall be for ever' (Eccles. iii. 14)."

14. "And the wall of the city had twelve foundations," *i.e.*, as

dations, and ᵇ in them the names of the twelve apostles of the Lamb.

15 And he that talked with me ᶜ had a golden reed to measure the city, and the gates thereof, and the wall thereof.

16 And the city lieth foursquare, and the length

ᵇ Matt. xvi. 18. Gal. ii. 9. Eph. ii. 20.
ᶜ Ezek. xl. 3. Zech. ii. 1. ch. xi. 1.

---

we suppose, a stone of immense length reaching from gate to gate and supported the wall; on them the names of the twelve Apostles of the Lamb, signifying that the Church in regard of doctrine and fellowship rested on the Apostles. One expositor, Lee, however, says, "It is far more consistent with the grandeur of the whole description to understand that the wall rests on a basis of twelve courses of stones, each course encompassing the entire city, and constituting one foundation."

We cannot help noticing that when Abraham, in Hebrews xi., is said to look for the glorious future, he is said to look for the city "which hath the foundations, whose builder and maker is God."

15. "And he that talked with me had a golden reed to measure the city, and the gates thereof, and the wall thereof." On three other occasions is a messenger of God said to have a reed wherewith to measure that which God reveals. First, in Ezek. xl. 3, "a man with a line of flax in his hand." Again, in Zech. ii. 1-2, "a man with a measuring line in his hand . . . . to measure Jerusalem." Again, in Rev. xi., where, however, the reed is given to the Apostle, and the angel commands him to rise and measure the temple of God. What is intended by this elaborate measuring? Evidently, I think, to impress upon us that the things revealed are not spiritual visions, beautiful dreams, signifying some spiritual grace or moral character in those who being pure spirits need no local habitation, but the exact contrary: measuring and measurements, and golden reeds, and furlongs, and cubits, pertain to the outward visible world rather than to the inward and spiritual, and we must, so far as we can, treat them as such. The outward and visible may be purified, sanctified, sublimated, but by these processes it is not resolved into mere thought, much less imagination.

16. "And the city lieth foursquare, and the length is as large

is as large as the breadth: and he measured the city with the reed, twelve thousand furlongs. The length and the breadth and the height of it are equal.

17. And he measured the wall thereof, an hundred *and* forty *and* four cubits, *according to* the measure of a man, that is, of the angel.

---

as the breadth." Aristotle is quoted as speaking of a perfect man being "tetragonos," as if the city was built square in order to set forth the virtue of those who dwelt in it; but if sufficient land was available any fortified city which was built upon it would be square. Such a city would afford straight streets, intersecting one another so as to give spaces for immense gardens planted with all natural products for the use or delight of the inhabitants. I do not for a moment say that St. John saw this in the New Jerusalem, but it is much more in accordance with the fitness of things than that he should use an Aristotelian metaphor to set forth a virtuous population.

"And he measured the city with the reed, twelve thousand furlongs. This, no doubt, must be taken as signifying the length and breadth of the great square, 3,000 furlongs each way, each side of the enormous square being above 350 miles.

"The length and the breadth and the height of it are equal." It can scarcely be supposed that the city is in the form of a cube, because in such a case the height of each house would be above 350 miles; and we are also told in the next verse that the walls are only 144 cubits, of course in height. Now in such a case the walls would not be observable, and there would not be even the appearance of protection; so that we must perforce understand the length and breadth to be equal, and the height uniform all around. Alford and others understand the height of the rock on which the city is supposed to be built to be taken into account, so that with the rock it is 350 miles high, but this is equally contrary to the description.

The highest mountain in the world is little more than five miles in perpendicular height.

17. "And he measured the wall thereof, an hundred and forty and four cubits, according to the measure of a man, that is, of the

18 And the building of the wall of it was *of* jasper: and the city *was* pure gold, like unto clear glass.

d Isa. liv. 11.

19 ᵈ And the foundations of the wall of the city were garnished with all manner of precious stones.

---

angel." This can only mean that the angel adopted a human standard of measurement. It is important as evincing the circumstantiality, and so the reality of the description. It is the description not of what is shadowy and invisible, but of what is material and visible.

18. "And the building of the wall of it was of jasper." The word "building" (ἐνδόμησις) is explained as the superstructure. The word occurs in Josephus, "Ant.," xv. ix. 6, who there applies it to the superstructure of a mole of a harbour. It is that part of the walls which is built on the foundations, *i.e.*, immediately above them.

"Was of jasper." Probably the most precious of stones, the diamond.

"And the city was pure gold, like unto clear glass." How are we to understand this? Gold is not transparent. Why is it described here as transparent? Bishop Wordsworth takes no notice of it. Bishop Boyd-Carpenter writes: "Gold has an inalienable reference to the sun itself; consequently to the symbol of the face of God or Christ, *i.e.*, to the manifestation of God's love." Dean Alford writes, "Ideal gold, transparent such as no gold is here, but surpassing it in splendour." Milligan, "Pure gold, the most precious metal known, but in this case transfigured and glorified, for it was like unto pure glass." This latter is, so far as we can judge, the interpretation most directly pointing to the truth. The Divine architect lavishes upon this city the most beautiful and costly of materials, but by His power renders these more beautiful still. I. Williams quotes the holy spiritualizing of St. Gregory: "By gold and glass we understand that heavenly country, that society of blessed citizens where the saints in the supreme brightness of bliss are as a city constructed of gold; and as that brightness is reciprocally open to them in each other's breasts, this very gold is described as like pure glass." (Gregory on Job xxviii. 17.)

19. "And the foundations of the wall of the city were garnished

The first foundation *was* jasper; the second, sapphire; the third, a chalcedony; the fourth, an emerald;

20 The fifth, sardonyx; the sixth, sardius; the seventh, chrysolite; the eighth, beryl; the ninth, a topaz; the tenth,

---

with all manner of precious stones." This does not mean, as we learn from the context which follows, that the foundations were merely ornamented with smaller stones, but that the foundations themselves were composed of such stones.

"The first foundation was jasper" (*iaspis*). This is the same in Hebrew, and is the last stone of the twelve in the high priest's breastplate. By the Septuagint translators it is rendered onyx. It is the stone of which the walls (upper part) were built. Bishop Boyd-Carpenter speaks of it as dark opaque green, but in verse 11 it is supposed to be "clear as crystal."

"The second, sapphire." Bishop Boyd-Carpenter describes its colour as opaque blue, said to be *lapis lazuli*. It is the second stone in the second row of the high priest's breastplate.

"The third, a chalcedony." This name is difficult to identify with any precious stone which we know. It is said to be a sort of emerald or an agate, brought from Chalcedon (Alford).

"The fourth, an emerald." The same as that now called by that name.

20. "The fifth, sardonyx." Probably the same as the second stone in the fourth row of the Aaronic breastplate. Sardonyx, or onyx, so called from its resemblance to the human nail. Its colour white and red, according to Boyd-Carpenter, and so also Wordsworth.

"The sixth, sardius." Supposed by some to be the ruby, by others the carnelian. It is the first, according to our translation, in the Aaronic breastplate.

"The seventh, chrysolite." Is described by Pliny as translucent with gold lustre; very probably the topaz.

"The eighth, beryl." The same (according to King) in composition with the emerald.

"The ninth, a topaz." Or, according to some writers, peridot, a sort of topaz, but not the more valuable one, in colour yellowish-green.

a chrysoprasus; the eleventh, a jacinth; the twelfth, an amethyst.

21 And the twelve gates *were* twelve pearls; every several

"The tenth, a chrysoprasus." Something akin to our aqua marina.

"The eleventh, a jacinth." Our sapphire, not the same as the second foundation stone which is called by this name.

"The twelfth, an amethyst." Perhaps the same as the last stone in the third row of the Aaronic breastplate. In colour violet, and in all probability the same as the stone now called by the same name.

The reader will see from the above how impossible it is to attempt to give a separate spiritual or moral meaning to each of these foundation stones, though we may be sure that they represent every spiritual grace bestowed upon God's faithful servants. In the variety and beauty of the precious stones is symbolized the πολυποίκιλος σοφία of God (Ephes. iii. 10), and His multiform love in supplying all the χαρίσματα, gifts and graces vouchsafed by Him to the several Apostles.

Equally impossible is it to assign to each of these stones the name of an Apostle. Thus Cornelius à Lapide, speaks of the first, the jasper, being inscribed with the name of St. Peter; the second, the sapphire, with St. Paul, or, as some suppose, with St. Andrew; the third, the emerald, St. John; but not a single valid reason can be given for such assignments. The one thing to keep in mind is that these stones are the most precious things of the earth; they are as rare as costly, and are assigned as the foundations of the city in order to illustrate how God builds it up with what must be new creations of His power.

Mark also the variety of the precious stones. "The precious stones," says Bede, "are adapted each severally to the foundations, because although all are perfect, shining with the light of spiritual grace, yet "to one is given by the Spirit the word of wisdom, to another the word of knowledge, to another faith," and so on.

21. "And the twelve gates were twelve pearls; every several gate was of one pearl." "Gates" are rendered by most "gate-towers," not being the doors of the gates which are hung upon hinges, and which open and shut, but the gate-towers which com-

gate was of one pearl: ᵉ and the street of the city *was* pure gold, as it were transparent glass.   ᵉ ch. xxii. 2.

22 ᶠ And I saw no temple therein: for the Lord God Almighty and the Lamb are the temple of it.   ᶠ John iv. 23.

---

mand them. Some consider that all these entrances are one. Christ is alone the door of the entrance, and all enter through Him. This is true; but if this eternal city is local, so as to be a fitting habitation for the glorified bodies of the saints, then we must be careful to adhere as far as possible to those outward and sensible conditions of it which God reveals.

"And the street of the city was pure gold, as it were transparent glass." See remarks on verse 18. It is noticeable that for the word clear or pure, καθαρος, is here substituted a word meaning more unmistakably transparent, διαφανής (or διαυγής).

22. "And I saw no temple therein: for the Lord God Almighty and the Lamb are the temple of it." The significance of the Jewish tabernacle or temple was that it was the house of God. But in the New Jerusalem God and Christ will be universally present, and will manifest their presence everywhere, so that there will be no temple, because all is temple. It must have been beyond measure astonishing to a Jewish believer to be told that in the perfect Jerusalem—the Jerusalem of which the former Jerusalem was but a shadow—there would be no temple. It would be Jerusalem without its one surpassing glory. In the eyes of a godly Jew Jerusalem existed for its temple. Even in Pentecostal times—in the full blaze of the light of the Holy Spirit— the Christians, and especially the Apostles, worshipped in the temple; but now St. John himself would understand that the Jewish temple betokened imperfection in access to God. God, instead of shining forth, was behind a veil; the sacrifices betokened imperfect and uncompleted atonement. No sacrifice imparted life. They all pointed to Him Who was to come. Now that He had come He had made a perfect reconciliation. And now the prayer was being fulfilled. "Father, I will that they also, whom thou hast given me, be with me where I am; that they may behold my glory" (John xvii. 24). Even in our churches the presence of Christ is veiled; then it will be unveiled. Not only spiritually, but sensibly, we shall worship in God and in Christ.

23 ᵍAnd the city had no need of the sun, neither of the moon, to shine in it: for the glory of God did lighten it, and the Lamb *is* the light thereof.

24 ʰAnd the nations of them which are saved

ᵍ Isa. xxiv. 23. & lx. 19, 20. ch. xxii. 5. ver. 11.
ʰ Isa. lx. 3, 5, 11. & lxvi. 12.

---

23. "Is the light;" rather the lamp. Greek is not φῶς, but λύχνος.

24. "Of them which are saved" omitted by ℵ, A., B., &c., and read, "and the nations shall walk in the light of it."

23. "And the city had no need of the sun, neither of the moon, to shine in it: for the glory of God did lighten it, and the Lamb is the light thereof." This was very clearly predicted in Isaiah lx. 19, "The sun shall be no more thy light by day; neither for brightness shall the moon give light unto thee: but the Lord shall be unto thee an everlasting light, and thy God thy glory."

All this is in strict accordance with the fact that God and Christ will be manifested in this glorious place. If in this city there is the effulgence of His presence Who dwelleth in the light which no man can approach unto; Whom because of that exceeding brightness no man hath seen or can see—if in this city of walls, transparent as glass, His presence is manifested of Whom it is said that "His countenance is as the sun shining in his strength," then it is plain that such light would extinguish that of our material sun—all other created light would be as darkness before it. And in this light we hope to live. If this be so, then assuredly it is the very truth that every one that hath this hope in Him "purifieth himself, even as he is pure" (1 John iii. 3).

"The Lamb is the light thereof." It is again to be noticed that the emblem of the Lamb is used to describe our Lord in this verse and in the last, as it is also in verse 14. The memory of Christ's work on earth is never obliterated. In the intense splendour and joy of that city of light, the remembrance of Him Who was led as "a lamb to the slaughter," gives depth and fulness to its joy.

24. "And the nations of them which are saved shall walk in the light of it: and the kings of the earth do bring their glory and honour," &c. The reader will see that almost all authorities omit the words, "Of them which are saved," and read "the nations

shall walk in the light of it: and the kings of the earth do bring their glory and honour into it.

---

shall walk by means of its light." Who are these nations? Whence sprang they? What was their origin? For we were led to suppose, by the last verses of the previous chapter, that none would in future be living upon earth except the saints in their state of reward; but it seems from this Divine declaration that the earth is peopled with nations who are not dwellers in the New Jerusalem, and yet are permitted to enter into it to bring, through their kings, their glory and honour into it. This, however understood, is one of the most remarkable revelations of this wonderful book, and it is repeated in the 26th verse: "And they shall bring the glory and honour of the nations into it." And we learn from the next chapter, verse 2, that these nations will require, and apparently continue to require, healing: "The leaves of the tree [of life] were for the healing of the nations." How came these nations to exist? They must have been survivals of the general judgment, and yet in what condition did they survive? Not as saints raised up in their glorified bodies, for in such a case they would have belonged to the New Jerusalem as its citizens, which they evidently do not. They are in some sense, if we may reverently use the term, outsiders, and yet friendly, evidently holy, fearing God, and believing in Jesus.

An immense number of questions may be asked about them. If they are human beings they must be descended from Adam, and yet do they partake of original sin? They require in some sense healing, for it is expressly said so. It is disappointing to find commentator after commentator passing this extraordinary revelation over as if there was nothing extraordinary, nothing worthy of deep thought or questioning in it. Wordsworth, for instance, refers to such places as "The Gentiles shall come to thy light, and kings to the brightness of thy rising" (Isaiah lx. 3). But how did these kings or nations survive the passing away of the old earth and heaven, and appear in the new? So Bishop Boyd-Carpenter, "All nations and peoples flock within the walls;" but how did they exist before they flocked in? I mean on the renewed earth. They could not be the offspring of those in the city, for the Lord so expressly declares "that they who attain

25 ¹ And the gates of it shall not be shut at all by day: for ᵏ there shall be no night there.

26 ¹ And they shall bring the glory and honour of the nations into it.

27 And ᵐ there shall in no wise enter into it any thing that defileth, neither *whatsoever* worketh abomination, or *maketh* a lie: but they which are written in the Lamb's ⁿ book of life.

ⁱ Isa. lx. 11.
ᵏ Isa. lx. 20. Zech. xiv. 7. ch. xxii. 5.
ˡ ver. 24.
ᵐ Isa. xxxv. 8. & lii. 1. & lx. 21. Joel iii. 17. ch. xxii. 14, 15.
ⁿ Phil. iv. 3. ch. iii. 5. & xiii. 8. & xx. 12.

---

27. "That defileth;" rather, "unclean," κοινόν instead of κοινοῦν. "Whatsoever worketh abomination;" rather, "He that worketh" (Mosc.).

to the Resurrection life neither marry, nor are given in marriage, but are equal to the angels." Alford writes, "If, then, the kings of the earth and the nations bring their glory and their treasures unto her, and if none shall even enter into her that is not written in the book of life, it follows that these kings and these nations are written in the book of life. And so, perhaps, some light may be thrown on one of the darkest mysteries of redemption. There may be—I say it with all diffidence—those who have been saved by Christ, without ever forming a part of His visible organized Church." But this does not answer the question, how did these nations or their ancestors survive the judgment and the passing away of the old heavens and the old earth, to make way for the new state of things?

25. "And the gates of it shall not be shut at all by day: for there shall be no night there." If, then, the gates shall never be shut—never in the day, and not at night, "for there shall be no night," why are there gates at all? Evidently to keep out of it anything which might defile; aught that worketh abomination. I cannot imagine any other reason.

26. "And they shall bring the glory and honour of the nations into it." This is a repetition of part of verse 24. It seems incredible that they should bring gold into a city of gold, or precious stones into a city whose very walls are of jasper and emerald, and amethyst. Must not this glory and honour be the relations or memories of good deeds, for which, mysterious though it be to us, there will be ample scope on the renewed earth?

27. "And there shall in no wise enter into it any thing that

defileth," &c. This a shortened repetition of verse 8. But the question arises, if the whole earth is purged and renewed, and there is "a new earth, wherein dwelleth righteousness," there seems an impossibility of conceiving any thing unclean or abominable as dwelling in it. Yet it would seem that original sin yet remains among those that dwell in the earth outside the city.

I cannot help drawing attention to the words, bearing upon and, I think, elucidating the whole contents of this chapter, of one who has made a considerable mark on the sacred literature of the Church of England: "In the first place, none can deny that after the Resurrection and the final judgment, the just made perfect will not be, as angels, simply spiritual essences, but be endowed, as when on earth, with material bodies. Now material beings necessarily presuppose a material locality: material sights would be simply useless unless there were material substances to see; material hearing, unless there were material sounds to hear. This obviates one great objection to what I am saying, that the whole Apocalyptic description is only the lowering of heavenly ideas to earthly minds. If a mere spiritual state were being described, doubtless it would so be; but when, to say the least, much that is material must be mixed up with it, the argument vanishes. Consider, again, the remarkable terms in which the abode of the elect is mentioned, after the final doom: 'A new heaven and a new earth.' And lest anyone should think that this is a mere casual expression of St. John's (granting that such things might be), St. Peter also and Isaiah speak of 'new heavens and a new earth.' If, now, there were no analogy between the old and the new, between the first and the second earth, to what purpose this particular and thrice repeated expression? And most remarkably it is said, 'There was no more sea.' There is, therefore, so strong a resemblance between the two earths that the absence of the sea in the second is thought a point worthy of notice. Therefore, all the varieties of natural beauty, besides this, it may be presumed, still will exist. If of one thing in a series it is recorded that it is abolished, the natural presumption about the others is that they remain. And in the mystical descriptions of heaven with which Holy Scripture abounds we find frequent references to other most remarkable components of earthly scenery. To trees, for there is the tree of life; to mountains, for there is the utmost bound of the everlasting hills; to lakes, for there the glorious Lord will be a place of broad streams; to rivers, for there is the river of the water of life. Surely it is impossible to believe that these things are purely metaphorical; nor can it be even said that the expressions are used in a sacramental sense" (From "The Unseen World," by the Rev. J. M. Neale).

CHAP. XXII.

^a Ezek. xlvii. 1. Zech. xiv. 8.

^b Ezek. xlvii. 12. ch. xxi. 21.

AND he shewed me ^a a pure river of water of life, clear as crystal, proceeding out of the throne of God and of the Lamb.

2 ^b In the midst of the street of it, and on either

---

1. "Pure" omitted by ℵ, A., B., D., most Cursives, Vulg., Copt., Syr., Æth. "Pure" read by only twelve Cursives.

1, 2. "And He shewed me a pure river of water of life, clear as crystal, proceeding out of the throne of God and of the Lamb. In the midst of the street of it, and on either side of the river, was there the tree of life, which bare twelve manner of fruits," &c. It is very difficult here to distinguish between what is spiritual and what is outward and physical, if one may use such words. A river of water of life proceeding out of the throne of God and of the Lamb seems to signify the Holy Spirit and Him alone. For, as we believe, He proceeds from the Father and from the Son. What can proceed from the throne of Deity except the Lord, the Life-giver. And yet it may not personally be the Holy Spirit, but be typical of Him; for if the city be a real city it cannot be accounted perfect except it has a river. In the visions of the New Jerusalem vouchsafed to Ezekiel we read (xlvii. 1), "Afterwards he brought me again unto the door of the house; and, behold, waters issued out from under the threshold of the house eastward." Then as he followed their course the waters increased till they became a river impassable by the prophet; waters to swim in, a river that could not be passed over, and that this was the river of life; he further asserts that these waters healed the waters of the sea. "And

side of the river, *was there* ᶜthe tree of life, which bare twelve *manner of* fruits, *and* yielded her fruit

ᶜ Gen. ii. 9.
ch. ii. 7.

---

it shall come to pass, that every thing that liveth, which moveth, whithersoever the rivers shall come, shall live," but of course with a new and better life. And this also is a river; and it may be ordained for the physical needs of the inhabitants of the New Jerusalem. It may be to them a sacrament of eternal life; an outward and visible thing ordained to communicate or increase life both of body and soul.

Now we cannot dissociate this river of the water of life from the tree of life which grows on each side of it, and whose roots are fed by this water of the river of life. This tree of life is apparently not a spiritual but a real tree—answering to the tree of life of the garden of Eden—the tree of which if Adam had tasted, even after his fall, he would have lived for ever: which tree was not destroyed but fenced round about with cherubim and a flaming sword. According to all analogy of God's dealings the various forms of life have to be sustained by nourishment, and here God provides the water of life as well as the fruit of the tree of life to sustain the eternal life of His people.

How are we to understand, " In the midst of the street of it, and on either side of the river, was there the tree of life, which bare twelve manner of fruits." The river of life is evidently one, but the tree of life seems evidently more than one—manifold; because it is on either side of the river, which a single tree cannot be. The trees would be all the same, of one kind, but it seems impossible to suppose that one single tree would supply so immense a city as one river might. All the attempts to explain the fact that there is but one single tree, and that on either side of the river, seem to me to fail utterly. Williams writes: " It certainly seems more natural to consider ' the tree of life ' to be but one ; it is more suitable to the whole description, where all is returning to the unity of God, more agreeable to our Lord's words, ' To him that overcometh will I give to eat of the tree of life which is in the midst of the paradise of God ' (Rev. ii. 7)." Then he proceeds : " But the construction of the Greek would very well allow it to be understood as, ' in the midst of the river which flowed on this side and on that

every month: and the leaves of the tree *were* ^d for the healing of the nations.

3 And ^e there shall be no more curse: ^f but the

^d ch. xxi. 24.
^e Zech. xiv. 11.
^f Ezek. xlviii. 35.

---

side of it.'" And thus it is taken by Dean Woodhouse, "The river which was on one side and on the other."

But this is dividing the river. It seems impossible and contrary to the nature of things that one single tree should supply the inhabitants of so immense a city. So we must acquiesce in the fact that the tree of life being on each side of the river of the water of life must be manifold.

"Which bare twelve manner of fruits, and yielded her fruit every month." These twelve manner of fruits are explained as being "the manifold rewards of the righteous," but why should they not be for the sustenance of the glorified bodies of the saints? They seem to be brought forth for that. Bishop Wordsworth seems to understand these trees as the Cross merely because this tree and the Cross are both ξυλον. This description of the tree of life with its variety of fruits seems to be taken from Ezek. xlvii. That is, the Holy Spirit first inspired Ezekiel to write it, and then inspired St. John to repeat it, "And by the river upon the bank thereof, on this side and on that side, shall grow all trees for meat, whose leaf shall not fade, neither shall the fruit thereof be consumed: it shall bring forth new fruit according to his months, because their waters they issued out of the sanctuary: and the fruit thereof shall be for meat, and the leaf thereof for medicine" (verse 12). In St. John we learn, "And the leaves of the tree were for the healing of the nations."

Who are these nations (see xxi. 26, 27). We assume that the inhabitants of the city are all the saints of God; but who are the inhabitants of the earth? They walk in the light of the city; their kings bring their glory and honour into it; but—deepest of mysteries —they require healing; and they receive it from the tree of life and, doubtless, through the ministrations of the glorified dwellers in the city. We cannot explain all this. The words are there as we have written them, and we must leave their interpretation to the good time of God.

3. "And there shall be no more curse: but the throne of God and of the Lamb shall be in it." In the next few verses there

throne of God and of the Lamb shall be in it; and his servants shall serve him:

4 And ᵍ they shall see his face; and ʰ his name *shall be* in their foreheads.

ᵍ Matt. v. 8.
1 Cor. xiii. 12.
ʰ 1 John iii. 2.
ʰ ch. iii. 12.
& xiv. 1.

---

is a repetition of what has been described in the foregoing chapter. "There shall be no more curse," or, as we are told that we ought to render it rather, "no accursed thing:" but an accursed thing depends upon a curse. This seems a repetition of xxi. 4: "And there shall be no more death, neither sorrow, nor crying, neither shall there be any more pain: for the former things are passed away."

But the throne of God and of the Lamb shall be in it. The throne of God is also that of the Lamb. "I have overcome and am sat down with my Father on his throne." Where God reigns in Person there can be no more curse. It is because He reigns in His glory in heaven that there is supreme blessedness there.

"And his servants shall serve him." This seems to be a repetition of the words in xxi. 3: "He will dwell with them, and they shall be his people." Being like the angels, they shall serve Him as do the angels. God's will will be done on earth—on the renewed earth—as it is in heaven.

4. "And they shall see his face; and his name shall be in their foreheads." Does this mean that they shall actually see the face of God the Father, or will it be perfectly fulfilled by their seeing Christ in His glory, as He said, "He that hath seen me hath seen the Father"? And yet the Lord says of the guardian angels of little children: "In heaven their angels do always behold the face of my Father which is in heaven" (Matt. xviii. 10).

"And his name shall be in their foreheads." Christ promises to those who overcome, in the Church of Philadelphia, "I will write upon him the name of my God, and the name of the city of my God, which is new Jerusalem, which cometh down out of heaven from my God, and I will write upon him my new name" (iii. 12). And the 144,000 who were with the Lamb on Mount Sion had His Father's name written on their foreheads. This, whatever be its literal interpretation, indicates that, as no other creatures did, they absolutely belonged to God. There may also

5 ¹And there shall be no night there; and they need no candle, neither light of the sun; for ᵏ the Lord God giveth them light: ˡand they shall reign for ever and ever.

6 And he said unto me, ᵐThese sayings *are* faithful and true: and the Lord God of the holy

¹ ch. xxi. 23, 25.
ᵏ Ps. xxxvi. 9. & lxxxiv. 11.
ˡ Dan. vii. 27. Rom. v. 17. 2 Tim. ii. 12. ch. iii. 21.
ᵐ ch. xix. 9. & xxi. 5.

---

5. "There any more" (ἔτι), with ℵ, A., P., Vulg., Syriac, but a few Cursives have ἐκεῖ.
"Need." "Shall need," A. "Giveth." "Shall give."
6. "Of the holy prophets;" rather, perhaps, "of the spirits of the prophets," ℵ, A., B., P., thirty-five Cursives, Copt., Syriac, &c.

be an allusion to the writing on the forehead of the High Priest indicating their high-priestly functions and honours.

5. "And there shall be no night there; and they need no candle, neither light of the sun; for the Lord God giveth them light: and they shall reign," &c. This is difficult for us to realize, for night is the season of refreshment.

As Williams says, "There shall be no more night; for there is no frailty of body. The night is often taken as betokening the withdrawal of the light of God's countenance for a season; this shall be no more, and God will always shine upon them: they shall ever rejoice without weariness in His Light."

And if they need not the light of the sun, they shall need no lesser light. The uncreated Light will shine everywhere, and extinguish all created lights.

"They shall reign for ever and ever." "Not," as some one has said, "as the saints reigned in the thousand years, whatever that signifies, but for ever, with no intermission."

Over whom shall they reign? Perhaps over countless worlds which God has created, and will create. Again, let us remember that the one great distinctive employment of those who have overcome will be reigning. An employment which will exercise throughout eternity their highest and best faculties.

6. "And he said unto me, These sayings are faithful and true: and the Lord God of the holy prophets [or 'of the spirits of the holy prophets'], sent his angel to shew unto his servants the things which must shortly be done." This is a similar message from God to what we read in chap. xix. 9, "Write, Blessed are

prophets ⁿ sent his angel to shew unto his servants the things which must shortly be done. ⁿ ch. i. 1.

7 °Behold, I come quickly: ᵖblessed *is* he that keepeth the sayings of the prophecy of this book.   ° ch. iii. 11. ver. 10, 12, 20. ᵖ ch. i. 3.

---

they which are called unto the marriage supper of the Lamb. And he saith unto me, These are the true sayings of God." And, again, chap. xxi. 5, "And he that sat upon the throne said, Behold, I make all things new. And he said unto me, Write: for these words are true and faithful." They are faithful and true sayings then that there shall be no more curse; that they shall see God's face, that there shall be no night in the New Jerusalem, and that they shall reign for ever and ever.

"And the Lord God [of the spirits] of the holy prophets hath sent his angel to shew unto his servants the things which must shortly be done." And yet, whatever plan of interpretation we give to the contents of this book, they have occupied well-nigh two thousand years. "Shortly," then must be understood in the light of the saying, one thousand years is with the Lord as one day; or, "shortly," must be taken as compared with the ages of eternity. Amazing as the events are which are contained in these visions they are as nothing to that eternity which God inhabits. This verse the reader will remember is a repetition of the first verse of this book, "The Revelation of Jesus Christ, which God gave unto him, to shew unto his servants things which must shortly come to pass; and he sent and signified it by his angel unto his servant John."

7. "Behold, I come quickly: blessed is he that keepeth the sayings of the prophecy of this book." Three times in this chapter is this repeated; in verse 12, "Behold, I come quickly: and my reward is with me," and in verse 20, "He which testifieth these things saith, Surely I come quickly."

"Blessed is he that keepeth the sayings of the prophecy of this book." What are the sayings of this book which men are required to keep? They have by some been supposed to be the words to the Seven Churches, which are all the moral and practical instructions of this book which are capable of being *kept*. The rest of the book is mostly composed of visions which cannot well be kept as moral precepts can be. Now in what I am about to say respecting

8 And I John saw these things, and heard *them*. And when
I had heard and seen, ^q I fell down to worship before the feet of the angel which shewed me these things.

^q ch. xix. 10.

9 Then saith he unto me, ^r See *thou do it* not: for I am thy fellowservant, and of thy brethren

^r ch. xix. 10.

---

8. "Saw these and heard;" perhaps, rather, "heard and saw."

this, I confess I can scarcely name any one who seems to agree with me; nevertheless, I think it is worthy of some consideration. It is that these words from verse 7 to 21 are not only the conclusion of this book of the Apocalypse, but the concluding chapter of God's whole Revelation. In the Greek, Latin, and Syriac Bibles this chapter forms the conclusion. I cannot help regarding this as brought about by the good providence of God, and so I conceive that the sayings of this book are the sayings of God throughout the whole Bible. If the visions of this book are only meant, no two commentators agree in their interpretation, but if the whole Bible be meant by the sayings of this book, then it agrees with what has been the fact, that every copy of the whole word of God concludes with this chapter. I do not say for a moment that the whole order of the books as contained in our copies is inspired, but this I say, that this chapter is a fitting conclusion to the whole sacred volume, and not only to a book of visions. I may have more to say on this when I come to verses 18 and 19.

8, 9. "And I John saw these things, and heard them. And when I had heard and seen . . . the sayings of this book: worship God." This is the second time that the blessed and holy Apostle was exposed to this temptation and all but succumbed to it, and as it is twice recorded, it is evident that God intends us to take notice of it and dwell upon it.

Some expositors out of a desire to acquit so great an Apostle of anything approaching to idolatry have hazarded the conjecture that St. John thought that the angel who had showed him these things was Jesus Christ Himself, but St. John at the commencement of these visions saw the Lord surrounded with such wondrous glory that it overwhelmed him—he "fell at his feet as dead." It

the prophets, and of them which keep the sayings of this book: worship God.

---

never then could have entered into his mind that the angel which showed him these things, bright and glorious though he might be, was the Lord Himself. Again, another commentator says that St. John intended merely an act of civil honour or homage, and the angel declined it out of humility and in order to give occasion to no scandal. The lookers-on might have misunderstood the meaning of the act as being one of Divine worship, whereas the Apostle merely meant to honour the angel with the honour which in the east men pay to their superiors in rank. But this cannot be allowed as an explanation, for the angel evidently supposes that the Apostle intended to pay him some unlawful honour, and so he directs him to pay his adoration to the only Being worthy of it—"worship God."

This incident is very decisive against any thing approaching to saint or angel worship, but it yields a still deeper lesson suited to our times, which is this, that the best, the most devout, the holiest of men may be betrayed into thus falling. When we consider the state of things in the modern Church of Rome, and we are called upon to do this in some way or other almost daily, two things strike us with astonishment. The first of these is the length to which this Church goes in encouraging the invocation of angels and departed saints. This is an increasing evil. It is greater now than ever it has been before. In Romish countries the worship of the Virgin in the way of Invocation far exceeds that of the worship paid to any Person in the Ever Blessed Trinity. Theologians, it is true, make a distinction between the worship paid to the Virgin and saints and that paid to the Persons in the adorable Trinity, but the vast mass of worshippers know of no such distinction.

This, then, is the first thing; but another matter which fills us with astonishment, and some even with misgiving, is this, that notwithstanding this idolatry, so many devout minds have been won to this corrupt Church, and have themselves gone very far in this direction. How can it be, we ask, that men who know Scripture, and who unquestionably have their souls alive to the things of God and of Christ, can yet pay this idolatrous worship. This is

10 ᵇ And he saith unto me, Seal not the say-

ᵃ Dan. viii. 26. & xii. 4, 9. ch. x. 4.

staggering to some, but not if we read aright this very place of Scripture. For here we have an Apostle, full of the Holy Ghost, called and taught by Christ Himself, one of those who had drank in His profoundest teaching. Here we have him twice needing the reproof, "See thou do it not: ... worship God." If *he* was exposed to the temptation, and was actually beginning to yield to it, and would have unquestionably committed sin if he had gone a step further, is it anything wonderful that in the nineteenth century men infinitely his inferiors in the possession of the Spirit and knowledge of the will of Christ should yield to it?

So that the fact that men of very deep devotion and knowledge of the mysteries of God have yielded to the seduction of a system plainly idolatrous in some of its main features is no proof of the truth of the system. All of these put together, multiplied many times over, are not to be compared to St. John, and yet he twice required to be told, "See thou do it not."

Now let us ask for a moment in passing, How could St. John have been exposed, even for a moment, to such a temptation?[1] I suppose none of you have ever been tempted to do such a thing as worship an angel, or a saint, or the Blessed Virgin? It is the very last temptation you are likely to be troubled with. You are tempted to do other things bad enough. You are tempted to do dishonest things, base things, unclean things, spiteful things; you are tempted to be proud, to be envious, to be untrue; none of which temptations touched the Blessed Apostle, and yet you think, perhaps, you can look down upon him, even if it be only for a moment, because he was tempted to fall down at the feet of the angel.

How, then, was it possible that this temptation should assail an Apostle? Because, I answer, he had a revelation granted to him such as you or I are not likely to have, because we are utterly unworthy of it. He had the unseen spiritual angelic world set before him in all its glories, and it was set before him through the instrumentality of one of these heavenly beings, and so the temptation assailed him.

---

[1] This is taken from a sermon preached to a large middle-class congregation, and is reproduced verbatim.

ings of the prophecy of this book: ᵗ for the time is at hand.

ᵗ ch. i. 3.

11 ᵘ He that is unjust, let him be unjust still: and he which is filthy, let him be filthy still: and

ᵘ Ezek. iii. 27. Dan. xii. 10. 2 Tim. iii. 13.

---

11. "Let him that is unjust, let him commit injustice still: and he that is polluted, let him pollute himself still: and he that is righteous, let him still do righteousness."

It is not for us who have never been so favoured, who, perhaps, some of us, have never believed in an angel at all—who have never realized or tried to realize our companionship with angels, or how God works by them—it is not for us to judge this Apostle; but it may be well for us to learn somewhat from him. How grand then, beyond expression, must these visions of the New Jerusalem and its inhabitants have been if they could so affect an Apostle who had lain in the bosom of Jesus Himself.

And who was this angel? What was his dignity? He tells us. "I am thy fellowservant, and of thy brethren the prophets, and of them which keep the sayings of this book: worship God."

Here is a mighty angel claiming to be the fellow-servant, not only of an Apostle, but of all those who obey the word of God. All those who obey God, no matter what their position in the universe, are His servants. And the highest and the lowest are fellow-servants. This bond unites them all as one family, one household, and the Son of God is their chief in service. He Who left His throne not to do His own will, but the will of Him that sent Him.

10. "And he saith unto me, Seal not the sayings of the prophecy of this book, for the time is at hand." When (in chap. x. 4) the seven thunders had uttered their voices he was told to seal up those things which the seven thunders had uttered, *i.e.*, they were not to be divulged, they were to be like a book which being sealed cannot be read; now he is told not to seal them up, for the time of their fulfilment is at hand. Men have but a short time to prepare —so short that it is no time at all for so great a work, and they must continue as they are.

11. "He that is unjust, let him be unjust still: and he which is filthy, let him be filthy still: and he that is righteous, let him be

he that is righteous, let him be righteous still: and he that is holy, let him be holy still.

12 ˣ And, behold, I come quickly; and ʸ my reward *is* with me, ᶻ to give every man according as his work shall be.

ˣ ver. 7.
ʸ Isa. xl. 10. & lxii. 11.
ᶻ Rom. ii. 6. & ch. xiv. 12. xx. 12.

---

righteous still," &c. This has been explained as said in a sort of solemn irony, as if it were the reflex of that written in the book of Proverbs: "They hated knowledge, and did not choose the fear of the Lord. They would none of my counsel, they despised all my reproof. Therefore shall they eat of the fruit of their own ways." Were then those to whom these words are addressed shut out from repentance by God? No; they had shut themselves out. They had become incapable of repentance. As the saying is, they are become Gospel hardened. As Alford says, "The lesson conveyed is 'Change while there is time,' to which we may add, change while you can, before you become incapable of changing—before your habits of ungodliness have become hardened into settled character."

But what then must we understand by "He that is righteous, let him be righteous still: and he that is holy, let him be holy still"? In connection with the announcement that the time is at hand, it seems to be this:—No matter how short the time is, slacken not in your efforts to preserve righteousness and holiness. The Lord has not come yet; take care that when He comes you may be found of Him as He would have you to be.

12. "(And) behold, I come quickly; and my reward is with me, to give every man according as his work shall be." When the Lord comes He will not postpone the rewards of His servants to the far future, but will at once say to them on His right hand, "Come, ye blessed of my Father, inherit the kingdom prepared for you from the beginning of the world." He brings with Him the New Jerusalem. At His voice men rise up in their glorified bodies. He then says to each faithful servant, "Enter thou into the joy of thy Lord."

"To give every man according as his work shall be." Again the judgment according to works; again the assertion, "Every man shall receive his own reward according to his own labour." Again

13 ᵃ I am Alpha and Omega, the beginning and the end, the first and the last.

14 ᵇ Blessed *are* they that do his command-

ᵃ Isa. xli. 4. & xliv. 6. & xlviii. 12. ch. i. 8, 11. & xxi. 6.
ᵇ Dan. xii. 12. 1 John iii. 24.

---

13. "And" omitted by אּ, A., B., &c.
14. "That do his commandments." So B., most Cursives, Copt., Syr., Arm.; but אּ, A., Vulg., Æth., read, "who wash their robes."

the truth, "He that soweth little shall receive little, and he that soweth plenteously shall reap plenteously." No truth of God is more insisted upon both by Christ and His servants than this.

13. "I am Alpha and Omega, the beginning and the end, the first and the last." Before this seems to be said by God the Father. Now it is said by God the Son. We confess the co-eternity of the Son with the Father when we say in our creed, "The Father Eternal, the Son Eternal, and the Holy Ghost Eternal." And yet they are not three eternals, but one eternal. Some have thought that here it has reference to the eternal reward. "My reward is with me, and it is an eternal one, as I myself am eternal."

"The beginning and the end, the first and the last," are expansions of the Alpha and Omega.

14. "Blessed are they that do his commandments, that they may have right to the tree of life, and may enter in through the gates into the city." There is a very important difference of reading here. Some MSS., as B., read as in authorized; others, as A., read, "Blessed are they that have washed their robes [in the Blood of the Lamb]." Both these readings taken together represent the whole truth. None can enter into eternal happiness except those who have kept the commandments of God ("If thou wilt enter into life keep the commandments"); and none can enter into eternal happiness except those who have washed their robes in the Blood of Christ. How are men to wash their robes? Evidently by applying to God both by word of mouth and through the means of grace. What commandments are men to keep? Not merely "thou shalt do no murder; thou shalt not commit adultery; thou shalt not steal;" but believe in Me; abide in Me; come to the Father through Me; take up thy cross and follow Me. "If thy hand, thy foot, thine eye offend thee, cut it off, or

ments, that they may have right ᶜto the tree of life, ᵈand may enter in through the gates into the city.

15 For ᵉwithout *are* ᶠdogs, and sorcerers, and whoremongers, and murderers, and idolaters, and whosoever loveth and maketh a lie.

ᶜ ver. 2. ch. ii. 7.
ᵈ ch. xxi. 27.
ᵉ 1 Cor. vi. 9, 10. Gal. v. 19, 20, 21. Col. iii. 6. ch. ix. 20, 21. & xxi. 8.
ᶠ Phil. iii. 2.

---

15. "For without." "For" omitted by ℵ, A., B.

---

pluck it out, and cast it from thee." "Receive me, even to the eating of my flesh, and drinking of my blood, that thou mayest have my life in thee."

His commandment is, "Come unto me, look unto me, follow me." His commandment is, "lay up for yourselves treasures in heaven," "Make to yourselves friends of the mammon of unrighteousness," "Forgive and ye shall be forgiven," "Eat ye my flesh and drink my blood, that ye may have my life in you."

If He washes us with His Blood, He washes us with no mere external washing; He washes us from all filthiness of spirit, from all selfishness, from all unbelief, from all disobedience of will, from all that is contrary to His own and to His Father's will.

"That they may have right unto the tree of life." A strong expression to signify the privilege of being able to eat of the tree of life. A man can only have the power over a fruit tree that he may eat its fruit. It is as if there was added, no man forbidding him—no one able to hinder him.

"And may enter in through the gates into the city."

15. "For without are dogs, and sorcerers, and whoremongers, and murderers," &c. The gates have angels stationed at them to guard them, and keep out everything that would defile. We should have thought, from chap. xxi., verse 6, that all here said to be excluded, would have been shut up in Gehenna; but it seems not to be so. This bears upon the deep mystery that the nations outside of the city, as distinguished from the citizens, have sin yet lingering among them.

"Dogs." Taken as the type of all that is unclean and lecherous. Thus St. Paul writes (Phil. iii. 2), "Beware of dogs, beware of evil workers." "The allusion to the dogs outside the city is hardly appreciated by Westerns. In the East, however, troops of

CHAP. XXII.] THE BRIGHT AND MORNING STAR. 295

16 ᵍ I Jesus have sent mine angel to testify unto you these things in the churches. ʰ I am the root and the offspring of David, *and* ⁱ the bright and morning star.

17 And the Spirit and ᵏ the bride say, Come.

ᵍ ch. i. 1.
ʰ ch. v. 5.
ⁱ Nu. xxiv. 17.
Zech. vi. 12.
2 Pet. i. 19.
ch. ii. 28.
ᵏ ch. xxi. 2, 9.

---

hungry and semi-wild dogs used to wander about the fields and streets of the city, devouring dead bodies and other offal, and thus became such objects of dislike that fierce and cruel enemies are poetically styled dogs in Ps. xxii. 16-20 " (Bishop Boyd-Carpenter.)

16. "I Jesus have sent mine angel to testify unto you these things in the churches." Thus the angels of God, the angels of heaven, are the angels of Jesus. He is "far above all principality, and power, and might, and dominion, and every name that is named, not only in this world, but also in that which is to come" (Ephes. i. 21).

"I am the root and the offspring of David." "I am the root," because He is from everlasting, and all existence is derived from Him. "Without him was not any thing made that was made."

"And the offspring." Because he was made of the seed of David, according to the flesh. Note how He expresses His eternity and His human nature in words which must have been so peculiarly grateful to a child of Israel.

"And the bright and morning star." The star which ushers in the morning, which knows no evening. This day-star has not only to arise on the mystical horizon, but in each of our hearts, as St. Peter writes, "Until the day dawn, and the day-star arise in your hearts" (2 Pet. i. 19).

17. "And the Spirit and the bride say, Come." It is only the Holy Spirit of God which can inspire the bride—the Church—throughout all the world to desire and to pray for the coming of the Lord. It is the very mark of the bride to desire the coming of the Bridegroom. The bride is the blessed company of those who love his appearing (2 Tim. iv. 8); of those who look for and haste "unto the coming of the day of God" (2 Pet. iii. 12).

"Let him that heareth say, Come." Let this word "come" be taken up by all who have within them the voice of the Spirit, and who hear the voice of the Church. It is the Advent cry. It is

And let him that heareth say, Come. ¹And let him that is athirst come. And whosoever will, let him take the water of life freely.

18 For I testify unto every man that heareth the words of the prophecy of this book, ᵐ If any man shall add unto these things, God shall add unto him the plagues that are written in this book:

19 And if any man shall take away from the words of the book of this prophecy, ⁿ God shall take away his part ǁ out of the book of life, and out of ᵒ the holy city, and *from* the things which are written in this book.

<small>¹ Isa. lv. 1. John vii. 37. ch. xxi. 6.

ᵐ Deut. iv. 2. & xii. 32. Prov. xxx. 6.

ⁿ Ex. xxxii. 33. Ps. lxix. 28. ch. iii. 5. & xiii. 8.
ǁ Or, *from the tree of life.*
ᵒ ch. xxi. 2.</small>

---

19. "The book of life;" rather, "from the tree of life." ℵ, A., B., most Cursives, Vulg. (Amiat.), &c

"Which are written" omitted by ℵ, A., B.

the cry of those who say aright, and in the Spirit, Christ's own prayer, "Thy kingdom come."

"And let him that is athirst come." One thing only is requisite on our part—desire. "If thou knewest the gift of God, and who it is that saith to thee, Give me to drink; thou wouldest have asked of him, and he would have given thee living water" (John iv. 10).

We must not wait till the last time to receive this water at the hands of Christ; we must receive it now, "Whosoever will, let him come—not wait, but come."

18-19. "For I testify unto every man that heareth the words of the prophecy of this book, If any man shall add unto these things, God shall add unto him the plagues that are written in this book: And if any man shall take away . . . . God shall take away his part out of the book of life," &c. Like a vast number of sayings in this book, this is a repetition of what we find in the Old Testament, in the book of Deuteronomy, "Ye shall not add unto the word which I command you, neither shall ye diminish ought from it" (Deut. iv. 2). Are these words applicable only to the visions in the twenty-two chapters of the Apocalypse, or are they the fitting conclusion to the words of all Scripture. I cannot help

20 He which testifieth these things saith, ᵖ Surely I come quickly. ᵠAmen. ʳEven so, come, Lord Jesus.

ᵖ ver. 12.
ᵠ John xxi. 25.
ʳ 2 Tim. iv. 8.

---

thinking the latter. It is equally, we should have thought, a sin against God to add to any of His words, no matter in whose book they are written, whether the book of a Jewish prophet, or of an evangelist, or of an apostolical letter. So that these words, though especially true of the Apocalypse, form a fitting conclusion to the whole Bible. How are men in danger of adding to the words of Scripture? I answer, by unauthorized traditions. These traditions may be traceable to remote ages as Mariolatry, or they may be traceable only to the Swiss Reformation, to Calvin and others, as that Christ died for a few, and the way of salvation is open only to a very small proportion of the whole race of mankind.

And where now is the danger of taking away from the words of the book of this prophecy. I answer, by criticisms, falsely so called. There are persons who tell us that St. Paul wrote only four of the thirteen Epistles reckoned as his in the canon. If he was inspired by God to write many more, and the Universal Church has believed from the first that he was, what a sin against God, the Inspirer of Scripture, for men to say, relying only on self-will, and what they consider right for him to have written, that such letters, or even Gospels, are no part of the inspired volume, and consequently not profitable for doctrine, for reproof, for correction, for instruction in righteousness.

As Isaac Williams has noticed, the severity of the curse against taking away from the Word of God (or of this prophecy) is much greater than that of adding to it. If a man adds, certain plagues are added to him: if a man takes away from them, his part in the book (or tree) of life is taken away.

20. "He which testifieth these things saith, Surely I come quickly." No matter when I come, I come quickly, for I come unexpectedly. I take all by surprise. Even on the waiting Church I come when all slumber and sleep (Matt. xxv. 5). On the wicked I come on a day that he looketh not for Me, and at an hour that he is not aware of. And no matter how I hasten, or how I delay, I come quickly.

And the answer of the renewed and ready soul is, "Come when

21 ᵃ The grace of our Lord Jesus Christ *be* with you all. Amen.

ᵃ Rom. xvi. 20, 24. 2 Thess. iii. 18.

---

21. " Be with you all." " Be with all the saints."

Thou wilt. Come in Thine own good time, for notwithstanding its terrors, it will be a good time. For Thou doest all things well. Thy time is the fulness of time. When Thou comest, if Thou givest us grace, we will say, ' Lo, this is our God ; we have waited for him, and he will save us: this is the Lord ; we have waited for him, we will be glad and rejoice in his salvation' (Isaiah xxv. 9)."

21. " The grace of our Lord Jesus Christ be with you all (or with all the saints) Amen." This is the conclusion of most of the Pauline Epistles. Nothing can be fitter; for all the power and will to keep the Word of God, and do what is written therein, is through the grace of Jesus. And so especially is the grace to wait for Him, and look for His appearing, the grace of Jesus. Assigned to us by the love of the Father, and sealed to each one by the Holy Spirit.

THE END.

CHURCH COMMENTARY ON THE NEW TESTAMENT.

WITH NOTES, CRITICAL AND PRACTICAL.

By the Rev. M. F. Sadler,
Late Rector of Honiton and Prebendary of Wells.

THE GOSPEL OF ST. MATTHEW.
Sixth edition. Crown 8vo, 7s. 6d.

THE GOSPEL OF ST. MARK.
Fourth edition. Crown 8vo, 7s. 6d.

THE GOSPEL OF ST. LUKE.
Fourth edition. Crown 8vo, 9s.

THE GOSPEL OF ST. JOHN.
Sixth edition. Crown 8vo, 7s. 6d.

THE ACTS OF THE HOLY APOSTLES.
Fourth edition. Crown 8vo, 7s. 6d.

THE EPISTLE TO THE ROMANS.
Third edition. Crown 8vo, 6s.

THE EPISTLES TO THE CORINTHIANS.
Second edition. Crown 8vo, 7s. 6d.

THE EPISTLES TO THE GALATIANS, EPHESIANS AND PHILIPPIANS.
Third edition. Crown 8vo, 6s.

THE EPISTLES TO THE COLOSSIANS, THESSALONIANS AND TIMOTHY.
Second edition. Crown 8vo, 6s.

THE EPISTLES TO TITUS, PHILEMON, AND THE HEBREWS.
Second edition. Crown 8vo, 6s.

THE EPISTLES OF SS. JAMES, PETER, JOHN, AND JUDE.
Second edition. Crown 8vo, 6s.

THE REVELATION OF ST. JOHN THE DIVINE.
Second edition. Crown 8vo, 6s.

LONDON: GEORGE BELL AND SONS, YORK STREET, COVENT GARDEN.

OPINIONS OF THE PRESS.

THE GOSPELS.

From THE CHURCH QUARTERLY, *October*, 1883.

"It is far the best practical Commentary that we know, being plain-spoken, fearless, and definite, and containing matter very unlike the milk and water which is often served up in [so-called] practical Commentaries. ... For solid Church teaching it stands unrivalled. Nothing could be better than the notes on the Sermon on the Mount, and the practical lessons drawn with convincing clearness from our Lord's words on the subject of Almsgiving, Prayer, and Fasting. Throughout the whole book the writer is ever on the watch for general principles and teaching applicable to the wants of our own day, which may legitimately be deduced from the Gospel narrative."

From THE CHURCH TIMES, *February* 23rd, 1883.

"The question of the origin of the Four Gospels is well treated, and a more succinct account of the real standing of the Evangelists with respect to each other, or to a supposed original document from which all copied, could scarcely be found than that contained in these few pages. Some few pages introductory to the critical portion of the volume, and explaining the elements of textual criticism, bring us to the text of the Commentary itself. Throughout the whole of its pages the same evidence of scholarship and critical acumen, which distinguishes all the author's work, is apparent; while the faculty of conveying such knowledge to the minds of the least learned in a simple and forcible manner, is abundantly preserved, and will procure for this work the position of one of the best of popular commentaries. Many of the notes extend beyond the scope generally implied by the term, and become full explanations of doctrinal subjects such as will prove of immense value to the student as well as to the general reader. We may cite as an instance of this exhaustive process the lengthy note on St. Matt. xvi. 18, and those notes on the Parables, which, severally treated in their entirety, present a more intelligible meaning than when explained in short disjointed notes. Finally, it remains to mention the fact, which, however, goes without saying, that the tone of the Commentary is thoroughly Catholic, so that the reader will find here a firm defence of the supernatural and divine character of the Gospel story, which never condescends to the tone of much of modern criticism, but remains true to primitive Catholic teaching."

From CHURCH BELLS, *November* 18th, 1882.

"It is written in a clear and sensible style, with a healthy tone; and its practical portions are devout without being wearisome or 'goody.'"

From THE CHURCH REVIEW, *November*, 1883.

"A valuable and substantial contribution to the literature of the New Testament is made by Mr. Sadler in the volume now before us. ... It might be said that every page of the work lights up the grand historical character of the Church as the one supreme authority for the authenticity and interpretation of the books of Scripture."

From THE CHURCH TIMES, *December 21st*, 1883.

" We have much pleasure in announcing the issue of 'The Gospel according to St. John, with Notes, Critical and Practical,' by the Rev. M. F. Sadler (George Bell and Sons), a companion volume to his gloss on St. Matthew, and a redemption of the pledge he gave therein to carry on his labours to the remaining Gospels. This is admirably done, being exactly what is wanted for that large and increasing class of readers who need the results of genuine scholarship and sound vigorous thought, but who are repelled by any surface display of erudition, and still more by dryness of treatment, ... The admirable lucidity, which is the distinctive quality of Mr. Sadler's style, comes out markedly in his annotations, whether they take the form of pithy clearings up of verbal difficulties or more elaborate dissertations on important points of doctrine; and he is a good judge in selecting the best matter supplied by his precursors, such as Olshausen, Stier, Godet, and, above all, St. Augustine, whose commentary on St. John is one of that Father's ablest works. This is much less of a mere grammatical inquiry than Professor Westcott's volume in the 'Speaker's Commentary,' but it is much more of a theological explanation, and that of a far sounder and deeper school."

From THE LITERARY CHURCHMAN, *December 7th*, 1883.

" . . . Apart from these longer and more continuous glosses, the reader constantly meets with single pithy notes, which by their clear common sense solve a difficulty at once, and satisfy the understanding promptly, so that this is quite the best popular commentary on S. John we know, without implying by that epithet that even advanced students of Biblical literature will not find ample profit in consulting it."

From THE CHURCH TIMES, *October 3rd*, 1884.

" We gladly chronicle the third instalment of Prebendary Sadler's clear and sensible Commentary on the Gospels, which exactly meets the needs of that large and increasing class, which, without pretending any interest in the more abstruse problems of scholarship in connection with the Greek Testament, is desirous of having in its hands a trustworthy guide to the actual meaning of the sacred writers, and some plain statement of the results accepted by that calmer type of scholars who understand the nature of evidence, and are not disposed to admit the validity of unsupported conjecture, however original and brilliant, as proof. . . . . The notes, as always with Mr. Sadler, are singularly lucid, pithy, and to the point."

From CHURCH BELLS, *November 22nd*, 1884.

" This is a work of a veteran scholar and divine to whom the Church owes much. Prebendary Sadler's writing is characterized by great clearness of style, and he has a remarkably persuasive way of putting things. His sermons, as well as his 'Church Doctrine Bible Truth,' &c., have done much towards furnishing the parochial clergy with materials for feeding their flocks. In this commentary he aims at a yet more important object, the instruction of the educated classes. He has carefully compared the original Scriptures with the authorized and revised versions, and has set himself to meet objections of scientific sceptics, and he has achieved great success. . . . . The volume is full of thoughts and suggestions for preachers as well as for general readers."

From THE SATURDAY REVIEW, *February* 21*st*, 1885.

"We can recommend his book to devout and cultivated Churchmen who want to read the Gospels for instruction as well as for edification."

From THE CHURCH QUARTERLY, *January*, 1885.

"The Notes are, like all Mr. Sadler's works, straightforward and to the point. The difficulties are not shirked, but are fairly stated and grappled with, so that the volume forms a welcome addition to the literature of the Second Gospel. In reading the notes upon the text, the feature which strikes us most in their intensely practical character. Mr. Sadler has a remarkable faculty of bringing the teaching of the incidents of our Lord's life on earth to bear upon the circumstances of our own time. Even where the points brought out are well worn and familiar, there is a freshness in his manner of treating them which adds greatly to the charm and value of the Commentary."

From THE CHURCH TIMES, *July* 3*rd*, 1886.

"Indeed, one great merit in this commentary and its companion volumes is the frequency with which notes are found, which are capable of being each expanded into useful sermons. They are like very strong essences or tinctures, which will bear considerable dilution before being employed medically, though for convenience they are usually kept in the more portable form."

From THE CHURCH QUARTERLY, *July*, 1886.

"We must begin our notice of this volume by offering Prebendary Sadler our hearty congratulations on the completion of his work on the four Gospels. The previous volumes were all reviewed in our columns as they appeared, and we have no hesitation in extending the welcome which we gave to them to their present companion. It is no slight distinction for a writer, after having made his reputation by what is confessedly the best popular work on Church doctrine, to have produced what we hold to be the best popular commentary on the Gospel narrative. There is no other occupying quite the same ground, and we cordially recommend these four volumes, in the now familiar blue binding, as for practical purposes the most useful to the general reader."

From CHURCH BELLS, *July* 2*nd*, 1886.

"Mr. Sadler's excellent qualities as a theological writer and expositor are so well known that we need only introduce the reader to this, his last Commentary on the Gospels, completing the series, by saying that it presents the same features as its predecessors. It is somewhat longer than any of the other three, a circumstance quite intelligible to those who consider how a commentator's view of his responsibility must enlarge as he proceeds with his work. To begin at the beginning, the Introduction is excellent, clear, concise, and full. In short, it says all that need be said on the authorship of the Gospel, and says it well."

From THE IRISH ECCLESIASTICAL GAZETTE, *Nov.* 6*th*, 1886.

"Originality of treatment, depth of insight, and thorough grasp of the practical side of Divine truth characterize these commentaries of Mr. Sadler on the four Gospels."

THE ACTS OF THE HOLY APOSTLES.

From THE GUARDIAN, *July,* 1887.

"We find, however, in the notes on St. Luke and the Acts the same freshness in thought and style, the same direct and independent consideration of the themes brought up on the sacred pages, the same knowledge of what has been said by others, the same masterly use, alike without subservience and without neglect, of the great and varied stores which our predecessors have left to us of these days who study the New Testament. The result is that Mr. Sadler's Commentary is decidedly one of the most unhackneyed and original of any we have. It will often be found to give help where others quite fail to do so, and its special value will be to the preacher or teacher who has to give oral and practical instruction; Mr. Sadler's strong point being decidedly in pointing the application to contemporary thought and to life, its trials and its duties, of the divine words with which he has to deal."

From CHURCH BELLS, *July 8th,* 1887.

"We can hardly imagine a commentary better adapted than Mr. Sadler's for giving to the reader an antidote to that unsettling influence which is now going about in the world, making people have a different set of religious opinions every month or so."

From THE CHURCH QUARTERLY REVIEW.

"There is vigour and freshness about his writings which makes it a pleasure to read them, while there is certain to be much that is instructive, and their tone and tendency are equally certain to be sound and edifying. This short commentary on the Acts of the Apostles is no exception to the rule, and it well supports the established reputation of its author."

From THE CHURCH TIMES, *August 26th,* 1887.

"Prebendary Sadler's useful commentary on the New Testament is advanced another important stage by the issue of this volume on the Acts of the Apostles, a part of Scripture whose interest and value seems to increase daily, as investigation into the beginnings of the Christian Church are pressed on with fresh vigour, alike by those who wish to prove Christianity a mere human evolution out of materials lying to hand in the Augustan era, and those who accept it as a divine revelation. Much of the work which has been done of late years in connexion with the Acts and other Pauline records has been devoted chiefly to the externals of history, geography, antiquities, and the like, rather than to the religious teaching which they contain; and this fact makes a gloss from a theologian like Mr. Sadler all the more welcome."

THE EPISTLES.

From CHURCH BELLS, *May* 18*th*, 1888.

"Mr. Sadler carries on his work with unabated vigour, and now we have some hope of his being able to give us a commentary on the whole of the New Testament. Undoubtedly such a work when completed will be of great value, as giving a well-thought-out exposition of the whole of the sources from which we derive the history of the founding, as well as the doctrines, of the Christian Church, and this, too, an exposition which supplies, not the mere personal opinions of its writer, although it is everywhere tinged by his individuality, but the historical meaning of the teaching of individual writers and of the Church at large. The 'introduction' to the present volume is excellent, giving all the requisite information without any unnecessary waste of words."

From THE CHURCH TIMES, *June*, 1888.

"There are three excursuses at the end of the volume, on Justification, on Election, and on the Christology of St. Paul, all carefully written, but with most pains bestowed upon the second. We do not know a better book than this Commentary to put into the hands of an intelligent Evangelical who is beginning to doubt the soundness of the system he has heretofore accepted, and is striving to find his way out and up into a higher and clearer atmosphere."

From THE CHURCH QUARTERLY REVIEW.

"We hail with pleasure this addition to the Commentary on the New Testament. . . . . . We think this volume will certainly sustain the high position which Mr. Sadler has gained as a practical interpreter of Holy Scripture."

From THE IRISH ECCLESIASTICAL GAZETTE, *April* 18*th*, 1890.

"Incomparably the best Commentary on the New Testament extant."

From THE BANNER, *May* 23*rd*, 1890.

"Ordinary readers could hardly have a better exposition of the sacred books."

From THE LITERARY CHURCHMAN, *February* 6*th*, 1891.

"This volume will be found to present all the characteristic excellences of Mr. Sadler's method; and it would be hard, indeed, to find any points of objection to these terse, thoughtful, Church-like notes."

Uniform with the Church Commentary.

Second edition.   Crown 8vo, 5s.

SERMON OUTLINES
FOR THE CLERGY AND LAY-PREACHERS.
321 OUTLINES ARRANGED ACCORDING TO THE CHURCH'S YEAR.

This book, a book of suggestions rather than of mere divisions, or skeletons as they were formerly called, has been composed with a view to meeting the objection heard on all sides that sermons at the present day are very deficient in setting forth Christian doctrines.

From THE GUARDIAN, *April 12th, 1893.*

"It is easy to prophesy a considerable sale for this volume. . . . We meet here all the well-known characteristics of his writings. The style is straightforward and vigorous. There is never any doubt about his meaning. His remarks are always pointed, and the arrangement of his material is excellent."

From THE CHURCH TIMES, *February 17th, 1893.*

"This volume differs in three respects from most similar volumes: (1) It aims, primarily, at supplying sketches of sermons on Christian Doctrine, couched in clear, definite language. (2) It is a book of 'suggestions, rather than of mere divisions or skeletons.' (3) It includes lists of texts and subjects for courses of Lenten and other sermons. The well-earned reputation of its author will be a sufficient guarantee for the soundness and usefulness of the work."

From CHURCH BELLS, *December 16th, 1892.*

"They are adequate, and they are helpful; they set forth the elementary teaching of the Church's seasons, the redemption, salvation, and sanctification of mankind. Each Sunday of each Church season has several appropriate texts and heads of discourses, and these are rich in wise suggestions as to helpful teaching. There is much simplicity and strong meat for learners. Prayer-book lines are made the rule throughout—the best rule of all."

From THE ROCK, *November 4th, 1892.*

"We should think that it would be difficult to find anywhere such a real help for preachers as these outlines afford. . . . Such depth of spiritual teaching is seldom to be found."

From THE IRISH ECCLESIASTICAL GAZETTE, *Nov. 11th, 1892.*

"This should be among the most popular and useful of Prebendary Sadler's writings."

From THE CLERGYMAN'S MAGAZINE, *December, 1892.*

"These outlines are both Evangelical and doctrinal. They occupy exactly one page of the book, and therefore afford ample opportunity for the preacher's own powers of expansion."

WORKS BY THE REV. M. F. SADLER,

Rector of Honiton and Prebendary of Wells.

49th Thousand.

CHURCH DOCTRINE—BIBLE TRUTH. *Price 3s. 6d.*

"Mr. Sadler takes Church Doctrine, specifically so called, subject by subject, and elaborately shows its specially marked Scripturalness. The objective nature of the faith, the Athanasian Creed, the Baptismal Services, the Holy Eucharist, Absolution and the Priesthood, Church Government and Confirmation, are some of the more prominent subjects treated. And Mr. Sadler handles each with a marked degree of sound sense, and with a thorough mastery of his subject."—*Guardian.*

Thirteenth Edition, completing Forty-sixth Thousand.

THE CHURCH TEACHER'S MANUAL OF CHRISTIAN INSTRUCTION. Being the Church Catechism expanded and explained in Question and Answer, for the Use of Clergymen, Parents, and Teachers. *Price 2s. 6d.*

"Far the best book of the kind we have ever seen."—*Literary Churchman.*

CONFIRMATION: An Extract from the "Church Teacher's Manual." 70th Thousand. *Price 1d.*

11th Thousand.

THE ONE OFFERING: a Treatise on the Sacrificial Nature of the Eucharist. *Price 2s. 6d.*

"A treatise of singular clearness and force, which gives us what we did not really possess till it appeared."—*Church Times.*

Second Edition, Revised.

JUSTIFICATION OF LIFE: its Nature, Antecedents, and Results. *Price 4s. 6d.*

12th Edition.

THE SECOND ADAM and THE NEW BIRTH; or, The Doctrine of Baptism as contained in Holy Scripture. *Price 4s. 6d.*

"The most striking peculiarity of this useful little work is that its author argues almost exclusively from the Bible. We commend it most earnestly to Clergy and laity, as containing in a small compass, and at a trifling cost, a body of sound and Scriptural doctrine respecting the New Birth, which cannot be too widely circulated."—*Guardian.*

7th Edition.

THE SACRAMENT OF RESPONSIBILITY; or, Testimony of the Scripture to the Teaching of the Church on Holy Baptism. *Price 2s. 6d.* Cheap Edition. 9th Thousand. Price 6d.

114th Thousand.

THE COMMUNICANT'S MANUAL; being a Book of Self-Examination, Prayer, Praise, and Thanksgiving. 32mo. *Price 1s. 6d.*
Cheap Edition for Distribution. Price 8d.
A Larger Edition. Red rubrics. Fcap. 8vo. Price 2s. 6d.

SERMONS. Plain Speaking on Deep Truths. 8th Edition. *Price 6s.*
Abundant Life, and other Sermons. 2nd Edition. *Price 6s.*

C. P. 2.96.—5000.

www.ingramcontent.com/pod-product-compliance
Lightning Source LLC
Chambersburg PA
CBHW031859220426
43663CB00006B/689